D1447285

Elizabeth Hayes

Pioneer Franciscan Journalist

Franciscan Life Center
116 Eighth Avenue SE
Little Falls, MN 56345-3597

To my parents
Kathleen Margaret and Robert Hastings Shaw
with love and gratitude

Elizabeth Hayes

Pioneer Franciscan Journalist

PAULINE JOAN SHAW

Foreword by M. Rosa MacGinley

GRACEWING

First published in 2009

Gracewing
2 Southern Avenue, Leominster
Herefordshire HR6 0QF

ISBN 978 0 85244 209 8

Typesetting by
Action Publishing Technology Ltd, Gloucester, GL1 5SR

Contents

Abbreviations

AOLA	*Annals of Our Lady of the Angels*
CSMVAW	Congregation of St Mary the Virgin Archives Wantage
FMASB	Franciscan Mission Archives Santa Barbara
FSAG	Franciscan Sisters Archives Glasgow
FSALF	Franciscan Sisters Archives Little Falls
MFICAA	Missionary Franciscan Sisters of the Immaculate Conception Archives Australia
MFICAE	Missionary Franciscan Sisters of the Immaculate Conception Archives England
MFICAR	Missionary Franciscan Sisters of the Immaculate Conception Archives Rome

Illustrations

Foreword

The publication of this book is timely with much scholarly as well as religious interest focusing on historical issues. There is a growing realization that so much affecting our social and political experience today has deep and still active living roots in the past; there are also instructive parallels and models worth reconsideration. In this ongoing movement over time of human endeavour and idealism, there have been the underlying tides, environmental and economic, carrying human societies from one stage of evolution to the next. But riding these forces and shaping outcomes within them have been individuals and groups whose decisions and actions are the essential subject matter of history and on whose agency coming generations build.

In the case of the Church, its ongoing history is essentially part of the unfolding of original Revelation, with the insertion of a divine power and providence in guiding its destiny. The immediacy and agency of this presence have been evidenced down the centuries, within the matrix of historical currents, through remarkable lives whose focus was the continuing action of God in His world. Light and shadow mix, as do good and evil – these personalities and their positive action for the triumph of good remain bright and ever relevant beacons of hope.

So with Elizabeth Hayes and her remarkable story. Her life spanned all but the first two decades of the nineteenth century and a few remaining years at the century's close – our recent past in historical perspective but already receding with the urgent press of current challenging developments and multiform responses. It is an era being intensively explored today and this book re-captures, through the experiences of this one woman, much that was characteristic of the century. Born on the island of Guernsey, this daughter of an Anglican clergyman, on coming to England, found herself drawn into the Oxford Movement, became acquainted with its leading figures, joined one of the newly emerging Anglican

Sisterhoods and was next led, with influential companions, to form a Catholic religious community.

The twists and turns of history take her to a French-founded Franciscan Third Order community in Glasgow and then, with her developing missionary attraction, to a daughter community founded from Glasgow in Jamaica. All along, Elizabeth, with her keen intelligence, her literary interests nurtured from childhood and her unshaken conviction of the religious call at the heart of her being, was being led to further horizons. Finding the Jamaican experience unfulfilling in its restrictions and community difficulties, she returned to Europe. In an older pattern, while retaining her viewed religious identity, she was individually able, through the protective jurisdiction of several supportive bishops, to seek the type of Franciscan community she wished to form around her. This took her to France and then, following the disbandment of her community there during the Franco-Prussian War, together with many accompanying war-related experiences, to the United States where, in late 1872, she was able to found her lasting missionary Franciscan Sisterhood at Belle Prairie in Minnesota. She was now in her fiftieth year.

Through these vicissitudes, Elizabeth elicited strong and enduring loyalty, as well as much active support, among many friends, both men and women – among them many eminent names of the period and the circles in which she moved. Only from the base of her Belle Prairie foundation was she now able to undertake, as an effective vehicle for her missionary objective, the apostolate that would consume her energies for the remainder of her life: the promotion, explanation and defence of Christian values through the press. Beginning her *Annals of Our Lady of the Angels* in Minnesota, she later transferred her printing operation to a house she opened in Georgia for a ministry to the lately emancipated and needy African-American people there. She was soon led to establish the central house of her religious institute in Rome and to continue the regular publication of her *Annals* from there. Among contributors in its successive issues, we find leading names, internationally known, in the Church, distinguished literary figures in Europe and North America and other religious as evangelically committed as herself in the nineteenth-century burgeoning of new spiritual movements. Elizabeth's journal evidences a high level of literary merit, wide acquaintance with historical and contemporary writings and an efficient method of production and distribution through the devoted work of her Sisters.

Pauline Shaw has given many years, among educational and

missionary commitments, to uncovering the story of Elizabeth Hayes, her earlier work stemming from the Vatican Council's mandate to religious institutes to seek, research and reclaim their founding inspirations in a fresh interpretation of their relevance for today. This has led Pauline to follow literally in Elizabeth's footsteps – in Guernsey, England, Jamaica, France, Germany, the United States and Italy and to explore many archives. Elizabeth Hayes' story has challenged several biogaphers to produce carefully referenced and fascinating accounts, but always Elizabeth herself remained a little elusive, even enigmatic. Pauline became convinced that only an in-depth exploration of her commitment to her Apostolate of the Press would throw further revealing light on the true woman. In *Elizabeth Hayes – Pioneer Franciscan Journalist*, she leads us on her own pathway of discovery, in a task that came to involve a monumental exercise in research, with its sifting of accumulating information and situating in context remarkable nineteenth-century figures whose lives intersected with Elizabeth's; she finally reflects on the significance of her contribution. In the light of this unique study, Elizabeth Hayes should no longer remain an unknown and obscure figure among her towering literary contemporaries.

Rosa MacGinley, PVBM
Australian Catholic University
McAuley at Banyo Campus
Brisbane

Introduction

Elizabeth Hayes (1823–1894) is a fascinating woman who, with her love of reading, culture and journeys, sought to serve her God through outreach to others in unique ways. The book initially introduces Elizabeth before situating her within the outpourings of nineteenth-century periodical literature, in order to appreciate her work as editor-publisher. It is argued that this Guernsey woman was a significant contributor to the 'Apostolate of the Press' and that she used her journal as a tool for adult education and entertainment. The youngest child of English parents, with an Anglican schoolmaster and clergyman father, she became a follower of St Francis of Assisi and capably led an international journal of religious ideas to stability and longevity. Through her Franciscan *Annals of Our Lady of the Angels*, Elizabeth left evidence in the literary field of a contribution to history that acknowledges professional women who enriched society with religious periodicals.

This book originated from a doctoral dissertation and is not a flat chronological biography of Elizabeth yet does contain biographical elements. It is hoped that strangers can meet her for the first time and friends can see her in a new light through the journalistic contributon she made to the religious and Franciscan periodical press. A few biographers appear to see Elizabeth's work in journalism as an adjunct to her life. This is far from the truth and it is time to revise this thinking. Hopefully now Elizabeth's publication will become recognized as an essential component of her life and mission with her truer character revealed through it. The text is dominated by the search for facts that prove not only her pioneering role in Franciscan journalism but also show the high achievement of the publication and the eminent contemporary contributors it attracted.

Elizabeth was passionate about all things Franciscan. Her personality, capacity for applied effort, single-hearted Franciscan approach and her view of the Franciscan contribution within the Church, all speak of the energy and perceptiveness of her being. Her capacity to mingle comfortably with key religious and literary figures of the period in England, Paris, Rome and North America, set her apart. Having a bold, broad vision, she ventured confidently into an arena where most women writers struggled for acknowledgement. Elizabeth was no minor player in Victorian Catholic journalism as she wrote, edited, published and distributed, through her Sisters, the first English Franciscan journal which she commenced in 1874. She continued these roles for twenty-one years until her death yet her periodical itself continued for a century.

Overview

Nothing equals the thrill of discovering persons of special interest from the past by walking in their footprints, visiting the places where they lived and reliving their social setting. Chapter one provides this experience and discovers that Elizabeth's family tree bore religious and literary fruit. Her early life in the Channel Isles, her involvement with leaders of the Oxford Movement, educational achievements and membership in the Wantage Anglican sisterhood are revealed. After her conversion to Catholicism, she embraced the Franciscan movement and as Sr Mary Ignatius Hayes, she made her vows before Dr H. E. Manning in London when a neo-monastic revival found enthusiasts in both the Catholic and Anglican Churches. Elizabeth learnt to follow the Franciscan way through her life with the Bayswater Franciscan Sisters and then with the French-influenced Glasgow Franciscans.

Chapter 2 provides a summary of Elizabeth's quest for mission beginning in 1864. Besides continuing to note the significant literary developments in her life, this chapter shows her as a missionary in Jamaica desirous to serve the needy and dedicated to following the Franciscan Rule. Situations change and other mission alternatives follow in France until the outbreak of war. Then Germany beckons with opportunity for further mission quests and responses. Elizabeth made numerous transatlantic crossings and her zeal for the accomplishment of God's reign was suppported by hard work and purposeful activity. When she ventured into the mission territory of Minnesota, she entered fully into the world of journalism. Highly active and fruitful years are underway as this chapter brings her story into 1874.

Elizabeth in the Age of Journalism is examined in chapter 3 by looking at secular and religious periodicals in the English language. The inquiry situates Elizabeth's *Annals* in the contemporary Catholic periodical press in countries where she lived and toiled, namely England, France, North America and Italy. The history of Catholic Victorian periodical literature is highlighted because Elizabeth's *Annals* invite search into its relations with the pontificate of Pius IX, in Rosminianism, activities of Mermillod, Leo XIII, Ludovico da Casoria and Cardinal Parocchi. Elizabeth's involvement in the Catholic periodical press in North America includes awareness of the *Ave Maria* Press, the central influence of New York, Isaac Hecker, Orestes Brownson, Irish American relations, 'Knownothingism' and migrant influences.

Elizabeth as pioneer in the Franciscan periodical press is the focus in chapter 4 which defines the pre-1874 European Franciscan journals. The dearth of research on Elizabeth's *Annals* in the past meant that they lacked comparison with any contemporary periodicals and this is ventured now. European Franciscan periodicals 1874–94 and Franciscan periodicals in North America in the same period are investigated. Elizabeth's love of Franciscanism led her to become committed to the 'Apostolate of the Press' in North America. Her Franciscan periodical has twin aims for it was published not just for Franciscan readers but also for the 'general reader'. The story of Elizabeth's Roman interval is intertwined with the involvement of Poor Clares who accompany her on her return to the USA. Developments there and a pause in the *Annals* carry the chapter to 1877.

Analysis of Elizabeth's *Annals* is found in chapter 5 and achieved through her themes which for the 'general reader' include original tales and historical and biographical sketches, together with stories of saints, pilgrimages, missionary activities and devotions. Elizabeth was passionate about the Franciscan way of following Christ; she loved Franciscan history and literature. She was interested in Franciscan foreign missions and admired Franciscan saints and holy people, in particular, St Anthony of Padua. The chapter also provides a chronological account of other mounting activities between the years 1878 to 1882.

Chapter 6 shares an understanding of Elizabeth and her contributors through women religious like Sr Brett and Mother Drane, while clergymen include Léon de Clary, T. Bridgett, H. Rawes and F. W. Faber. Third Order Secular Franciscan contributors are highlighed through the Hon. Mrs Fanny Montgomery, Lady G. Fullerton and Lady M. E. Herbert while other lay contributors to

Elizabeth's *Annals* include A. Procter, M. Howitt, E. Bowles, and A. de Vere. The chapter is rounded off chronologically with the further evolution of Elizabeth's institute.

Elizabeth's strategies in the production and distribution of her journal are discussed in chapter 7 with emphasis on her editing skills and printing and publishing procedures – including finance, distribution and readership. Like a technician attempting to climb the mountain of modern information technology, Elizabeth wrestled with the impact not only of intellectual and social ferment but with new printing techniques and mounting costs. The institute's story (1889–90) brings the chapter to a close. The book moves into the eighth and last chapter in order to appreciate Elizabeth's final challenge through the events of 1891–94. The leadership of three women, Angela Chaffee, Annie Thomas and Adzire Doucet, from 1894 to 1913, are presented in order to reveal Elizabeth's rich and on-going legacy.

Acknowledgements

First to Sisters Marian Bandille and Helene Byrne who ensured that the *Annals of Our Lady of the Angels*, held in the archives of the Roman Motherhouse of the Missionary Franciscan Sisters, for the years 1874–94, was transferred from fragile print to CD-ROM to provide easier access and mobility. Special thanks to Dr Patrick Colbourne, an Australian Capuchin scholar, who provided numerous personal introductions to enable research visits to European Franciscan archives and libraries in 2000–1 and who has encouraged and supported the whole project to the end. Wherever research was conducted, Franciscan Friars showed generosity and helpfulness, especially in Oxford, Erith (Kent), Killiney, Fulda, Rome and elsewhere. Some research was only possible through the kindness and hospitality of women religious and their friends in Paris, Nancy, St Wendel (outside Saarbrüken), Düsseldorf, Fulda, Stuttgart, and in the UK and the USA.

Thanks are due to librarians and archivists in Minnesota, especially to those in Franciscan and other religious houses, diocesan offices and in historical societies in St Paul, Bloomington, St Cloud, Little Falls, St Joseph and Brainerd. Special thanks also to the Poor Clare nuns of Santa Barbara, California and to their neighbours for enabling research in the archives of the Santa Barbara Mission. Translations done by Sr Bernadette Howes in Rome on parts of early Italian Franciscan journals are acknowledged. Appreciation is expressed regarding sections from Mario Finauro's 1997 doctoral dissertation on the Italian *Franciscan Annals* (1870–1900) that were translated by Sr M. Jeanne La Spina, late of Perth, Western Australia.

Assistance received during the initial thesis work at Notre Dame University, Fremantle, through Dr Catherine Kovesi, must be gratefully acknowledged. When circumstances changed for both of us, continuity was maintained through her support at the University of Melbourne. Very special thanks must be given to Dr M. Rosa MacGinley who has not only been a genuine advisor and collaborator in the preparatory publication process but who was also thesis supervisor in the final stages. Those who know of Rosa's *A Dynamic of Hope* and her other publications, monographs and journal articles, will recognize in the text her guiding hand, especially in historical and canonical matters associated with the evolution of life for vowed women religious.

Last, but not least, because there are too many names to mention, thanks are due to all the Missionary Franciscan Sisters in Australia and elsewhere, in Rome, Braintree (Essex), Dublin, Montreal and the USA, who helped to turn a project spread over eight years into this publication. Sincere thanks also to friends and family members who have walked the journey as well, with both understanding and assistance.

A final note

When entering the Missionary Franciscan Sisters noviciate in Kedron, Brisbane, Queenland, it was the story of Elizabeth Hayes, found in the 'Blue Book', that was inspirational for me. The book entitled *Mother Mary Ignatius of Jesus: Foundress of the Missionary Franciscan Sisters of the Immaculate Conception, 1823–1894*, and written 'by a Sister of the Institute' was printed in Rome (1954). It was based on the life of Elizabeth as recorded in the 'Memories' of Mother Chaffee. She presented her handwork to Mother Doucet as a gift for one of her feastdays. Mother Doucet gladly accepted it for she believed that Mother Chaffee 'of all our Sisters had lived most closely to our dear Mother Foundress'. Chaffee's 'Memories' have influenced this new publication which hopefully will carry further the stories of the wonderful women who pioneered a Franciscan journal. It has been a privilege to research and record their lives. May we, Sisters, associates, friends and young students in Franciscan colleges and institutions, continue to strive to live their inspirational Gospel vision and Franciscan values – enriched by the spirit of Elizabeth Hayes.

Pauline J. (Sr M. Francine) Shaw, MFIC

Chapter 1

Elizabeth Hayes and her Earlier Years

A young woman boarded a passenger ship anchored in picturesque St Peter Port harbour in the early 1840s. The ship lay in readiness to transport Elizabeth Hayes from her island home of historic Guernsey to the English mainland; she was never to return. Waving farewell to relatives and friends, she had no idea of what the future held yet she was calmly confident that this voyage heralded the beginning of an exciting adventure. Elizabeth watched old Castle Cornet gradually disappear and soon felt the swell of a current that was taking her in the direction of Weymouth. In her heart she sensed she was returning to her English roots where her family once made a significant contribution, to music and religion in particular, and she pondered how her life was to unfold and continue to honour the family story.

Family Background

Beginning with her great-grandfather, three generations of Elizabeth's Oxford forebears ushered in her life whose yet unknown achievements would one day equal or surpass theirs. Dr William Hayes (1708–1777) was an important eighteenth-century English musician who 'possessed considerable genius and abilities'.[1] The respected name of Dr William Hayes appeared in eighteenth-century journals and newspapers. He held Oxford's Heather Professorship of Music and his writings on music were widely circulated, including his works on every musical genre except opera. As a member of London's Royal Society of Musicians and a celebrity, William was responsible for directing many performances of George Frederick Handel's vocal works. In Holywell Street, Oxford, not far from his impressive house, William built the first freestanding music room in Europe and ensured Oxfordians enjoyed performances by Handel in it. In the periodical press he championed the famous composer when he judged that unfair criticism was directed at him. One of William's sons, Philip, followed closely in his father's footsteps and published his biography. Philip also earned a reputation for his substantial musical and literary works.[2] In the 1840s and 50s when Elizabeth visited Oxford, besides seeing the names of William and Philip Hayes displayed on the organists' board of St Mary's University Church, she admired her forebears' large portraits hanging in the Music Faculty. Elizabeth had ancestors of whom she could be justly proud and they broadened her own horizon of possibilities in life.

Elizabeth inherited from her grandfather, William Hayes the second (1741–1790), a talent for singing and an interest in church music and hymns. Her grandfather received his MA at New College and as organist moved to Worcester Cathedral where he published in the *Gentleman's Magazine* (May 1765), 'Rules necessary to be observed by all Cathedral-Singers in this Kingdom'.[3] Elizabeth's grandfather became a Minor Canon at Saint Paul's Cathedral, London, and later an Anglican clergyman who published a number of sermons and preached at All Hallows in Barking. The familiarity of Reverend William Hayes with the *Gentleman's Magazine* is noteworthy; this long-popular English periodical (1731–1914) stood with *Blackwood's Edinburgh Magazine* in the top six acclaimed periodicals of his day. The *Gentleman's Magazine* featured an assembly of essays and articles culled from numerous sources for each monthly issue. Probably the *Gentleman's Magazine* was a favourite of the Hayes family just as in the same period the *Quarterly* was favoured by the May family as described by Charlotte Yonge in *The Daisy Chain*. When the Reverend William died these facts and many more were recorded in his obituary in the *Gentleman's Magazine*.

Elizabeth's father, the Reverend Philip Hayes (1781–1841), attended Magdalen College, Oxford, and was a chorister from the age of ten to fifteen. He gained his BA, became an Anglican clergyman yet embraced the teaching profession and educated London boys for some years. Philip and Elizabeth's mother, Mary (née Thomasine Rainals), married in England and after the birth of their first son, William, moved to Guernsey. Elizabeth's father established his successful school in the Plaiderie where boys were prepared for matriculation. The rest of Philip and Mary Hayes' ten children were born on Guernsey with Elizabeth, their youngest surviving child, born in 1823.

Guernsey

The Channel Island of Guernsey provided a rich and diverse environment for Elizabeth in her developmental years. Wealthy Guernsey, proud of its history and culture, boasted five-storey buildings along the harbour waterfront of St Peter Port when Elizabeth was baptized at the Anglican 'Town Church'. Girls' education was not ignored on Guernsey and Elizabeth's parents developed her early love for reading. Besides books, clergymen read not only general magazines but usually ordered Church of England and other clerical publications. There is no reason to believe Philip Hayes did otherwise. His London lifestyle and regular visits there exposed him to London's growing journalistic developments. Also Guernsey received its share of London's books and newspapers, along with many other goods, via sailing ships and later steamships. Literary wise this Channel Island was in an advantageous position.

When Elizabeth was aged eight, St Peter Port's population was almost 14,000, trading ships filled the harbour and the town was a stimulating place with people aware of contemporary movements. Guernsey was no backwater. The covered market was packed with French-speaking buyers while its architecture contributed beauty to match the natural surroundings. As a child looking from the town toward the thirteenth-century Castle Cornet, then standing on a small island not yet connected to the mainland, Elizabeth must have asked many questions. In later years her fine handwriting, excellent spelling and grammar, noteworthy command of the English language, accompanied by an impressive vocabulary, were attributed to the foundations laid by her teacher, Aunt Sophie Hayes, who conducted the Allez Street young ladies' seminary.[4] While Elizabeth's French nurse was a devout Catholic, her family attended services in St James Anglican Church where the minister was a close family friend.

The French Catholic Church of Notre Dame du Rosaire on Burnt Lane was not far from Elizabeth's home in Sausmarez Street. When her nurse, of whom she was fond, returned home from services, at which incense was used generously, Elizabeth loved to wrap herself in the folds of her clothing in order to inhale the 'mysterious perfume'. The general environment in Guernsey was distinctly Protestant with Catholicism just beginning to creep back in spite of some violent opposition. Elizabeth's siblings enjoyed Guernsey's social life but apparently Elizabeth often preferred to remain at home to enjoy her reading.[5] She was so fluent in French that her father called her his 'little French girl'.[6] Revd Philip Hayes and his wife, Mary, made it possible for their daughter to be immersed in the surrounding French culture and language. Later in life this influence would prove invaluable.

Elizabeth's father rented the family house in an upmarket area and the parlour boarders attending his school shared the sizeable residence with family and servants. In spite of the relative obscurity of Elizabeth's life on Guernsey, we are certain that she was pre-occupied with reading, but precisely what she read in the 1830s can only be surmised through what was available to a clergyman's daughter and a young lady of her class. It could have included the works of William Blake, Robert Burns, William Wordsworth, Sir Walter Scott, Jane Austen, Thomas Carlyle, Edward B. Pusey or John Henry Newman. Family reading, besides family musicals, was part of orderly life in the Hayes home; there were plenty of jour-nals from which they could choose and to which a new generation of writers was contributing. By 1829, for example, the young William Makepeace Thackeray was already a contributor to the *Edinburgh Review*.[7] Elizabeth's mother did not enjoy robust health as she suffered from some kind of bronchial malady. Breathing for her was easier in a steam-filled room where Elizabeth, whose own health was thus damaged, often kept her company. Mary died at the age of fifty-six when Elizabeth was only fifteen, a painful time for all the family.

Benedictine monks, Norbertine canons and Franciscan friars had lived on Guernsey long before local people developed their interest in botany and geology or in visits to the nearby islands of Jethrou, Herm and Sark. When Elizabeth visited her mother's grave she walked close to the Rue des Freres and may have been told that, before 1537, the Franciscans had lived and worked nearby.

Elizabeth's later teenage life had necessarily to adjust to giving most of her attention to her much loved father. However, a final illness led to his death in August 1841. He was buried beside his wife in Candie Road Cemetery where a headstone still clearly marks the place and recalls part of the family story. Many years later, Elizabeth shared the great grief of this time with her friend and confidante, Angela (Sr M. of the Angels) Chaffee. Her written memories record that Elizabeth long cherished words of her father, especially, 'Never deviate from the principles in which you have been brought up. Say your prayers regularly.' Reflected in Elizabeth's own life, the advice portrays a simple Christian message, whether Anglican or Catholic, that the young woman from Guernsey never forgot. Elizabeth left Guernsey between 1843 and 1845; a more precise date cannot be established since Guernsey's shipping records indicate arrivals but not departures.

Life in England – Oxford and Wantage

Elizabeth arrived safely in England and in the next phase of her life, up to 1856, her subsequent London, Oxford and Wantage experiences included not only working as a teacher but also activities that enriched her personally and shaped her thinking. Religion was a popular and widely debated topic in nineteenth-century England and confusion over beliefs abounded, not only between different religions but also between different Church of England teachings. The numerous avenues available to join in the controversies included discussions at dinner tables, in coffee-rooms and on railway stations, besides meetings, pulpits, newspapers and periodicals. Elizabeth witnessed the 'Literary London' that boasted a newly developed magazine-publishing industry along with the thriving publication of books and newspapers. She was advantaged by this greater access to publications and, even if her lowly teacher's income inhibited her, the practice of relatives and friends lending to one another sufficed. Elizabeth saw the great difficulties that faced English women writers since journalism was considered basically a male profession. Some female writers felt that the only way readers would accept their work was to make it sound masculine. Marian Evans used the pseudonym George Eliot; Harriet Martineau, when volunteering to write an article for the *Edinburgh Review,* used the phrase, 'I'm your man', while the three Brontë sisters submitted their 1847 manuscripts to publishers under male names.

The power of the periodical press was witnessed by Elizabeth as people read increasingly; publications on religion were often fuelled by the Oxford Movement's attempts to restore to the Church of England certain Catholic teachings and practices. Lady Georgiana Fullerton's novel, *Mrs. Gerald's Niece,* caught the contemporary mood through her characters who discussed the division between 'Roman Catholics' and Oxford Movement followers. Elizabeth followed the controversies often published by periodicals as in the *London Review, Edinburgh Review* and the *British Critic.* She had a first cousin, Reverend William Hayes, living in London, who was an assistant master at King's College School and chaplain at St Katharine's Hospital, Regents Park. Her relatives introduced her to Dr Edward B. Pusey and Reverend John Keble, the two remaining leaders of the Oxford Movement after Hurrell Froude's death and John Henry Newman's conversion to Catholicism. As a Puseyite Elizabeth read the Oxford Tracts, some of which were written by Newman while he edited others. Elizabeth was conscious that he once declared that 'through Pusey the character of the tracts was changed', thereby attributing to Pusey much of the success of the publications. Newman regarded Pusey highly and wrote of him:

> I had known him well since 1827–8, and felt for him an enthusiastic admiration ... His great learning, his immense diligence, his scholarlike mind, his simple devotion to the cause of religion, overcame me; and great of course was my joy, when in the last days of 1833 he showed a disposition to make common cause with us. ... He at once gave to us a position and a name.[8]

As with Newman, Pusey impressed the very logical mind of Elizabeth; however she was her own person, confident in herself. One day, Elizabeth listened to Pusey as he preached against practices of the Church of Rome, in particular against confession and vows. Afterwards she went to him in the vestry to put forward her questions and objections.[9] To be able to confront a person of Pusey's theological, linguistic and literary stature indicates something of Elizabeth's strong character and personality. Elizabeth loved poetry and like many other Puseyites was influenced by Keble's *The Christian Year*, a widely used volume of poems for Sundays and festivals of the church year. 'To quote Keble's poetry was like a profession of faith in Anglicanism',[10] and this was her faith until 1856.

Elizabeth's interest grew in the Anglican Sisterhoods which, as part of the general religious renewal movement, were initiated and supported by Dr Pusey, a handful of other clerics, Lord John Manners and William (later Prime Minister) Gladstone.[11] The taking of religious vows by Anglicans was considered a daring step as this had been forbidden since the Reformation. In 1841 Marian Rebecca Hughes, under the guidance of Pusey, had been the first woman to take Anglican vows even before Puseyite communities commenced with St Katharine's near Regent Park in 1844. A circle of women Puseyites, including Elizabeth Hayes, interacted with the pioneer Anglican Sisters and she resolved to join them. Elizabeth looked to Lydia Priscilla Sellon's community in Devonport, as did other well-educated women like Fanny Taylor and Catharine

Chambers,[12] but after an interview with Mother Sellon, she decided to wait. She watched developments in the Oxford diocese, under Bishop Samuel Wilberforce, where future growth looked promising in the sisterhoods in Wantage (outside Oxford), in Clewer (near Windsor) and in Oxford itself where Marian Hughes lived and was caring for her elderly parents before establishing her community. Elizabeth formed a firm friendship with Marian that lasted for many years.

Wantage, an ancient town situated in the foothills of the Berkshire Downs and familiar to readers of *Tom Brown's Schooldays*, initially gained its fame through King Alfred the Great who was born there around AD 849. Literary conscious Tractarians whose friendships interconnected with other enclaves of well-educated friends encircled the Wantage Sisterhood venture begun in 1848 by the local vicar, Reverend William Butler.[13] This zealous man, with plenty of common sense and in sympathy with the Oxford Movement, had arrived two years earlier, accompanied by his young wife, who came from a respected banking family, and their first child. He showed unflagging energy for his church and the town. The Wantage project, which encompassed both a school and a shelter for unmarried mothers and ex-prostitutes, would not have been possible, however, without the cooperation and finances of a certain likeable and well-educated wealthy woman. Her name was Elizabeth Lockhart (1811–1870) and, despite the conversion to Catholicism of her famous half-brother, William, and of her step-mother, she became the founding sister in the Anglican Wantage project. Elizabeth Lockhart, whose father was a clergyman, was the only child of loving parents. Her mother died when Elizabeth was a child and her father remarried. The second Mrs Lockhart show-ered much affection on her stepdaughter and, at one period in their lives, they both helped Archdeacon Henry Edward Manning in his Anglican parish by teaching the children. Elizabeth Lockhart, now known as a religious sister, worked hard for two years in Wantage until she also decided to convert to the Catholic faith. When she departed from the Wantage foundation in 1850, Dr Pusey recommended to Reverend William Butler that Elizabeth Hayes should replace her.

This was the same year in which everyone was talking about the Gorham Judgement, a major event of the time with significant consequences, for it brought to a climax the struggle between Church and State and demonstrated that authority, even in matters of doctrine, resided in the Crown. It was a time when *Punch* cartoons poked fun at the Puseyites and, along with *The Times*, lampooned the Catholic Church which had, also in 1850, restored its hierarchy of bishops under the leadership of Cardinal Nicholas Wiseman. *Punch* delighted in humouring its readers with sketches of Newman and Wiseman as 'Mr Newboy holding up Mr Wiseboy's tail' and in publishing suggestions that the 'Catholics were preparing to blow up all England'. Meanwhile, in her own place, Elizabeth Hayes accepted the offered position which involved the care of the Wantage shelter. Far less dramatic yet of significance for her was the experience of having her educational talents recognized and, within a month of her beginning at Wantage, in July 1850, she replaced Elizabeth Ashington in the school which had begun initially with twenty-four students in two cottages in Mill Street.

Elizabeth Hayes was initially a lay teacher while Sr Harriet Day continued to care for the Wantage shelter. Two groups of helpers emerged. With reference to one of these, the April 1851 census indicates that Elizabeth Hayes, now aged twenty-eight, was head of the household in Newbury Street and three other lay women lived with her. Elizabeth worked tirelessly to develop the different types of schools needed; the following year she opened a Work School in the parish so that some students could learn needlework and household duties. Just after Easter 1852, Elizabeth was in Clevedon where she undertook and passed an examination to gain a government certificate for headmistress in a parish school. School life in Wantage was not all hard work. William Butler recorded in his diary that Miss Hayes and her assistant, Miss Watkins, were known to leave Newbury Street for Oxford with students for an all-day outing. Visits to Oxford were reciprocated by Marian Hughes who stayed with 'Miss Hayes who had charge of the parish school', who lived in a 'most picturesque house' and 'was herself a most charming and accomplished lady'.[14] Wantage travellers who wished to visit London could use the Great Western Railway which passed within two and a half miles of Wantage. Perhaps this was used by Elizabeth for more distant travels.

William Butler wrote that Miss Hayes was a person of tireless industry with the capability of managing the girls who were rough and disobedient. By February 1854, Sr Harriet was recognized as ecclesiastical superior of her small group while Elizabeth continued to establish the education complex on a firm foundation. This now included a separate Middle School because the local tradesmen objected to sending their children to the same school as the poverty-stricken ones.[15] In time the whole educational complex grew to become, and has remained, a respected Wantage institution. Elizabeth's ability to be abreast of rapid advances in the educational field was exemplified by her introduction of pupil teachers. In a period of the growing sense of professionalism and professional identity,[16] Elizabeth studied the educational publications of her time. The Tractarian-inspired atmosphere around Elizabeth in Wantage, enriched with regular clerical visitors from Oxford, further increased her thirst for reading and academic development and enhanced her understanding of writing, publishing and editorship.

Elizabeth moved from being called 'Miss' to 'Sister' on 25 July 1855 when she became the Anglican Sister Superior of St Mary the Virgin School and School Sisterhood. On this unique occasion Bishop Samuel Wilberforce presided and formally approved the vows professed by Elizabeth, Mary Puttock and Lucy Power. Dr Pusey preached at the ceremony while Elizabeth was called on to state publicly:

> I, Elizabeth, elected superior of the sisterhood established in this place for the education and training of children, do hereby, in the presence of God and of this congregation, promise and vow all fidelity and due subjection, obedience and reverence to my Mother the Church of God in England, and to thee Samuel, Lord Bishop of this diocese, in all matters connected with this work.[17]

In the bishop's formal reply he gave Elizabeth authority to rule and reminded her to be 'just and righteous in that state of life to which it hath pleased God to call thee'. The Wantage Sisterhood developed to become the Anglican Church's largest in England[18] and to this day the Sisters are friends of the spiritual daughters of Elizabeth Hayes.

In 1855, not long after the formal event, the Vicar of Wantage who had only good things to say about Miss Hayes up to this point, including his delight in her contribution to beautifying Saints Peter and Paul Church, now commenced negative diary jottings about her and the work. He was most annoyed when Elizabeth, because of overwork, cancelled one class without asking him. A situation developed due to differences over authority and finance for the vicar was not a man who believed that a woman was capable of organizing an establishment independently of himself.

The School Sisters in Newbury Street, including Sr Elizabeth, Sr Mary and Sr Lucy, prayed the Divine Office together and lived a religiously committed, mortified and refined lifestyle. In her desire to procure more Catholic literature for herself and the Sisters, one day Elizabeth took her pony chaise and drove to visit a clerical

friend.[19] Local news in a small town travels fast and it quickly
reached the vicar. Relations between Elizabeth and the vicar
became more strained because Elizabeth took seriously the authority and responsibility given to her by Bishop Wilberforce. Then in
her continual efforts to improve the school, Elizabeth incurred
much higher than anticipated expenses and William Butler was
most displeased.

   Elizabeth's widowed blood sister, Mrs Anne Dynham, came to
live in Wantage in a house adjoining the 'Blue Boar Inn'. It was
possible that some of the outstanding expenses calculated by a Mrs
Purdue, in Stroud's shop in Market Place, actually related to Anne.
It will never be known, but what is known is that after some time
the vicar and Elizabeth did not see 'eye to eye' any longer.[20]
Between February and April 1856, the strained relationship moved
Elizabeth to make a painful decision. She resigned as leader of the
Schools and the School Sisterhood and, while still believing that
her life was given to God, she left Wantage with the resolution to
follow another path.

In London – Greenwich and Bayswater

Arriving in London, Elizabeth found herself in the Catholic revival
scene which proved to be for her a fresh period of religious and
literary initiation. The return to England of Religious Orders and
Congregations in the 1850s was significant. While some of the 'old
Roman Catholics' and those opposed to Catholicism entertained
suspicion about the new Catholic life of London, it was a time when
many returned to the pre-Reformation Catholic religion of a
country that traditionally was called 'Our Lady's Dowry'. The religious groups that touched Elizabeth's life included the Jesuits who
opened their church in London in 1849, the Rosminians of whom
Fr William Lockhart was a member, and the future members of the
English Oblates of St Charles Borromeo. Elizabeth knew also of the
presence of Fr Frederick William Faber's Oratorians who had
moved into Brompton and of the return of the Franciscan Friars.
The Catholic renewal was enriched by a significant number of
Tractarian convert clergymen of literary giftedness, churchmen like
Henry Manning, John Newman and F. W. Faber, and well-educated
convert women, including ex-Anglican Sisters. Some joined religious houses while some men joined the secular clergy or followed
an academic career with Christian dedication. Elizabeth was aware
of the many publications of these author-converts.

Having read her way into Catholicism, Elizabeth made her decision and after making her abjuration of heresy was conditionally baptized in the Jesuits' Mayfair Church. This place was generally known as 'Farm Street', a place popularly chosen by converts and central to London Catholic life only since its 1849 foundation.[21] She listened to famous preachers who delivered their sermons from the pulpit of Farm Street and heard converts like Fathers Manning, Newman and Faber as well as the Cardinal, Nicholas Wiseman. It was Dr Manning who would sustain the strongest spiritual influence on her. Besides the religious atmosphere created by the Farm Street Jesuits and their many new convert friends, the place was encircled by a great interest in, and the ability to produce, religious and periodical literature. Elizabeth like others watched as this centre grew in literary strength to the extent that it gradually earned the name of the 'Scriptorium'. Known to her were Farm Street's respected contemporary Jesuit writers including Fathers Coleridge, Hathaway, Gallwey, Parkinson and Harper. One day in the future their names and writings would enrich her journalistic work, especially in the 1880s.

Elizabeth discussed with Dr Manning, now her spiritual director, the possibility of joining a Franciscan Poor Clare community or Catherine McAuley's Sisters of Mercy but, through Manning's guidance, she selected the educated convert women who had gathered under the leadership of Elizabeth Lockhart. Sister Lockhart, the former pioneer sister in Wantage, and her stepmother, Martha Lockhart, were now Rosminian Sisters and in 1852 they had purchased a large Greenwich house at number 66 Crooms Hill to use as a Catholic convent and home for women converts. In choosing to join this new Rosminian group of Sisters in Greenwich, who by now also owned two other houses in the street near the church,[22] she re-situated herself within the Lockharts' influential literary circles of friends, relatives and connections.[23] Included among the Lockhart's relations were Sir Walter Scott and his son-in-law, John Gibson Lockhart, successful editor and author. The extent of the Lockhart connection is evident in numerous sources through the names of religious and secular friends, letters quoted in books, lists of contributors to Catholic periodicals and biographies of literary or otherwise significant figures. One interesting example is William H. Anderdon who began his literary apostolate by publishing Catholic tales, and later wrote for newspapers and religious journals, including the English *Messenger of the Sacred Heart*. Elizabeth read this journal and in later years would refer to it.

In this same year of 1856, Fr William Lockhart's life changed from an itinerant one of preaching missions to a settled life in North London where the Rosminian Fathers of Charity established a new house at Kingsland. So William Lockhart had parish responsibilities for schools and many pastoral activities, yet his journalistic enterprises continued to please his circle of friends. Lockhart's literary undertakings included the institution of St Joseph's Press for the training and employment of journeymen printers and pressmen, and the purchase and editorship of *The Lamp* and *Catholic Opinion*.[24] Elizabeth Hayes was surrounded by a religious environment where writing journal articles, translating books and publishing were recognized as the Apostolate of the Press. These activities were practised compatibly with teaching poor children, caring for orphans, assisting converts and visiting the sick. Men and women like Manning, the Lockharts, Lady Georgiana Fullerton and others in Elizabeth's circle were of high moral and intellectual endowments; she saw how they used their gifts to combat the perceived evils of the time and the enemies of the Catholic Church. Elizabeth was in the right place at the right time to experience the intensity of their Apostolate of the Press enterprises.

In 1857 Dr Henry Manning and the Oblates he had inaugurated needed help in the new Bayswater Parish of Our Lady of the Angels and he turned again to his former helper in Anglican days, Elizabeth Lockhart. Elizabeth Hayes accompanied Mother Elizabeth Lockhart, six professed Sisters and four other postulants to Bayswater where the community established themselves in three Elgin Street houses.[25] Two weeks later the postulant Elizabeth and other community members were teaching in the poor school for girls attached to the parish church, preparing converts for reception into the Church and doing charitable works. When Manning visited Rome, the Jesuit who temporarily replaced him observed that the Sisters might not be fully approved by Roman authorities. The Sisters were following a Rosminian Rule at a time when some Italian spokesmen were questioning the philosophical writings of Fr Antonio Rosmini. Up to the twentieth century, legislation from the Fourth Lateran Council in 1215 directed new religious communities who wished to be recognized canonically to adopt the accepted Rules of Basil, Benedict, Augustine and then later Francis.[26] On his return Dr Manning recommended that the Sisters look to the Franciscan Rule and observances and suggested contact with a community of Franciscan Sisters in Glasgow.[27] Events that followed were to influence Elizabeth Hayes for the rest of her life. Mother Elizabeth Lockhart and Sr M. Francis Burton went to Glasgow while three Glasgow Sisters came to assist the Bayswater group in the transition period, which proved difficult for them all; some Sisters opted to leave the convent while Elizabeth Hayes remained.[28]

One of the Glasgow Sisters was recalled, so the Bayswater Sisters and postulants, Elizabeth being one, were offered the opportunity to travel to Glasgow to join the larger and more firmly established Franciscan house there.[29] Elizabeth knew that the Glasgow Sisters had a mission in Jamaica and so, with her heart now set on being a foreign missionary, she gladly received the Franciscan habit, and the new religious name of Sr Mary Ignatius, in a reception ceremony presided over by Dr Henry Manning on 25 November 1858. A novice now, she departed immediately with a group for Glasgow.[30] Elizabeth Hayes had left Bayswater before Mother Elizabeth Lockhart published her translation of *The Life of the Curé of Ars* and later works,[31] but her vocational determination had been strengthened and she had witnessed the influence of Apostles of the Press; both had been valuable experiences.

Experiences in Glasgow and Jamaica

In Glasgow, Elizabeth Hayes was introduced to the poor end of town and in particular to the Franciscan Sisters in the Charlotte Street Convent. The growth of this religious group was due to the arrival of two French Franciscan Sisters, Mother Adelaide Vaast and Sr Veronica Cordier who were accompanied and financed by one of their pupils, Mademoiselle Constance Marchand, who later became a Sister. Having accepted an invitation to come and help the Glasgow mission only eleven years earlier, they were now welcoming young Irish and Scottish women who desired to be Franciscans. Elizabeth took her place among them and learnt that the extended Franciscan family, often described as a tree with three main branches, called the First, Second and Third Orders, traces its history back to St Francis of Assisi and his first group of brothers in 1209. As the Franciscan movement developed, their priests and affiliated brothers were labelled the First Order, the nuns the Second Order and associated lay people the Third Order. Among the latter, groups came together to form communities and hence were described as Third Order Regular. Individual lay people formed the Third Order Secular.

The Glasgow Sisters shared with Elizabeth the story of their origins from St Francis to Angela of Foligno's 1397 (Third Order) foundation. As the group spread, they became known as the Grey Sisters, who established a community in Commines in 1442. From there four Sisters were sent in 1630 to Tourcoing and this community sent the two Sisters to Glasgow in 1847.[32] Mother Veronica Cordier, who survived the hardships of the first years, believed that if the problem of the city's poverty was to be overcome, education was the solution and hence the sisters opened schools. Elizabeth's education and experience were recognized and she was called on to assist the educational ministry and undertook a strenuous teaching workload. Sisters walked daily to and from poor parish schools to teach the children while in the cold foggy evenings they returned again to teach working girls. This gradually caused Elizabeth to suffer from exhaustion.[33]

Before Elizabeth's arrival in Glasgow, Mother Veronica Cordier with three other Sisters had set out in 1857 to establish a mission in Jamaica for she believed that the Church existed for mission. The home mission, with assistance from Catholic periodicals and literature, had been promoting and developing Catholicism in the first half of the century,[34] but Jamaica was considered a foreign mission and this was what particularly attracted Elizabeth. When she made her Glasgow profession of the vows of poverty, chastity and obedience, she added a voluntary fourth vow, 'to devote myself to the foreign missions'.[35] The Sisters on the community Council approved of her making this fourth vow as well as her transfer to join the Jamaican community. Elizabeth travelled to Southampton and boarded the *Atrato* which sailed on 2 December 1859 for St Thomas and Jamaica.[36] She may have already known of the *Atrato* because engravings depicting the ship's launching had been published some years earlier.[37]

With the voyage over and a safe arrival in the natural harbour, Elizabeth's bright blue eyes surely misted when she saw the conditions in Kingston town. She realized that most of the people lived in great poverty and discovered that only a handful of missioners ministered to the Catholic population.[38] No sooner had she unpacked than she was back in the classroom again. Instead of teaching the poor children as some of the Sisters were and as she desired, she was given the task of educating the daughters of wealthy plantation owners in the Immaculate Conception Academy. It was also the Sisters' responsibility and had been opened only in early 1858. The Academy was a private boarding and day school for young ladies and it consisted of two main streams. In one stream the classes were taught in French for the Haitian students with English as a foreign language, while in the other stream Jamaican girls were taught in English with French as a foreign language. The income from payment of fees at the Academy enabled the Franciscan Sisters to offer free educational opportunities to poor children. Bishop Dupeyron, Vicar Apostolic in Jamaica, recorded in 1862 that the Sisters educated 400 children but he did not indicate the proportion of fee-paying students to those who paid nothing. A few Sisters from the Academy also helped at St Joseph's Elementary free school which was conducted in an assembly room attached to Holy Trinity Church. Elizabeth rose early each morning because Academy classes commenced at 7.30 a.m. and, while there was a mid-morning break and a long noon meal break, students were not dismissed from classes until 4.30 p.m. Besides the usual academic subjects, there were classes in music, painting and needlework.[39]

Elizabeth recorded that religious community life in Jamaica posed frustration for her. The Sisters' Rule and Constitutions, followed strictly by Mother Veronica Cordier and the mainly French-speaking community, were unclear as to whether the Sisters' vows were solemn or simple which meant that the degree of cloister to which the Sisters were bound was uncertain. Mother Veronica had trained in Tourcoing where the French convent of Grey Sisters was not only rooted in genuine medieval origins but, was also quite conservative. For greater legal security as well as canonical recognition, some Third Order groups like the Grey Sisters were accorded solemn vows in the early sixteenth century but later legal uncertainty arose and the actual status of such groups was questioned.[40] Elizabeth experienced great stress and disappointment, for in trying to fulfil her fourth vow, her efforts met with obstacles, failure, illness and discouragement. She wrote in her diary:

> My soul [is] in a martyrdom of loneliness and misery but I resolved
> to offer this suffering, this very absence of all support of any friend
> on earth, as part of the penance taken when the vow was made.[41]

Two-thirds of what later became known as Elizabeth's Diary was written in Jamaica and since, before her death, she burnt her personal letters from key people like Dr Manning, Dr Pusey, numerous archbishops and bishops and the Hon. Fanny Montgomery,[42] these Jamaican writings remain very significant.

To understand Elizabeth's missionary heart and mind, attention to her diary is essential; without this understanding it is difficult to appreciate her later life. Diary entries include, for example, an

incident with a Jesuit cleric and former Crimean War chaplain, Fr
J. Sidney Woollett, which displays her strength of character. The
incident was occasioned by what Elizabeth called the 'false logic' of
Fr Woollett who 'argued on false premises' and apparently was not
totally open and honest with the Sisters. Elizabeth wrote:

> Father Woollett may lay down the law and insist as much as he
> pleases but a Sub-Prioress, chosen by the Prioress and appointed by
> her in her place, is not the duly constituted Superioress elected by
> the voice of the Community, as recognized in our Holy Rule.[43]

The Diary also contains quotations from French spiritual books for
Elizabeth's versatility in French provided her with wider reading
opportunities. However, she found reading indoors, especially in
her room, less enjoyable in Jamaica's 'intolerable' heat and yet this
was part of the cloistered life expected of her. How she must have
longed to feel the sea breezes of Guernsey!

The Jamaican interval proved a time of interior suffering for her.
She experienced a deeper conversion in her interior life as she
searched intensely for God. Her Diary reveals that, influenced by
her readings, she grew in spiritual insight. Unable to have a spiritual director of her choice in Jamaica, she personally strove to
deepen her interior life and direct it toward closer union with God.
Again and again, Elizabeth prayed for the fruits of the Holy Spirit.
She earnestly sought to be more patient, compassionate, loving
and gentle in daily events during this difficult period of her life.
Like St Augustine, Elizabeth prayed, 'Lord teach me to know
myself that I may know thee.' She wrote:

> I think that much that befalls us is sent to teach us to know
> ourselves, and so we are permitted thus to learn our own weakness.
> This ought not to make us despond. Grace would be stronger than
> nature if we were faithful in seeking diligently for it.[44]

Toward the end of 1862, Elizabeth discerned for herself that she
was not obliged to stay in her situation and drafted a letter to the
Vicar Apostolic in Jamaica, Bishop Dupeyron, to obtain the necessary ecclesiastical permission to leave Jamaica. The letter asked
him to treat her as he had dealt with Mother Veronica Cordier
when poor health forced her return to France. She asked him to
give her liberty to leave, so long as she obtained the consent of
another bishop to receive her vows.[45] In the following May, Bishop
Dupeyron authorized Elizabeth, still known as Sr M. Ignatius

Hayes, to leave Jamaica; Sr M. Francis de Sales O'Neill was to accompany her. They hoped later to either return to a mission on St Thomas Island or to affiliate themselves with a French Franciscan community.[46] As a vowed religious of the Glasgow community, Elizabeth returned to the jurisdiction of Bishop Murdoch of Glasgow, who would now have the authority to sanction her next move.[47]

Notes

1 Simon John Heighes, 'The Life and Works of William and Philip Hayes (1708–77) & 1738–97)' {Ph.D. Oxford (Bodleian), 1990} vol. 1, abstract, 17, vol. 3, iii.

2 Brian de Breffny, *Unless the Seed Die: The Life of Elizabeth Hayes (Mother M. Ignatius O.S.F.). Foundress of the Missionary Franciscan Sisters of the Immaculate Conception*, 14. Heighes, 'The Life and Works of William and Philip Hayes', vol. 1, 15, 62, 71, 85; vol. 2, 6, 11–13, 17–18, 113; vol. 3, 89, 91, 200.

3 Ibid., vol. 1, 14, 86; vol. 2, 6.

4 de Breffny, *Unless the Seed Die*, 23.

5 Angelica (Mother M. of the Angels) Chaffee, 'Memories of the Life and Works of Mother Mary Ignatius of Jesus, Foundress of the Institute of the Missionary Franciscan Sisters of the Immaculate Conception', *c*.1912, unpublished typescript, MFICAR, box 13, section B, folder 5, 2.

6 Ibid., 1.

7 John S. North (ed.), *The Waterloo Directory of English Newspapers and Periodicals, 1800–1900. Edinburgh Review (or the Critical Journal)*, North Waterloo Academic Press, http://www.waterloodirectory.com/default.asp accessed 12 August 2002.

8 John Henry Cardinal Newman, *Apologia Pro Vita Sua*, 40–1.

9 Chaffee, 'Memories', 3.

10 Lady Georgiana Fullerton, *Mrs. Gerald's Niece*, 300.

11 Owen Chadwick, *The Victorian Church, Part One, 1829–1859*, 506–8.

12 Mother Sellon established her first communities at Devonport and then Ascot; later she became leader of the Park Village community. For Fanny Taylor's story see Francis C. Devas, *Mother Mary Magdalen of the Sacred Heart (Fanny Margaret Taylor: Foundress of the Poor Servants of the Mother of God (1832–1900)*. For more on Catherine Chambers, see Jennifer Cameron, *A Dangerous Innovator: Wary Ward (1585–1645)*, 255.

13 For more on Butler see Sr A. F. Norton, 'A History of the Community of St Mary the Virgin, Wantage: Foundation and Early Development' (MA, Oxford, 1974), 81.

14 Phrases used are taken from the diary of Marian Rebecca Hughes, p. 69. The hand script was seen by the writer in Oxford's Pusey House Collection in 1994, along with memorabilia from the Anglican Society of the Holy and Undivided Trinity which 'Mother Marian' founded in

Oxford. Much loved and still in charge, she died in 1912. Her former main convent at 24 St John Street houses St Anthony's College; Elizabeth visited Marian at her house at the corner of the present St John and Pusey Streets.

15 Until educational reforms in the later nineteenth century, schools traditionally catered for different social classes: boarding colleges for the well-to-do; middle schools for the lower middle class; and free or 'poor' schools for the poor. Wantage came to cater for these latter two types.

16 For nineteenth-century growth of professionalism, see J. Don Vann and Rosemary T. VanArsdel, eds, *Victorian Periodicals and Victorian Society*, 7.

17 A copy of Elizabeth's vows are recorded in CSMVAW and in Norton, 'A History of the Community of St Mary the Virgin, Wantage', 81.

18 Kathleen Philip, *Victorian Wantage*, 20.

19 Chaffee, 'Memories', 3.

20 On Elizabeth's deprivation of speaking her mind and her lack of freedom at this time, see Sr M. Cuthbert McCarthy, 'Elizabeth Hayes – a Woman of Her Time. An Examination of the History of Victorian England and an Attempt by an Englishwoman to Trace Its Influence on Mother Mary Ignatius Hayes, 1823–1894', in *Passageways*, ed. Helene Byrne, 147.

21 George Andrew Beck, ed., *The English Catholics, 1850–1950: Essays to Commemorate the Centenary of the Restoration of the Hierarchy of England and Wales*, 443.

22 'Dowry Register', in *Bayswater Franciscan Records*, MFICAE. The Rosminians moved into no. 70 and in 1856, the year Elizabeth Hayes joined the community, they purchased also no. 72. (Property Records, Blackheath Historical Library.) Years later Ursuline Sisters from Germany used the property and in 1882 sent a community of Sisters to Armidale, Australia. Franciscan Sisters on pilgrimage there have renewed old connections.

23 For more on the Lockharts, see *Father Lockhart of the Institute of Charity (1819–1892)*. Sr M. Agatha McEvoy, *A Short Life of Mother Mary Elizabeth Lockhart and Brief History of Her Franciscan Sisters*, 8–9.

24 *Father Lockhart*, 26–7. One source claims Mrs Martha Lockhart as the founder of *Catholic Opinion* with her son, Fr William Lockhart, as its editor. Josef L. Altholz, *The Religious Press in Britain, 1760–1900*, 105.

25 'Chronicles 1857–1904', in *Bayswater Franciscan Records*, n.d., MFICAE.

26 M. R. MacGinley, *A Lamp Lit: History of the Poor Clares Waverley Australia 1883–2004*, 18. Founders of new religious communities added their own constitutions to the chosen historic Rule.

27 On this community, see 'Origin and Development of the Third Order of St Francis' in Sr M. Dolores Cochrane, 'In the Beginning', in *Franciscan Sisters of the Immaculate Conception* (Glasgow: unpublished, 1994), 1–7. John Watts, *A Canticle of Love: The Story of the Franciscan Sisters of the Immaculate Conception*, 52.

28 'Franciscan Convent of the Immaculate Conception Glasgow: The Establishment of Our Foundation and the Subsequent History of Our House', n.d. 7, FSAG.

29 These Franciscan Sisters represented the first Religious Order to settle in the West of Scotland since the Reformation. *Franciscan Sisters of the Immaculate Conception. Celebrating 150 Years in Glasgow: 1847–1997*, 122. The sister recalled was Sr M. Gertrude Foley.

30 'Clothing Records' and 'Chronicles 1857–1904', in *Bayswater Franciscan Records*, MFICAE: n.d. on either. A 1979 source claims there were six others besides Elizabeth Hayes. M. Gabriel Palmer, FSAG.

31 Lockhart was staff writer for the *Dublin Review*, contributor to the *Lamp*, and translator of several books. 'Chronicles 1857–1904', in *Bayswater Franciscan Records*, MFICAE. McEvoy, *A Short Life of Mother M. Elizabeth Lockhart*, 20.

32 *Franciscan Sisters of the Immaculate Conception. Celebrating 150 years in Glasgow: 1847–1997*, 95, 189.

33 Bishop Alexander Smith, Letter, 30 Nov. 1858. Chaffee, 'Memories', 7.

34 An account of Scottish Catholics' response to periodical literature, the involvement of Revd P. Forbes (staunch friend of the Glasgow Sisters) and Bishop Murdoch's controversy with McGavin of *The Protestant* is found in the Catholic press as recorded in 'Emancipation and Catholic Revival 1793–1878', in Leslie J. Macfarlane and Revd J. McIntryre, eds., *Scotland and the Holy See. The Story of Scotland's links with the Papacy Down the Centuries*, 13.

35 Elizabeth Hayes, 'Act of Profession of Sister M. Ignatius Hayes', in 'Profession Register, 1859', FSAG. Recorded at the end of the Act: 'Left for Jamaica, December, 1859'.

36 J. M. Wraight, Letter from Greenwich Maritime Information Centre to P. J. Shaw, 3 October 1994, MFICAA.

37 *Illustrated London News*, 1853, vol. 22, 352.

38 See Francis X. Delaney, *A History of the Catholic Church in Jamaica B. W. I. 1494 to 1929*, 68–9. Also Francis J. Osborne, 'Jamaica', in *New Catholic Encyclopaedia*, 804.

39 Cochrane, 'In the Beginning', 50.

40 The evolving currents that brought the simple-vow groups into full canonical recognition are a major factor in tracing their history. See M. R. MacGinley, *A Dynamic of Hope. Institutes of Women Religious in Australia*, 2nd edn, 26–7, 59–60, 172.

41 Elizabeth Hayes, 'Diary of Sister Mary Ignatius Hayes', n.d., manuscript, MFICAR, section B, folder 3, 24. Pauline J. Shaw, ed., *Diary. Sister Mary Ignatius of Jesus (Elizabeth Hayes)*, 26.

42 Chaffee, 'Memories', 7.

43 Shaw, ed., *Diary*, 39. M. Veronica Cordier had returned to France because of ill health. For Woollett and women involved in the Crimean conflict see Francis J. Osborne, 'J. Sidney Woollett, S.J., and His Times', in *History of the Catholic Church in Jamaica*, 231–3.

44 Shaw, ed., *Diary*, 57.

45 Ibid., 33.

46 Ibid., 41–3.

47 Bishop Murdoch was ecclesiastical superior of the Glasgow Franciscan

community and was empowered, in the canonical understanding of the time, to enable Elizabeth to transfer the ecclesiastical authorisation of these vows to another bishop.

Chapter 2

Quest for Mission

Having previously made a fourth vow to devote herself to foreign missions, in this period after Jamaica and before she reached Minnesota in late 1872, Elizabeth was on a quest to follow her perceived God-given vocation through serving others. The year 1864 was famous for the publication of Newman's *Apologia* in London and of the Holy See's controversial *Syllabus of Errors* in Rome. It was the year that Elizabeth travelled to Paris and at the time she wrote in her diary, 'Now the question is what to do with myself?' The previous year during the voyage to England, Elizabeth felt that Sr M. Francis de Sales O'Neill was not the right person with whom to open a new mission. They had decided on parting, with her former Jamaican companion joining the Poor Clares in York. Later events were to prove that Elizabeth's intuitions were accurate.[1]

Mission Alternatives and Consequences

Elizabeth intended to meet Mother Cordier, now living in Tourcoing, regarding their shared plan to open a new mission. However, Mother Cordier changed her mind, or had it changed for her by medical and religious authorities, and the plan was aborted. While making a retreat in Paris, Elizabeth jotted a few lines about her struggle as to whether she should enter the well-established Franciscan Convent in Calais or return to the island of Saint Thomas in the West Indies.[2] The Parisian convent where she was staying may well have been the Franciscan Convent of St Elizabeth, re-established in 1815, and apparently the heir of the famous convent suppressed during the French Revolution. To this convent back in 1852, Cardinal Wiseman directed three English novices, future Franciscan founders in his diocese and later at Drumshanbo in Ireland, to be trained there. Sarah Walmsley

(Mother Marie of St Cecile), another English convert, was abbess of this convent before her death in 1856. Elizabeth, like these other English women converts, listened to the Spirit of God, and then decided against both the possible ministry options she had considered.

At the time the Archbishop of Paris was Georges Darboy, former professor at the Grand Seminaire of Langres. He had published numerous religious books from 1845–58, and was recognized for his contributions to the *Correspondant* (1847–55) and directorship (1850) of *Moniteur Catholique*. Elizabeth visited this highly respected ecclesiastic, putting forward a proposal to found a Franciscan community that would serve the needs of his city's poor immigrants. The archbishop liked her plan but expected her to purchase a convent and not to use a rented house.[3] Without the necessary finance for this kind of project in Paris, she looked for another place to carry out the same ministry while contemporaneously building a religious community which would have the capacity to send sisters to foreign missions.

Amid Parisian political unrest, Elizabeth was acting with a definite purpose for she wanted to establish a stable Franciscan community along with achieving the fulfilment of her fourth vow to foreign missions. She had clear objectives from the time she made her decision to go to Glasgow; they remained a constant, namely stability, a sound authorization for her ministry and the missionary horizon.[4] Exposure to French Catholic mission annals at this time and in the late 1860s provided a model for Elizabeth's later mission-orientated periodical. She and her Parisian Catholic friends were surrounded daily with Catholic foreign mission news which was widely published in French Catholic newspapers, journals, reviews, pamphlets and books. *L'Univers*, founded in 1833, was one of the best-known Catholic newspapers while *Le Correspondant* was considered a very popular review. The most widely known French mission periodical, published in Lyons since 1822, was *Annales de la Propagation de la Foi*. This organ belonged to the Society for the Propagation of the Faith and had been conceived by Pauline Jaricot whose work for the support of foreign missionaries grew into a worldwide major mission-financing project. The *Annales de la Propagation de la Foi* contained letters from missionaries, news of the missions, and reports of all money received and apportioned by the Society.[5]

Elizabeth decided to approach the Bishop of Orléans, Felix Antoine P. Dupanloup. Known as one of the ablest French bishops of his day and a prolific writer, he was pleased to welcome

Elizabeth into his diocese and Bishop Murdoch approved of the new developments. However, within a month more changes overtook Elizabeth, adjustments were necessary and Murdoch sent a letter of recommendation to another French ecclesiastic, the Bishop of Versailles, which included a telling commendation to be borne out in later years:

> During some years that she [Elizabeth] lived in this city under my obedience she has shown herself in every respect a good religious, pious, humble and full of fervour and conspicuous for her love of regular observance and obedience. She has lately been living in the missions of the West Indies ... I testify that she is endowed with natural capacity which is not mediocre, by no means mediocre, and with prudence and zeal in executing business.[6]

The situation changed yet again, Bishop Murdoch gave another approval and the earlier plans for a foundation in Orléans were restored and completed. In late July that year, Elizabeth was in Lyon collecting money for her Orléans foundation,[7] and this city, well known for its numerous Catholic printing houses, also gave her an opportunity to see Apostolate of the Press activities.

Then surprisingly her plans for the Orléans foundation were obstructed when Bishop Dupanloup questioned the validity of the Glasgow Franciscan Rule and Constitutions that she intended to implement. So Elizabeth travelled south to Marseilles in order to go onto Rome to seek definite clarification on this issue.[8] Having obtained a passport on 12 September, she arrived two days later at Civitavecchia, the port of Rome, in the company of Bishop Dupeyron from Jamaica who, it appears, stopped for her en route to the beatification of Margaret Mary Alacoque.[9] Elizabeth continued to correspond with Bishop Murdoch and on the 27 September 1864, he forwarded her leave to transfer her obedience and vows to Bishop Dupanloup. However, until a foundation was made in France later, she remained under Murdoch's jurisdiction while in Rome.

Period in Rome

Roman ecclesiastical authorities decided that a complete revision of the Glasgow Rule and Constitutions was essential. Elizabeth was invited by the authorities to undertake the painstaking work, which would require living in Rome, reading volumes of material,

researching and rectifying the reason for the dubious status of the
Glasgow Rule and Constitutions, besides attending meetings with
Franciscan and ecclesiastical authorities. She accepted the challenge, aware that her French foundation was impossible without a
pontifically approved Franciscan Third Order Rule and
Constitutions. This cosmopolitan woman was a leader by nature
and, with zeal and courageous determination, she forged ahead
regardless of what others viewed as impossible obstacles. During
the course of her lonely work, Elizabeth lived in a convent as a
parlour boarder and suffered from the extremes of heat and cold,
as noted in her diary. By persevering in her task, Elizabeth was also
responding to the Glasgow Sisters' desire to access and use the
more authentic Rule and Constitutions. The Bayswater Franciscan
Sisters, who remained in touch, also asked to be able to benefit
from her work.[10]

During this period Elizabeth's hand and pen were always busy.
She unearthed the truth of diocesan bishops' interference in the
earlier Rule and Constitutions, going back as far as the seventeenth
century.[11] A Tourcoing letter of 1864 clearly admitted, 'Our Holy
Rule is not a Rule of the Third Order of St. Francis'.[12] In his
response to Elizabeth, the Minister General of the Friars Minor
clarified the necessity of leaving intact the Rule of the Third Order
approved by the Holy See, with freedom to write Constitutions in
accordance with the Franciscan Rule and Church laws.[13] So
Elizabeth wrote in her introduction to the Rule and Constitutions:

> The Rule for a religious community is like a ray of divine light; it is
> the expression of the evangelical counsels and the foundation of a
> religious life. The Constitutions, which are ordinarily attached to
> the Rule, are its explanation and development. The Rule, says St.
> Francis de Sales, is the road, and the Constitutions are the road
> posts or indications by which it becomes known, and which are
> placed for the direction and assistance of those who travel on it; or,
> as some holy and learned men have expressed it, the Rules propose
> the means of arriving at perfection, while the Constitutions point
> out how these means are to be employed.[14]

Elizabeth's writing indicates her wide reading of the masters of the
spiritual life while in her segment on education she shows her
knowledge of the writings of the celebrated French bishop,
Francois Fénélon (1651–1715). Her Roman experience of almost
two years provided her with invaluable opportunities to be introduced to influential literary ecclesiastics of her own calibre. She
also enjoyed reunions with numerous literary and educated

English churchmen and laity living in Rome or visiting the city. Elizabeth would continue to correspond with quite a number of her friends of this period, and follow with interest their activities and publications.

Finally Elizabeth's work on the Rule and Constitutions was presented to the Sacred Congregation of Propaganda Fide;[15] being assured that Pope Pius IX would sign the approbation of the Rule and Constitutions soon, she left for France in August of 1866.[16] Due to Elizabeth's work while at the Vatican, Cardinal Alexander Barnabo signed a new Decree for the Glasgow Franciscans in August and a Rescript for the Bayswater Franciscans in September.[17] In the following year her written work was printed and bound.

Return to France

Elizabeth returned to Orléans only to discover that another religious community had commenced an educational ministry there, so she resurrected a former alternative plan for Sèvres, a town adjacent to Paris and then in the diocese of Versailles. She broached this with the bishop who gave her 'a house, chapel and chaplain' with his blessing to establish a school for boarders and a noviciate.[18] On 8 December 1866, the special feast of Mary's Immaculate Conception under whose patronage Elizabeth's community was founded, Mass was celebrated in Sèvres' convent chapel. With delight Elizabeth wrote to Monsignor Talbot, rector of the English College in Rome, saying, 'We shall only be a quarter of an hour's distance from Paris and directly in a line with the Champs Elysees and the English Mission.' A week later Monsignor Talbot replied at length to her letter from her convent at '13 Bellevue Avenue, Sèvres, près Paris',[19] and three early communications between these two English friends provide the main facts about the foundation. Besides the letters, few other details about the convent and school are available yet Elizabeth did commence a boarding school that welcomed French and English students and she fully intended to provide special assistance to English converts.

Knowledge about the composition of her community is scant, however novices appear to have been French except for a young Leicestershire convert, Alice Mary Peet. She would continue to live, move and minister beside Elizabeth for some years as the talented Sr M. Clare. A Sr M. Aloysius MacIntosh from Glasgow hoped to join Elizabeth when the Orléans project was anticipated, but fortunately she did not become a permanent member of the Sèvres community. Conflicting accounts exist about this woman, yet it seems that, unlike her hard-working Franciscan Sisters in Glasgow, her lethargic divisive style would have hampered the new foundation.[20] From a letter of the Honourable Mrs Fanny Montgomery to Monsignor Talbot in February 1868, it is clear that 'three young English ladies' were expected yet whether they were for the school or the noviciate it is unclear. What is certain is that during her years at Sèvres, Elizabeth joyfully witnessed the reception of her own niece, Mary Sophie Claire Dynham, into the Catholic Church in the Sisters' chapel.[21]

Elizabeth's new Sèvres mission needed financial assistance so the Hon. Fanny Montgomery collected funds and involved Monsignor Talbot in the project.[22] Elizabeth's proximity to Paris, with Fanny's presence on Rue St Honore close to the Louvre, provided her with opportunity to share and observe French Catholic periodicals such as *L'Avenir* and *Le Correspondant,* and to read publications from outstanding Catholic writers like Gaspard Cardinal Mermillod (1824–1892), Henri Lacordaire, OP (1802–1861) and Felicité de Lamennais (1782–1854). She was aware also of the irreligious press that France, like other countries, was producing. Elizabeth (Sr M. Ignatius) and her community flourished for over three years until the outbreak of the Franco-Prussian war in 1870 when the convent was forced to close and the community was disbanded.[23]

War Period, Consequent Activities, Germany

Elizabeth, accompanied by three English-born companions, the novice Sr M. Clare Peet, the Hon. Fanny Montgomery and Rosalie Thomas, a young orphan, set out toward the French-German border. Railway authorizations testify that the English group was permitted to travel first to Nancy, the city between Paris and Strasbourg. Since Nancy was not bombed in either of the twentieth-century great wars, some of the historic sights seen by Elizabeth remain, including the famous world heritage La Place Stanislas with its eighteenth-century fountains and its impressive gold and iron gates. Elizabeth no doubt visited the old cathedral in Nancy which to this day honours the famous French missionary and writer, Cardinal Lavigerie (1825–1892), who had founded only two years earlier the French Missionaries of Africa, known as the White Fathers. Elizabeth had a special interest in this community.

Taking advantage of Germany's good railway system, Elizabeth

and her companions moved on to the city of Saarbrüken on the
Saar River in southwest Germany. Before the war Saarbrüken was
considered a little known, sleepy country town but during the war
it became a hive of activity with great numbers of soldiers in full
battle dress. Around this same time the railway station was visited
by Elizabeth's old Anglican associate of Wantage days, the
Reverend William Butler, who was moving around France and
Germany. This station, with its horrific conditions in war time, was
described by the vicar in his letters to his wife back home. Revd
Butler's experiences of Red Cross work in places where Elizabeth
moved were published in 1897 along with his wartime letters. The
pages give one an understanding of what Elizabeth saw and
endured, including the awful smells of rotting human flesh, of
carbolic acid and of terrible open drains.[24] Butler wrote of seeing
French convents being turned into hospitals, noting that in one
the Mother Superior was an 'intelligent German from Munich'.
The vicar worked on a Red Cross Commission in Saarbrüken,
Cologne and other towns in the area. Elizabeth was also to work for
the Red Cross and nurse wounded French soldiers.

Saarbrüken's present Red Cross headquarters are still in the
heart of the old city. Attendants at the headquarters were shown a
photo of Elizabeth's 1870 Red Cross arm bands and were provided
with details of her Red Cross accreditation number and passport,
but additional specific information about Elizabeth in Saarbrüken
proved elusive. Today's visitors to the battlefield of Saarbrüken,
where 21,000 soldiers lost their lives, can begin to comprehend the
terrible event by reading a detailed description provided by a
soldier who fought in the battle.[25] Elizabeth moved on toward
Berlin, leaving behind the Saarland area where Franciscans had
ministered for centuries. To be a Red Cross worker, training and
accreditation have always been required, so this may explain why
Elizabeth, Sr Peet and Fanny Montgomery made their way to the
capital where their 'Accreditation for voluntary care of the sick'
was signed on 24 October. Later in January 1871 in Berlin, they
were given passports, signed by Lord Augustus Loftus, as British
subjects travelling on the Continent.[26] In between those dates, they
were 'just outside Berlin' as Sr Chaffee later recorded, but exactly
where?

Wounded soldiers numbered many, many thousands in hospitals, formerly large chateaux, castles and convents, or in village
hotels and homes. Where did Elizabeth and her companions nurse
the wounded near Berlin? The answer has lain hidden for over a
hundred and thirty years in an issue of Elizabeth's publication, the

Annals, in an article contributed by Fanny, entitled, 'Corpus Christi: The Feast of the Most Blessed Sacrament'.[27] Fanny requests her readers to allow her to share a personal experience, explaining first the fervour of Fr Herman Cohen when distributing the Eucharist to French soldiers during the Franco-Prussian War. Fr Cohen was a German Carmelite convert from Judaism, an accomplished musician, and author of *Thabor* (five collections of sacred songs with musical accompaniment) published in 1870. He had ministered to London Catholics in the early 1860s and was well known by Cardinals Wiseman and Manning, also to other Londoners, including Elizabeth and Fanny, who had read the headline news about his conversion years before. Then the author provides a unique insight into her ministry with Fr Herman Cohen, Sr Elizabeth Hayes and Sr M. Clare Peet. Where and doing what? – 'at Spandau, near Berlin, when they nursed sick and dying French prisoners of war'. Fanny's article went on to say that Fr Cohen planned to write music for her concluding poem in her *Annals'* article on the Eucharist, but sadly he had died while ministering in Spandau. Revd Butler's letters resonate with this account for he wrote, 'Heaps of prisoners at Spandau, the Fortress not far off . . .'[28]

To continue Elizabeth's adventure, her exact movements in Germany and France for many months remain obscure; however, we know that other English groups, including doctors, nurses, religious Sisters and Red Cross volunteers, helped many wounded soldiers. Elizabeth and Fanny, with their interest in literature, particularly the periodical press, were also much inclined to closely observe people and events. With the outbreak of the *Kulturkampf,* whose secularization drive consolidated the Catholic counter resolve,[29] they witnessed first hand the necessity for and power of the Catholic press. This ecclesiastico-political struggle caused numerous small papers to spring up. While Elizabeth had been in Protestant Berlin, a Catholic newspaper, *Germania,* commenced, developing into the most important organ of the Catholic Centre Party. It appears from a broad examination of events that in 1871 Franciscanism and literary interests guided some of the activities of Elizabeth Hayes and Fanny Montgomery.[30] Both women were committed to Franciscanism and interested in literature and writing while Montgomery's wealth and influence, plus the presence of Sisters in Franciscan habits, made possible the pursuit of, and strengthened, their common interests.

The record of Elizabeth's visit to Fulda, when she was in Europe later in 1875–6, indicates an earlier visit and previous knowledge of the Fulda Franciscans. The city was a place of special attraction to nineteenth-century English visitors because of its associations with, and being the burial place of, the English missionary, St Boniface (673–754). The place was also of interest to Franciscans because St Francis' followers first arrived here in 1273, were later forced to leave for some time and then returned. Today a Franciscan friary still overlooks the city as it has done since 1623. Elizabeth probably knew that the English foundress, Mary Ward, established a convent in Cologne in the seventeenth century and that her Sisters worked for centuries in Fulda where they were traditionally called the 'English Ladies'. Their Fulda convent offered an opportunity for Elizabeth to take advantage of their hospitality and preferred accommodation.

While Elizabeth was moving through Germany, she heard about religious Sisters who were being sent by their congregations to new missions in North America.[31] Just two years earlier in 1869, another English foundress, Fanny Taylor (who had nursed with Florence Nightingale and the Sisters of Mercy in the Crimean War) was visiting German convents to learn about religious life because she planned to open a new convent in England. She stayed in Düsseldorf, wrote that there she met Sisters called 'The Maids of Christ', while in nearby Cologne she met Third Order Regular Franciscans called Poor Sisters of St Francis. Fanny Taylor pointed out that many German foundations of Sisters had begun around 1849–51 so, twenty years later, Elizabeth surely availed herself of their hospitality.[32]

Düssseldorf at the time was another important Franciscan centre with both Friars and Sisters working there. The OFM Capuchins were strong in numbers in Cologne while the OFM Observants were more numerous in Düsseldorf to where the Poor Clares came in 1859. These Poor Clares trace their history back to St Colette and the house in Ghent which she founded in the fifteenth century.[33] In the nineteenth century, Düsseldorf on the east bank of the Rhine River, about twenty-five miles downstream from Cologne, was one of the largest industrial cities in west-central Germany. The city gained interest for English visitors after Florence Nightingale came to Kaiserswerth, a suburb of Düsseldorf, to study nursing.[34] German hospitals were numbered among the world's best with Düsseldorf held in high esteem; during the Franco-Prussian War wounded solders were sent there via Cologne in Rhine River steamboats.

Fanny Montgomery, who later contributed constantly to Elizabeth's *Annals*, wrote *Misunderstood* the year after her 1871 experiences and her book was published in Germany at Leipzig.

Though some distance from the major battlefields, this Saxon city played a significant role in the transportation of soldiers, including the movement of wounded soldiers to numerous German destinations.[35] Fanny Montgomery was not the only English Catholic writer and friend of Elizabeth to use Leipzig for publishing purposes for Fr William Lockhart also had connections there. Wherever Elizabeth and her companions moved in 1871, they obviously kept away from Paris where the Commune, which lasted barely two months, brought about the massacre of thousands of citizens and was directly responsible for the deaths of Archbishop Darboy (whom Elizabeth knew in Paris) and five Jesuits. Events of this historic period were to have a profound influence on the development of socialism and communism, and as we shall later see, on subsequent developments in their associated press and literary influence.

Further Mission Quests

Following these momentous events and experiences, Elizabeth knew by early 1872 that it was time to listen again and respond to the insistent call of a foreign missionary life. She accepted the invitation of a Belgian Redemptorist, Fr Louis de Buggenoms, to return to the West Indies, this time to the Island of St Thomas.[36] Sisters Hayes and Peet duly arrived in the port of St Thomas where passengers were quarantined; unfortunately Elizabeth was given a room in which the former occupant had died from yellow fever and she became seriously ill.[37] Conflicting accounts about numerous difficulties at the Redemptorist mission have circulated over the years, but the outcome at the time was that the two Sisters withdrew and headed for New York. Again, no time to 'cry over spilt milk'!

It is not known precisely why Elizabeth chose New York as a destination. However, factors such as the availability of shipping, knowledge of Franciscan hospitality there, insights gained in Germany about the pastoral needs of their people in Minnesota and the financial backing of Fanny Montgomery, may well have contributed to her significant decision. While it was well known that bishops urged the need for missionaries in the Midwest of North America,[38] no written record exists to explain exactly why, in New York, Elizabeth Hayes and Daniel Mason of Belle Prairie, Minnesota, signed a deed dated 6 September 1872 for the purchase of land in Belle Prairie.[39] White settlers came to northern

Minnesota in 1851,[40] and the next year Fr Francis Pierz came to labour among the Chippewa Indians. In the following years the railroads gradually supplanted the horse and carriage as the main means of transport; Elizabeth with her companion availed themselves of both in order to reach Belle Prairie.

By 1872 the presence of many German people in Minnesota may have been the attraction for Elizabeth, as well as the fact that the Catholic community at Belle Prairie was under the care of German-born Fr Joseph Buh who was to prove a sterling friend. Elizabeth's ten-acre purchase was beside the St Paul Northern Pacific Rail Road,[41] and later she purchased land on the opposite side of the railway line beside the church and reaching down to the Mississippi River. It was on this site that Elizabeth would build her first convent. Before Mark Twain wrote his Mississippi River stories, *The Adventures of Tom Sawyer* (1876), *Life on the Mississippi* (1883) and *The Adventures of Huckleberry Finn* (1881), Sisters Hayes and Peet were living in their Belle Prairie log cabin close to this great river's upper reaches, well beyond the unnavigable St Anthony Falls at St Paul, yet still in Minnesota. Today this State attracts countless tourists in the summer season because of its beauty and its opportunities for numerous activities on the many lakes. However, the winter months in this part of the Midwest are extremely cold and snow-falls thickly blanket the countryside. The newcomers experienced harsh conditions on their arrival. Back in 1872 Belle Prairie was in the St Paul diocese, under Bishop Grace, but in the following years the diocesan boundaries were to change and Elizabeth was to negotiate successfully with later church authorities, including Bishop Rupert Seidenbush, Bishop John Ireland and Bishop Otto Zardetti.[42] Bishop Grace resigned in 1884 and was replaced by Bishop John Ireland, already known to Elizabeth, who in 1888 became the first Archbishop of St Paul.

The construction at Belle Prairie of four new wooden buildings, erected around an open courtyard, was initiated by Elizabeth to firmly establish her missionary venture. The *Saint Cloud Times* of 12 February 1873 announced the names of the builder and material supplier from Saint Cloud, and explained that the buildings would be used as two boarding houses, a schoolhouse and 'a dwelling two stories high'. One large room was multi-purpose and had sliding partitions allowing for an extension of the chapel, for classrooms or other purposes. Elizabeth took advantage of Minnesota's newspapers to announce that St Anthony's Academy for young ladies, offering an impressive curriculum and boarding facilities, would be opened at Belle Prairie on 1 January 1873.[43] Subjects available at the school were 'English language, writing, arithmetic, geography and history in all their branches', also needlework and private lessons in French and German, music, drawing and painting.[44] The front of the new complex faced a narrow dirt road and beyond it the planned route of a railway line, while the land behind the buildings was tree-covered and on the bank of the Mississippi River. Elizabeth thought big and so the front steps led into a corridor with parlour rooms on both sides; on the right side, rooms were capable of becoming later a printing office and behind that a bookbinding area. The February newspaper article concluded with, 'The school is in fine running order, and already has quite a large attendance.'

Travel with Purpose

California now beckoned with further possibilities, so in July 1873 Elizabeth travelled to the West Coast to obtain financial assistance on the Californian gold fields. It was a long distance but widows and women whose husbands were on the gold diggings were also travellers so Elizabeth did not lack company. She also planned to visit the old Santa Barbara Mission which was part of the chain of over twenty-one Franciscan missions along the West Coast established by the Spanish Friars mainly in the eighteenth century. The famous Franciscan, Fr Junipero Serra (1713–1784) had worked among the Indians and founded nine missions from San Diego to San Francisco and dreamt of one more at Santa Barbara. After many hours of rough travel, Elizabeth walked up the front steps of the well-established Santa Barbara Mission in order to visit Franciscan educators, who had organized a day and boarding college, to discuss with a senior friar her now maturing dream of publishing a Franciscan periodical.

Elizabeth talked with Fr José Maria Romo, the Guardian of the community; she, or her friends, may have known Fr Romo previously, judging by descriptions of his many travels prior to this time.[45] This meeting was most significant for it confirmed Elizabeth's resolve to proceed with her plans to move into the lively and highly competitive world of the periodical press. A few accounts of this meeting have given Fr Romo credit for suggesting a Franciscan periodical to Elizabeth, but these accounts rest on interpretations of the written 'Memories' of Sr M. of the Angels Chaffee. She actually wrote that Fr Romo 'urged' Elizabeth (Mother M. Ignatius) to proceed, as there was 'no Franciscan periodical at that time printed in America'.[46] Elizabeth read, or was aware of, the mere handful of existing European Franciscan journals, printed in France, Italy and Spain, and she was fully aware that not only was there no Franciscan journal published in North America but that no Franciscan journal had been published in the English language to date. Elizabeth was about to change this.

Fr Romo's 1870s diaries show no record of the meeting between Elizabeth and the author. If Fr Romo had seen himself as instigator of Elizabeth's journal then surely he would have recorded it in his diary.[47] Besides affording affirmation for her project, the wisdom of Elizabeth's visit would be indicated in later years. She had further positioned herself in the North American Friars' networks, especially where they lived in the regions of St Paul-Jordon in Minnesota, St Louis and Indiana. As Elizabeth's story unfolds, these connections will become clearer for, after 1884, the Santa Barbara community was annexed to Indiana. The leadership of the Santa Barbara friars at one stage was given to Fr Ferdinand Bergmeyer, OFM who was significant in Minnesota at the time some Sisters of the institute would later form their own diocesan community at Little Falls.[48] Elizabeth continued communications with the Santa Barbara Friars and her interest in the developments of the State of California and the Church there did not fade.[49] The fact that within months of the Santa Barbara visit, Elizabeth's first issue of her *Annals of Our Lady of the Angels* was printed in Brainerd in January 1874, is evidence to support the findings that for years Elizabeth's experiences had been preparing her for editorship. Now her preparation was sufficient.

Outreach and Challenges

When Elizabeth returned to her mission in Belle Prairie, she faced not only back-to-school responsibilities but, being a woman with a broad vision, she undertook two major projects, each with a range of new activities. Belle Prairie had been the starting point of Fr Pierz's outpost mission. The log cabin on church property was used initially by Elizabeth until a section of the new convent-school complex, authorized for her by Bishop Grace, was available. Now Elizabeth felt free to inquire about other property options in Brainerd, a railroad town twenty-eight miles further north, which was mushrooming and was expected to become one of Minnesota's major centres. Her new project there included another school as she knew how the railways were influencing expansion and bringing more people, and she also knew that printing houses existed there.[50] Today Brainerd's Historical Museum throws light on life in the town in 1873–4, including its people, the central railway station, the occupations including printing and the Catholics of St Francis of Assisi parish whose church was near the courthouse. Elizabeth's other new project was her Franciscan periodical for which much preparation was necessary, including contact with a publisher and communication with Bishop Grace to gain his permission to initiate this major undertaking in the diocese.

An article on Elizabeth's intention to open a school in Brainerd appeared in *The Brainerd Tribune* in November 1873 and other articles relating to their educational involvement followed.[51] On 25 November 1873, Elizabeth began directing the school which was situated at the corner of Tenth and Main (now Washington) Streets. According to a local newspaper, it offered a curriculum similar to the Belle Prairie convent school. Since French Canadians and German migrants were numerous in the area, the language skills of Sisters Hayes and Peet were valued. Elizabeth wrote to a Mr T. H. Canfield of the Lake Superior and Puget Sound Company asking for lots in block 131,[52] knowing it was the Christian practice of this Company to donate land to charitable organizations. For her projected periodical, she waited for the letter of approval from Bishop Grace who was known to possess publishing experience and expertise. In his reply he gave his approval to her enterprise but he feared that the periodical would not survive. He wrote:

> My fears are not as to your ability to make the publication such as will be worthy of a large patronage; of your capability I am fully convinced; but the knowledge I have of the fate that has awaited so very many efforts of the kind, made under the most favourable circumstances, causes me to fear that you will only embarrass yourself and perhaps others.[53]

So the bishop fully recognized Elizabeth's ability to become the successful producer of a journal while his fears for her enterprise were based on his knowledge of numerous Catholic periodicals plagued with financial troubles. The bishop's letter also indicated his recent meeting with Elizabeth's intended printer, Morris Russell of Brainerd, who assured the bishop that 'he would be willing to stop publication' and release her 'from the obligation of the contract at any moment' if necessary.

Besides the financial risks, Elizabeth, though encouraged by the success of English Catholic women writers, was also aware of the competitive market created by established periodicals. However, she had other factors in her favour as she embarked on this momentous undertaking, absolutely committed as she was to the Apostolate of the Press which is evidenced later in her publishing of Monsignor Mermillod's ideas:

> It is necessary to baptize the press, and to consecrate it, and herein lies a great work for women to do. Women shall come to the assistance of the Press as they came in former days to the assistance of Jesus Christ, of His apostles, and of His martyrs. They shall help in this apostolate, as they have helped in all others, by their heroism, their generosity, their prayers, their labours, and their lives.[54]

Another factor in Elizabeth's favour was indicated in Morris Russell's *The Brainerd Tribune* newspaper when he not only seconded the bishop's conviction regarding Elizabeth's capability, by describing her as 'a lady of extraordinary attainments', but in his also adding, 'and great piety',[55] as seen in her following decisions.

In December 1873, it was time for the novice Alice (Sr M. Clare) Peet to pronounce her vows. She was the first to take vows in Belle Prairie and Elizabeth chose her favourite feast of the Immaculate Conception (8 December) for the event. Three years later and in winter again, when a group of postulants were to receive the Franciscan habit, Elizabeth invited Bishop Seidenbush OSB, Vicar Apostolic of Northern Minnesota residing in Saint Cloud, to officiate at the ceremony, as Belle Prairie, from 1875, was in his vicariate. He replied, 'Send me a sleigh and I'll come.' On the special day he arrived safely to everyone's delight.

Unfortunately Elizabeth's application for land was unsuccessful and this appears to have been the reason why the Brainerd school venture was short lived; it ended in February 1874. In her 1977 analysis of these events, Sr M. Assumpta Ahles made an insightful observation when she indicated that Elizabeth wanted to make Brainerd her main centre. For just how long, following her first visit, the foundress lived in Brainerd is hard to determine but she did advertise her Brainerd Post Office number in the 1874 *Annals*. Today the only buildings that have survived from Elizabeth's era in Brainerd are the nineteenth-century Crow Wing Courthouse with its County Jail and the Post Office building with 1870 clearly marked on its stone face. The most important outcome of Elizabeth's Brainerd experience was that she had the opportunity to become friendly with the town's respected newspaper printer, Morris C. Russell, who became not only the first printer of the *Annals of Our Lady of the Angels* but also the Sisters' advocate. Together he and Elizabeth planned and ensured that Volume I of a new Franciscan journal would roll off his Brainerd press in January 1874.

Busy Fruitful Years

Elizabeth's three major biographers, Mother M. of the Angels Chaffee, Sr M. Assumpta Ahles and Brian de Breffny, have provided different perspectives on, and insights into, the life of this very energetic and highly achieving woman. Elizabeth was by nature industrious, and was at the peak of her physical and mental powers during the next stage of her life; it began in January 1874 in Belle Prairie and continued in different places for approximately the next ten years. This assessment is based on the knowledge that during part of this period, she worked incessantly in Belle Prairie and Brainerd, travelled across the Atlantic to Europe, searched untiringly in Rome to strengthen her home base, finally returned to New York with high hopes, and then survived a major disappointment before returning again to Belle Prairie. During these challenging years, a unique story unfolds of just what kind of a woman she really was. Elizabeth the Franciscan, leader, teacher, builder, editor, publisher, traveller, communicator, spokesperson at the highest ecclesiastical level, and faith-filled woman are all encapsulated in this time. Endeavouring to tell the story in sequential order is quite challenging. However, it is in seeking to comprehend the number and variety of activities that demanded her attention and energy simultaneously, that this multi-skilled woman is seen at her best.

Elizabeth was a 'lady' in the nineteenth-century sense of the word and had spent much of her life living among and associating with upper-class ladies and gentlemen. She had worked with and among poor people but her education and background provided her with ready entry into another social and literary world. What a contrast to this was presented by the 1874 Minnesota environment, especially in Belle Prairie and Brainerd. Most secular history books overlook Belle Prairie; it is rarely found on maps in illustrated texts, was often perceived in the 1870s by outsiders as part of the Wild West, and yet for Elizabeth, she saw it through different eyes. Certainly life was primitive and was not easy but the little settlement of Belle Prairie was in communication with the outside world through its Post Office. It did have a small store and a staging post where the coach arrived a number of times per week, prior to the coming of the railroad in 1877, while five miles away was the town of Little Falls where most basic services were offered.[56] That Elizabeth could embrace and move easily in different environments, as if by right, is a testimony to her calibre.

Elizabeth had come to assist the Catholic Church in a pioneer situation and she knew that while Fr Buh called Belle Prairie his mission centre (1865–78) and serviced Brainerd, most of his time was spent visiting his flock in far-flung places. He was an exemplary missionary who strongly desired more priests to join him and implored church authorities to send them. Bishop Grace especially wanted Franciscans from Germany to come and assist the small number of hard workers already there, including Benedictine Fathers along with the Benedictine Sisters. Since 1857 these religious women ministered as teachers in St Cloud on the Upper Mississippi and had spread to other places in the vicinity. The Northern Minnesota of the 1870s had only four cities and approximately twenty-four villages or fair-sized settlements.[57]

During the first six months of 1874, Elizabeth coped with the demands of the Belle Prairie foundation which was only in its second year, and carried on with her teaching commitments and shouldered the responsibility for the school, including more building projects. Simultaneously, she ensured the monthly publication of her periodical, besides preparing for forthcoming issues in the future. Then halfway through the year, because of the critical need for more personnel for her mission, she asked for and gained written permission from Bishop Grace to travel to Europe. This approval was dated 12 June and later in the same month, she would travel to the East Coast in order to make the transatlantic journey.

What awaited Elizabeth was an extended rich and colourful adventure with moments of frustration, surprise, disappointments, challenge, and unexpected results. But what about the school? It seems that Sr Peet was left in charge and, if not, then responsibility was delegated to others. What about the *Annals*? The staggering reality is that not only was Elizabeth to move through this overseas adventure, but for the first twelve months of her time in Europe, she was a mobile editor and organizer of all the material for her *Annals*. Sr Chaffee's memories confirm this extraordinary achievement:

It is worthy of note also that our Mother furnished Mr. Russell of Brainerd with material for publishing in the *Annals of Our Lady of the Angels*, from Rome and her other stopping places, during all the months of her absence; which was a source of wonder and admiration to Bishop Grace. Such was her industry and intellectual capacity.[58]

Elizabeth certainly shows industry and intellectual capacity, to put it mildly, and, impossible as it may seem, she continued to edit her high-standard journal and Mr Russell to print it during this long physical absence. As to the content of her publication, when an article throws light on her experiences or when her travels influenced a particular article, it will be noted in due course, while later her chosen themes in the *Annals* will be uncovered.[59] However before the story of the Roman interval is recounted, it seems appropriate to look next at the wider milieu in the 'Age of Journalism'.

Notes

1 Sr O'Neill's inconsistent and dubiously motivated behaviour caused problems in the community. Known as Sr M. Dominic (and Dominick) in her years in York, Baddesley (Warwickshire) and Skidaway (USA), she finally set herself up as abbess of an irregular community whose activities were questionable.

2 Elizabeth Hayes, 'Diary of Sister Mary Ignatius Hayes', 47. Pauline J. Shaw, ed., *Diary. Sister Mary Ignatius of Jesus (Elizabeth Hayes)*, 46.

3 'Personnel File Card of Sister Ignatius' in Folder of Mother Mary Ignatius Hayes, n.d. MFICAR.

4 M. R. MacGinley, 'Elizabeth Hayes: Religious Foundress' (paper presented at the 'Elizabeth Hayes: Woman of Her Time – Woman for the Future' workshop, Mt Alvernia College, Kedron, Brisbane, 7 May 1994).

5 Also the earlier Society of the Foreign Missions of Paris grew rapidly again in the nineteenth century and its publication provided much mission content, especially stories about their many missionary martyrs in the East.

6 Brian de Breffny, *Unless the Seed Die. The Life of Elizabeth Hayes (Mother M. Ignatius O.S.F.). Foundress of the Missionary Franciscan Sisters of the Immaculate Conception*, 96.

7 Fr Armand de Charbonnel, 'Testimonial from Fr Amand de Charbonnel for Sr M. Ignatius', 1864, MFICAR, section B, folder 2, item 23.

8 Elizabeth was in Marseilles on 12 September as indicated by the Passport 'Issued to Mary Ignatius Hayes', held in 'Passports (1864–6, 1871) and papers relating to the Franco-Prussian War', MFICAR, section B, folder 3, item 1.

9 Angelica (Mother M. of the Angels) Chaffee, 'Memories of the Life and Works of Mother Mary Ignatius of Jesus, Foundress of the Institute of the Missionary Franciscan Sisters of the Immaculate Conception', 14. A fuller explanation of what transpired and of Dupeyron's confidence in Elizabeth is given by Canice Mooney, Benignus Millet, and Redempta Power, 'First Instalment of Facts About the Life of Mother Mary Ignatius Hayes, Foundress', unpublished (Rome: Cause of Mother M. Ignatius Hayes – Missionary Franciscan Sisters, 1976), 16. MFICAA .

10 'Personnel File Card of Sister Ignatius'. 'Franciscan Convent of the Immaculate Conception Glasgow: Records', n.d., 118, FSAG.

11 Detailed evidence in 'Bayswater: Rule and Constitution History', n.d. MFICAE. Further explanation by Sr M. Dolores Cochrane, 'In the Beginning', Franciscan Sisters of the Immaculate Conception. Glasgow, 1994 draft, 34–5, 44.

12 Sr M. Alphonsine Liefquint, 'Letter from the Franciscan Prioress of Tourcoing Convent', in Bayswater Franciscan Records, ed. Franciscan Father, 1864, MFICAE. As noted earlier, Elizabeth Hayes had belonged to the Glasgow Franciscan Sisters who traced their roots to the Tourcoing tertiary Grey Sisters who, because of Pius V's *Circa pastoralis*, were required to take solemn vows and accept enclosure. Elizabeth lived in a time of ambiguity before simple-vow communities obtained a clear canonical validation.

13 Raphael Pontecchio, 'Letter from the Franciscan Minister General to Sr M. Elizabeth Hayes', 1865, MFICAE.

14 'Rule and Constitutions Written by Mother Mary Ignatius Hayes', 1866, MFICAR, section A, folder 11.

15 This Roman Congregation dealt with all affairs in foreign mission areas and countries with non-Catholic rulers.

16 'Passport Issued to Mary Ignatius Hayes'. This passport's reverse side indicates Elizabeth Hayes returned to France on 8 August 1866.

17 'Franciscan Convent of the Immaculate Conception Glasgow: Records', 119.

18 'Sister Mary Ignatius of Jesus (Hayes) to Monsignor George Talbot', 1866, in 'Talbot Papers', ECAR. Mooney, Millett, and Power, 'First Instalment of Facts', 23.

19 'Letter from Monsignor George Talbot to Soeur Marie Ignace', 1866, MFICAR, section B, folder 1, item 17. Chaffee, 'Memories', 21–2.

20 de Breffny, *Unless the Seed Die*, 103–5. John Watts, *A Canticle of Love: The Story of the Franciscan Sisters of the Immaculate Conception*, 34, 47, 55. (Chapter 2 of this text contains some inaccuracies about Elizabeth Hayes.) For the surname of Sr M. Aloysius, Watts has Mackintosh, de Breffny has MacIntosh, Ahles has McIntosh while my research in the Glasgow Franciscan archives supports MacIntosh.

21 Copy of the certificate of adjuration and conditional baptism, MFICAR, section B, folder 1, item 18.

22 Talbot was asked by Montgomery to obtain a cameo from the Pope. Even Empress Eugenie and Napoleon III were expected to assist. de Breffny, *Unless the Seed Die*, 108.

23 Chaffee, 'Memories', 23–4.
24 Arthur J. Butler, *Life and Letters of William John Butler. Late Dean of Lincoln and Sometime Vicar of Wantage*, 251–72.
25 Ibid., letter of 1 October 1870.
26 'Passport Issued to Mary Ignatius Hayes', in 'Passports (1864–66, 1871) and papers relating to the Franco-Prussian War', MFICAR, section B, folder 3, item 2: 1871.
27 Hon. Mrs. Fanny Montgomery, 'Corpus Christi, the Feast of the Most Blessed Sacrament', *Annals of Our Lady of the Angels* I, no. vi (1874): 187–92.
28 Much later than Butler's times, Anthony Beevor in his *Berlin: The Downfall 1945*, wrote about Spandau and its Fortress. Maev Kennedy, in a London article, wrote of Rudolf Hess at Spandau, referred to Spandau's prison grounds and the death of Hess in 1987.
29 Bismark's *Kulturkampf*, through measures such as the closure of convents and the dispersal of religious communities, produced consolidation among Catholics in consequence. Cf. Gerard Manly Hopkins' poem, 'The Wreck of the *Deutschland*', as an example of its effect in Britain.
30 German Franciscan friars impressed Elizabeth Hayes, for only three years later she asked for them to be sent to Minnesota and to be attached to the Cologne mission in Missouri.
31 An example is provided by Sisters from the Catholic town of Olpe in Germany from where two Franciscan groups, who were founded in 1860 and in 1863 respectively, sent sisters across the Atlantic to open new houses in 1872 and 1875.
32 Francis Charles Devas, *Mother Mary Magdalen of the Sacred Heart (Fanny Margaret Taylor. Foundress of the Poor Servants of the Mother of God 1832 – 1900)*, 95–6.
33 This Düsseldorf community in 1875 sent nuns to the USA where they in turn were to join two Italian Poor Clares who will be introduced later in Elizabeth's story. Together they formed the Cleveland foundation in 1877.
34 Nightingale's story was widely published but not the fact that she was introduced to the Deaconess Institute through reading its Annual Reports, a gift from London's Prussian ambassador. Anna Sticker, *Florence Nightingale Curriculum Vitae*, 8.
35 Examples that endow Elizabeth's experience with stark realism can be found today in John Lace, *Leipzig-Dresden Railway Line through Time – the Line During the War of Unification (1870–71)*, The European Railway Webring, http://easywab.easynet.co.uk/~jjlace/part14.html; accessed 12 December 1998.
36 Sisters Hayes and Peet were expected by Buggeonoms in February of 1872. (de Breffny, *Unless the Seed Die*, 111–12; Mooney, Millett, and Power, 'First Installment of Facts', 27–9.)
37 Chaffee, 'Memories', 24.
38 Carol K. Coburn and Martha Smith, *Spirited Lives: How Nuns Shaped Catholic Culture and American Life, 1836–1920*, 100.

39 'Warranty Deed', 1872, MFICAR, section A, folder 11, item 14.
40 Coburn and Smith, *Spirited Lives*, 100.
41 An old plat (handmade map with a scale of 2 inches to the mile) shows 'E. Hayes. 10' marked on the corner of Rosenkran's huge property. 'Plat of Belle Prairie Township 41 North, Ranges 31–32 West', n.d., Morrison County Historical Society Museum archives, Little Falls, Morrison County, Mn.
42 In 1875 Bishop Rupert Seidenbush became Vicar Apostolic of Northern Minnesota residing at St Cloud, while in 1889 Belle Prairie came into the new diocese of St Cloud with the Bishop Otto Zardetti its first bishop. John Ireland was to become the famous Archbishop of St Paul.
43 The newspapers included *St. Cloud Press, The Brainerd Tribune, St. Paul Northwestern Chronicle* and *The Minneapolis Daily Tribune* – copies in FSALF and MFICAR.
44 Morris C. Russell, 'News Item on Brainerd School', *The Brainerd Tribune*, 22 November 1873, 1, col. 7. This was the typical curriculum of a convent high school of the time.
45 For Romo's travels see Zephyrin Engelhardt, *Santa Barbara Mission: The Missions and Missionaries of California*, 414–15.
46 Chaffee, 'Memories', 25.
47 José Maria Romo, 'Diary. Romo, José Maria. 1871–1885', FMASB.
48 Englehardt, *Santa Barbara Mission*, 416.
49 Fr Gonzalez Rubio, OFM sent Elizabeth a translation of an eighteenth-century manuscript written by Fr Junipero Serra about the missions. She wrote an introduction for it and published it in 1874 under the title of 'A Chronicle of the Early Californian Missions' and 'The Mission to San Diego'. In 1878 Elizabeth published 'A Sketch of the Catholic Church in Upper California', plus a series of articles in the same year called 'California a Century Ago'.
50 Veronica (Sr M. Assumpta) Ahles, *In the Shadow of His Wings: A History of the Franciscan Sisters*, 77. How the railways encouraged expansion in Minnesota, including the development of Brainerd, see William E. Lass, *Minnesota – a History*, 138–50.
51 *The Brainerd Tribune* 22 November 1873, 6 December 1873 and 7 March 1874, FSALF and MFICAR. Ingolf Dillan, *Brainerd's Half Century*, 31.
52 Elizabeth Hayes, Sisters of St. Francis, to T. H. Canfield, letter of 1874, n.d.. MFICAR.
53 Bishop Thomas Grace, St Paul, letter to Rev. Sister Mary Ignatius, Superior, Sisters' Institute, Brainerd, Minnesota, 18 December 1873, MFICAR.
54 Hayes, 'The Apostolate of the Press', AOLA XV, no. ii (1890): 37.
55 Morris C. Russell, 'News Item', *The Brainerd Tribune*, 27 December 1873, p. 1, col. 5.
56 Ahles, *In the Shadow of His Wings*, 100.
57 de Breffny, *Unless the Seed Die*, 118, 120–1.
58 Chaffee, 'Memories', 30.
59 This 'Roman Interval' (July 1874–September 1875) has been related in

detail in Sr Ahles' well researched and documented 1977 book, *In the Shadow of His Wings*, 86–104. With fluent Italian-speaker, Sr M. Redempta Power MFIC, Sr Ahles of Little Falls spent years researching Rome's Propaganda Fide documents in order to grasp the essence and sequence of this period. Besides using Elizabeth's Diary (really jottings at different times and mostly written in Jamaica, yet with one very important entry in this Roman interval) she had access to Sr Chaffee's 'Memories', to unpublished typescript of Benedictine Fr Albert Kleber about the Poor Clare Bentivoglio sisters (including chronicles, letters, rescripts), and to data from noted Franciscan historian, Fr Marion Habig, OFM. Brian de Breffny's text for the same period is based on Sr Ahles.

Guernsey grave of Elizabeth Hayes' parents and Aunt Sophie. A plaque
honours Elizabeth also.

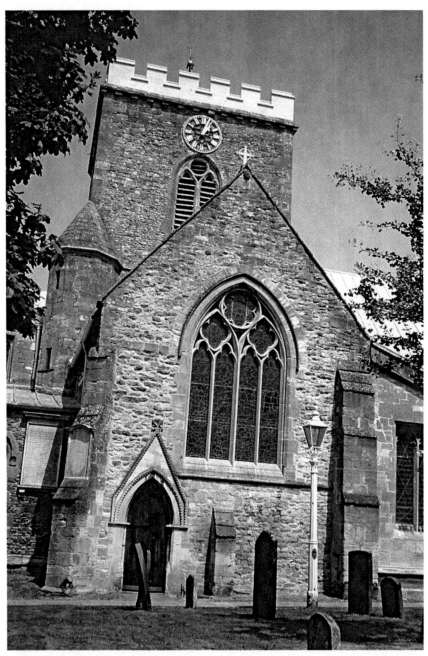

Sts Peter and Paul, Wantage. In this thirteenth-century church Elizabeth attended Anglican services. (She assisted in the care of the altar and arrangement of the flowers.)

Holywell Music Hall, Oxford, built by Dr William Hayes. Known as the first 'free standing' music hall in Europe.

The Jesuit Mayfair Church in Farm Street, London. Here Elizabeth was received into the Catholic Church.

Embroidered Mass vestments used in Sévres' convent chapel, France.

Elizabeth's Red Cross arm-bands, accreditation number, passport and details, Berlin, during the Franco-Prussian war.

Chapter 3

Elizabeth in the Age of Journalism

Nineteenth-century periodical literature, with its immense power for good or evil in society, came in retrospect to characterize the era as the age of journalism. In a world so influenced by the growth of periodical literature, Elizabeth experienced its vitality and she changed and developed with it. By stepping into journalism for the final twenty-one years of her life, she exemplified a type of womanly confidence and ability that differed from the dominant stereotype of Victorian women. Recently historians of Victorian literature have exposed a flood of nineteenth-century journals that have been hidden away in the dust of time, so now it is opportune to uncover Elizabeth's publication and allow it to take its place in the age of journalism.

Elizabeth had a sound knowledge of European and North American nineteenth-century journals. Greater awareness of these journals can help one appreciate her capabilities and capture the richness of her international place in this field. New research into secular, religious and Catholic journals, each division like layers of an onion, contributes to the understanding of the journalistic milieu into which Elizabeth ventured, and so these categories will be explored here.[1] At least, by watching in particular the activities of some of Elizabeth's contemporary women journalists, new understandings of her and her writings will emerge.

A fraction of the broad range of countless secular and religious periodicals in the English language will be touched upon, followed by some history on periodical literature produced by the Catholic press. To appreciate Elizabeth's awareness of, and clear associations with, the Catholic periodicals of England, France and Italy, attention will be given to surprising discoveries. Finally it will be enlightening to explore and observe Elizabeth in the North American arena when editors of Catholic periodicals take advantage of the 'power of the press'.

Setting the Scene

In the 'Age of the Periodical', the editor of the *Colonial Times,*
Robert Montgomery, voiced an insight into the importance of the
periodical press, not only in Europe but also in other countries:

> Periodicals are amongst the peculiar characteristics of the present
> age: emanating from the womb of circumstances, and imbued with
> the vitality of existing events, they direct the current of living
> thought and active energy, and give a form, a tone, and hue to
> society.[2]

The merits and demerits of the secular periodical press were recognized by the publishers of religious journals. Editors wished to
counterbalance the evil perceived in certain non-religious, sensa-
tional or scandal-filled magazines. As the monthly periodical
became more and more the arena for serious discussion of life's
problems, it was logical and necessary that this literary form
become popular for propagating religious ideas. While, technically
speaking, Elizabeth's potential was well positioned in the kind of
journalistic milieu around her, commitment to the Apostolate of
the Press essentially challenged her to produce high quality literature to partially counteract these perceived irreligious and secular
outpourings. Could she do it?

Subjects like work and wages, commerce and finance, exploiting
and exploited, were of keen interest to many nineteenth-century
people in an era of intellectual and social ferment. Although religious journalistic literature had been taking shape in the
eighteenth century, only in the next century did an increased
number of individuals gain a greater realization of the power of
the press and were able to lead their religious followers into journalistic action; others fearfully still held back.[3] As a committed
Anglican for thirty-three years, Elizabeth had been surrounded
with religious literature, especially Tractarian, and was aware of the
growing desire for periodical literature. She realized the need for
her *Annals* years before Stead claimed that:

> The monthly magazine or review represents the higher thought of
> our time, and, hence, a good monthly magazine is as indispensable
> for the culture of a democracy as a well-endowed University, or a
> good common school.[4]

To deal with the enormous volume of nineteenth-century periodicals, a selection of particular writers and journals that were known

to Elizabeth, or influenced her in some way, have been chosen.

In a high proportion of nineteenth-century journals Elizabeth and other readers were provided with references to *The Times*; for example, this influential newspaper published a social justice article in which Dr Manning stated that 'every man has a right to work or to bread'. The article was widely denounced as socialistic and anarchistic.[5] This reaction to *The Times'* article indicates something of the prevailing climate in which Elizabeth lived, a period of change, revolution and transition. Dr Manning, the 'Dockers' Cardinal', concerned for poor workers and their families, negotiated in the Workers Strike of 1889. This, so-called, clerical interference in the workers' question was disliked by Karl Marx who wrote to Friedrich Engels regarding the German clergy, 'We have to combat the clerics vigorously, especially in the Catholic areas ... the scoundrels are flirting with the worker's question whenever it seems appropriate'.[6] Elizabeth knew that the first volume of *Das Kapital* was published in 1867, and together with the Communist First International, formed in the same year, was having great influence on the development of communism and socialism.

In her *Annals* Elizabeth defined the 'Internationale' which originated from Marx and his friends, as 'a sort of international trades-union founded upon socialistic and anti-religious principles' and recognized its widespread influence.[7] She was impressed by Canon Schorderet who realized that the Catholic press needed to be completely 'independent of free-masonry and socialism'. In nineteenth-century Europe and other countries the influence of Marx, who with Engels had produced the *Communistic Manifesto,* was spreading. In Cologne Marx took advantage of the power of the press by establishing and editing a communist periodical.[8] In London he contributed articles on contemporary and social events to republican European and American newspapers and maintained contact with followers whose aim was to form revolutionary organizations. In the 1860s when Marx's activities and writings were given much press coverage, Elizabeth lived and moved around France, Italy and Germany, where European events influenced her and shaped her ideas on the powerful influence of the press.

The *Annals* that Elizabeth published formed part of the wider Christian response to the period's socialist and anti-religious literature. The Industrial Revolution brought new kinds of world products and a new style of world economy. Elizabeth was aware that a new working class suffered from appalling conditions and she read about the rise of trade unions and the socialist philosophers who denounced capitalism. Elizabeth also knew of writers who raised public awareness and of social workers who alleviated suffering. Added to this scene were scientists such as Charles Darwin who, through the publication of *The Origin of Species* and later *The Descent of Man* with its theory of evolution by natural selection, undermined traditional religious beliefs. Darwin's work challenged the way the Bible had been interpreted and the churches strongly opposed his theory. One famous 1860 debate was between Thomas H. Huxley and the Bishop of Oxford, Samuel Wilberforce, whom Elizabeth knew in her Wantage days. Every epoch displays what many at the time regard as a wedge of evil. In the nineteenth century good periodical literature appeared to Elizabeth and her literary friends to be a remedy for contagious secularism which could threaten deeply held religious and social values.

The nineteenth-century marketplace around Elizabeth was flooded with literature on 'isms' including Socialism, Darwinianism and Malthusianism; many were indifferent or hostile to traditional Christian religion. While conversions to Catholicism, like Elizabeth's own personal experience, were numerous in England, many Europeans, including English Christians, listened to other 'literary prophets' of the day. The religious press struggled against its secular critics while the Catholic Apostolate of the Press clarified its purpose and tried to counterbalance what Elizabeth called, 'irreligious publications'. For her and other contemporary Christian thinkers, religion – belief in a superhuman power – involved faith in a personal God who was entitled to obedience, love and worship. Literature published contrary to this was seen by committed Christians as irreligious.

Secular Periodicals in English

The link between the three mentioned 'isms' was only a small part of the whole scene, but it can, with the help of a major Victorian journalist, provide an insight into the period's turbulent intellectual atmosphere, the world of journals, and into Elizabeth's growing understanding of the 'immense power for good or evil which in these days is inherent in the Press'.[9]

Harriet Martineau (1802–1876) lived when many intellectual women were challenging the view that women were mentally inferior to men, especially in regard to scientific knowledge.[10] Harriet embraced scientific materialism and her advanced views on social, economic and religious questions caused considerable controversy. Scientific pamphlets and journals of the 1860s were proclaiming atheism and many like Harriet joined the rationalists who put their faith in the capacity of science to provide adequate solutions to life's queries. For growing numbers, religion and science were seen as incompatible and many chose to emphasize human self-sufficiency, achievement and production. This contradicted the Christian concept of a Creator God who invites collaborators to transform history into God's reign of justice and love. Secular journals that acclaimed human achievement as the central concern of life were seen by many Christians as irreligious.

On reading the Martineau-Atkinson *Letters on the Laws of Man's Nature and Development* (1851), Charlotte Brontë, a clergyman's daughter like Elizabeth Hayes, was shocked by the scientific approach and wrote:

It is the first exposition of avowed atheism and materialism I have ever read; the first unequivocal declaration of disbelief in the existence of a God or a future life I have ever seen. In judging of such exposition and declaration, one would wish entirely to put aside the sort of instinctive horror they awaken ...[11]

Charlotte's words provide an example of the reaction of committed Christian people on seeing such irreligious publications and of their anxiety that the Christian understanding of Truth be upheld. Elizabeth expressed her concern by quoting Monsignor Mermillod, exiled Bishop of Geneva:

Truth is held captive by the revolution throughout the world; the press is enslaved, and at the mercy of error; but it can be sanctified by sacrifice and prayer. Good literature, he said, can carry the bread of Truth to a society, which is dying of sheer want of justice, and peace, and liberty.[12]

Marian Evans, alias George Eliot and an acclaimed novelist who had cast off her Evangelical faith under the influence of biblical criticism, moved in Harriet's circle of friends. Marian's family was torn asunder, as were many other Victorian families, when a member converted to another Church or to outright agnosticism. Elizabeth had suffered also and knew the pain of being cut off from family and friends. In essence, she wished to bring to the periodical press her particular kind of convert zeal. In this age of the periodical, publications spread new insights about economics, commerce, women's issues, the need for temperance and the struggle of workers, and also addressed student and children's needs.[13] Developing technology, faster distribution and lower prices made the purchase of periodicals possible for a greater number of readers.

Among major British secular periodicals that were flooding the market, outstanding were *The Edinburgh Review* (1802–1929)[14] and *Blackwood's Edinburgh Magazine*. Amongst the European periodical equivalents were the *French Revue des Deux Mondes* (founded 1829) and the German *Literarisches Wochenblatt* (1820–98). Well-known British secular journals were shipped to America, Australia and other countries and included *Punch, The English Family Herald, Household Words, Tit-bits, All the Year Round* and *Illustrated London News*.[15] To ascertain if these publications, which arrived at many nineteenth-century coastal ports in the United States, reached the American Midwest, a visit to some Minnesota libraries was undertaken by the present writer and this revealed the literary situation Elizabeth's *Annals* encountered.[16]

The number, variety and readership of attractively designed periodicals grew enormously in the United States around 1850, 'America's Golden Age'. American literary reviews and magazines that reached Australia and were readily available included the *North American Review*, the *Atlantic Monthly*, *Harper's Monthly Magazine* and *Scriber's Magazine*, so what was available in the State of Minnesota? What periodicals were advertised for sale in the city of St Cloud, situated south of Belle Prairie township and between Elizabeth's convent and the twin cities of Minneapolis/St Paul? Of the four periodicals quoted, three were advertised in the 1872–3 St Cloud newspaper, the *St. Cloud Journal*.[17] The *North American Review* (1815–1940), named in the early part of the century as one of the most important serious periodicals circulating in the United States, was absent; probably it was so popular that it did not need advertising. Much information about train and boat travel, points on farming and guidance for health care were among 'Literary Notices' that encouraged the purchase of periodicals. In central Minnesota Elizabeth had been surrounded by a large number of secular journals, some twenty-six at least.[18] No reference was found to any journal published in Minnesota, a fact noted by Elizabeth's printer who wrote in his *Brainerd Tribune*, 'It [Elizabeth's *Annals*] is the only monthly magazine now published in Minnesota.'[19]

Central Minnesota press records indicate that in the 1870s there was no shortage of local printing houses, male editors and news-papers.[20] Elizabeth chose initially to avail herself of a Brainerd printing house rather than one at St Cloud where the controversial newspaper editor, Mrs Jane Grey Swisshelm (1815–1884) worked.[21] Known as the St Cloud firebrand, the first and only other local woman editor at the time, she experienced opposition resulting in mob violence, demolition of her press and disposal of its remains in the Mississippi River.[22] Eventually Jane sold her *Visitor* and the newspaper became the *St. Cloud Journal;* Elizabeth advertised her school in it but avoided its printing services.

Among the host of secular American periodicals that reached the environs of St Cloud and the Mississippi River settlements, the most popular were *Godey's Lady's Book, Peterson's Magazine* and *Vick's Illustrated Magazine.*[23] The lengthy table of contents of *Godey's Lady's Book* shows a breadth of interests and even covered 'Selections from the Writings of Fénélon', whose famous reflections on the education of girls were familiar to Elizabeth.[24] The first volume of *Vick's Illustrated Monthly Magazine,* in response to a potential market, commenced four years after Elizabeth launched her periodical. Elizabeth resonated with the wishes of *Vick's* readers for she also had begun with a monthly periodical. *Peterson's Magazine* provided a sample of the flavour of the times. By 1888 its contents showed a special interest in English life; everything in an account it published by Revd Charles Kingsley (1819–1875) was familiar to Elizabeth and other English immigrants and showed how an American publication could successfully market English content. *Peterson's Magazine* was studded with poetry, a popular nineteenth-century practice in secular periodicals which Elizabeth also employed successfully.

Religious Journals in English

In the field of non-Catholic religious journals, it is clear that writer-converts to Catholicism had often written previously for Church of England journals, continued to read them, and made reference to them in later articles. Elizabeth read the *Guardian,*[25] described as the most intelligent weekly among the churches and the leading journal of the Church of England.[26] She also read *The Quarterly Review,*[27] that according to *The Month* was 'top of the list' and she knew of *The Christian Work,*[28] published by the London Mission Society.

This study, in looking at the non-Catholic religious journals, favours a chronological approach, guided by Elizabeth's presence in England (1840s-50s). The approach, combined with some major denominational movements and related journals, can move us through the turbulent century so that Elizabeth's contribution can be better situated. Early in the century, traditional religious views were weakened by the general spread of knowledge and discussion, aided by the publication of sceptical secular and anti-Christian periodicals.[29] Religious and sincere minds in general struggled with the difficulty of discriminating truth from error as more and more journals flooded the fast-growing market. Periodicals came to constitute a literature in their own right in the nineteenth century; not only did output increase on such topics as politics, literature, science and art, but the periodical press multiplied the number of publications related to other professions and occupations.[30] Many Victorians, according to John Henry Newman, were:

> Simply perplexed, – frightened or rendered desperate, as the case may be – by the utter confusion into which late discoveries or speculations have thrown their most elementary ideas of religion ... Let them be fierce with you who have no experience of the difficulty with which error is discriminated from truth, and the way of life found amid the illusions of the world.[31]

Early in the century, denominations began to face internal struggles which undermined their readiness to respond adequately to a faith crisis; the real point of conflict was the inadequate response of the churches. Both the critical spirit and the will to believe were further influenced by scientific journals and related publications. 'The Bible and the Bible alone' was the watchword of English Protestantism. A faith that interpreted the Bible literally, without understanding of deeper symbolic and metaphorical meaning, faced a crisis when confronted with the new scientific findings. Elizabeth captured this struggle in the story of a young Englishman:

> We Protestants do not find much strength in our religion to keep us from evil, and help us to practise what is good. It is very difficult for us to find what is the right true religion, and what we should do to obtain the certainty of salvation. All is darkness and confusion, and in the midst of a multitude of teachers that there are among us, each holding different opinions, how is it possible to find one who can guide us into the truth? It creates in us a despair of ever discovering it ...[32]

Through periodicals, assisted by lectures and sermons, one prophet after another helped to create a 'climate of opinion', and so scepticism and the habit of doubt were unconsciously bred.[33] The Church of England's answer to this and to Charles Knight's famous *Penny Magazine* (1832–45/6) was the *Saturday Magazine* (1832–44) published by John Parker for the Society for Promoting Christian Knowledge. It combined general information and religious instruction with portraits of churchmen, scenes from the Holy Land, biblical illustration, and pictures of cathedrals and churches. In the same year the Methodists produced their *Evangelical Penny Magazine and Bible Illustrator* with the first issue displaying a woodcut of John Wesley while extracts from his religious diary were scattered throughout the journal. Elizabeth employed the stories of saints' lives in the same way as this Methodist journal promoted the biographies of evangelical holy men.

Contemporary religious journals, including *The Evangelical Spectator, The Evangelist* and the *Evangelical Magazine,* continued in the market even when William and Robert Chambers with their *Chamber's (Edinburgh) Journal* (1832–1955) strengthened competition.[34] From 1834, the aim of the *Christian Keepsake and Missionary Annual* (1834–39) was the promotion of piety and the diffusion of authentic information respecting the progress and effects of Christianity in different quarters of the globe. Its purpose was much the same as that of many other Victorian missionary periodicals published in London by denominational missionary societies or by missionary societies serving a group of denominations. Missionary magazines were a lively part of the religious press before the temperance journals entered the publishing scene in the mid-nineteenth century.

The *Christian Lady's Magazine* (1834–49), launched beside the new serious monthly and quarterly literary reviews, *The Southern Literary Messenger* and *Graham's Magazine,* exemplified Protestant religious journals which were 'Christian' in tone, anti-slavery and also anti-Catholic. *Christian Lady's Magazine* published an essay on 'Reasons for Leaving the Church of Rome' and its pages spoke of 'taking the Christian message to the Irish and removing them from the influence of Rome'. Charlotte E. Tonna, editor for most of the magazine's life, sought to enhance women's power through this instructive and educational magazine, yet she castigated the writings of Mary Wollstonecraft (1759–1797). Also published at this time was the *Baptist Reporter* (1836–57; 1864–65), a quasi-temperance periodical offering church news, cautionary anecdotes, and practical advice including suggestions for Sunday Schools.[35] The Unitarian's accessible journal, *The National – A*

Library for the People (1839) was short-lived even though Tennyson, Wordsworth, Keats and other famous poets contributed to it. *The Christian Teacher* (1835–39), first a monthly and then a quarterly, was intended for all denominations despite its strong Unitarian control. Many journals provide evidence of the short life span of religious periodicals.

In the 1840 to the 1860s, writers of the Oxford Movement tracts gradually became contributors to Tractarian journals. In the early 1840s their *British Critic* published articles by Dr William G. Ward (1812–1882) who soon converted to Catholicism and then contributed to its journals. While Tractarians dwelt on doctrines, the Broad Church Camdenians, the Cambridge Camden Society, focused on ritual solemnities, founding *The Ecclesiologist* in 1841 to support their views.[36] Anne Mozley was the editor of the 'moderate' Anglican journal, the *Christian Remembrancer* (1841–68). Her literary skill was such that in later life, John Henry Newman – a relative – invited her to edit his letters of Anglican days. Mozley also contributed reviews to three prominent secular periodicals of serious pretensions: *Blackwood's Edinburgh Magazine*, the *Saturday Review* and the short-lived *Bentley's Quarterly Review*. However, since theology was a male preserve, neither Anne's name nor her sex appeared. She exemplified the blurring of distinctions between religious and secular journals; she contributed religious topics to a secular journal as seen in her Blackwood's articles on 'English Converts to Romanism' and 'Convent Life'. John Henry Newman, as a Catholic, continued to read the Anglican *Christian Remembrancer* and evidence suggests that Elizabeth Lockhart and Elizabeth Hayes read it in their Wantage Anglican Sisterhood days.[37]

In the 1840s Elizabeth Hayes was surrounded by a kaleidoscope of journals, when religious ones had to compete with periodical giants including the *London Journal, Westminster Review,* and *Punch,* the weekly magazine famous for its satirical cartoons, jokes and puns devoid of compassion for churchmen and politicians. *The Ecclesiologist* 'monthly/bi-monthly' was published between 1841 to 1868,[38] while *The Rector Magazine* maintained its publication from 1845 to 1862 and was assisted by contributions from young Revd Charles Lutwidge Dodgson, alias Lewis Carroll of *Alice in Wonderland* fame. While the *Clergy List* struggled for survival, Transcendentalists in England watched the rise of an American New England journal, *The Dial* (1840–44), edited by Margaret Fuller and Ralph Waldo Emerson.[39] In 1848 the Christian Socialism movement published a weekly journal, *Politics for the People,* and with

Charles Kingsley's help, supported working people and promoted the formation of workers' associations with consequent social improvement. In the 1850s amid the religious ferment of the age, Elizabeth was encircled by the press when quarterly, monthly and daily periodicals taught people what to think and say.[40] The huge success of Charlotte Yonge's novels, the most famous being *The Heir of Redcliff* (1853), propelled the success of the Tractarian journal for youth, the *Monthly Packet*, which Charlotte edited for almost fifty years. Charlotte, the same age as Elizabeth, belonged initially to the Keble-Lockhart-Dyson-Butler circle of friends,[41] and then later to the Butler-Wantage enclave,[42] who were literary people full of admiration for Tractarian leaders well known to Elizabeth.[43] Charlotte Yonge, above all other women and editors, provided the present writer with insights into Elizabeth's mid-century literary world, hitherto unacknowledged by her biographers.

Religious journals were challenged by the popular secular magazines to present serial articles and illustrations, such as in Charles Dickens' family journal, *Household Words,* and his *All the Year Round.* Dickens' periodicals could not be described as 'religious' yet, as his social-reformer activities increased, his serialized periodical contributions appeared to hold a greater power for good. This was evidenced in the 1852–3 serialization of *Bleak House* and in *Little Dorrit,* serialized monthly in 1855–7. Later in *All the Year Round, A Tale of Two Cities* appeared in serial form also. Elizabeth recognized the success of serialization in periodicals and from her first volume serials were included. Major serialized contributions in Elizabeth's *Annals* include numerous lives of saints, stories for the young, fiction, Franciscan history, 'Souvenirs of Mgr de Segur', 'The Royal Recluse', Manning's 'Confidence in God' and Vansittart's English history.

As a London teacher, Elizabeth knew that most Victorian temperance societies had youth sections that tried to inculcate temperance ideals in children, along with the practice of charity, thrift and self-discipline. The largest and most successful of these groups was the non-denominational Band of Hope which in the late 1840s published regional and local temperance periodicals and newspapers for working-class children. In 1851 its London-based organization launched its official journal, *Band of Hope Review,* and since its first priority was abstinence from alcohol, it provided young readers with moralistic tales, anecdotes, poems, and songs which promoted temperance values and the qualities of self-control, diligence and providence. This large-sized *Review* also reflected the organization's close connection with Sunday-school work and its commitment to the Ragged Schools Movement, anti-slavery and peace.[44]

By 1854 the journal, *Sunday at Home*, was published by the Religious Tract Society and was similar to many Sunday magazines that offered appropriate Sabbath reading such as articles about foreign missions, religious poetry, Bible tales, and uplifting fiction. When Elizabeth published her *Annals* she included these same four elements. *Sunday at Home* had accompanying illustrations, included many high quality wood engravings, some on tinted paper and a few colour lithographs. One of Elizabeth's biographers quoted a contemporary *Brainerd Tribune* newspaper extract which remarked that Elizabeth also chose fine 'tinted book paper'.[45] The introduction of mass production by the giants of periodical literature did not deter smaller adventurers; *Cassell's Illustrated Family Bible*, packed with illustrations, was sold to thousands of poor people in separate instalments for a penny each week. *The Quiver* (1861–1916), initially edited also by Cassell and a weekly publication, contained general fiction and non-fiction with strong religious and moralistic overtones. Cassell's publications provide examples of secular periodicals attempting to mitigate perceived evils in society through the influence of religion.[46]

As industrializing society moved through the 1860s, Elizabeth observed that the newly literate classes increasingly found that periodicals became their primary source of entertainment, instruction and information. Recognizing the power of the press, the Church of England Total Abstinence Society launched its own official organ, the monthly *Church of England Temperance Magazine* (1862–72).[47] The United Kingdom's religious magazines, like the long-running monthly *Good Words* and *The Quiver*, were the first sixpenny magazines and were illustrated throughout. *Good Words* edited by Presbyterians and featuring eminent English writers, including William E. Gladstone, mixed religious content overtly with entertainment in the form of serial fiction and short essays on general subjects. Other Protestant journal organs were *The Church Builder*, a successful quarterly from 1862 for those interested in church architecture, the *Church Times* from 1863, the *Rock* founded in 1868 and the *St. Paul's Magazine* (1867–74). The last named was initially edited by Anthony Trollope and was noted for its collection of serialized novels, including a contribution from Trollope. It was illustrated and contained poetry, criticism and reviews. The name of this publication alone would have meant much to Elizabeth Hayes as family members had been associated with St Paul's. Religious periodicals were overshadowed from 1864 by one of the great nineteenth-century reviews, *Fortnightly Review* (1864–1954), to whose pages churchmen such as Newman at times contributed.

In the nineteenth century's last quarter, with journals far outnumbering printed books, the churches became more fully aware of the power of the press.[48] Religious journals, sometimes called 'weekly papers', struggled harder against the increased tide of secular periodicals and sought to broaden their appeal; the *Church Times*, the *Rock* and the *Record* now fell under this category. Of greater circulation, however, and still not narrowly ecclesiastical were the *British Weekly* and the *Guardian*. The Anglican clergyman, J. Erskine Clarke, introduced *The Parish Magazine* which proved a launching pad for local parish magazines. By 1885 many Anglican parish clergymen were committed to organizing their own monthly magazines, Revd Butler of Wantage included, as his parish had its own printing press.[49]

Catholic Periodical Press in the Age of Journalism

Turning now to focus on Elizabeth's contribution within the Catholic periodical press in Europe and North America, it is significant to note that many nineteenth-century Catholic writers appreciated the potential for good that was achievable in periodical literature. Church history of this period is punctuated with the names of leading Catholic figures, men and women, clerical and lay, who made mighty efforts to combat the flood of anti-Christ, anti-Pope and anti-Church literature. In order to situate Elizabeth in this arena so as to appreciate her contribution, there needs to be at least a look at this broad Catholic periodical response. Despite finding a number of primary resources, there is a shortage of critical secondary materials in this area.[50] The most fruitful results emerge through an examination of selected journalists whose lives and writings shed light on Elizabeth's period and the environment she experienced 1874–94.

By walking in Elizabeth's footprints through the *Annals* one becomes aware of the surprising breadth of her international interests and concerns. Because of her extraordinary web of literary connections in different countries, she also reveals much of her Apostolate of the Press commitment through individuals in her circle of associates. Like other educated nineteenth-century women, Elizabeth wrote many letters but since these are no longer extant,[51] there is need to rely on others with similar backgrounds and experiences and to draw parallels.

The Catholic Press in England

The full flourishing of Catholic life was possible in England only after the Catholic Emancipation Act of 1829. Outstanding among the women who understood the power of periodical articles for the Catholic cause was Fanny Margaret Taylor, former Crimean War nurse, once Elizabeth's Bayswater neighbour and one who also appreciated Manning's spiritual direction.[52] Fanny, like a number of other women writers, had eased her way into the literary scene by contributing translations, and discovered that it was unnecessary to translate or write a book in the 1860s when periodical literature was flourishing.[53] She wrote for the high profile Catholic periodical, *The Dublin Review*. This quarterly, read by prominent figures involved in the period's great religious, literary and scientific movements and founded in 1836 by Nicholas (later Cardinal) Wiseman and Daniel O'Connell, the Irish parliamentary leader, had a territorial title that was influenced by Blackwood's *Edinburgh Review's* fame yet, from the beginning, it was edited and published in London. The influence of *The Dublin Review* may be judged by its effect on Newman who claimed that one of its articles on St Augustine became a turning point for him. Three other English Catholic periodicals known to Elizabeth were *The Lamp*, *The Month* and *The Messenger* and their connections with her are worth consideration.

The Lamp was a monthly penny magazine founded in 1846 and numbered among its contributors Elizabeth Lockhart – respected writer, translator of religious books and staff writer for *The Dublin Review* – and her half-brother, William Lockhart, one-time editor of *Catholic Opinion* and theological editor for *The Universe*. The latter was London's first Catholic penny paper, commenced in late 1860, after Cardinal Wiseman expressed the urgent need for a paper, like Louis Veuillot's *L'Univers* in France, to contradict press articles against the Holy See. As noted earlier, the Lockharts' friendship with Elizabeth Hayes secured literary connections for her. Other contributors to *The Lamp* included Lady Georgiana Fullerton, close friend of Fanny Taylor,[54] Augusta T. Drane, Henry E. Manning (later Cardinal), and Fathers Edward Caswell and Henry A. Rawes. All of these writers in time contributed to Elizabeth's *Annals*. In 1862 Fanny Taylor became the successful proprietor and editor of *The Lamp*. She was encircled with influential literary friends including the Farm Street Jesuits, most of whom were known to Elizabeth, also John H. Newman (later Cardinal), Dr Edward B. Pusey, Fathers Gallwey, Goldie, and Formby, Mrs Parsons, Cecilia Caddell, and Bessie R. Parkes, many of whom contributed to other Catholic periodicals as well. Newman's most famous contribution to Fanny Taylor's periodical was his *Dream of Gerontius* (1865). After a visit to Ireland, she published a series of articles for *The Lamp* which were reissued under the title of *Irish Homes and Irish Hearts* and advertized in *The Dublin Review* of 1867.[55] Catholic journals co-operated with one another to help their common cause. In the 1870s the Hon. Fanny Montgomery clearly adopted this growing serialization style in her major contribution to Elizabeth's *Annals*.[56] Due to financial difficulties – the perennial Catholic struggle – *The Lamp* was abandoned in 1871.

Fanny Taylor's *Eastern Hospitals and English Nurses* (1856) had been well accepted; however in 1859, when she related the English martyrs' story, *Tyborne, and Who Went Thither;* this made her so famous that afterwards she could simply sign her publications 'Author of Tyborne'. Lady Georgiana Fullerton, considered the period's most distinguished Catholic woman writer, was full of praise for it.[57] *Tyborne* is said to have won its place immediately as a standard Catholic story, and it ensured the acceptance of Fanny Taylor as a leading contributor to Catholic periodicals. In 1887–88, almost thirty years later, Elizabeth published from Rome her version of 'The English Martyrs' in a series of eight articles. It commenced with the new 'Decree of the Congregation of Sacred Rites' and referred to Cardinal Manning and other English bishops who had recently petitioned Pope Leo XIII on this matter.[58] Elizabeth's series concluded with a personal exhortation to her readers:

> Let us so live, and let us so die, that we may be with the martyrs in Heaven. In living and in dying, we, like them, must be on God's side always, cost us what it may.[59]

The lines have two layers of meaning, for Elizabeth was aware also of the 'martyrs of the Press' and they suggest how seriously she wished to carry out her evangelizing press ministry.

The Month was a magazine and review, whose aim was to deal with important questions and to take a Catholic stance on historical, religious, scientific and literary subjects. It was firmly founded in 1864 by Fanny Taylor in cooperation with the English Jesuits. It was hoped that *The Month* could be of a kindred nature to *The Dublin Review* and, once under way, its editorship and ownership were taken over by the Jesuits. Expenses were always an owner's greatest problem since, besides the cost of printing and paper, contributors

– some of whom were known to Elizabeth – had to be paid, with the exception of Lady Fullerton who donated her *Constance Sherwood*.[60] It became common practice for articles to appear in Catholic journals first in serial form and then later to be published in book form. Fanny (Mother M. Magdalen) Taylor, continued to write numerous stories, articles, and sketches for *The Month* and other contemporary Catholic periodicals.[61]

Elizabeth in her 1880s *Annals* clearly acknowledged her use of *The Messenger of the Sacred Heart of Jesus* as her resource for 'The Holy Man of Tours',[62] 'Scenes in a Soldier's Life',[63] 'Reparation by Religious Orders'[64] and 'Story of a Recent Conversion'.[65] *The Messenger's* history is another example of Fanny Taylor's editorial influence and is also of significance to our story because of its French connections. The journal's title was sub-headed 'Organ of the Apostolate of Prayer'.[66] The 'Apostolate of Prayer or League of the Sacred Heart' had been founded at Vals, near Le Puy, in France in 1844 and was introduced into England in 1865 by a Jesuit priest, William Maher. The periodical's circulation fell into decline until in 1882 Fr Dignam, well known to Fanny Taylor, planned a new approach and sought her assistance. In 1884 *The Messenger* was restyled by Fanny and it became the *Penny Messenger* which then could be purchased by the poor. The periodical's most zealous promoters were the Poor Servants of the Mother of God, the religious congregation founded by Fanny. Wherever these Sisters were found, the Apostolate of Prayer flourished and there is seen in them, along with the Jesuit printer, Br James Stanley, a leading example of commitment to the English Catholic periodical press.

The Catholic Press in France

The French Catholic Press had a major influence on those Catholics who contributed to periodicals in the 1870s and it is worth reflecting on the French influences on Elizabeth, earlier French literary influences, the French influence on the Catholic press of other countries and missionary activities linked to Catholic periodicals in order to better understand Elizabeth's work. Besides the traditional influence of the French Church on Irish Catholics, Elizabeth brought to her *Annals* her unique set of French experiences – life on French-speaking Guernsey, living with French Sisters in Glasgow and Jamaica, and living for some years near Paris. When her publishing project began she already had a deep conviction about the power of the press. This conviction grew out of her knowledge, not only of her English friends' literary success, but also of the immense influence for good or for evil seen by her in the French press.

This French influence in the *Annals* is seen, for example, when Elizabeth devoted a series of three articles to 'The Apostolate of the Press'.[67] Her series informed readers of the French origins and activities of the press apostolate of Canon Schorderet. Elizabeth proceeded in the articles to draw attention to the fact that Fr Kleiser arrived in England in 1874 for the same apostolate. Finally, she introduced her readers to an account of courageous young French women, namely Marguerite Durantet, Marie Weber and Catherine Sturney, who committed their lives to the Apostolate of the Press. A fourth article on the Catholic press affirmed the importance of what Elizabeth and other editors of Catholic periodicals had been doing, namely, the dissemination of good writings. Elizabeth wrote:

> The immense power for good or evil which in these days is inherent in the Press, is too obvious to require our dwelling upon it at any length. In these days of universal decay, the Press is the one human power which holds its own. We see in it the rapid universal agent of human thought, overflowing with fire and energy, welcomed alike by rich and poor, and possessing complete and irresponsible freedom of action. These capabilities have been recognized by the enemies of Christianity, and they have turned the Press into a huge instrument for the propagation of infidel, immoral, and revolutionary principles.[68]

The 1870s' response of the French Catholic periodical press leads one to glance back at earlier French literary activities. Three significant figures in French Catholic literature were Louis Veuillot, Count de Montalembert and Fr Henri Lacordaire. All were intellectuals and distinguished writers with Veuillot seen as committed to Catholic authoritarianism while the other two were more prominent for their adherence to French Catholic liberalism. There is significant difference in the meaning of the French form of liberalism from the English one, as Newman once noted.[69] Veuillot, the champion of the conservative French press, was at age seventeen the editor of a Rouen newspaper and because of his talent, style and wit was able to enter Parisian journalism. A friend of Veuillot took him to Rome, he converted to the Catholic faith and, on his return to Paris, devoted himself to the Catholic cause.

Many French people had been influenced by the anti-religious ideas diffused by Voltaire and the Revolution. In contrast, Veuillot wrote a number of works entirely devoted to the beauty of

Christian doctrine and life; he discovered *L'Univers,* a little known newspaper lacking financial resources. Position and money were offered to Veuillot, but he refused both to take the path of Catholic journalism. Around the second half of the 1840s, a major French discussion topic was the Catholics' thrust for liberty in education and teaching, which was spearheaded by Montalembert. Veuillot resurrected *L'Univers,* Montalembert was associated with it and *L'Univers* became a major Catholic organ with a distinctly Roman emphasis. Later Veuillot found himself in conflict with his former friend, Montalembert, with some bishops and especially with Bishop Dupanloup of Orléans. Elizabeth in 1864 received the approval of this same Bishop Dupanloup to make a foundation at Orléans after Bishop Murdoch of Glasgow had licensed her transfer of vows to another bishop.[70] Afterwards, Murdoch wrote approvingly that she would be in the diocese of a prelate of international renown. Dupanloup was influential in the highest educational circles and his writings regarding the needs of students were well ahead of his times.[71] Elizabeth never lost interest in French Catholic education; in her 1880 *Annals* she published 'The Bill against Religious Education in France'.[72]

Press-related writings provide evidence that many bishops, clergy and editors read widely.[73] Bishop Grace of St Paul, Minnesota, and Elizabeth followed events in the Catholic press with great interest, including education issues and the topical history of the infallibility claim, especially in the periodicals from France, Rome, England and Germany. The writings of Veuillot were familiar to them since he contributed enormously to the political and religious debate. He, along with the future Cardinal Ledochowski (Nuncio at Brussels), the future Cardinal Pie (Bishop of Poitiers), Monsignor George Talbot (private Chamberlain to Pius IX and English friend of Elizabeth)[74] and *Civiltà Cattolica's* Jesuit editors, had been alarmed by Montalembert's opinions expressed in the well-known review *Le Correspondant.* However, Montalembert was supported and defended by the future Cardinals Lavigerie and Guibert, Cardinal Sterckx (Archbishop of Mechlin), many well-known Parisian Jesuits and especially by Bishop Dupanloup. Elizabeth's later articles – on Archbishop Ledochowski and his imprisonment,[75] contribution by Ledochowski on Leo XIII's Jubilee[76] and the mission-related articles of Cardinal Lavigerie – indicate her interest in the activities of these French ecclesiastics.

French missionary enthusiasm experienced a peak period in the nineteenth century. Catholic periodical output was influenced not only by the revival of older French religious congregations but also by the founding of new missionary ones, several of which were known to Elizabeth. The Association for the spreading of the Faith, initiated in 1819 by the young Lyonnaise woman, Marie-Pauline Jaricot, had developed quickly throughout Europe and America.[77] The Association's official publication, *Annales de la Propagation de la Foi*, had begun to appear regularly in 1824 and was disseminated widely.[78] Mission literature with vivid accounts of missionary experiences read by the early Sisters in Belle Prairie apparently included these *Annals of the Propagation of the Faith*. Sr Chaffee wrote, 'Our dear Mother [Elizabeth], who had such love for the Foreign Mission work, would, in order to cultivate in us this spirit, often let us read magazines devoted to them'.[79] It is reasonable to believe that Elizabeth was influenced by this particular French production, the *Annals of the Propagation of the Faith*, the most widely known of these publications.[80]

Cardinal Lavigerie, founder (1868) of the French Missionaries of Africa (the 'White Fathers') and friend of foundress, Hélène de Chappotin, appealed to women with literary gifts to help the anti-slavery cause. After contact with de Chappotin's Franciscan Missionaries of Mary in Salzburg, young Mary Theresa Ledochowska read of Lavigerie's crusade.[81] In 1889 Mary Theresa began a periodical called *Echo from Africa*, which was to become known worldwide and which still continues. In 1894 Mary Theresa founded the Missionary Sisters of St Peter Claver, a community of lay and religious women for the African missions. She purchased a property outside Salzburg and renamed it 'Maria Borg'; it became the centre of an extensive press apostolate. In the same year that Cardinal Lavigerie influenced Mary Theresa, Elizabeth published two translations related to him.[82] The second translation followed a communication from Lavigerie to the pope and was related to a ceremony involving twenty new missionaries who where about to leave Algiers for remoter parts of Africa.[83]

Another contemporary French missionary initiative that linked Lavigerie, missionary activities, and the Apostolate of the Press was that begun by Hélène de Chappotin de Neuville, mentioned above.[84] After the example of the Franciscans in Mexico in the sixteenth century and later the Jesuits in India, China and Paraguay, this foundress wanted her missionary sisters to utilize printing presses. Hélène de Chappotin knew that the press apostolate would ensure the diffusion of Christian teaching and propaganda for the new missions in need of wide support.[85] Every two months after 1886 the trained Sisters produced and printed in Paris their own Annals of the Institute. It seems that some of the

bold initiatives of Hélène were part of the missionary dream of
Elizabeth but that, given her situation and her age by this time, it
was impossible for her to realize them.

Since 1863 the Franciscan Capuchin Friars had been publishing *Annales Franciscaines* in Paris and their story will be told later.
Other religious congregations in France, whose periodicals had
been suspended as a consequence of the decrees of 1880 against
religious congregations, re-established their publications later in
the century and a range of Catholic periodicals were associated
with Catholic universities and the movement of socially-oriented
journalism.

The Catholic Press in Italy

What was happening in the 'Age of the Periodical' in Italy and how
was Elizabeth implicated in Catholic publications there? To investigate these questions, a little background will be provided, then
Pius IX's pontificate and Rosminianism will be considered,
followed by acknowledgement of connections involving the pope,
Mermillod and Elizabeth's *Annals;* next attention needs to be given
to Leo XIII in the 'Age of Encyclicals', and finally, there will be an
observation of Elizabeth's friends, Fra Ludovico da Casoria and
Cardinal Parocchi.

The Italians' creative genius and their long history of literature
are impressive; earlier Jesuit writings in Italy, for example,
provided a prelude to their famous nineteenth-century Catholic
paper, *Civiltà Cattolica.* Here, however, we must confine ourselves
to the period of Pius IX and Leo XIII, a time of 'material loss and
spiritual gain'.[86] A search by the writer for a directory of Italian
Catholic periodicals published in Elizabeth's lifetime proved difficult; however, an Italian Franciscan library provided a document
containing a catalogue with an alphabetical collection of weekly
magazines.[87] The latter consists of a listing of 1291 titles accompanied by brief descriptions of magazines from Italy and other
countries. Despite the title, monthlies were also listed including,
for example, *The Month, Annales Franciscaines* and Elizabeth's
Annals.[88] A distinction between newspapers and regular periodicals in these Italian entries proved unsatisfactory so the term
'periodical' has had to suffice. One historian astutely saw the
Italian periodical press scene as '*Civiltà Cattolica,* the *Osservatore
Romano* and the rest of the Catholic press'.[89] Selection consists of
these two major papers, other papers/periodicals and individual

contributors, in order to situate Elizabeth's journal in these often 'troublesome times'.

Pius IX's pontificate and Rosminianism

Civiltà Cattolica, widely quoted in books, periodicals and papers, was called a 'Jesuit journal' and 'Jesuit paper'. After the Jesuits were restored to their full liberties in Rome, Pius IX encouraged the founding of a new periodical and so they launched *Civiltà Cattolica.*[90] It became and has remained an authoritative, but not the official, organ of Catholic thought on religious and political matters. Elizabeth, moving among the key ecclesiastics and religious in Rome, read *Civiltà Cattolica* when the encyclical *Quanta Cura* of December 1864 was released. The encyclical was accompanied by the famous *Syllabus Errorum,* a table of eighty propositions considered erroneous; these were derived from the scientific mentality and rationalism of the century. According to the *Syllabus,* modern religious errors could be grouped under a number of 'isms' including rationalism, socialism, communism, and religious liberalism. In the Catholic press the 'errors' encapsulated the evils it was trying to combat and *Civiltà Cattolica* strongly defended the pope's condemnation of these perceived evils.

As national borders changed, due to wars and political upheavals during a complex time in Italian politics, so did periodicals. Before the division of Church and State, all periodicals were called Catholic. In Italy's 'Reign of Terror', the publication of Catholic journals became impossible, and then during the period of papal restoration from 1850, the Italian government censored the press in political matters but allowed periodicals explaining and defending Catholicism to continue. The conservative periodical, *Voce della Verità,* arose to be followed by others of more liberal tone and, with Pius IX's return to Rome in 1850, the *Giornale di Roma* was founded. To this publication was added the evening 'paper' that was to become the Vatican's voice, *L'Osservatore Romano.*

Elizabeth obviously kept herself abreast of contemporary journals and Italian events. She was disturbed in 1874 that one hundred Franciscans had been evicted from San Francesco-a-Ripa and others from the Ara Cœli, both locations known to her. To give news of the persecution in 'The Convents of Rome and the Revolution', she quoted the French source, *Semaine Religieuse de Rennes:* 'peaceful and defenceless inhabitants of the Roman Monasteries have been robbed of their own and driven out homeless upon the streets by the Italian Junta'.[91] Elizabeth's 1874 *Annals* also carried 'Extracts of News from Rome' and related that on 27 November the previous year, the Franciscan Father General 'has been forced to quit the Ara Coeli' by 'a hostile and sacrilegious hand'.[92]

A window into Elizabeth's awareness of Italian events and press connections can be gained also in an *Annals* article where she shows her knowledge of the 1867 battle of Mentana.[93] Cardinal Antonelli, a leading figure known to Elizabeth, was charged with the temporal rule of Rome for some twenty-seven years. He recognized that the defence of the pope rested upon the French Government's good will. France was compelled to withdraw her troops during the Franco-Prussian War and so around 1870 there was a new wave of governmental and sectarian opposition to the Catholic press. This occurred not only in Rome but also in regional parts of Italy with a resulting increase in the Catholic reaction and, in particular, that of periodicals. Comparably with French Catholic periodicals around the time of the Vatican Council, *Civiltà Cattolica* caused vibrations by implying the liberals of Dupanloup and Montalembert's school were not fully Catholic. The Catholic press was accused of stirring up passionate feeling about the infallibility issue and *Civiltà Cattolica* was later credited with helping to bring about the success of Ultramontanism.[94]

In 1860 the pope helped to establish *L'Osservatore Romano* in order that Catholics worldwide might be informed of his intentions, opinions and attitudes. Among numerous other periodicals, Milan's *Osservatore Cattolica* (founded 1864) was known not only for its fidelity in advocating papal policy but also for its refutation of Rosminian interpretations. Since Elizabeth was once a Rosminian postulant with Mother Elizabeth Lockhart in Greenwich, she followed events concerning Rosminianism in numerous Italian newspapers and other periodicals which adverted to the writings of Fr Antonio Rosmini. Several volumes of Rosmini's works were translated either by Fr William Lockhart or under his supervision.[95] Rosmini continued to explain his system of philosophy in articles for periodicals even though all his previous works had been denounced to the Holy See and some 300 censures had been circulated against him. A church authority took a different view and, in a letter to *L'Osservatore Romano* (16 June 1876), reminded the editor of the silence enjoined on both parties and stated that no theological censure could be inflicted.[96] A month later, the *Osservatore Cattolico* of Milan acknowledged its interpretation to be erroneous and for a time the Rosminian controversy ceased to be an issue for the press.

The pope, Mermillod and Elizabeth's Annals

A strong connection involving the pope, Monsignor Mermillod and Elizabeth's *Annals* is interesting. In the year when Leo XIII created Swiss-born Gaspard Mermillod a cardinal, Elizabeth's *Annals* carried a story of this strong advocate of the Apostolate of the Press.[97] As a young curate Monsignor Mermillod had established two periodicals in Geneva in the late 1840s: *L'Observateur Catholique* and *Les Annales Catholiques.* 1864 marked the year he was appointed auxiliary to the Bishop of Lausanne for the canton of Geneva. The next year Pius IX felt the need of a politico-religious organ for the support of his own ecclesial programme, to refute 'pernicious doctrines' and to serve as a medium of official communication to all Catholics. This was achieved through the *Acta Sanctae Sedis* and the *Correspondance de Rome*, the latter's purpose being the support of the Holy See and opposition to those labelled Liberal Catholics and Opportunists. In 1870 Bishop Mermillod moved the *Correspondance* to Geneva. The radical government of the canton protested when the Holy See appointed Mermillod the independent Administrator of Geneva; he was expelled from Switzerland and went to live in Ferney on French soil. In the first issue of Elizabeth's *Annals* her readers learnt that Mermillod, only months earlier, was in Paray Le Monial with English pilgrims.[98] The same year, *The Month* and *Catholic Review* praised Lady Herbert of Lea, a contributor to Elizabeth's *Annals*, for her translation of Mermillod's Conferences, published as *The Supernatural Life.*[99]

Elizabeth introduced readers to Mermillod's story set around 1876, which indicated he was in favour of the new Institute of Saint Paul, also known as Apostolate of the Press, founded by Canon Schorderet in Fribourg, Switzerland. In Elizabeth's words:

> For many years Canon Schorderet had been greatly occupied with the subject of the ravages wrought among all classes by the spread of bad literature. In order to counteract the evil effects of the Press in his own country he had started a paper 'La Liberte', now the chief organ of the canton of Fribourg. But he soon realised that the Catholic Press could never hope to vie with its adversaries unless it was supported by some apostolic institution, animated by the spirit of faith and of true devotion, and unless it could render itself independent of free-masonry and socialism.[100]

Elizabeth's *Annals'* article recalled how the printing workers, affiliated to Marxist-influenced international trade unionism, as were many other groups of workers on the Continent, were under pressure to strike time and time again. Union leaders planned to bring about the ruin of the Catholic *La Liberté*.

While this struggle was going on, seven young Fribourg women wanted to dedicate their lives to God through prayer and active ministry. Monsignor Mermillod offered advice and proposed that there could be no greater ministry than to devote themselves to the cause of Catholic literature. Canon Schorderet seconded Mermillod's words; Elizabeth wrote of the founder:

> He represented to them the beauty of a life of combined labour and contemplation, and showed them how, whilst working with their hands in the production of books for the glory of God, and the service of the Church, they might sanctify their own souls by constant prayer and meditation, and invest the Press with somewhat of the supernatural, by the free and continual immolation of their lives for the good of souls.[101]

The young women responded positively and on their way to Lyon to learn the skill of typography,[102] they stopped at Ferney to visit the exiled Mermillod who encouraged them strongly, saying:

> The Press is perhaps the greatest power that exists in these days. Ideas govern the world, and ideas are spread abroad by the Press, which acts as the great artery of human thought.[103]

From the article's convincing tone and the number of quotations from Mermillod endorsed by Elizabeth, it is fair to conclude that his views about the power of the press were hers also.

Elizabeth wrote more on this Apostolate of the Press story. About the time of the women's return from Lyon, a personal communication informed Canon Schorderet that his private plan to provide Institute of Saint Paul workers had been discovered and the printers' union demanded a permanent strike. However, there were women compositors in a Roanne printing office, including a Mademoiselle Marguerite Marie Durantet, who were interested in the Institute of Saint of Paul. At Schorderet's urgent plea for help, Marguerite, two companions and the newly trained members from Lyon joined forces, and *La Liberté* was printed on time.[104]

Elizabeth's publication relates how the Institute of Saint Paul grew from strength to strength, opening successful printing houses in Paris and Bar-le-Duc, publishing 'several important Catholic journals', receiving the sanction of Pius IX and the protection of Cardinal Parocchi, Archbishop of Bologna.[105] Pius IX personally encouraged Schorderet who pledged to further 'the spread of the pure doctrines of Christ's church'. Elizabeth concluded her first article on this topic by saying that in subsequent years Pius IX 'testified his interest in the work by no less than five separate Briefs'.[106] This, combined with the attention Elizabeth gave to papal writings in her *Annals*, emphasizes her belief that the popes in her time were calling writers to use their gifts in the Apostolate of the Press.

During the closing years of Pius IX's life, the 'Liberal' Press insinuated that at the time of the next papal election, the Italian Government would take a hand in the matter and occupy the Vatican. However, the press had not foreseen the Russo-Turkish War or the death of Victor Emmanuel II in early 1878 and their prognostications were thus buried under other issues. At the death of Pius IX (1878), the condition of Catholic journals was described as very favourable and among them *Unità Catttolica* was especially distinguished. The Catholic papers have been acknowledged as possibly inferior in format, but unrivalled as to the ability of their writers and the vigour and intelligence of the polemics.

In this year also Leo XIII was elected and so the Catholic world welcomed a prelate who even as a teenager had gained a classical facility in the use of Latin and Italian, a skill that would later be admired in his official writings and poetry. During his earlier life this pope-to-be worked in and around Perugia, known as a 'hotbed of the anti-papal revolutionary party' and later he was appointed bishop of this town, a place traditionally linked with the youthful Saint Francis of Assisi. The significance of the bishop's experiences for the Franciscan movement and Elizabeth's *Annals* will become apparent.

Leo XIII in the 'Age of Encyclicals'

Pope Leo XIII heralded the 'Age of Encyclicals'. 'Religious errors' and 'false liberalism' were still rampant and the Catholic world looked to Rome for leadership on the important issues of the day. Besides his letters and other writings on philosophical, theological and spiritual matters, Catholic periodicals and papers became great instruments for diffusing the pope's teachings, and Elizabeth, like numerous other Catholic editors and journalists, contributed significantly to this apostolate. In Leo XIII's first year in office he lamented the oppressive evils of society and that socialism was still prevalent thirty years after the Revolution of 1848. In 1879 he produced *Aeterni Patris*, on restoring Christian Philosophy, which gave pre-eminence to the works of Saint Thomas Aquinas and opened the floodgates for a new set of papers and periodicals which often reflected in their titles the content of the encyclical.[107] Politics and encyclicals were intertwined in the historical events of the period and periodicals engaged in spreading the battle of words. When Fr William Lockhart visited Leo XIII, he was assured by the pope that it was never his intention to condemn the works of Rosmini or his followers, and Fr Lockhart assured Leo XIII that Rosminians were not the *Liberali* that they were reported to be in Italian periodicals.[108]

An examination of selected Catholic monthly periodicals (1874–94) in England, Ireland and Australia, show that *Civiltà Cattolica* was the most popular source quoted under 'Foreign Catholic Periodicals'. Leo XIII realized the need of a 'papal journal' through which he could communicate with the foreign press so he created the *Journal de Rome* but this paper disappointed him so it was superseded by *Moniteur de Rome* (1881–95). Each year Leo XIII wrote new encyclicals, the greatest number being published in 1888. While Elizabeth's *Annals* kept abreast of these publications, the editor ensured that her readers were not swamped with them. Elizabeth's selection and handling of Pope Leo's writings and those of a few key ecclesiastics provide an insight into her amazing reading capacity. As her time in Rome lengthened, so too did her reliance on Italian publications and by 1893 the quantity of translations from these reached a maximum.

Reference has been made to Leo XIII's links with Perugia and Saint Francis of Assisi. On the feast of the Stigmata of Saint Francis, 17 September 1882, Leo XIII issued *Auspicato Concessum* with its focus on Saint Francis. In March the following year, Elizabeth's *Annals* carried the news that Cardinals Parocchi, Bartolini and sixteen other prelates had written to Leo XIII after a gathering in Assisi where many had celebrated 'the seventh centenary of the lawgiver and patriarch Saint Francis'. In Elizabeth's article the pope is quoted as expressing his pleasure that these prelates evinced devotion and love for the Seraphic Father Francis, and his hope that this devotion would spread so that the fruits of faith and charity would be 'revived among the men of this century'. The pope believed that membership in the Third Order of Saint Francis was a remedy for the social ills of the time, saying that nothing 'could be more agreeable' than 'the wide diffusion of the sacred army of the Third Order because it opposes powerfully the evils of our century, and promises decided blessings both in public and private life', thus bringing about 'justice and peace' in the world.[109] This praise of the Franciscan Order brought about

dramatic increase in membership in the branches of the Order –
the friars, contemplative nuns, religious Sisters (Third Order
Regular) and lay men and women (Third Order Secular).
Elizabeth caught the wave of opportunity, coupled it with her own
giftedness, and successfully provided readers with Franciscan spirituality, history and mission news.

In April that year, Elizabeth printed 'Leo XIII and the Third
Order', announcing the pope's recommendation, this time at an
audience with various Roman arch-confraternities, 'to inscribe
yourselves in the Third Order of Saint Francis'. The words 'now
first given to the Press' reminded people that in the previous
month 'the entire Catholic World celebrated ... the seventh
centenary of the birth of Saint Francis'. The quotation included,
'Its scope is to preserve civil society from the corruption of the
world by the sole means of sanctifying the most common and ordinary actions of life in shaping them after the true spirit of Jesus
Christ'. The pope was quoted as saying how the Rule of Saint
Francis is basically the observance of the Gospel and that for Third
Order members 'it proposes to heal social wounds'. The article
concluded with a statistical claim that 1,736 of those present had
already joined the Third Order.[110] Again in 1885 in Elizabeth's
usual 'Franciscan Record' segment, she inserted 'The Pope and
the Third Order' which echoed the pope's same sentiment and in
which he told Franciscan Generals how he himself prayed the
Franciscan devotions.[111] The pope, as a member of the Third
Order of Saint Francis, preached what he practised and the publication of this commitment appears to have influenced the sale of
Franciscan journals.

Fra Ludovico da Casoria and Cardinal Parocchi

In the 1884 *Annals*, Elizabeth linked the names of her Italian
friends, Fra Ludovico da Casoria and Cardinal Parocchi in her
regular news segment.[112] The article provided the news that
Ludovico and his helpers had established a successful free extern
school, as well as an intern orphanage, with workshops for several
crafts and trades, including printing.[113] The following year, Fra
Ludovico died in Naples so Elizabeth's May edition announced his
death, provided a short summary of his holy life and gave other
information. The editor promised 'to give a fuller account of this
true Son of the Seraphic Saint Francis whom Our Holy Father Leo
XIII tenderly named his beloved friend, il mio prediletto

amico'.[114] Elizabeth kept her promise, printing Lucovico's own
'Testament'[115] and three articles of which two provide insight into
Ludovico's Apostolate of the Press as well as into her own similar
commitment. She claimed that Fra Ludovico, who had formerly
been a Franciscan teacher in philosophy and mathematics, understood the 'evils which are caused every day by bad literature and
false science'. One remedy was his establishment of schools, the
other – 'in 1867 he founded a review called *Charity* and a periodical called *The Orphan*'. Elizabeth wrote, 'he promoted the religious
press with its typography, and erected stands for the sale of books
of piety as against bad publications'.[116] For Elizabeth also, education and the Apostolate of the Press were major time-consuming
commitments. In the November *Annals* she quoted at length Fr
Bonaventure[117] who recorded that Fr Ludovico had also founded
'a musical periodical of Christian melodies, of his own composition' and undertook 'the publication of another religious
periodical, entitled the *Religious Indicator of Naples*'.[118] At the
funeral service for Venerable Ludovico da Casoria, he was
described according to Elizabeth, 'as the revived St. Francis of the
nineteenth century'.[119]

Besides knowing Fr Ludovico, for years Elizabeth had communicated with numerous other leading ecclesiastics in Rome, London
and Paris. Like her, these ecclesiastics often travelled from one city
to another and kept in contact with friends. While the names of
these men have found their way into so many books, and today's
websites, Elizabeth Hayes' name has not. In the mere handful of
books, papers and websites that refer to her, information is often
inaccurate. Even current publications, or conference papers on
nineteenth-century women or journalism, omit her when her journalist achievement could appropriately be noted. How a person
who knew so many key church and literary figures during her lifetime has been overlooked is difficult to explain. However, while
many notable nineteenth-century women have been overlooked
simply because they were females, it is hoped that this present
publication concerning her will help to establish her rightful
place, not only in the history of women journalists, but also in
Franciscan and Church history. The following true story strength-
ens this hope.

The Vicar of Rome, Cardinal Parocchi, was a scholarly man who
in 1878 had founded the *Scuola Cattolica* embracing all branches of
theology and ecclesial discipline. Elizabeth and her Sisters, including those who had worked on the *Annals* in Rome since 1883, had
gained the attention of church authorities, including that of

Cardinal Parocchi. He asked Elizabeth in 1886 to publish a very large work in Latin that would be used in the vicariate and by the bishops. Besides this and at the same time, Parocchi asked for a book, *Against Heresy*, to be translated from Italian into English and then to be printed.[120] In the July's *Annals* of the same year was a striking article by Parocchi, 'Against Heresy in Catholic Garb', subtitled with 'Notification of the Most Eminent Lord Cardinal Parocchi, Vicar General of His Holiness the Pope', and followed by 'Translated and published by order of His Eminence'. The seven-page article deals with 'These heretical teachers desiring to destroy the Catholic education of our people' and who 'raise the standard of discord'. It condemned strongly a group calling itself 'Catholic and Italian' who were 'heretical and foreign'. Besides describing the group whose 'notions' were affiliated to a heretical sect of some fifteen years earlier, the article linked the culprits to the 'so-called Gallican Church and to Hyacinth Loyson'.[121] It concluded with a reminder of the Church's desire for justice, love and clemency. This article, the translation and the book's printing provide an insight into the confidence placed in Elizabeth by Parocchi and church authorities. Cardinal Parocchi and the Prefect of Propaganda Fide, Cardinal Simeoni, visited Elizabeth's convent in Via Alfieri this same year and inspected all the departments of the printing work, the press and the bindery.[122] No wonder then when Elizabeth later petitioned Leo XIII for a Rescript that would classify the printing and sale of the *Annals* as a 'Work of Spiritual Mercy' for the 'propagation of good books', not a commercial venture or industry, her request was granted. Elizabeth's lengthy letter of petition actually acknowledged the encouragement that she had received from the pope and Cardinal Parocchi.[123]

The *Annals* of 1888 reflected the special celebrations in Rome of the Sacerdotal Jubilee of Leo XIII. Elizabeth published the 'Encyclical Letter of His Holiness Pope Leo XIII'[124] and chose the Jubilee theme for four articles.[125] However, she allotted the most space, nineteen pages, to the pope's Brief on the abolition of slavery.[126] This topic touched the heart of Elizabeth who had witnessed both in Jamaica and Georgia the sufferings inflicted by slavery, and she published the complete text. Another encyclical this year was *Libertas* which had political implications since it explored the nature of human liberty. Elizabeth published, not the encyclical itself but, considerate of her many lay readers, she called on her friend Cardinal Manning to present a commentary, 'On the Pope's last Encyclical'.[127] Manning noted that in a world tossed by anti-Christian movements, 'ideas have governed the world', an echo of Bishop Mermillod's words. Again, the spread of ideas by the press gave it acknowledged power for good or evil, and it was this understanding that drove Elizabeth on in her task as a journalist.

Constraints of space will not allow a fuller examination of all of the pope's writings published by Elizabeth in the *Annals* (1874–94), nor of the articles that show the influence of other Italian writings. Perhaps the brief overview that follows can indicate to some degree the extent of the Italian press' influence on Elizabeth and her periodical, and how she in turn spread the 'good news' in her effort to counterbalance 'bad literature'. In 1891, besides printing a number of papal writings, Elizabeth entertained her readers with illustrations and articles on famous historical places in Rome.[128] Then in 1892, the *Annals* printed what may be interpreted as an acknowledgment of its own Franciscan roots in America, 'The Papal allocution on Columbus'.[129] Four major writings on the Rosary devotion were promulgated by Leo XIII, one each year 1891–4,[130] and Elizabeth published in full, almost 'hot off the press', the September 1892 encyclical, *Magnae Dei Matris*, in the following month.[131] Taking the pope's message to heart, Elizabeth edited for her 1892–4 issues, a series of articles entitled 'Sanctuaries of Our Lady' which were acknowledged as based on a 'translation from the Italian'. The articles were sub-titled with the names of many Italian Marian shrines.[132] Amongst these Marian articles during the same three years was a series called 'The Holy Angels', and again the editor acknowledged that they were translations from a nineteenth-century Italian source.

Cardinal Manning predicted:

> The Pontificate of Leo XIII will be known in history as the time when upon a world torn and tossed by anti-Christian and anti-social revolutions, the abundant seed of Divine truths, sown broadest, revived the conscience of Christendom.[133]

Elizabeth was impressed and inspired, not only by how the pontiff sowed 'the abundant seed of Divine truths', but also by the quality of his writings which were considered models of classical style, of clarity and convincing logic. While Leo XIII exemplified what it was to be an 'Apostle of the Press', so too did Catholic writers and journalists like Elizabeth Hayes, Cardinal Manning, the Lockharts, Monsignor Mermillod, Fr Ludovico da Casoria and Cardinal Parocchi. Elizabeth's *Annals* helped to neutralize the anti-Catholic evil 'exercised by the irreligious Press', and she saw her mission as being one with the Italian Pontiff who wrote, 'Our first duty is to spread the name and reign of Christ more widely.'[134]

Elizabeth and Catholic Periodical Press in North America

The rapid expansion of the nineteenth-century Catholic Church in the United States, due especially to Irish and German immigration, was reflected in its periodical literature. It is within this context that we look at Elizabeth's contribution. This was the period when, for the first time, the pope and the Roman Curia took into account the significance of American Catholicism for the Church as a whole. The nineteenth century in America, as in England, witnessed the conversion of numerous writers to Catholicism and when some turned their attention to the cause of their new Faith, the results were significant as demonstrated in writings of Orestes A. Brownson, Maximilian Oertel, R. A. Bakewell and Isaac T. Hecker. The ephemeral nature of Catholic newspapers and magazines was characteristic of the period, as was the variety of the publications (ranging from dailies, weeklies, semi-weeklies to monthlies, semi-monthlies, by-monthlies, quarterlies and annuals), and the clear dominance of New York and the Eastern press over 'the West' and 'the South'.

While Catholic periodical resources do not always clearly distinguish between newspapers and magazines, there exists sufficient information to indicate a flood of journalistic literature. Between 1809 and 1911 statistics claim that 550 Catholic periodicals, newspapers and magazines were begun in the United States, yet only five of these published in the first half of the century survived.[135] Many Catholic bishops and clergy strongly advocated the value of Catholic papers and magazines and supported Catholic press initiatives. After the 'hungry forties', Irish immigrants brought about marked development in Catholic periodical literature with Irish names recorded as editors, publishers, printers and contributors.[136] The same may be said of the contemporary secular press as numerous secular publications also advocated Irish interests. Names such as George and Isaac T. Hecker, Orestes A. Brownson and Patrick Donohoe first appeared in relation to newspapers and later reappeared with significant magazines or reviews. The Third Plenary Council at Baltimore (1884) furthered developments in periodical literature by stating that 'Catholic papers should be fostered and encouraged'.[137]

The struggle to maintain Catholic papers is exemplified by *The Pilot* which changed its name seven times in order to stay alive between 1829–1836. This paper, initiated by Bishop Fenwick, finally became the most important Catholic paper of national circulation and influence. One contributor was Irish-born Michael Hennessy, under the penname of 'Laffan' and a member of the *New York Daily Times* editorial staff, while a significant editor at one period was Revd John P. Roddan, member of Orestes Brownson's circle and contributor to his *Review*. In the year when Elizabeth stayed in New York before her westward journey to Minnesota, she probably read Hickey's newly established newspaper, *The Catholic Review*. Years later at Hickey's death, he was acknowledged as Brooklyn's Apostle of the Press and his *Catholic Review* lived on. The editor-owner had surrendered the promise of a brilliant career and its financial rewards in order to found *The Catholic Review* under disheartening circumstances that he finally turned into success.[138]

Elizabeth, Ave Maria *Press and Fr Daniel Hudson*

It is time to uncover the story of the link between Elizabeth, *Ave Maria* Press and Fr Daniel Hudson. After achieving this, attention will be given to the influence of New York in this arena, to connections involving Hecker, Brownson and Elizabeth, to Irish-American relations and 'Knownothingism', and finally, the focus will turn to the German migrant contribution. Co-operation, not competition, was the hallmark of the two Catholic publishing houses selected for this periodical press story, and long-forgotten correspondence with Elizabeth has guided the choice. The *Ave Maria* (dating from 1865) was 'the best known and most widely circulated Western publication' and 'a Catholic Journal, devoted to the honour of the Blessed Virgin, published weekly at Notre Dame, Indiana'.[139] The *Ave Maria* was published weekly in a magazine form, with sequential numbers of volumes, issues and pages. Brother Stanislaus Clarke, the *Ave Maria's* correspondent with Elizabeth, was to refer to her *Annals* as an 'excellent periodical'.

Ave Maria's early editor and contributor was American-born Fr Neal Henry Gillespie while his sister, Eliza Maria (Mother Mary St Angela) provided its initial 'moving spirit' and was a major contributor. Elizabeth probably knew Eliza, an outstanding educator and leader, for according to extant letters Elizabeth was in contact with the Holy Cross Sisters at Notre Dame from 1878 to 1879 and she most likely took advantage of their hospitality during her visits. Five months after Elizabeth restarted her *Annals* in January 1878, the *Ave Maria* editor was Fr Daniel E. Hudson, Professor of English Literature at Notre Dame University. Elizabeth and another Sister visited the campus in the early half of 1878,[140] and Fr Hudson published the following in the *Ave Maria* of 8 June that year:

> *The Annals of Our Lady of the Angels* is the title of a neat little monthly magazine of thirty-two pages published at Belle Prairie, Morrison Co., Mn., by the Sisters Regular of the Third Order of St. Francis. It is well edited and neatly printed – being, by the way, exclusively the work of the Sisters themselves. It is, we see, in its third year, although new to us, for until now we had not been sent a copy of it and saw no notice of it in the Catholic Press. The subscription price is $1.25 a year. Contrary to what its title would seem to indicate, *The Annals* is not an exclusively devotional or ascetic work; a great portion of its contents is made up of interesting stories and sketches which cannot fail to make the magazine attractive to the general reader, and thus in a measure to counteract the growing appetite for nonsensical trash. The Contents of the present number are: I, The Gifts and Graces of Mary; II, Clare, or the Child of Our Lady of the Angels; III, Hail Mary; IV, Thoughts of a Tertiary Priest; V. California a Century Ago; VI, A Convert's Gratitude (Poetry); VII, Life of Mary Cherubina Clare of St. Francis; VIII, Alone in the Far West; IX, Franciscan Record.[141]

Fr Hudson's name is mentioned in five of the seven letters that came from *Ave Maria's* Office to Elizabeth during 1878–79 and provide evidence of exchanged articles between Fr Hudson and Elizabeth (Mother M. Ignatius) Hayes. Br Stanislaus Clarke wrote on behalf of Fr Hudson, 'So if you like, he will send you the *Ave Maria* containing the Sketches in exchange for 'Clare, or the Child of Our Lady of the Angels''.[142] Clarke's letter also conveyed information regarding rights to publish since the *Annals* articles were written by the Hon. Mrs F. Montgomery. It reads in part:

> Rev. Mother, Since I last wrote you I spoke so enthusiastically of the story in your magazine, 'The Annals', to Rev. Father Hudson, that I tempted him to the desire of republishing it in the 'Ave Maria', and crediting the 'Annals' with it. This would be a good way of making your magazine known to many, and perhaps of obtaining several subscriptions for it; but I also reminded him that you might not be free to permit its publication outside your own magazine. He said no difficulty could arise in this way, as the book was to be brought out on the other side of the Atlantic. But even if it were published in book form in this country it would but add to its popularity, as we

> know from the stories heretofore published in the 'Ave Maria'.
> Those who had read them or read portions of them wished to obtain
> them afterwards in book form ...[143]

When Fr Hudson asked for all back copies, ranging from January 1874 to June 1875, a hand note of Elizabeth's on the letter indicates that, along with other periodicals, she 'put the *Ave Maria* in the exchange list of the *Annals*'.[144] In an 1880 article, 'The Tomb of St. Peter of Alcantara',[145] Elizabeth acknowledged another exchange article.[146] Other exchanges probably followed but no proof exists. The *Ave Maria's* contribution to the Apostolate of the Press, which Elizabeth appreciated and travelled a long distance to see in action, was recognized in its 1879 letterhead that carried the new 'Approbation of and Blessing of Our Holy Father, Leo XIII'. It reiterates for the Catholic periodical scene in general, and for hard-working pressroom individuals, their belief in the power of the press for good and its ability to counterbalance evil.

Elizabeth's wisdom in turning to *Ave Maria* for advice, not to one of Saint Cloud's secular publishing houses, highlights her deeply religious interests, and it also produced practical results. When she planned to open a new Southern mission for the Afro-American people, it was the *Ave Maria*, through Fr Hudson, which quickly offered to include articles that would generate assistance.[147] Living, reading and publishing in the South from 1878, Elizabeth knew that New Orleans of 'the South' produced the *Morning Star* paper (founded 1867) which she acknowledged in 1880 when she printed her translation of Paul Feval's article.[148] Elizabeth's *Annals* always carried poems and two of the contributing poets, the Revd Abram J. Ryan and James R. Randall, were editors of the *Morning Star* for some time.

New York's influence

Among the Eastern magazines New York led the field, yet because of the ephemeral nature of Catholic journals, one could not know which journal might respond to the plea of a missionary which Elizabeth printed in her mission news: 'Would to God that a Catholic journal of New York might express our thanks', for the Catholic generosity which so impressed him on returning from the United States to his foreign mission field.[149] It was 1883 and the visitor, by calling on New York's Catholic journalists, gave himself what he felt was the best chance of being heard. However, the first

Catholic magazine in the United States, the *Metropolitan* or *Catholic Monthly Magazine*, was not born in New York but in Baltimore; it struggled to survive. Twelve years later, Baltimore published the *Religious Cabinet*, which after a year changed its title to the *United States Catholic Magazine;* it enjoyed respected contributors but survived only until 1847 or 1848.[150] The list of failures also included the New York *Catholic Expositor*, the *Young Catholics' Magazine*, the short-lived monthly *National Catholic Register* of Philadelphia and the *Metropolitan* which surfaced again in 1853 but failed to make a permanent contribution.

Nearer to the period when Elizabeth launched her magazine, included in an 1868–78 failures' list was the *Catholic Record* of Philadelphia, *Central Magazine* of St Louis and the *Young Crusader* of Boston. High profile editors, Revd James A. Corcoran, George D. Wolf and Archbishop Patrick J. Ryan, launched the *American Catholic Quarterly Review* in 1876 but its life span was not long and the *Ecclesiastical Review* in Philadelphia, founded in 1889 mainly to provide professional material for the clergy, struggled to survive. It was in late 1873, in this period of eastern failures, that Elizabeth asked Bishop Grace for permission to commence her *Annals*. The basis of the bishop's fears about the success of Elizabeth's venture was, as he wrote, 'knowledge of the fate that has awaited so very many efforts of the kind, made under the most favourable circumstances'.[151]

Within a year, however, the secular Saint Paul *Northwestern Chronicle* published:

Annals of Our Lady of the Angels. A Monthly Bulletin of the Third Order of St. Francis of Assisi. This is a little monthly published by the good Sisters at Brainerd, on the Northern Pacific R.R. and, naturally, filled with the most pious writings and edifying selections. It is printed by our friend Russell, of the Brainerd *Tribune*, and certainly speaks well for the workmanship of his office. We do not see how it could be done much better in the east. This monthly is interesting, besides its good reading, as a tide mark of the advance of Catholicity and Catholic literature in this country.[152]

Meanwhile, more permanent Catholic periodicals were emanating from New York, the birthplace of its famous son, Isaac Thomas Hecker (1819–1888) author, missionary and founder of the Paulists who were to play a significant role in Catholic journalism. Fr Hecker was a friend of Elizabeth and his name was linked with a number of important nineteenth-century journalists. By looking at his life and friendships, a window is opened into the challenges and successes of American Catholic periodical literature. Only by looking into these challenging times can Elizabeth's extraordinary success be comprehended.

Elizabeth, Isaac Hecker and Orestes Brownson

We will now follow Elizabeth's connection with Fr Isaac Hecker, Orestes Brownson and others because our appreciation of the literary influences on Elizabeth is impoverished without knowledge of these relationships. In his youth Isaac Hecker was a friend and correspondent of Orestes A. Brownson (1803–1876), a philosopher and social reformer, later known also as essayist, influential convert, reviewer and intrepid advocate among New York's immigrant Catholics.[153] Brownson founded *The Boston Quarterly Review* in 1838 which attracted literary contributors of note and later he merged it with New York's monthly *U.S. Democratic Review,* with himself as a contributor. By 1844, he began his own *Brownson's Quarterly Review* which became until 1875 the most significant Catholic quarterly in the USA. Also in 1844, New York's Bishop McCloskey baptized Issac Hecker who later studied in Belgium to become a Redemptorist and was ordained later in London by Cardinal Wiseman.[154] Fr Hecker returned to New York in 1851 to serve the rapidly increasing migrant population. Later, a misunderstanding with his congregational leaders in Europe caused Fr Hecker and four companions to be released from their vows by Pius IX. At this same time the pope gave them approval to begin the new Missionary Society of Saint Paul in the State of New York. The new community grew but became involved in the 'intangible heresy' called 'Americanism' which was unpopular with the ultra-conservative clergy from Europe.[155]

In the 1860s the Paulists, led by the zealous Fr Hecker, preached, wrote and delivered missions – especially to the 'Gentiles' – and were seen also to be 'setting new standards in Catholic journalism'.[156] Fr Hecker in 1865 founded the successful journal, *Catholic World,* and for the first five years John R. G. Hassard was the editor.[157] Fr Hecker notably promoted the Apostolate of the Press among Catholics in America, and besides his work for the influential *Catholic World,* he organized the Catholic Publication Society, directed a children's paper called *The Young Catholic* and thus created a new movement in Catholic literary activities. Elizabeth also did not forget children and at times included an article for them in her publication.

Now Hecker's friend Brownson had helped to allay New York

Catholic immigrants' fears when he boldly defended the Faith and challenged the 'political atheism of Catholics'. Brownson basically contributed one or two articles a month to Hecker's *Catholic World* and he also wrote several articles for the weekly *Ave Maria* of Notre Dame.[158] Elizabeth was aware of all these literary happenings. While Hecker wrote only three books in comparison with Cardinal Newman's long list, nonetheless Newman observed that 'we had both begun a work of the same kind, he in America and I in England'. Newman made Catholic dogma and practices more acceptable to English people while Hecker brought the Catholic Faith closer to the democratic temper of the American people.

Another English connection, also interconnected with Elizabeth, was Fr William Lockhart's friendship with Fr Isaac Hecker. Lockhart wrote that 'the idea of throwing Catholic doctrine into the form of conversations, and combining them together by a thread of narrative so as to form a tale', was first suggested to him by Hecker. The first chapters of Lockhart's book, *The Old Religion*, appeared in Hecker's *Catholic World,* while in England the story was published initially in Lockhart's journal, *Catholic Opinion.* By following Hecker's suggestion, Lockhart found that his journal increased in circulation and that he received 'many letters of encouragement' with even more suggestions.[159]

Elizabeth's opportunity to see Fr Hecker again came when she and Sr Chaffee were in New York in 1885. Having visited their American convents they were travelling back to Rome, so they 'called at the Monastery of the Paulist Fathers to see her [Elizabeth's] old friend Father Hecker'.[160] Sr Chaffee recorded that Hecker 'was exceedingly infirm, and very seldom came down' but he did so to see Elizabeth.[161] Hecker indicated he understood the difficulties that were being experienced by Elizabeth, and other religious congregational leaders, who had head houses in Europe during the 'Americanism' controversy.[162] Unfortunately Chaffee did not record any discussion about the *Annals,* the *Catholic World* or other periodical literature. However she did remember Fr Hecker's advice to Elizabeth about going to see Bishop Wigger regarding Elizabeth's desire to open a Franciscan convent in New York.[163] Recently another insight emerged from the Franciscan Sisters' Union City chronicles to confirm the friendship of Elizabeth and Fr Hecker.[164] Neither of these Apostles of the Press was to know that later, in 1915, the *Annals* begun by Elizabeth would be printed and circulated in Union City, New Jersey, and continue until the centennial of publication in 1974.

Another significant literary connection linking Elizabeth and Fr

Hecker was their mutual friendship with Archbishop John Ireland who was among the most influential episcopal leaders in the USA. Fr Hecker had striven unceasingly to recommend the Catholic Faith to the democratic sense of the American people, who in general had been reared in hostility to the Catholic Church on the pretence that 'she' was foreign and anti-democratic. As a convert and a European, Elizabeth understood the situation. Both Fr Hecker, an ardent native-born American thinker, and Archbishop Ireland, an Irish immigrant, were full of admiration for American institutions and probably Elizabeth was also. When *The Life of Father Hecker* was published in New York in 1891, it carried an introduction of approval by Archbishop John Ireland who was also a subscriber to and admirer of Elizabeth's *Annals*. One aspect behind the success of Elizabeth's *Annals* may well have been her ability to speak to the heart of democratic Americans who made up the bulk of her subscribers.

In his lifetime Fr Hecker won the highest approval from the papacy, but the controversy over 'Americanism' was associated with his name after his death.[165] The Catholic press added fuel to the fire, the flames being extinguished only after the bishops of the United States replied to the pope's cautionary letter, *Testem Benevolentiae* on the disputed issue.[166] Catholic periodical literature in the USA was coloured to some degree not only with 'Americanism' and this controversy but also with Irish-American relations. A look at the latter, and some significant journals, should cast further light on the search to explain how Elizabeth was able to contribute successfully to periodical literature in these challenging times.

Irish-American relations and 'Knownothingism'

This topic is worthy of consideration for it was the latter that indirectly caused Elizabeth so much pain and suffering in the final years of her life. A few years ago the history of nineteenth-century Irish-American relations was highlighted by the *Irish Gazette's* article on 'the way the Irish have influenced history and participated in events that have shaped' American lives.[167] The Irish immigrants' involvement in New York was recalled, for example, by the laying of St Patrick's Cathedral foundation stone in 1809, Bishop John Hughes' need later to gather parishioners to prevent the anti-Catholic and anti-immigrant mob from burning the church, and Bishop John McCloskey's reception of the cardinal's 'red hat' in 1875. Alongside the Irish-American relations that coloured periodicals, historians suggest that Catholic publications also broadcast the 'Irish versus the Native Americanism' struggle. During 1851–58 the Catholic press was busily engaged in responding to the charges made against the Church by the 'Knownothing' party in a revived version of the Native American Movement of the earlier quarter century.[168] Secular and religious newspapers of the 'Knownothing' party in the 1850s demonstrated the power of the press for evil in the form of encouraging violence against and bitter intolerance of innocent 'foreigners'. Brownson described the history of 'Knownothingism' as a period when a prejudiced political party which was basically anti-Catholic, opposed chiefly to the Irish, wished to prevent them from having the rights of free citizens. The Catholic press responded, mainly through newspapers, to the books and anti-Catholic papers that were aimed at inflaming the passions of the mob against their Irish neighbours. Bishop Spalding's letter to Bishop Kenrick told of 'a reign of terror'.[169]

As the years moved on the Catholic periodical press continued to challenge readers to infuse the political arena with basic Christian principles. In an issue of *Donahoe's Magazine*, the words of Elizabeth's patriotic friend, Archbishop John Ireland, headed the front page. It stated, 'The future of the Irish people in this country will depend largely upon their capability of assuming an independent attitude in American politics'.[170] Bishop Fenwick, long connected with Donahoe and admired by Fr Lockhart, started *The Jesuit or Catholic Sentinel* in 1829, and after acknowledging in his prospectus the rapid increase of Catholics in Boston, he stated clearly his intention to present traditional Catholic views.[171] Like other publications it passed through a series of name changes, evolving finally into *The Pilot* which advocated Catholic and Irish interests, and grew into a significant paper of national circulation and influence.

Two prominent figures in the periodical press, Archbishop John Hughes of New York together with Orestes Brownson, were associated in 1856 with St John's College founded in Fordham, New York.[172] As time progressed, Brownson issued a rousing call for a new vision of the relationship between Catholicism and American civilization, one that directly challenged the more traditional view formulated by Archbishop John Hughes, Archbishop Martin Spalding and Bishop John N. Neumann of Philadelphia.[173] Brownson encouraged the ideal of American citizens being led by God's Spirit, similarly to some writings of his friends Isaac Hecker,

John Keane and John P. Roddan.[174] Hecker's apologetic, founded on a combination of the American concept of natural rights and the Catholic teaching on justification, would not have occurred to Hughes, Spalding or Neumann.[175] Hecker's forward-thinking interpretation of the 'Knownothing campaign' evidenced his belief in the providential course of history, while Hughes and his fellow thinkers held to an apologetic that looked back to the past. Hecker's writings evidence his belief that the first principle of American constitutionalism was that 'man was capable of governing himself' – a principle that sat comfortably with Elizabeth's words on governance – 'What right have any of us to claim authority and not take responsibility?'[176]

In this American struggle, the quarterly *Dublin Review* played a significant role in supporting Irish-American acceptance for it was read in America by prominent Catholics, Bishop Ireland included.[177] It was founded by Cardinal Wiseman and Daniel O'Connell, as noted earlier, following Catholic Emancipation when Irish Catholics discovered the power of the press.[178] Though published in London, the *Dublin Review* was general in character and Irish in more than name.[179] Its list of editors was impressive including Dr C. W. Russell, Dr W. G. Ward, W. Michael Quin, W. Henry R. Bagshawe, John Cashel Hoey and Monsignor Moyes, some of whom were Irish-born. Besides this review, Irish journals and papers, including the popular monthly *Irish Ecclesiastical Record,* circulated in USA and they contained articles bearing on Catholic Irish-American-English relations.[180] Contributors' names appearing in this *Record* as well as in Elizabeth's *Annals* were Fr T. Bridgett, Aubrey de Vere and Knowles; this must have pleased her large number of Irish-American subscribers. The *Irish Monthly* boasted the longest continuous existence of all Irish Catholic magazines and it had the same Jesuit editor, Matthew Russell, for thirty-eight years. The names of the editor and of some contributors to this monthly are found in Elizabeth's *Annals* which she published in the USA between 1874 and 1883.[181]

Cardinal Manning, longstanding contributor to the *Dublin Review,*[182] was much admired by Minnesota's Archbishop Ireland and became his trusted friend.[183] Manning was a contributor to Elizabeth's *Annals* and Ireland, for over fifty years a dominant figure in the religious, social and political life of the United States, was a subscriber as we saw earlier. When sending his initial *Annals'* subscriptions to Elizabeth, Bishop Ireland as he then was wrote, 'I feel a pride in the fact that such talents as God has blessed you with has [sic] chosen our State as its field of labour.'[184]

German migrant contribution

Besides the Irish immigrants' influence on American Catholic periodical literature, the large number of Catholic German
immigrants had led to 'periodicals', many weekly papers, and a
good number of magazines in their own language. Bishop Ireland
'more than anyone else guided a vast flood of Catholic immigrants
into the mainstream of American life'[185] and among them many
Germans came into his beloved Minnesota. In St Paul, the German
newspaper *Der Wanderer,* on 11 January 1873, advertized the
Franciscan Sisters' presence in Belle Prairie, Morrison County,[186]
while *Der Nordstern* (1876–1885, 1887–1913) was another nearby
German publication in St Cloud.[187] The English version of the
German publication, the *St. Paul Northwestern Chronicle,* carried
news of 'Mother Hayes' on a few occasions with one article (5
January 1878) advertizing the 'Annals of Our Lady of the Angels
published by Members of the Third Order of St Francis of Assisi –
Belle Prairie'. Another article (4 January 1879) said of Elizabeth, 'a
convert to our Holy Faith, [she] is a lady of fine mental culture,
and her zeal and devotedness are unlimited'.[188] When this
Minnesota news item was published, Elizabeth was preparing the
fourth volume of her *Annals* and by then she had more Sisters to
assist her in the work of printing, publishing and distributing while
she continued to do all the preparatory reading and editing
herself.

Evidence of not only the Minnesota literature but of the fifty-
one German periodicals, the second highest ethnic number in a
total of 321 in the United States, is provided in the 1911 Catholic
Directory. The first German Catholic paper *Der Wahrheitsfreund,*
founded 1837, rolled off the press regularly until 1907 while the
famous Bavarian convert, Dr Maximilian Oertel, considered one
of the most brilliant editors the Germans ever produced in
America, founded the successful weekly, *Katholische Kirchenzeitung.*
The record for the largest circulation among all Catholic week-
lies was awarded to Fr Jos Jessing who founded the *Ohio
Waisenfreund* in 1873. The Germans in fact appear to have had two
Catholic dailies before a Catholic one appeared in English in the
United States.

As a young Puseyite, Elizabeth was aware of the German influence on her distinguished spiritual adviser, Dr E. B. Pusey.[189] Pusey
was greatly influenced by the writings of the Fathers of the Church
whose works he brought back from Germany, through the influence of Augustus Neander.[190] New research, especially that of

American William H. Franklin, places the Oxford Movement in a wider perspective and highlights the impact of Germany on the Anglican Catholic Revival of the nineteenth century. Elizabeth's Wantage pastor, William Butler, was wholly devoted to the Oxford Movement's principles and overall stance, and he had an immense regard for Pusey. How Elizabeth viewed the German Catholic press in the 1870s is not recorded but her journey to Berlin after the Franco-Prussian war, and the Belle Prairie presence of Sr M. Alice Peet who spoke German fluently, facilitated the consideration of translations in her *Annals*.[191] During the 1860s, amid numerous other periodicals in Germany, a famous Jesuit organ, *Stimmen aus Maria-Laach*,[192] appeared at irregular intervals and made its way to America, in particular to Minnesota.[193]

In conclusion it seems fair to make the following observation. Many German immigrants would have been aware of past and present happenings regarding the Catholic periodical press in Germany after the 1848 events,[194] and after 1871 with the fierce onslaught of the *Kulturkampf*.[195] The Germans gave the American Catholic press brave apostles, men and women who understood the immense power of the press and its potential for 'good and evil'. The *Irish Ecclesiastical Record* told of an Irish desire to have such Apostles of the Press. If only 'we had an organ of Irish opinion, conducted with the energy and singleness of purpose which characterise the management of the *Germania*',[196] – and again, 'It is from Germany, too, that we get our best defence and our ablest expositions of Catholic doctrines'. Yet these German apostles of the press were not alone; there were other apostles in England, France and Italy, as well as distinguished converts in the USA and Irish Americans. These journalists understood the violent challenge issued to revealed doctrine by pantheists, rationalists, materialists, Kantians, Hegelians, evolutionists and others. These apostles of the press appear to have grasped that the violence done to truth, as they understood it, was best answered by the propagation of good periodical literature. This could be achieved by a press utilising orthodox articles on doctrines of faith and morals, Church history and liturgy, sound education at different levels, spiritual and devotional exercises, and all else good belonging to faith in a loving God. Among these nineteenth-century apostles of the press, Elizabeth stands tall and it is clear that she was not a minor player among them.

Notes

1 For more exhaustive research into categories of nineteenth-century journalism, see Ph.D. thesis by Pauline J. Shaw, 'Mission Through Journalism: Elizabeth Hayes and the *Annals of Our Lady of the Angels*', 2006, chs. 2–4. The Australian Catholic University has made the thesis available online.

2 Judy McKenzie in her review of two publications – *Periodicals of Queen Victoria's Empire: An Exploration* edited by J. Don Vann and R. T. VanArsdel; *Disreputable Profession: Journalists and Journalism in Colonial Australia* by Denis Cryle in *Australasian Victorian Studies Journal* 3, no. 2 (1998): 136. The *Colonial Times* newspaper was published in Tasmania (1 July 1825 – 22 August 1857).

3 Owen Chadwick, *The Victorian Church, Part Two, 1860–1901*, 426. 'Nonconformists were quicker than the Anglicans'.

4 W. T. Stead, 'To the English-Speaking Folk under the Southern Cross. Why the *Review of Reviews* Takes Root in Australia', *Review of Reviews*, Aust. edn 1, no. 1 (1892): 11.

5 V. A. McClelland, 'Manning's Work for Social Justice', *The Chesterton Review* XVIII, no. 4 (1992): 534.

6 J. Derek Holmes and Bernard W. Bickers, 'The Church, Revolution and Reaction, 1789–1914', in *A Short History of the Catholic Church*, 228.

7 Hayes, 'The Apostolate of the Press', *AOLA* XV, no. ii (1890): 35.

8 Charles Sowerwine, 'Marxism and History' (paper presented at the History Unit 131084, Methods and Research, University of Melbourne, 15 August 2001). Marx's periodical was the *Neue Rheinische Zeitung*.

9 Hayes, 'The Apostolate of the Press', *AOLA* XV, no. iii (1890): 74.

10 Sarah Lumley, 'A Tale of Bad Times; or, Ecological, Sustainable Development and Harriet Martineau', *Australasian Victorian Studies Journal* 6 (2000): 65.

11 Elizabeth Gaskell, *Life of Charlotte Bronte*, ch. 23, 329, in Houghton, *The Victorian Frame of Mind 1830–1870*, 68.

12 Hayes, 'The Apostolate of the Press', *AOLA* XV, no. ii (1890): 37–8.

13 J. Don Vann and Rosemary T. VanArsdel, eds. *Victorian Periodicals and Victorian Society*, 7.

14 It numbered among its contributors Sir Walter Scott, Thomas Carlyle and Matthew Arnold.

15 See Lurline Stuart, *Nineteenth Century Australian Periodicals: An Annotated Bibliography*, 1–2.

16 Libraries included public and convent ones in St Paul, Minneapolis, St Joseph, St Cloud, Little Falls and Brainerd.

17 Records in the Stearns History Museum and Research Centre, St Cloud, Mn., microfilm.

18 Records of newspaper pages and 'Literary notices' in the *St. Cloud Journal*, 1872–3, microfilm.

19 Morris C. Russell, 'News Item', *Brainerd Tribune*, 26 September 1874, 1, col. 7.

20 Joseph A. A. Burnquist, ed., *Minnesota and Its People*, 68–71. The city of

Minneapolis/St Paul alone published 127 papers.

21 William E. Lass, *Minnesota – A History*, 129.

22 Burnquist, ed., *Minnesota and Its People*, 69.

23 The Brainerd library also held the contemporary *New Monthly Magazine*, *Public Opinion*, *The Household* and *Browning's Magazine*.

24 Elizabeth Hayes' Rule 2, Constitution 2, contained Fénélon's remarks on education. Old typed copy of Rule and Constitution, 5, MFICAR.

25 Hayes, 'The Church of St. Francis at Madrid', *AOLA* XIV, no. xii (1889): 382.

26 Chadwick, *The Victorian Church, Part Two, 1860–1901*, 125, 420.

27 Hayes, 'Extracts from a Letter of the Poor Clares', *AOLA* I, no. v (1874): 154.

28 Hayes, 'The Life of the Catholic Church', *AOLA* I, no. x (1874): 312.

29 Houghton, *The Victorian Frame of Mind: 1830–1870*, 95. Houghton quoted from 'The Age We Live In' in *Fraser's Magazine* 24 (1841): 8.

30 Van and VanArsdel, eds, *Victorian Periodicals and Victorian Society*, 7.

31 Newman, *Apologia Pro Vita Sua*, 176.

32 Hayes, 'A Speaking Picture', *AOLA* II, no. i, ii (1875): 390.

33 Houghton, *The Victorian Frame of Mind 1830–1870*, 95.

34 The *Chamber's Journal* went on to reach a circulation of 90,000 in 1845.

35 Rosemary Taylor, 'English Baptist Periodicals, 1790–1865', *Baptist Quarterly* 27 (1977): 50–82. Van and VanArsdel, eds., *Victorian Periodicals and Victorian Society*, 265.

36 Chadwick, *The Victorian Church, Part One, 1829–1859*, 213.

37 Charlotte M. Yonge, 'Miss Yonge's Recollections', in *Life and Letters of William John Butler. Late Dean of Lincoln and Sometime Vicar of Wantage*, ed. Arthur J. Butler, 286–90.

38 Vann and VanArsdel, eds, *Victorian Periodicals and Victorian Society*, 56.

39 Donna Dickenson, ed., *Margaret Fuller: Woman in the Nineteenth Century and Other Writings, The World's Classics Series*, publisher's note.

40 Newman, 44 – 'Christ upon the Waters' (1850) from *Sermons Preached on Various Occasions* (1898 edition) in Houghton, *The Victorian Frame of Mind: 1830–1870*, 148–9.

41 Letter from 'W. J. Butler to Miss C. M. Yonge' in Butler, *Life and Letters of William John Butler*, 285–6.

42 Norton, 'A History of the Community of St. Mary the Virgin, Wantage', 42.

43 Letter written at 'The Deanery, Lincoln' from 'W. J. B. to Miss Yonge' in Butler, *Life and Letters of William John Butler*, 338.

44 Vann and VanArsdel, eds, *Victorian Periodicals and Victorian Society*, 268–9.

45 Ahles, *In the Shadow of His Wings*, 86.

46 Vann and VanArsdel, eds, *Victorian Periodicals and Victorian Society*, 140.

47 Olsen, 'The Church of England Temperance Magazine', *Victorian Periodicals Newsletter* 11 (1978): 38–49, in Vann and VanArsdel, eds, *Victorian Periodicals and Victorian Society*, 264.

48 Chadwick, *The Victorian Church, Part Two, 1860–1901*, 426.

49 Canon A. M. Allchin, 'W. J. Butler – Sacraments and Society' (paper

presented at the Chapter Meeting of the Community of St Mary the Virgin, Wantage, Oxenfordshire, 31 May 1994), 6.

50 One resource for nineteenth-century Catholic periodical literature is in the classic 1912 edition of *The Catholic Encyclopaedia* available on website and CD-ROM.

51 Chaffee, 'Memories', 7–8.

52 While it appears very likely that Elizabeth Hayes knew Fanny Taylor, or knew of her through Manning, no proof has been found.

53 Joyce Sugg, *Ever Yours Affly. John Henry Newman and His Female Circle*, 157.

54 See Francis Charles Devas, *Mother Mary Magdalen of the Sacred Heart (Fanny Margaret Taylor. Foundress of the Poor Servants of the Mother of God (1832–1900)*, 247.

55 Ibid., 69.

56 The Honourable Mrs Alfred (Fanny) Montgomery contributed 'Clare; or, The Child of Our Lady of the Angels' in 1874–75 and 1878–79 issues of *AOLA*.

57 Devas, *Mother Mary Magdalen of the Sacred Heart*, 65.

58 Hayes, 'The English Martyrs', *AOLA* XII-XIII, no. iii-vi, ix, xi, xii; ii (1887–88: (1887): 91–5, 112–16, 158–60, 171–4, 282–88, 336–45, 366–73; (1888): 44–7.

59 Ibid., 47.

60 Devas, *Mother Mary Magdalen of the Sacred Heart*, 320.

61 Ibid., 316.

62 Hayes, 'The Holy Man of Tours', *AOLA* V, no. iv-ix (1880): 106–10, 129–33, 161–4, 193–7, 225–30, 257–61.

63 Hayes, 'Scenes in a Solder's Life', *AOLA* V, no. iv, v (1880): 101–5, 134–5.

64 Hayes, 'Reparation by Religious Orders', *AOLA* V, no. v, vi (1880): 136–40, 169–73.

65 Hayes, 'Story of a Recent Conversion', *AOLA* V, no. iv (1880): 120–1.

66 Original copies researched in Braintree library, MFICAE.

67 Hayes, 'The Apostolate of the Press', *AOLA* XV, no. ii, iii, vi (1890): 35–40, 73–6, 164–9.

68 Ibid., 74.

69 Newman, *Apologia Pro Vita Sua*, 191.

70 Bishop Murdoch, letter to Sister M. Ignatius, 27 September 1864. MFICAR. Murdoch was ecclesiastical superior of the Glasgow Franciscans; Elizabeth required a letter of authorisation from him re transfer.

71 Dupanloup's writings encouraged the total development of the student, disapproved of 'mug-jug' methods, embraced the concept of learning as process and recommended utilising games.

72 Hayes, 'The Bill against Religious Education in France', *AOLA* V, no. v (1880): 149–50.

73 In the 1870s Fr Robert Dunne, later first Archbishop of Brisbane, received at his Toowoomba presbytery each week fourteen French, Australian, English, Italian and Irish newspapers. Neil Byrne, 'Dunne's Vision: Catholic Press Teacher of Humanity', *The Catholic Leader* (Brisbane), 28 October 1992, 15.

74 Monsignor Talbot was formerly a priest in St George's, London. His Roman correspondence with Elizabeth in Sèvres is extant.

75 Hayes, 'Archbishop Ledochowski Visited in Prison', *AOLA* I, no. x (1874): 316–17.

76 Cardinal Ledochowski, 'The Sovereign Pontiff on His Jubilee', *AOLA* XIII, no. xi (1888): 321–4.

77 Holmes and Bickers, 'The Church, Revolution and Reaction, 1789–1914', 230. Holmes and Bickers dated the establishment as 1822 but 1819 was stated more recently as the date of its genesis. M. R. MacGinley, *A Dynamic of Hope. Institutes of Women Religious in Australia*, 93.

78 MacGinley, *A Dynamic of Hope*, 255.

79 Chaffee, 'Memories', 54.

80 Observation expressed by religious historian, MacGinley, 'Elizabeth Hayes: Religious Foundress'.

81 MacGinley, *A Dynamic of Hope*, 304.

82 Hayes, 'Letter of Cardinal Lavigerie Archbishop of Carthage to Cardinal Manning Archbishop of Westminster. (Translated from French)', *AOLA* XIV, no. iv (1889): 107–9.

83 Hayes, 'The Holy Father to Cardinal Lavigerie', *AOLA* XV, no. x (1890): 308–12.

84 Although her institute of Franciscan Missionaries of Mary was founded in India in 1877, later initiatives of French-born de Chappotin took place in France. Her institute spread quickly to many other countries.

85 Georges Goyau, *Valiant Women: Mother Mary of the Passion and the Franciscan Missionaries of Mary*, trans. Mgr George Telford, 191.

86 *Loss and Gain* was Newman's contemporary book.

87 Friars Minor, '*Elenco Alfabetico Delle Riviste Presenti Nel Catalogo Electtrónico Della Biblioteca Dell'Antonianum*' (Rome: Franciscan University Library, Pontificium Athenaeum Antonianum, n.d.).

88 Listed numbers in the Catalogue included: no. 89 for *Annales Franciscaines*, no. 97 for Elizabeth Hayes' *Annals of Our Lady of the Angels*, and no. 737 for *The Month*.

89 Hales, *The Catholic Church in the Modern World*, 144.

90 Holmes and Bickers, 'The Church, Revolution and Reaction, 1789–1914', 240.

91 Hayes, 'The Convents of Rome and the Revolution', *AOLA* I, no. vi (1874): 172.

92 Hayes, 'Extracts of News from Rome', *AOLA* I, no. ii (1874): 60–1.

93 Hayes, 'Christmas Day in Rome', *AOLA* I, no. xi (1874): 327–30.

94 Denis Meadows, 'Loss and Gain in the 19th Century', in *A Short History of the Catholic Church*, 202. Holmes and Bickers, 'The Church, Revolution and Reaction, 1789–1914', 240.

95 Rosmini's works and material by W. Lockhart are available at the Rosminain Fathers library, Glencomeragh, Kilsheehan, County Tipperary. Among Lockhart's publications is his *Life of Rosmini* (1886).

96 In 2001, *L'Osservatore Romano* published an article that included: 'The Decree stated: 'All the works of Antonio Rosmini Serbati that have

recently been examined, are to be dismissed *(Dimittantur opera Antonii Rosmini)* and this examination in no way detracts from the good name of the author, nor of the religious Society founded by him, nor from his life and singular merits towards the Church'.' Richard Malone, *Historical Overview of the Rosmini Case* (*L'Osservatore Romano*, English Edition, Baltimore, MD).

 97 Hayes, 'The Apostolate of the Press', *AOLA* XV, no. ii, iii, vi (1890): 35–40, 73–6, 164–9.
 98 P. C., 'A Tertiary's Account of the English Pilgrimage', *AOLA* I, no. I (1874), 6–10. Australians are interested in knowing that Mother Mary MacKillop was a member of this pilgrimage.
 99 *The Month and Catholic Review* (1874) June, 245.
100 Hayes, 'The Apostolate of the Press', 35.
101 Ibid., 36.
102 Lyon was the headquarters of Society of the Propagation of the Faith where Pauline Jaricot's Annals, *Missions Catholiques*, were published.
103 Hayes, 'The Apostolate of the Press', 36.
104 Ibid., 38–9.
105 Cardinal Parocchi was known to Elizabeth Hayes. This connection will appear later in the period when she lived permanently in Rome.
106 Hayes, 'The Apostolate of the Press', 40.
107 Examples were *Eco di S. Tommaso d'Aquino* in Parma (1879) and *Divus Thomas* in Piacenza (1880), while *La Sapienza* of Turin (1879–86) led the field in igniting a new debate on non-Thomistic works.
108 The papal audience is described in William Lockhart, ed., *Life of Antonio Rosmini Serbati: Founder of the Institute of Charity*, 337–9. The pope knew that Rosmini had sent to England some of his most talented and committed young Italian preachers. Rosminians at Prior Park, aware of the power of the press, had a printing press by 1840.
109 Hayes, 'Franciscan Record', *AOLA* VIII, no. iii (1883): 92–3.
110 Hayes, 'Franciscan Order in England', *AOLA* VIII, no. ii, iii (1883): 97.
111 Hayes, 'Franciscan Record: The Pope and the 3rd Order', *AOLA* X, no. iv (1885): 128.
112 Franciscan friar Lucovico (Archangelo Palmentieri) was described by Elizabeth in her *Diary* – 'like an angel from heaven' – she appreciated his support in a critical decision in Rome.
113 Hayes, 'Franciscan Record: Rome', *AOLA* IX, no. iv (1884): 127–8.
114 Hayes, 'Padre Ludovico Da Casoria: Obituary', *AOLA* X, no. v (1885): 160.
115 Ludovico da Casoria, 'The Testament of Padre Ludovico Da Casoria, 1877', *AOLA* X, no. vii (1885): 218–20.
116 Hayes, 'Padre Ludovico Da Casoria', *AOLA* X, no. x (1885): 316–20.
117 Fr Bonaventure was a member of Ludovico's Grey Brothers community. The Sisters founded by Ludovico were Elizabettines, a name taken from the Franciscan, St Elizabeth of Hungary.
118 Hayes, 'Padre Ludovico Da Casoria: His Last Days', *AOLA* X, no. xi (1885): 346–51.

119 Hayes, 'Funeral and Obsequies of Father Ludovico Da Casoria', *AOLA* X, no. xii (1885): 381–83.

120 de Breffny, *Unless the Seed Die*, 180.

121 Hyacinth Loyson (1827–1912) had been a popular French Carmelite preacher who refused to accept the definition of papal infallibility at the First Vatican Council (1869–70) and left the Church.

122 de Breffny, *Unless the Seed Die*, 181.

123 Ibid., 182. The Rescript was absolutely necessary for the *Annals'* distribution to continue in America.

124 Pope Leo XIII, 'Encyclical Letter of His Holiness Pope Leo XIII', *AOLA* XIII, no. vii (1888): 219–22.

125 Hayes, 'The Jubilee of Our Holy Father', *AOLA* XIII, no. i (1888): 1–16. Hayes, 'The Jubilee Mass at St. Peter's', *AOLA* XIII, no. iv (1888): 124–28. Cardinal Ledochowski, 'The Soverign Pontiff on His Jubilee', *AOLA* XIII, no. xi (1888): 321–24. Hayes, 'The Jubilee of the Dead', *AOLA* XIII, no. xi (1888): 351–2.

126 Pope Leo XIII, 'The Pope and the Slaves: Brief Addressed to the Bishops of Brazil', *AOLA* XIII, no. viii (1888): 233–51.

127 Henry E. Cardinal Manning, 'On the Pope's Last Encyclical', *AOLA* XIII, no. xi (1888): 399–45.

128 Titles of articles: 'The Famous Cascade of Tivoli', 'The Quirinal Palace and Monte Cavallo', 'The Arch of Constantine', 'The Forum of Trojan', 'The Roman Forum' and 'Temple of Concord'.

129 Pope Leo XIII, 'The Papal Allocution on Columbus: Letter to Archbishops and Bishops of Spain, Italy and the Two Americas', *AOLA* XVII, no. viii (1892): 239–46. Columbus was a Franciscan Third Order Secular member.

130 *Octobri Mense* (1891), *Magnae Dei Matris* (1892), *Laetitiae Sanctae* (1893) and *Jucunda Semper* (1894).

131 Pope Leo XIII, 'The Holy Rosary: Encyclical on the Devotion of the Holy Rosary', *AOLA* XVII, no. x (1892): 289–99.

132 E.g., 'Our Lady 'Ad Rupes'' – one of 7 articles in 1892; 'Our Lady of St. Apollinaris, in Rome' – one of 9 in 1893; 'Santa Maria di Montorella, in the Diocese of Tivoli, near Rome' – one of 6 in 1894.

133 Manning, 'On the Pope's Last Encyclical', 339.

134 The introductory words of *Christi Nomen* on the Propagation of Faith and Eastern Churches (24 December 1894).

135 The survivors were *The Irish American* (New York), the *Catholic Telegraph* (Cincinnati), *The Pilot* (Boston), the *Freeman's Journal* (New York) and the *Catholic* (Pittsburg).

136 E.g., Irish names included Thomas O'Connor of the *Shamrock*, or *Hibernian Chronicle*, James W. and John E. White, nephews of Irish novelist Gerald Griffin, editors of *Freeman's Journal*; Patrick Lynch from Kilkenny who founded *The Irish American*; Thomas D'Arcy McGee, founder of *The Nation* and *The American Celt*; Revd Patrick Cronin, *Catholic Union and Times* editor for many years.

137 Editors spread the statement as in *Donahoe's Magazine* article, 'Parochial Schools' (1884), 570.

138 *Donahoe's Magazine* (June 1889), 622.

139 *Ave Maria* office letterhead of 1879, MFICAR. The University of Notre Dame du Lac in Northern Indiana, also the head house of the Holy Cross Fathers since 1842, established a university press which issued two weekly publications, a literary and a religious magazine. The latter was the *Ave Maria*, 'contributed to by the best writers of Europe and America'.

140 Stanislaus Clarke, Notre Dame, Indiana, letter to Mother M. Ignatius Hayes, 27 May 1878, MFICAR.

141 Daniel E. Hudson, 'The Annals of Our Lady of the Angels', *Ave Maria* XIV, no. 23 (1878): 370.

142 Stanislaus Clarke, Notre Dame, Indiana, letter to Mother M. Ignatius Hayes, 16 June 1878, MFICAR. What Hudson received was very lengthy, it included Fanny Montgomery's 23 articles in 1874, 1875, 1878, with one in 1879 that we know of and probably more in the 1879 series.

143 Clarke, letter to Mother M. Ignatius Hayes, 27 May 1878, MFICAR.

144 Daniel E. Hudson, Notre Dame, Indiana, letter to Mother M. Ignatius Hayes, 6 June 1878, MFICAR.

145 'The Tomb of St. Peter of Alcantara', *AOLA* V, no. iii (1880): 78.

146 The original printing of the name, *Ave Maria*, in the Elizabeth's extant 1880 index initiated the present writer's research since the 1880 contents of her *AOLA* are not extant. It provided the key to other material in MFICAR.

147 Stanislaus Clarke, Notre Dame, Indiana, letter to Mother M. Ignatius Hayes, 6 January 1879, MFICAR.

148 Paul Henri Corentin Feval, 'The Miraculous Cross', *AOLA* V, no. iii (1880): 82. Feval was a novelist who contributed to important Parisian newspapers and who held the position of President of the 'Société des Gens de Lettres'.

149 Hayes, 'Missionary Notes', *AOLA* VIII, no. iii (1883): 94.

150 Contributors included Archbishop M. J. Spalding, Bishop Michael O'Connor, the Revd Dr C. C. Pise and B. N. Campbell. Spalding (1810–72) was once editor of the *Catholic Advocate* (1835), devoted much time to lectures and controversial writings in the Church's defence, published books and became the 7th Archbishop of Baltimore. Authorities disagree on closure date, 1848 appears most likely.

151 Bishop Thomas Grace, St. Paul, letter to Revd Sister Mary Ignatius, Superior, Sisters' Institute, Brainerd, Minnesota, 18 December 1873, MFICAR.

152 N. Bures, 'Annals of Our Lady of the Angels: A Monthly Bulletin of the Third Order of St. Francis of Assisi', *Northwestern Chronicle*, 1 August 1874, 5.

153 Browson in his Protestant days edited religious newspapers and periodicals, e.g., New York's *Free Enquirer*, a Western New York journal, *The*

Gospel Advocate and *The Philanthropist,* and contributed to others including *The Christian Examiner,* the most significant of these publications.

154 Cardinal Wiseman was known to have encouraged a number of young
writers, including Isaac T. Hecker, Margaret A. Cusack and Fanny
Taylor, to commit their lives to the cause of Catholic literature.

155 Elizabeth Hayes did not enter into this controversy. A central tenet of
'Americanism' was separation of Church and State, an idea unacceptable
to European political conservatives.

156 Meadows, 'Loss and Gain in the 19th Century', 214.

157 Meadows claims that Hecker was editor from the beginning of publication until his death in 1888. Ibid.

158 On the high profile network to which Brownson and Hecker belonged,
see Patrick W. Carey, *Orestes A. Brownson: American Religious Weathervane.*
Brownson as a Catholic also wrote leading articles in the New York *Tablet;*
his last article was contributed to the *American Catholic Quarterly Review*
(January 1876).

159 William Lockhart, ed., *The Old Religion; or How Shall We Find Primitive
Christianity?,* preface, n.p.

160 Chaffee, 'Memories', 51–2.

161 Hecker was sixty-six at the time but worn out; he lived another three
years.

162 Chaffee's words were. 'As soon as he saw Mother Ignatius [Hayes], he
understood the reason of this secret internal movement'. The difficulties
and consequences for the *Annals* will be considered later.

163 Chaffee recorded Hecker's words: 'Go to Wigger; Wigger is a good fellow
and he will help you ...' Sr Chaffee explained that Elizabeth Hayes
wanted to open a house in New York 'for the convenience of receiving
postulants' and that 'when we opened a house later on in Jersey City, it
was with the kind help of Bishop Wigger ...' Chaffee, as Mother General,
was to open a house on 13 June 1899 in Sixth Street, Jersey City; two
Sisters from the community were assigned as 'zelatrices' (sisters who
canvassed for subscriptions) for the *Annals.* Eileen Cahalane, *History of
the Immaculate Conception Province,* 21–2. From 1891 a new group of zelatrices had come to USA from Rome.

164 'New Jersey State was the place chosen by Mother M. Ignatius Hayes after
conferring with her friend, Father Isaac Hecker, ... for a *pied à terre*' – as
described in the chronicles. She wanted a 'foothold' on the continent so
that when the sisters arrived by ship in New York, they would have some-
where to stay. 'Fr. Hecker advised against New York itself as Manhatten
Island could be difficult to travel back and forth from'. MFIC Union City
chronicles.

165 Rome's suspicion at the time was that American Catholics desired a
different style of Catholicism from the rest of the world – rooted in the
initial separation of Church and State, a situation Bishop Ireland, e.g.,
saw as advantageous.

166 The controversy was brought to a head when in the preface of the
French translation of the *Life of Father Hecker,* an incorrect interpretation

had been placed on some of Hecker's publications. To clarify 'Americanism', Bishop Ireland commenced a three-month stay in Rome on 27 January 1899.

167 Kevin Shanley, 'Old St. Patrick's Cathedral Remembered by the Irish. Irish History ... A Look at the Way the Irish Have Influenced History and Participated in Events That Have Shaped Our Lives', *Irish Gazette*, March/April 2001.

168 The nickname 'Knownothing' originated from the party members' secrecy over naming its members and their standard reply to outsiders, 'I don't know'. The 'natives' referred to were the American-born descendents of European, mainly British, settlers.

169 Nearly 100 poor Irish people he claimed had been butchered or burned and some twenty houses burnt to the ground. Apparently damage and suffering was inflicted also on churches and religious organizations, including convents.

170 Patrick Donahoe, 'Editor's Note', *Donahoe's*, June 1889. Irish American and Catholic interests were the focus not only in *Donahoe's Magazine*, subtitled '*A Journal Devoted to the Irish Race at Home & Abroad*', but also in Donahoe's weekly paper, *The Pilot*.

171 Fenwick's first enterprise was in Connecticut where his short-lived journalistic venture was the *Catholic Press* begun in Hartford (11 July 1829). His aim next was to have 'a newspaper in which the Doctrine of the Holy Catholic Church, ever the same, from the Apostolic Age down to our time, may be truly explained, and moderately, but firmly defended'.

172 Hughes had become the first Archbishop of New York in 1850.

173 Joseph P. Chinnici, 'The Spirituality of Americanism, 1866–1900', in *Living Stones: The History and Structure of Catholic Spiritual Life in the United States*, ed. Christopher J. Kauffman, 87.

174 Both Hecker and Keane laboured to make people aware of the indwelling Spirit – Keane through his pastoral letters, his support of the Confraternity of the Servants of the Holy Ghost, and his diocesan visitations; Hecker through his numerous publications of mystical works, mission preaching and spiritual direction. Roddan, a Boston priest educated in Rome, was an editor of *The Pilot* and wrote for Brownson's *Review*.

175 Chinnici, 'The spirituality of Americanism, 1866–1900', 96.

176 Shaw, ed., *Diary*, 66.

177 Ireland, John Ireland Papers – Index Book (of Five Reviews) 1863–93.

178 Cardinal Wiseman, friend of Newman, was a constant contributor, contriving to supply at least one article to almost every number appearing in the 1850s when he was ceaselessly in demand in every part of England. His review articles covered almost every topic of the day including sociology, literature and the arts.

179 In the original series, at least half or more of its literary matter was produced in Ireland and its content contained Irish topics, political, social, educational and literary.

180 The *Dublin Review* (January 1868 issue) drew attention to the *Irish*

Ecclesiastical Record (founded October 1864) which in its opening page claimed that its 'character and scope' were summed up in its title, 'Ecclesiastical' and 'Irish'. The IER's contents evidenced Irish American connections under such titles as 'Irish Faith in America' and Archbishop Spalding's 'Lectures and Discourses' (1882), New York's publication of Capel's book (1885), and notices of religious books published by Benziger's of New York (1891).

181 Names included Fr Matthew Russell, Lady G. Fullerton, Aubrey de Vere, Fr T. Bridgett, Mother Raphael Drane and Rosa Mulholland.

182 Manning was still contributing at eighty-four years of age and writing with clarity of thought, e.g., 'If any man would protect the world of labour from the oppression of 'free contracts' or 'starvation wages', he is a Socialist. So obscure from want of thought, or so warped by interest, or so prejudiced by class feeling are the minds of men'.

183 Manning's trust in Ireland may be gauged from the fact that the former saw the latter as prospective editor of his manuscripts for a trilogy on the priesthood's rights and dignity that were to be published after his death. For Ireland's friendship with Manning see James H. Moynihan, *The Life of Archbishop John Ireland*, 321.

184 Revd John Ireland, St Paul, letter to Mother Mary Ignatius Hayes, 23 September 1874, MFICAR.

185 Revd Marvin O'Connell, 'James J. Hill and John Ireland', in '*You Shall Be my People*'. *A History of the Archdiocese of Saint Paul and Minneapolis: 150th Anniversary*, ed. John Christine Wolkerstorfer, 7.

186 Copies at FSALF and MFICAR.

187 Newspaper Time Index, Stearns History Museum and Research Centre, St Cloud, MN., microfilm.

188 Copies of both articles available, MFICAR.

189 It was said of Pusey by Dean Stanley, speaking of his 1838 lectures, 'The whole atmosphere of the Professor breathed the spirit of Germany to a degree which I am convinced could be found in no other lecture-room in Oxford'. {R. William Franklin, 'The Impact of Germany on the Anglican Catholic Revival in Nineteenth-Century Britain', *Anglican and Episcopal History*, Volume LXII, no. 3 (1993): 441, in E.G.W. Bill, *University Reform in Nineteenth Century Oxford 1811–1885*, 252–3.} Elizabeth Hayes was not in Oxford's lecture rooms but Pusey used the same approach in his public sermons.

190 Neander was 'a rather famous young German Church historian in Berlin'. Patristic theology and spirituality attracted Pusey, who had completed the equivalent of modern graduate studies over five years in German Universities in the 1820s. Pusey's Hebrew linguistic scholarship earned him a chair in Oxford and he was a brilliant Hebraist. (Allchin, 'W. J. Butler – Sacraments and Society', 5.)

191 Early 1890s *Annals*' translations from German included: Dr. Fisher, 'Address by the Most Rev. Dr. Fisher, Coadjutor-Bishop of Cologne, on the Occasion of Laying the Foundation-Stone of a New Monastery of the Franciscan Province of the Holy Cross, at Gladbach, North Germany, on

May 26th 1890', *AOLA* XV, no. x (1890): 286–91; P. Weiss, 'The Religious Orders: Extracts from the Speech at the German Catholic Congress Recently Held at Coblentz, by Rev. P. Weiss, of the Order of St. Dominic, Professor in the New Catholic University of Friburg', *AOLA* XV, no. xi (1890): 342–44; Elizabeth Hayes, 'Shrines of St. Anthony of Padua: The Miraculous Shrine at Kaltern in the Austrian Tyrol', *AOLA* XVII, no. i, iii (1892): 27–32, 90–6.

192 *Stimmen aus Maria-Laach* was still being published ten times a year by Herder at Freiburg, at the beginning of the twentieth century, issue 5200.

193 *Stimmen aus Maria-Laach*. Katholische Blätter. 1880, 1881, 1884 issues are available in the Benedictine Sisters Library at Saint Joseph, Mn., accessed in 2001; the 1880 issue was printed in Germany but the 1884 one was printed by Herder in St Louis, Mo. Its translated title, 'Voices from Maria Laach', was derived from the famous German Abbey.

194 Before 1848 German Catholic journalism did not prosper; then came the political and religious emancipation which were of immense importance for Catholic life and the Catholic press.

195 The *Kulturkampf*, instead of destroying the Catholic people's faith, brought about an expansion of power and scattered the Catholic laity, religious and clergy to other countries, especially North America.

196 Words of 'F.R.U.I.', 'A New Organ', *Irish Ecclesiastical Record*, V, 3rd Series (1884): 93. *Germania* (1871) was a Berlin newspaper founded by members of the Berlin Catholic Societies with the aid of Friedrich Kehler, embassy councillor. It was seen as the new, important organ of the political Catholic Centre Party.

Chapter 4

Pioneer in the Franciscan Periodical Press

Pioneers are trail blazers who make it possible for others to follow a new path and so, to appreciate the significance of Elizabeth among the earliest pioneers of Franciscan periodicals, we need to contextualize her journal within the wider Franciscan periodical scene, both at the time she began publishing in 1874, and over the twenty-one years of her editorship. In doing this one discovers that the pioneer Elizabeth made an initial contribution as the first person to edit and publish a Franciscan journal in English. Her early work spearheaded American Franciscan journals and later her *Annals* took its worthy place among respected European publications. While Elizabeth, like so many other religious women, shared in the ministry of education, she was one of the few nineteenth-century religious foundresses committed to the ministry of preparing periodicals for wide distribution.

To flesh out this nineteenth-century Franciscan periodical scene is challenging as a directory of nineteenth-century Franciscan journals produced for Europe, Canada or the United States, could not be located. The result of an extensive search of Franciscan library holdings and the first attempt to provide such a directory is provided in Appendix 1. Whilst not claiming to be complete, this listing provides a comparative setting within which to evaluate the contribution of Elizabeth's *Annals*.[1] It was noted earlier that Elizabeth's illustrated *Annals of Our Lady of the Angels,* initially appearing in 1874, was the first Franciscan periodical to be published in the United States. This claim, verified through recent research, received an earlier endorsement when, in 1873, Elizabeth visited Friar Romo at the Californian Santa Barbara Mission. Sr Chaffee recalled:

It was from the Father Superior of the Mission, Rev. Joseph Romo, that our Mother received her inspiration of printing the Annals of Our Lady of the Angels, the Father having urged it on the grounds of there being no Franciscan periodical at that time printed in America.[2]

When viewed in the context of the experience of her whole life, Fr Romo was not the primary source of her inspiration. Elizabeth already had the dream of a Franciscan periodical and her visit provided confirmation of it.[3] It was noted earlier that Elizabeth was fully aware that the Franciscans not only did not have their own journal in North America but that they did not produce one anywhere in the English language. So what European Franciscan journals were available to Elizabeth before 1874 and did she use them to enrich her *Annals*?

Pre-1874 European Franciscan Journals

In the Order's early days St Francis was convinced that a great number of men and women from almost every country would join the Order. According to his first biographer, Celano, Francis said, 'Frenchmen are coming, Spaniards are hastening, Germans and English are running, and a very great multitude of others speaking various tongues are hurrying.'[4] These words, quoted in an article by Elizabeth,[5] can be applied to the growth and propagation of Franciscan periodical literature in Europe in the second half of the nineteenth century. First, an overview of European Franciscan Journals that pre-dated Elizabeth's:

....

Overview of the pre-1874 European Franciscan journals[6]

1861 (Sept.) *Annales Franciscaines.* Paris. Capuchins.
1865 *Annales du Tiers-Ordre de Saint Francois d'Assise.* Avignon. Aubanel Frères.
1870 *Annali Francescani.* Milano. Capuchins.
1870 *Revue Franciscaine:* Bulletin mensuel du Tiers-Ordre de Saint Francois. Paris.
1871 *Letture Francescane:* peridico mensile religiso dedicato ai figli Terziarii di San Francesco d'Assisi. Cuneo.
1873 *L'eco di S. Francesco: periodico mensile sacro-francescano.* Napoli. Capuchins.

1873 *La Revista Franciscana.* Barcelona. Osservanti.
1874 *Annals of Our Lady of the Angels.* Belle Prairie, Mn. Third Order
   Regular Sisters.

....

Franciscans have a long and strong literary tradition developed over an 800–year history. In meeting the challenges of secular journals in the nineteenth century, Franciscan periodical editors drew on this strong tradition. Elizabeth referred to the learned doctors among the Franciscan scholars when she translated the following from the *Revue Franciscaine*:

> The Doctors and men of learning in this Order are more than ten thousand amongst which we do not comprehend any of those of the present day who notwithstanding are very numerous'.[7]

In another article Elizabeth wrote:

> Franciscan Doctors have occupied the first chairs of the most celebrated universities, such as Alexander of Hales, John de la Rochelle, St. Bonaventure, Adam de Marisco, Duns Scotus, Roger Bacon, Francis Mayronis, Nicholas de Lyre and many others. The Order, when still in its infancy, possessed the three-fold Aureola of martyrdom, apostleship and learning.[8]

Among *Annali Francescani's* four major contributors was the Third Order French bishop, Louis Gaston de Ségur, an authority on the Third Order and an important contributor to Elizabeth's *Annals* and other Franciscan journals. The editor of the monthly periodical, *L'eco di S. Francesco D'Assisi,* Friar Bonaventure, began the first volume with a greeting to Franciscans and Catholics everywhere, followed by a strongly worded claim that the journal would counteract the evils of the day – the same aim as Elizabeth hoped for her *Annals.* Elizabeth's *Annals,* as well as her diary, reveal that she was familiar with or knew of these earliest Franciscan journals and quoted from most of them on numerous occasions when they suited her topic. To let her readers know the difficult situation facing Franciscans in other countries, Elizabeth borrowed from the Parisian *Annales Franciscaines*:

> In our last number we announced the expulsion of these religious of the Third Order Regular of St. Francis, from Gnesen, in Prussia, by the government, we translate from the French Annals the following letter, assured that it will interest our readers.[9]

Drawing on the same journal for an article on missions, Elizabeth noted, 'A few quotations from the Annals published at the present time in Europe will satisfy our inquiries.'[10] Elizabeth's lifelong proficiency in French was invaluable for translating *Annales Franciscaines* which she probably read in Jamaica since French was the community's basic language. Also easy access to *Annales Franciscaines* was likely after Elizabeth's arrival in France, first in 1864 and then again from late 1866, until she left Sèvres, near Paris, around July 1870.

To demonstrate the flourishing state of the Franciscans in Italy, Elizabeth used statistical information from *Annali Francescani:*

> In Italy, according to the statistics published by the Franciscan Annals of Milan, there are 30,740 known Tertiaries, of whom thirty-eight are Prelates, 264 pastors of parishes, 832 Priests, 716 religious of different orders, more than 8,000 men and 49,840 women. Half of these have been admitted during the last two years, which shows the astonishing progress of the Third Order in Italy. At Gabinte, diocese of Milan, out of 450 families which form the entire population there are 866 Tertiaries; Milan itself counts 3,110. ... The Annals add that, including all the isolated members scattered in the different parts of the peninsula, the total number is estimated at over half a million![11]

In her diary in the early 1870s Elizabeth made reference to the 'Franciscan Annals of Milan' and hence indicated her awareness of the *Annali Francescani* before she engaged in the same Franciscan Apostolate of the Press.[12]

To highlight the political situation faced by some Franciscan publishers, Elizabeth quoted from *Revue Franciscaine* to tell the story of 'The Franciscans in Prussia'.[13] It told of Third Order Franciscan Sisters – 'several of the Sisters were French but the greater number were of Polish origin'- who were expelled 'for having published a collection of Hymns in honour of the Sacred Heart!' In the light of this, one wonders what was the penalty for publishing a journal during the *Kulturkampf* in places under German/Prussian control. When writing about missions, Franciscans or saints, Elizabeth at times called on *Revue Franciscaine*.[14] She was also aware of the Franciscans at Cuneo who published *Letture Francescane* as she recorded that 'At Cuneo there are 2,300 (Tertiaries)'.[15] When Elizabeth wanted to tell of the Order's development in Spain, 'notwithstanding that anarchy and revolution rend the country', she claimed that the commencement of *La Revista Franciscana* was 'evident proof the Third Order is spreading there'.[16] Of the seven European Franciscan journals commenced before her project, we know that she was familiar with six of them.

Roman Interval – Poor Clares

No matter where Elizabeth travelled, she always made time for reading, and so, as we follow the fascinating trail of her movements in the second half of 1874 – during which she remained editor of her publication – we move on to what has been called her 'Roman interval'.

Arriving in Rome, Elizabeth (Mother M. Ignatius) Hayes wasted no time before informing the Minister General of the Friars Minor, Fr Bernardine of Portogruaro, of her reason for being there and discussing with him her needs and plans for Belle Prairie, especially the need for a chaplain and for more sisters in her community. The Minister General normally resided at the Aracoeli; however while he retained this address on his letters, Elizabeth was aware of the government persecution and its takeover of the Friars' headhouse in 1873, so she visited Fr Bernardine in another part of Rome.[17] Fr Bernardine was not forthcoming with a suggestion regarding who might be a possible chaplain for Belle Prairie. Instead he directed Elizabeth to go to the heart of Germany to the Friars Minor in Fulda.[18]

With her sound knowledge of Franciscan history, Elizabeth was aware that a Greyfriars' house had existed in Fulda from 1273 until 1550.[19] To get to this gracious old town with rich reminders of its religious history, including St Michael's Church with a Carolingian crypt dating from Benedictine origins there in the early 800s – one of the most remarkable sacred buildings in the country – Elizabeth needed finance. She first visited Naples to seek help from Fra Ludovico da Casoria who ensured that she received enough money for the journey. Unlike today, when the traveller can fly into Frankfurt international airport, then drive by car or catch the inter-city-express train to reach Fulda within the hour, Elizabeth made her way there by slower means. Fulda, often called the 'City of St Boniface', welcomed the English traveller, for it was and is a place popular with English visitors since Boniface, an Englishman, died in 754 and was buried in Fulda Cathedral.[20]

After many efforts on the writer's part to learn with which religious community Elizabeth sought hospitality, the most likely appears to have been Mary Ward's Sisters.[21] Franciscan Friars came to Fulda in the time of St Francis and since 1623 a Franciscan friary has been situated in a park on one of Fulda's seven hills. After Elizabeth's climb to the top of this hill, which overlooks the city and the Rhön and Vogelsberg Mountains, the guardian, who in 1874–5 was Fr Xavier Post, no doubt first showed her the church attached to the friary. Built in the late Baroque period, Elizabeth would have appreciated its artistically remarkable interior. After that, it was down to business. It is hard to calculate just what kind of an impression Elizabeth made, but since other educated religious leaders recognized her talents and likeable personality, she was probably well received. She did not gain a chaplain at once; however, the name of Fr Aloysius Lauer of Fulda, who served as guardian (1859–63, followed by a short break, then again 1864–8) and who was local provincial (1867 to 1881, therefore including 1874–5),[22] weaves its way a number of times into the story of Elizabeth's life. Fr Lauer was a visitor to the United States of America in 1875 and his name will appear again later in Rome. Certainly, as mentioned earlier, after the Franco-Prussian War period, Elizabeth moved around Germany and was in communication with German friars. Sr Chaffee attributed some credit to her leader for the arrival in Minnesota of German Franciscan friars in 1875; however, most credit is due to Bishop Grace who sent the friars to Jordan, diocese of St Paul, at a distance from Belle Prairie. In the same year also Franciscans from Fulda came to the State of New York.

During the ensuing months following her return from Germany while she rejoiced in renewing old acquaintances living in Rome, Elizabeth focused on her main reason for being there. This Roman interval necessitated visits to many convents as she endeavoured to find Sisters to take to Belle Prairie. Elizabeth considered Belgium or France the appropriate countries in which to find workers for a mission, but instead, she clearly wanted a few mature Franciscan women from Italy who were saturated with the history, traditions and spirit of the Religious Life. Also Elizabeth still sought a Franciscan priest who would provide a spiritual ministry for the Sisters and for the local church, especially to provide Eucharist and administer the sacraments.[23]

Elizabeth was forced to spend much time waiting; she experienced the full meaning of the old saying, 'Rome is eternal'. However, as indicated by the numerous documents that exist in the archives of the Propagation of the Faith, her pen was busy while she waited. When she was writing to contacts back in North America, many of her letters, which were written to gain various approvals or to keep in close contact with key ecclesiastics, carry the Roman address, 45 Via Quatto Fontane. In particular, these included the Cardinal Vicar of Rome, Cardinal Patrizi, and the Prefect of the Sacred Congregation of the Propagation of the Faith (Propaganda Fide), Cardinal Alexandro Franchi. From all accounts it is obvious that Elizabeth looked for Sisters who belonged to the Third Order Regular of St Francis but, after finding none available, she was one day visiting the Poor Clare Convent of San Lorenzo-in-Panisperna where the enclosed nuns of the Second Order of St Francis resided. Elizabeth was able to feel in solidarity with these nuns who since the suppression of the religious in Italy in 1870 were restricted to a small portion of their convent while the rest of their building was appropriated by the government for a public school for medical students.

According to Marianus Fiege's account, a number of nuns at this Poor Clare Convent wanted to accompany Elizabeth to the United States while others opposed the idea.[24] A few from other Poor Clare communities also were interested and this is not surprising for, in the past, a few attempts had been instigated to introduce the Poor Clare nuns to the United States of America. Elizabeth was providing an opportunity to take a few nuns to North America, to provide them with a convent where their own Rule and Constitutions would be observed. She wished to share with them the fruits of the fertile property on the bank of the Upper Mississippi, while hoping they would be a prayerful spiritual support and be able to help with the requirements of a Eucharistic community, including Elizabeth's students and Sisters.[25]

One account says that the names of three Sisters were approved by the Franciscan Minister General, including two nuns from the convent of San Lorenzo and one from San Cosimato, in Tuscany. Petitions were written and given to Pope Pius IX to gain his apostolic sanction. Fiege wrote that in the petition presented by Elizabeth to the pope, she had set forth how favourable Belle Prairie was for the establishment of the Poor Clares.[26] The names of the two San Lorenzo Poor Clare nuns were Annetta and Costanza Bentivoglio, known in religion as Sr M. Maddallena (also called Magdalen) and Sr M. Constanza (who retained her baptismal name and was also called Constance).[27]

For Elizabeth, events in this Roman interval came to climax after months of searching, waiting and 'red tape'. There is in Elizabeth's diary a long and detailed account of this one very important day – the day when Elizabeth again encountered Rome's Cardinal Vicar, Eminenza Patrizi, and when she, with a strong display of confidence in God, argued again the need to take Poor Clare nuns to Belle Prairie. He and the others involved, representing an official view, hesitated, differed and stressed the human obstacles. The date in 1875 was stamped indelibly on Elizabeth's mind and she recorded it. For once she dated her diary entry and headed it, 'April 21st. A day of Anguish'. Those involved besides Cardinal Patrizi were: 'Nuns', Poor Clares who volunteered to go with Elizabeth; 'Confessor', Minister General who was Fr Bernardine of Portogruaro; 'Propaganda', Cardinal Alexander Franchi; 'Fr Ludovico', saintly Franciscan and friend of Elizabeth; 'Fr General', again Fr Bernardine of Portogruaro; 'Pope', Pius IX. Elizabeth's own words tell the story best for they convey the passion of her feelings and the strength her determination. (Elizabeth's account is in Appendix 3.)

What a picture: Elizabeth lecturing the Cardinal Vicar of Rome – an exceptional scene in which a nineteenth-century woman forthrightly defends what she believes. Elizabeth's words, 'Faith never changes. Confidence in God never changes' and again, 'it could only be done for God and in God', reveal the depths of her soul, her strong faith and her spirituality.[28] The virtue of 'great piety', attributed in the *Brainerd Tribune* to Elizabeth by Morris Russell, considered in the light of her encounter with Cardinal Patrizi, provides a picture of a pious woman fired with great faith in God. Elizabeth's piety sought to bring forth fruit through action; she was no 'shrinking violet' when the building of the reign of God was at stake. Neither was she, as John Watts described her – from his narrow interpretation of her diary-writing during the Jamaican situation – a 'delicate, highly strung perfectionist'.[29] Being a woman of prayer, she integrated her love for Christ with the giving of herself in service to others and nothing was going to deter her.

By April 1875, Elizabeth had been away from her Belle Prairie mission for close on ten months yet she still needed more time. During these ten months her *Annals'* publication continued to roll off the Brainerd Press and one wonders if her mobile editing work reflected what was happening during her Roman interval. Were her travels and experiences in Rome recorded in the articles that she was writing, editing, and translating for publication back in Minnesota? The items published during the period from July 1874 to April the next year include a continuation of six serialized stories begun in early 1874. There is evidence that in Rome Elizabeth had access to Italian and French material that she translated and edited. One article stands out in particular, 'Christmas Day in Rome', an account of her delight in sharing the festive season there. Elizabeth introduced her four-page article with:

> Every Christian man, to whom in any way it is possible, should, once in his life, go up to God's city of Rome. If he bring not back with him from that centre of grace a large treasure of blessing – and it will be his own fault if he does not – he will at least return with a store of happy memories, such as no other spot on this earth can give. For in Rome is written the history of the world. Once the capital of a vast Roman empire, centre of all natural civilization and order and learning, now the capital of Christ's wider and eternal kingdom, ...[30]

Elizabeth follows with an account of her own 'happy memories' of Rome's Christmas:

> Our first warning of the nearness of Christmas Day was an invasion of the city by shepherds or other peasants from without the walls, armed with a rude sort of pipe, wherewith they made music, more devout than tuneful, before the images of the Holy Child in His Mother's arms, which, at every street-corner of Rome, remind the passer-by how God, for his sake, came into the world. The music was wild enough, but no doubt the shepherds at Bethlehem made no better minstrelsy, when the angels sung them such glorious strains from heaven; and to see these simple Roman shepherds standing before image after image, and greeting, as best they could, the Mother and the Child with simple melody and simple devotion, woke in us thoughts that were no ill preparation for a happy Christmas.[31]

She went on to describe the Masses on Christmas day, and one sight in particular that impressed her:

> At the moment of consecration, the Pope's Noble Guard, who line both sides of the long sanctuary, fall down upon one knee, with swords drawn, as if ready to start up at once and give their lives in their Master's defence. Expressed in that act was the grand spirit of the old Crusaders; the spirit which, thank God! Has lived again in Mentana.[32]

Since Elizabeth saw Italy as the centre of the great religious Orders and cradle of the three Orders of St Francis of Assisi, it is not surprising that, while there, she continued to write articles about the Franciscans. Back in Minnesota she had written about the 'Progress and Development of the Third Order in Europe'; now in

Italy in July 1874, her *Annals* carried news of the 'New and Complete Edition of the Works of St. Bonaventure'. In October the same year, she published a historical and interesting 'Chronological Table of the Saints and blessed, from 1500 to 1791'. During this period Elizabeth had a copy of the French Franciscan Annals, *Revue Franciscaine*, and from this periodical she translated for her own publication an article on 'The Franciscan Order'. However Elizabeth did not swamp her readers with too much of any one theme; instead she maintained the aims and objectives of her *Annals* clearly outlined by her in her first issue. We will return to these later.

Developing situation in Rome

To continue the story of Elizabeth's Roman interval; Bishop Grace from Minnesota was in Rome and had communicated his approval of Elizabeth's enterprise to the pope who then blessed it. According to Sr Chaffee's memory of what Elizabeth told her, and with the later advantage to the researcher of access to a letter of Bishop Grace, Pius IX directed Fr Bernardine to select the two Poor Clares who would join Elizabeth's enterprise. After a novena of prayer his choice fell upon the two Bentivoglio blood sisters, Sr M. Maddallena and Sr M. Constanza. While Elizabeth had, years earlier, indicated her willingness to take these two fervent nuns to a foreign mission, one account suggests that 'in her secret heart she was dismayed at the impending arrangement'.[33] If this is the truth and if Elizabeth 'had recognised certain indications that the choice had doomed her plans', then this will have implications for our understanding of Elizabeth's coping strategies later in New York. The same account immediately records,

> However, submitting generously to whatever God might have in design in the matter, she [Elizabeth] forthwith devoted herself to get ready all that would be required in the matter of permissions and material. The latter she obtained with great outlay of money, furnishing them with all they required, of clothing, coverings, etc.[34]

When writing <u>her</u> memories of the situation, Sr M. Maddallena (Annetta) said that it was Pope Pius IX who decided that the two nuns from San Lorenzo should be chosen for the American foundation because they were blood sisters. She supplements her account by quoting the pope as saying, 'These Sisters will have many sufferings to endure, and many trials and hardships to pass through. And it is better to have two Sisters of the same family, as they can encourage and console each other better.'[35]

Finally, Cardinal Franchi of Propaganda promulgated the pope's decision in a Rescript dated 1 July 1875. The Minister General of the Franciscan Order was expressly told to appoint one priest to accompany the nuns on their journey, and to make all necessary arrangements. Not until 8 August was Fr Paolino of Castellaro named by the Minister General as the nuns' spiritual adviser/director; he was considered a learned and prudent friar, yet Sr Chaffee was later to recall bluntly, 'He failed her'. As Minister General, Fr Bernardine sent letters of obedience to Maddelena and Costanza who were to depart from their convent, move to their new and distant location, and establish a convent of the Poor Clares according to the primitive observance of the Rule of St Clare.[36] It is noteworthy that the nuns were answerable to Fr Paolino, not Elizabeth Hayes or anyone else; this would have significant consequences when they reached New York.

An insight into Elizabeth's behaviour is provided by Sr Maddalena in her chronicle. This was also recorded by Sr Chaffee, but without any detail. Before leaving Rome, the Poor Clares and Elizabeth (Mother M. Ignatius) were given an audience with Pius IX during which he handed to Maddalena and Constance a silver medal of the Virgin Mary. Maddalena wrote:

> When His Holiness observed that Mother Ignatius of Jesus also expected to receive a medal, he said: 'But you have nothing to do here.' Cardinal Franchi spoke: 'What? She has nothing to do, when she was the promoter of the work?' Whereupon His Holiness gave also to her a medal.[37]

It is clear that the Cardinal Prefect of Propaganda, Cardinal Franchi, had full confidence in Elizabeth since, before her departure from Rome, she was entrusted with Apostolic Briefs which raised Fr John Ireland of St Paul to episcopal dignity and coadjutor of Bishop Grace, as a later letter of 6 December 1875 from him testified. In this letter Fr John Ireland cordially invited Elizabeth to be present at the ceremony of his consecration. The circumstances of Elizabeth being the bearer of these Apostolic Briefs gave her, according to Sr Chaffee, a special place in Bishop Ireland's affection, and she claimed he was fond of alluding to it in after years.[38]

Return to USA

On 14 August 1875 the group left Rome and travelled first to Assisi, then on to Florence, Bologna, Venice and to Nice, staying at monasteries along the route. Also in Nice at this time was the Minister General, Fr Bernardine, who was in the area visiting his friars. So the Poor Clare Sisters renewed their vows according to the First Rule of St Clare in the presence of Fr Bernardine and, besides receiving spiritual support, were canonically inducted into their new role as the foundation members of their Order in the United States. Fr Bernardine officially named Maddelena the Mother Superior and Costanza the Vicaress and presented them with a formal Decree. From Nice the group travelled to Marseilles where the Bentivoglios spent eighteen days at the monastery of Poor Clares while waiting for the steamer to be ready for sailing.[39] During this time the abbess, Mother Theresa Tavera, wisely instructed them in the First Rule and so the Bentivoglios understood the rigors of the primitive observance, which was the tradition of Marseilles dating back to the days of St Clare.[40] One may well ask what Elizabeth did during this time of waiting. The long history of the Franciscans in Marseilles would suggest that, with her active and inquiring nature, she put the time to good use.

   Over one hundred and thirty years have passed since this historic transatlantic journey and today's readers would be interested to know how the steamer *Castalia* progressed between 27 September and when approaching land. Very little is recorded about the crossing, yet Sr Chaffee adds to her earlier comment about Elizabeth's fears for the success of the enterprise, 'The farther they proceeded, and the nearer they drew to America, the deeper our mother's convictions became that her plan was not thus to be realized.' According to Maddalena's chronicle, there was nothing of great interest to report, nothing extraordinary happened. However, there was excitement when land was sighted on 12 October 1875. Maddalena wrote:

> Oh, what happiness! Land! We talked of the joy that Christopher Columbus and his companions must have felt when they saw land after so long a voyage, when even our joy was so great, though we knew nearly the time of our arrival – with God's help.[41]

Carrying mainly merchandise and only a small number of passengers the *Castalia* docked in New York harbour in the early afternoon. The Poor Clares waited on board to disembark later for

Elizabeth obviously needed to attend to some arrangements on shore ahead of their landing. She called back for them in a few hours with a carriage to take them to 143 West Thirty-First Street where they were to stay with the Grey Sisters. After introductions, Elizabeth went on to the Franciscan Sisters at Spring Street, another Third Order Regular community which later became known as the Franciscan Sisters of Allegany, New York. Fr Paolino stayed with the Franciscan friars at Sullivan Street.[42] It probably would have been easier for the Poor Clares to have been in the same convent as Elizabeth, to see the preparations she was making for the next step of the journey and to be of assistance in some way. However, rules of enclosure for Poor Clares were strict and the waiting in another convent became too much for them and so they took themselves to see Fr Paolino. To their great surprise they found that he had unexpected news for them. Maddalena's own story is clear:

> He told us that he had made up his mind not to continue his journey with Mother Ignatius, but to remain in New York till he should hear from Father General; that he had good and solid reasons for what he was doing; that if we wished to continue our journey to Belle Prairie, we might do so, he would not oppose us; but that if we took his advice, we should do as he was doing.[43]

Ahles appears convinced that Fr Kleber knew why the chaplain, Fr Paolino, quit. The bottom line was that the friars needed help themselves. Sr Chaffee clearly wrote, 'The truth was that the good Fathers in New York had discouraged them against the sacrifice, representing the rigorous climate of Minnesota, and the poverty of the place.' On the other hand, Maddalena recorded:

> We knew we should grieve the poor lady who had been very good and kind to us; yet seeing no other way out of the dilemma, we broke the news to her as gently as we could. We told her that certain obstacles had arisen which for the present compelled us to remain where we were until further orders from Rome would arrive; otherwise we should have been very delighted to accompany her to Belle Prairie.[44]

Sr Chaffee certainly knew that the 'two Sisters Bentivoglio' were intended for the 'Minnesota foundation' and that in New York something changed their minds. She appears to be under the impression that the Poor Clare nuns were discouraged at the prospect of the poverty of Belle Prairie; however, she was not aware of the pope's Rescript of July 1875. It stated that Maddalena and Constance could proceed to Minnesota only 'under the express condition that they be accompanied by a Franciscan Friar', namely Fr Paolino, and that to him, and not to Elizabeth, was officially entrusted the responsibility for 'the execution of this undertaking'.[45] When Fr Paolino refused to continue on to Minnesota, Maddalena and Constance must have felt that they had little choice in the matter. This helps one understand why Maddalena wrote in her account, 'We begged of her [Elizabeth] not to bear us any ill will, as it was not our fault.'

We will probably never learn the whole story of events in New York when three of the group decided not to accompany Elizabeth to Belle Prairie. She shared her understanding of events in New York with Sr Chaffee, yet by 1912 we cannot be absolutely sure if the latter's memory of this event was totally accurate. Some of Sr Chaffee's memories could be coloured by her special admiration for Elizabeth and, as biographer, she says that at times she was writing with insufficient external documents. Maddalena's chronicle sounds genuine and sincere. Sr Chaffee read Maddalena's account, agreed with a particular paragraph, rewrote it as her final comment on the subject and acknowledged her source. It began:

> Poor Mother Ignatius felt our refusal very much. Yet having no binding claim upon us, she resigned herself to the inevitable, and departed from us with sorrow and grief in her heart.[46]

These words speak for themselves. One wonders how Elizabeth held the memory of that final day of separation from her three travelling companions. 'Day of anguish' would not be adequate to describe the day when, after all her long negotiations and all the hard-won approvals, she heard of their heart-breaking decision. However, Sr Chaffee believed that the news was not totally unexpected and maybe that helped Elizabeth to realize in hindsight how intelligently she often perceived situations and people. Over the years, others have reflected on the rest of the Maddalena's paragraph quoted by Sr Chaffee:

> How strange are God's ways; whatever may have been Mother Ignatius' personal intentions, it certainly must be said to her lasting credit, that she was instrumental in bringing us to this country. God made use of her for His own wise ends, without granting her the fulfilment of her own desires.[47]

How did Elizabeth feel as she made the journey back to Belle
Prairie, alone and empty-handed after her long absence? It seems
that she was able to overcome personal feelings and to believe that
God had another plan, both for her Third Order Franciscan Sisters
in Minnesota and for the Second Order of Poor Clares in America.
God had chosen Elizabeth to be the instrument to plant this
branch of the Franciscan Order in a new land. Could she have
imagined that one day her own followers would be enriched by the
American Poor Clares' fruitfulness, kindness and hospitality?[48]

There is a recent interesting article by Poor Clare Cecilia
Switalski which rounds off Elizabeth's Roman interval. Amid her
story of Mother Maddalena, she makes reference to two letters, of
1875 and 1876, from the Minister General, Fr Bernardine, to the
Bentivoglio Poor Clare nuns. One, dated 23 May 1876, finally gave
this advice, 'That the idea of Minnesota with that of Mother
Ignatius be definitively abandoned.'[49] And so 'the plot thickens'
again! As for Elizabeth's *Annals,* the pause in the publication at the
end of June 1875 continued and Mr Russell's circumstances in the
Brainerd printery changed. Sr Chaffee wrapped up this whole
account with, 'Having been disappointed in her plans for the Poor
Clares our mother's next step was to go to Canada, to seek for Irish
and French Canadian postulants.'[50] As Elizabeth did when she left
Wantage, Bayswater, Glasgow, Kingston, Sèvres and St Thomas, she
folded up her pilgrim tent and moved on, not giving herself time
to 'cry over spilt milk'.

The pause, the only pause, in the publication of Elizabeth's
Annals was extended because Elizabeth still needed recruits for
Belle Prairie. In the spring of 1876, she travelled to Montreal and
returned with five young women who wanted to receive the habit
of St Francis. The training of more new members, solicitude for
the academy, the opening of a new chapel, the development of the
self-supporting farm and concerns over local vandalism, prevented
Elizabeth from returning to her editorship until preparations for
the January 1878 edition of the *Annals.* Meanwhile other
Franciscans had stirred to the challenge of the Apostolate of the
Press and in England in 1877 the Capuchins with their *Franciscan
Annals* had begun publishing in Crawley.

It is not surprising that when Elizabeth restarted with her volume
three, she was clearly mindful of the new monthly *Franciscan
Annals,* a first for the Capuchins in the English language. Today
extant complete sets of the *Franciscan Annals'* year books are
housed in Oxford, Erith and Rome. Research in these Capuchin
libraries threw new light on Elizabeth *Annals.*[51] Difficulty is experi-

enced in identifying how Elizabeth used *Franciscan Annals* because firstly, extant texts of Elizabeth's *Annals* printed before the press office was established in Rome in 1883 are unevenly available today,[52] and secondly, because numerous Franciscan sources were used by Elizabeth and thirdly, because of the similarity of Franciscan titles used by numerous editors. One exciting benefit however was the opportunity to examine articles printed in the Capuchins' *Franciscan Annals* that led to a better understanding of some unavailable articles in Elizabeth's *Annals*. Among these between 1878 and 1883, for example, Elizabeth used the *Franciscan Annals* for two serials, 'The Franciscan Order in England' and 'Letters from the Holy Land'.[53] As our story continues, more Franciscan terms are being introduced so in Appendix 5 a reader will find how Elizabeth assisted her readers.

Hayes' *Annals* and the English *Franciscan Annals*

A deep probe into Franciscan journals indicated for the present writer the need to single out for particular comparison Elizabeth's *Annals* and the *Franciscan Annals*. The fact that they were contemporary and both in English and especially because Elizabeth read the Capuchins' journal, it is interesting to discover the degree to which Elizabeth's published selections, particularly her Franciscan serials, were influenced by them. How much advantage did Elizabeth take of the *Franciscan Annals* and did she edit the material from them? Elizabeth's sources for her major Franciscan items need to be divided into *Franciscan Annals* (acknowledged by her) and other sources (including other Franciscan journals).[54] Elizabeth's major Franciscan serials relied mainly on multiple other resources; however, it is also clear that the *Franciscan Annals* were the major single source of her use of Franciscan journals.[55]

Comparison of Elizabeth's chapters of 'The Franciscan Order in England', published 1878–83, with the Capuchins' introduction and with the thirty-four chapters of 'Chronicle of the Franciscan Order in England', printed in their *Franciscan Annals* 1877–82, is revealing. Elizabeth usually edited her sources carefully but for this particular series, which was based on Eccleston's *13ᵗʰ Century Chronicles,* she respected the original source and printed it word for word. Both texts include for example:

> The cathedral and monastic schools were enlarged and multiplied as need arose: a wider range of subjects was included in their course

of teaching, and the organisation was extended to keep pace with the growing intelligence of the age ... Men from all countries of Europe and even from the East congregated in the lecture-halls desirous either to teach or to learn, and a new phase of society arose in these centres of intellectual life ... For a long period the University of Paris was the most celebrated in Europe, but by the middle of the twelfth century [sic] Oxford rivalled Paris in renown, as the time when the Franciscans found their way thither the English University was famed throughout the known world. [56]

Where Elizabeth's *Annals* are extant other matching examples exist.[57] While the Capuchins reprinted the 'Chronicles' chapter by chapter, Elizabeth decided how many pages of the Chronicles she would give to her readers each month and made no reference to the chapter numbers. These two journals presented the chronicled history of the Franciscans in England beginning with their arrival at Dover in 1224 in St Francis of Assisi's lifetime.[58] It was appropriate that both the Capuchins and Elizabeth Hayes should publish a series of articles, 'Letters from the Holy Land', since St Francis went to the Holy Land 'to see for himself and experience the places where Christ had lived'. Franciscans 'established a friary in Jerusalem between 1222 and 1230', and their presence,

> cost the Franciscan Order not less than the lives of over ten thousand friars; four thousand of them having been martyred for the faith in defending the sacred shrines entrusted to their care; six thousand six hundred and forty having fallen victims to the plague, from the thirteenth century to the year 1834 when the calculations were last made.[59]

In 1880 Elizabeth acknowledged that she used the *Franciscan Annals* as the source for her 'Letters from the Holy Land'[60] so a search was conducted of the Capuchins' lengthy series, 'Letters from the Holy Land', published 1879–82.[61] However insufficient extant texts of Elizabeth's *Annals* around the same period foiled a comparison. Elizabeth regularly showed interest in the Franciscans of the Holy Land.[62] She published in 1875 'Franciscan Devotions and Works' while the *Franciscan Annals* (1882–3*)* printed 'Franciscan Works and Devotions'.[63] Comparison of the two journal series reveals that Elizabeth's articles preceded those of the Capuchins and therefore she used another Franciscan history source, which editors of both series did not acknowledge as their sources.[64] A different situation occurs when both journals published 'St Francis and Purgatory'.[65] The *Franciscan Annals* published this in 1880 and Elizabeth produced the same text, word for word, in 1885.[66] Elizabeth made no reference to the *Franciscan Annals* so she apparently used the same resource as earlier used by the Capuchins.[67]

In 1885 the Capuchins included in their publication the article, 'Wadding, the Historian' while Elizabeth printed 'Wadding the Historian' the following year (1886).[68] Elizabeth made no reference to the *Franciscan Annals* but she did say, in paragraph two of her single article, 'Besides this, and much more which must be passed over in our limited space, he established . . .', which suggests she culled a longer article. Elizabeth of course had access to other Franciscan resources including those at St Isidore's Irish Franciscan College in Rome. In 1886 she was editing in Rome, knew of Wadding's famous works and his close association with St Isidore's Irish College. Elizabeth's publication went there monthly for final theological approval.

A comparison of Elizabeth's *Annals* and the *Franciscan Annals* at times delivered unanticipated results. For example, the search related to Elizabeth's 1883 article entitled 'Leo XIII and the Third Order' uncovered similar titles and an instance of the same title in the *Franciscan Annals* (1881–85).[69] These examples highlighted once again the connection between Leo XIII, growth in membership of the Third Order and the publication of Franciscan journals. As mentioned previously, Leo XIII's call to follow the gospel example of St Francis of Assisi, and his proclaimed wish for the press to be an evangelizing instrument, gave the seal of approval to the ventures of the Franciscan editors. This had an incalculable influence on Franciscan periodical literature and the Catholic world. Together with Elizabeth, other Franciscan editors, especially the Capuchins, through their religious commitment, sharing of resources and hard work, were truly pioneering Apostles of the Press. What difference did these growing numbers of apostles make, in other parts of Europe and Canada and the United States?

European Franciscan Periodicals 1874–94

Elizabeth was aware of the 'growth and development of the Franciscan Order in Europe' which she had witnessed first-hand and recorded in her *Annals*.[70] Between 1874–94, the period when Elizabeth was publishing, at least another thirty-five European Franciscan journals were founded across Italy, France, Spain, Germany, Austria, Belgium, England and Ireland. A brief look at these journals can serve to illustrate the significance of Elizabeth's contribution.

Italy

In Italy the three journals already named continued and another sixteen were founded. The Italian Capuchins led the field in publishing journals and their 'Periodica' in *Lexicon Capuccinorum* named the Provinces of the Order where the journals originated.[71] It is not known how many of these Franciscan journals Elizabeth read while living in Rome from 1881. In her final editing years, Elizabeth sometimes simply introduced her article with the words, 'translation from the Italian'. Of these journals, a high proportion was short-lived. In 1888 the editor of *Annali Francescani* claimed that, besides his journal, there were only four others in circulation that were significant in Italy. To survive in the world of journalism was a great achievement; to be successful was extraordinary. Evidence indicates that these Italian journals existed to carry out the apostolate of instruction, encouragement and organization among the Franciscan Tertiaries, a mission to which Elizabeth was also totally committed.

France

In France the strong and continued success of the earlier wide-spread *Annales Franciscaines,* printed in Paris, meant decreased need for other French Franciscan journals and only five new ones were founded in this period.[72] The effects of religious persecutions after the Franco-Prussian war had taken their toll but the need to instruct the French tertiaries was urgent and important, as Elizabeth, who once lived in the diocese of Versailles, pointed out:

> On every side St. Francis finds new children. Special mention is made of the fervour of the congregations in the dioceses of Versailles, Moulin, Lucon, and Verdun. Tertiaries are also very numerous in Corsica. From Lille they write ... In the month of September (1873) last no less than 400 Sisters belonging to a congregation who have their Mother House at Bordeaux, entered the Third Order; another entire congregation gave the same example; the Ursulines do not forget that their saintly foundress was a Tertiary; and they also love to become the children of St. Francis. Thirty-eight of the religious of the convent of Dinan and three other

Communities were lately received. Many of the children connected with their academies, desiring to follow the example of their instructresses, were enrolled in the Arch-confraternity.[73]

The French journal, *Annals of the Franciscan Missionaries of Mary,* was written initially by the foundress, Hélène de Chappotin, beginning in 1886. In Paris, the Sisters set the text up in type from 1899 and, from simple beginnings, the printing equipment gradually improved to allow for greater artistic quality in their publications.[74] The content of their *Annals* contrasted with Elizabeth's *Annals* in that the latter did not record the activities of her Institute in her journal. The Missionaries of Mary certainly had more mission news to report but Elizabeth's *Annals* were published for a wider readership.[75] Some time before 1890 the Friars Minor started *La Voix de Saint Antoine* which continued after 1897.[76] The Franciscans in the city of Caen published the *Annales du Tiers Ordre Séraphique* which existed 1890–93 according to two sources.[77] The year before Elizabeth died, the Strasbourg Capuchins commenced the journal, *Grusse aus Nazareth,* but this lasted only three years, from 1893–6.[78]

Spain

In Spain, besides *La Revista Franciscana* which continued, three new journals entered the arena – *El Mensajero Serafico, El Eco Franciscano,* and *El Misionero Franciscano: revista religiosa.*[79] Perhaps Elizabeth knew of these Spanish journals through her neighbours, the Spanish Franciscans of San Pietro in Montorio, but there is no certainty.[80] However in 1889 Eliza Allen Starr's article on the Spanish 'San Pietro in Montorio' was included in the *Annals.*[81] Beginning in 1883 and continuing into 1885, Elizabeth published 'A Peep into Spain', a series of ten articles which were written by an unidentified 'Tertiary'. This series throws no direct light on Franciscan journals but it did coincide with Elizabeth and Sr Chaffee's visit to Spain in 1883 and places named by Sr Chaffee match places described in the articles, 'A Peep into Spain'.[82]

Germany and Austria

There is a paucity of material on Franciscan German and Austrian periodicals in the 1860s and early 1870s. This is in part a reflection of the Franciscan struggles in Germany around the period of the

Kulturkampf – a period when church property was seized, when laws restricted the Church's political and social role, and with many Franciscans forced to go to other countries. There were gains: for example, German Sisters and Friars made foundations in the USA and in turn a Cincinnati Franciscan periodical was published in German. Also German friars made an impact on Irish Franciscans who in turn encouraged Irish periodical literature. Nonetheless, there are some examples such as in Innsbruck, at times included under German publishing, while at others with Tyrolese or Austrian, where Friars Minor began publishing *Sanct' Francisci Gloecklein* in 1877.[83]

Elizabeth's interest in the Franciscans at Mönchengladbach – she called it M'Gladbach – was reflected in her 1890 publication of the address by the Coadjutor-Bishop of Cologne, Dr Fisher, when she quoted him as saying:

> 'Franciscan Convents are springing up once more in our native land, and growing constantly in number, especially in the industrial districts. And so I am so glad that the foundation-stone of a new Franciscan Monastery is being laid today in this thriving city ...'[84]

This renewed growth of Franciscan monasteries and convents in Germany, twenty years after the *Kulturkampf,* was a necessary preliminary before their later journals flourished on the Franciscan literature scene. What is interesting, however, is that Elizabeth was clearly aware of these publications also. In 1890 she published two other articles related to Germany, 'The Religious Orders. Extracts from the Speech at the German Catholic Congress Recently Held at Coblentz',[85] and 'A New Step of the Sovereign Pontiff toward Alleviating the Social Miseries. Letter of his Holiness to the Archbishop of Cologne'.[86] In 1892 Elizabeth published two separate German translations on 'Shrines of St. Anthony of Padua: The Miraculous Shrine at Kaltern in the Austrian Tyrol', and a letter to Elizabeth of 11 November that year links 'Kaltern M. Gladbach' with the Sisters' preparation and printing of a pamphlet for the President of St Isidore's College, thus opening a door to previously unexplored connections.[87]

Belgium, England and Ireland

Like the German Franciscan Provinces, the Belgian friar's Province was affected badly by the French Revolution and its aftermath; it seems that only two journals were founded. The Friars Minor produced *Le Messager de Saint Francois d'Assise: Revue mensuelle du Tiers-Order* (1875–1931), first in Brussels and also by 1890 in Antwerp.[88] This city also published *De Bode* but minimal reference to it suggests a short life.[89] Antwerp was the final resting place of the last Titular Guardian of Canterbury (England), Fr Leo Edgeworth, OFM who died in 1850, and it was from that city that the Belgian Recollect Province sent Friars Minor to England.[90] They opened houses in Gorton in East Manchester (1861), Glasgow (1868), and London and Stratford (1873). This paved the way for the 1880s English Franciscan revival. Elizabeth wrote of England and Ireland in her 1874 article on 'The Progress and Development of the Third Order in Europe':

> Not only on the continent but also in Great Britain and Ireland the Order has greatly increased within the last few years. In 1869 a new congregation of Tertiaries was erected in Cork, in the Church of St. Francis of the Friars Minor Obs [Observants]. It is very flourishing. The monthly reunion is made regularly … The fraternity possesses a good library where the brothers and sisters find an abundance of pious and instructive reading. In the Church of the Friars Minor Cap [Capuchins] in the same city, there is also a congregation under the direction of the Fathers … In Dublin, a new church, built by the Friars Minor Cap has been in the course of erection during the last three years, and was solemnly dedicated by His Eminence Cardinal Cullen, Archbishop of Dublin, on the 13th of October last.[91]

So the Irish stage was set for the entrance of English and Irish Franciscan periodicals – three in particular.

The Capuchins at Crawley (Sussex, England) entered the field in 1877 with the original cover page reading The *Franciscan Annals and Monthly Bulletin of the Third Order of St. Francis* and it became a highly respected and long running publication.[92] The sub-heading indicates the periodical's aims – it was clearly for the members of the Third Order of Saint Francis. The English *Franciscan Annals* contained a good deal of devotional and historical material: Franciscan news, lives of Franciscan saints, short stories, poems and other mixed material. In her *Annals* Elizabeth included some selections from the *Franciscan Annals*, as already noted, but she was not awed by them in any way. English *Franciscan Annals'* editors recycled some articles from old Franciscan literary sources and from the 'companion' Franciscan Annals of Italy and France.[93]

In the *Franciscan Annals'* 1882 August issue, 'The Miraculous

Tree of Sienna' was borrowed from the *Annales Franciscaines* of Paris.[94] The English editor was aware of *L'eco di S. Francesco* and included from it 'A Sermon by S. Lawrence of Brindisi'.[95] As the number of Tertiaries continued to grow so did the readership of the *Franciscan Annals*. A reader's 1882 question led to a listing of the Franciscan Monasteries, both Capuchin and Recollect/ Observant, indicating that this periodical was distributed in fifteen cities of the United Kingdom.[96] The periodical served as a vehicle of instruction and unity in Great Britain and Ireland, and readers also appreciated contributions from the well-known Lady Georgiana Chatterton who contributed long serials, including 'The Cathedral Chorister' and 'Old Nurse Eleanor; Or, Thirty Years Ago'.[97]

An 1890 inspection of the magazine and its printing works by the Minister General of the worldwide Capuchins, Fr Bernard of Andermatt, was reported. His observations supported the claim that Franciscan journals and their editors made a significant contribution to the Apostolate of the Press:

> We ... having learned all particulars concerning the 'ANNALS,' are highly pleased with the magazine – its object, religious tone, and high standard of contents for a publication of its class. We consider it a very useful and effective medium for diffusing among Tertiaries the true spirit of our Seraphic Father and Founder, St. Francis, so much needed in these days for the welfare of Religion and Society. We specially bless the periodical, and wish all prosperity and happiness to its promoters and subscribers. It is our earnest desire to see it spread on all sides.[98]

An 1887 copy of the Friars Minor *Franciscan Herald: Monthly Remembrance for English Speaking Tertiaries* had been published in Somerset by the Mercury Office, Clevedon,[99] and in 1890 the Dublin Friars Minor ushered in the *Irish Franciscan Teritary: A Monthly Journal for the Third Order of St. Francis*.[100] The aims of this journal basically reflected those of other Franciscan journals of the period. They were approved by the Minister Provincial, Fr Cleary, who encouraged Fr O'Reilly to proceed with the publication so that 'not only the Guardians and Directors of the Third Order' would benefit but that 'members of the Third Order in every part of Ireland' would be assisted by it.[101] Broadly, the *Irish Franciscan Tertiary's* contents consisted of articles on Franciscan shrines, conferences on virtues or beliefs, lives of Franciscan Saints called 'Monthly Patrons', Franciscan and religious articles, poetry, tales and literary notices. Outstanding contributors, most of these different from Elizabeth's contributors, were Katharine Tynan, Laura Grey, Agnes M. Manning, J. A. Jackman and Aubrey de Vere, with a little from Lady Georgiana Fullerton. From Waverley in Sydney, Fr Kennedy wrote, 'The monthly bulletin will be very welcome to every member of the Order, here as well as at home'. A New York friar significantly pointed out that 'this journal helped to spread the knowledge of our Third Order among the people which is just what the Holy Father wished'.[102] The latter comment is another confirmation of how many Catholics took to heart the pope's example and words in recommending Franciscan spirituality in order to evangelize.

News items in this *Irish Franciscan Teritary* confirm the regularity among Franciscan editors of promoting the international circulation of their journals.[103] By the thirteenth issue the Irish periodical introduced illustrations in its text besides on its cover, an action taken by Elizabeth early in her publishing career, but rarely imitated in the English *Franciscan Annals*. That the activities of Elizabeth and her community were known to the English Franciscans is indicated by the fact that this journal published in 1892 the news that the Little Falls Franciscan community in Minnesota had separated formally from Elizabeth's international institute.[104]

Franciscan Periodicals in North America 1874–94

Moving now the story of the Franciscan periodical press from Europe to North America. In Canada, Montreal's Third Order membership – after fluctuations over 200 years – in 1876 numbered over 2,000 Tertiaries. They also had their own journal; from 1869–1876 the tertiaries published the monthly *Gazette des Familles*.[105] As noted earlier, Elizabeth went to these Montreal tertiaries in 1876 to recruit women for her Belle Prairie mission.[106] By 1884 the Montreal Jesuits published a Franciscan journal, *Petite Revue du Tiers Ordre et des intérêts du Coeur de Jesus,* which continued until 1891 when it was taken over by the Tertiaries of Montreal and renamed *Revue du Tiers-Ordre.*[107]

For Elizabeth, the 'printing in America' continued when she transferred the printing work to Augusta in Georgia during 1878, but by late 1881 she was editing from Rome. Here Sisters printed, stitched and bound the *Annals* and shipped them to the United States. In cities, such as New York, Philadelphia, Boston and Chicago, Sisters canvassed for subscriptions, then personally delivered or mailed the *Annals* to the subscribers. In 1915 the *Annals*' publication resumed in its country of origin, this time in Union City, NJ, (formerly West Hoboken) and then finally was transferred to Tenafly, in 1921.[108] Elizabeth's *Annals* had initiated American Franciscan literature when the editor-publisher seized the opportunity for mission through a periodical.

The history behind the German influence in Pennsylvania on Franciscan journals was published by the *Franciscan Annals* in an article, 'The Franciscan Capuchins in North America'.[109] Yet, while the founding Capuchins arrived only twelve months after Elizabeth, the friars of Pennsylvania did not launch a journal until 1891 at Herman. It was known as *The Echo,* and while their membership grew, 'numbering about seventy religious and able to maintain itself as a distinct province of the Order' by 1886, little can be found about the life of their journal.[110]

Cincinnati was linked to United States Catholic periodical literature in the nineteenth century's final quarter and for Franciscan journals, it also became a strong centre. Influenced by German friars, *Der Sendbote des göttlichen Herzens Jesu* was founded by the Friars Minor in 1875 and continued to 1946.[111] *The Sodalist* was published 1884–1938 by the Friars Minor at St Francis Parish as 'A journal published monthly in the interest of Young Men's Sodalities'.[112] In 1892 the Friars Minor periodical, *St. Franziskus Bote,* established to spread knowledge about friars and tertiaries, was founded in Cincinnati and continued for twenty-six years.[113] Also founded in this city (1893) was the very successful *St Anthony's Messenger* which continues to the present and is also available online.[114]

Franciscan Sisters' activities in the United States in the period up to 1894 paralleled the missionary work of thousands of other Sisters.[115] The mission of journalism was not recognized as a mainstream ministry for women religious in the late nineteenth century yet Elizabeth dared to be different and her fruitful mission through journalism was enduring. Pope Leo XIII's example and call to the world to follow the gospel example of St Francis of Assisi, and his wish for the press to be an evangelizing instrument, had a great influence on the growth in tertiary membership and the publication of Franciscan journals. Active Franciscan networking was based on religious commitment, hard work and the sharing of resources, and Elizabeth, as a widely-read woman, thrived in the heart of this Franciscan periodical activity. Elizabeth, the first Franciscan woman to edit and publish a successful Catholic journal, and the first publisher of a Franciscan journal in the

English language, certainly was a trail-blazing pioneer in Franciscan periodical literature.

Notes

1 The Franciscan journals listed in this directory are of great interest, but those not interacting directly with Elizabeth's *Annals* or distracting from the main account are omitted in the analysis here. Directory in Pauline J. Shaw, 'Mission Through Journalism: Elizabeth Hayes and the *Annals of Our Lady of the Angels*' (Ph.D., Australian Catholic University, 2006).
2 Angelica Chaffee, 'Memories', 25.
3 Fr Romo continued his interest in Elizabeth Hayes' publication for in 1889 he wrote to her secretary, Sr Chaffee, requesting that the *Annals* be sent to his new address in Egypt.
4 1 Celano 27 in Eric Doyle, *Canterbury and the Franciscans 1224–1974*, 20.
5 Elizabeth Hayes, 'The Seraphic Order', *AOLA* XIII, no. iii (1888): 88–9.
6 Further commentary and resources are given in Appendix 2.
7 Elizabeth Hayes, 'The Franciscan Order', *AOLA* I, no. vii (1874): 244.
8 Hayes, 'The Seraphic Order', 92.
9 Elizabeth Hayes, 'The Franciscans of the Most Blessed Sacrament', *AOLA* I, no. iv (1874): 104.
10 Elizabeth Hayes, 'Foreign Missions', *AOLA* I, no. iv (1874):121.
11 Elizabeth Hayes, 'The Progress and Development of the Third Order in Europe', *AOLA* I, no. i (1874): 29.
12 Pauline J. Shaw, ed. *Diary*, 63.
13 Elizabeth Hayes, 'The Franciscans in Prussia', *AOLA* I, no. iii (1874): 94. *Irish Franciscan Tertiary* I (1891): 284.
14 Hayes, 'Foreign Missions', 121. Hayes, 'The Franciscan Order', 224. Elizabeth Hayes, 'Another Glorious Tomb', *AOLA* I, no. vii (1874): 223.
15 Hayes, 'The Progress and Development of the Third Order in Europe', 29.
16 Ibid.
17 Elizabeth Hayes, 'News from Rome', *AOLA* I, no. ii (1874): 60–1.
18 Chaffee, 'Memories', 26.
19 Michael Bihl, 'Das Gründungsjahr der estern Neiderlassung der Franziskaner in Fulda', *Fuldaer Geschichtsbätter*, 4 (1905), 30–2.
20 Boniface was born in Crediton, Wessex, about 673, educated by Benedictine Monks in Essex and sent as a missionary to Germany.
21 While St Mary's Benedictine Nun's Abbey, Abtei St Maria, was founded in 1626, the nuns were not in residence around 1874–5 but, according to the archivist, Sr Candida Elvert, they did return later.
22 Unseren Freunden und Wohltatern Gewidmet. *200 Jahre Kirche und Kloster: Frauenberg/Fulda 1763–1963*, 231.
23 The style of life of the Franciscan Sisters of Drumshanbo in County Leitrim, before changes in the twentieth century, seems to be what Elizabeth searched for in Rome. The foundresses of these Sisters have

already been referred to. They were sent initially by Cardinal Wiseman of London to St Elizabeth's Third Order Franciscan convent in Paris, worked for some time in London and later moved to Drumshanbo in the mid 1860s. Once they were called the Poor Clare Nuns of the Perpetual Adoration. One of the foundresses had the surname of 'Hayes'; not to be confused with Elizabeth. For Drumshanbo's story, see their website or Mrs Thomas Concannon, *At the Court of the Eucharistic King*.

24 A lengthy account of the Roman story from the Poor Clares' perspective is given by Fr Marianus Fiege, OFM Cap., *Princess of Poverty: St Clare of Assisi and the Order of Poor Ladies*, 220–65. This account sits well with Sr Ahles' 1977 publication and although she took advantage of Albert Kleber, OSB, 'A Bentivoglio of the Bentivoglio ... Poor Clare Abbess, Foundress of the Order of St. Clare of the strict Observance in the USA' (Unpublished typescript, n.d.), both author-priests relied on Sr Maddelena's chronicle. Sr Koster, writing on the Poor Clares in 1980, referred to the text of Fr Fiege who wrote only a few years after the deaths of the Bentivoglios.

25 Enclosed nuns have a long tradition of being suppliers of altar breads, linens and vestments for churches spread throughout surrounding regions.

26 Fiege, *Princess of Poverty*, 239.

27 Interesting data on the Bentivoglio family is available on websites.

28 Elizabeth's confidence in God is explored in Pauline J. Shaw's, *Companion to the Diary*: Sister Mary Ignatius of Jesus (Elizabeth Hayes), 52.

29 John Watts, *A Canticle of Love: The Story of the Franciscan Sisters of the Immaculate Conception*, 58. Watts' interpretation is plausible if parts of Elizabeth's Diary are not put into perspective with other primary resources. Most MFIC resources on Elizabeth Hayes have been circulated privately and have not reached the libraries of academics and most Franciscan houses.

30 Elizabeth Hayes, 'Christmas Day in Rome', *AOLA* I, no. xi (1874): 327.

31 Ibid.

32 Ibid., 329. The battle of Mentana took place in 1867 when Papal Zouaves foiled an attempt by Garibaldi to seize Rome.

33 Chaffee, 'Memories', 28.

34 Ibid., 29–30.

35 Fiege, *Princess of Poverty*, 239.

36 Ibid.

37 Maddalena Bentivoglio, 'Chronicle', in Kleber, 'A Bentivoglio of the Bentivoglio', 96; Ahles, *In the Shadow of His Wings*, 104.

38 Chaffee, 'Memories', 30.

39 Sr M. Camilla Koester, PCC, *Into This Land: A Centennial History of the Cleveland Poor Clare Monastery of the Blessed Sacrament*, 11.

40 Sr M. Maddalena's chronicle provides a first hand account of her experiences with Elizabeth and others. Fiege, Princess of Poverty, 257–8; Kleber, 'A Bentivoglio of the Bontivglio', 11; Ahles, *In the Shadow of His*

Wings, 104, f'n 166–67; Shaw, *Companion to Diary*, 53.

41 Maddalena's chronicle in Kleber, 'A Bentivoglio of the Bentivoglio'; Ahles, 105, f'n. 171.

42 Madddalena's chronicle, in Fiege, *Princess of Poverty*, 265; Maddalena's chronicle, in Kleber, 'A Bentivoglio of the Bentivoglio', in Ahles, *In the Shadow of His Wings*, 105.

43 Maddalena's chronicle, in Kleber, 'A Bentivoglio of the Bentivoglio', 131; Ahles, *In the Shadow of His Wings*, 106, f'n. 174.

44 Maddelena's chronicle, in Kleber, 'A Bentivoglio of the Bentivoglio', 132; Ahles, *In the Shadow of His Wings*, 107, f'n. 178.

45 Quotation from the Rescript, Udienze, 1875, Part 3 (182), f. 1499 recto-verso, APF; in Ahles, *In the Shadow of His Wings*, 101; Shaw, *Companion to Diary*, 53.

46 Chaffee, 'Memories', 29.

47 Ibid., from Maddalena's chronicle in Fiege, *Princess of Poverty*; Maddalena's chronicle in Kleber, 'A Bentivoglio of the Bentivoglio' 132; Ahles, *In the Shadow of His Wings*, 108, f'n. 180.

48 The Poor Clares of Santa Barbara, daughter house of the Cleveland Poor Clares, founded by Maddalena in 1877, provided the author with hospitality and assistance when doing research in 2001. Thanks are due to them for an accurate and interesting account of the initial days of these two pioneers in the USA and the fruits of their lives, in the book of Poor Clare Colletine, Sr M. Camilla Koester, *Into This Land*. Sr Koester's text confirms research not only on 1875 events but also on Franciscan history in Germany, especially re Düsseldorf. Special thanks also to another branch, the Bloomington Poor Clares in Minnesota for resources, hospitality and continued friendship.

49 'Religious Reflections' http:www.geocities.com/Heartland/Ridge/9280/reflections.html?20077. Accessed 7 October 2007.

50 Chaffee, 'Memories', 30.

51 Acknowledgement is due to Australian Capuchin scholar, Patrick Colbourne, who provided initial insights into the 'companion' *Franciscan Annals* and who tabled names and addresses of scholarly friars without whose assistance in Rome and England, my research on the *Franciscan Annals* could not have been undertaken so fully.

52 See Appendix 4, Elizabeth Hayes' *Annals* – Summary of availability.

53 How do we know this if articles are unavailable? Only for one year is nothing at all available; various clues are available for missing parts, e.g., through an index, by Elizabeth writing 'to be continued', serial articles or information given in particular texts.

54 Material related to 'other Franciscan journals', excluding the English *Franciscan Annals*, will be included later.

55 Sources for major serials included: 'The Third Order of St. Francis' (1874–6), series of 6 articles, chapters 'Translated from the French of Monseigneur de Ségur by a Franciscan Tertiary'. In 1883 the first 3 chapters were published again. 'Legacies of the Seraphic Father St. Francis' (1887), serial of 4 parts, taken from an unidentified source. 'Our Lady

of the Angels in Porziuncula' (1883), series of 5 parts, contributed by 'F.B. Assisi'. 'The Stigmata of St. Francis' – 2 articles in 1887. 'The Progress and Development of the Third Order in Europe' (1874), 2 articles, and 'The Seraphic Order' (1888–9), 7 articles, give indication that they were written by Elizabeth with the help of original documents.

56 'Chronicles of the Franciscan Order in England', *The Franciscan Annals and Monthly Bulletin of the Third Order of St. Francis* I (1877): 279; Elizabeth Hayes, 'Franciscan Order in England', *AOLA* IV, no. v (1879): 150.

57 'Chronicles of the Franciscan Order in England', *The Franciscan Annals and Monthly Bulletin of the Third Order of St. Francis* VI (1882): 123–7, 75–9; Hayes, 'Franciscan Order in England', 46–50, 70–4.

58 'Chronicles of the Franciscan Order in England', *The Franciscan Annals and Monthly Bulletin of the Third Order of St. Francis* I-VI (1877): 6 parts; (1878): 9 parts; (1879): 5 parts; (1880): 5 parts; (1881): 6 parts; (1882); 4 parts. Hayes, 'Franciscan Order in England', *AOLA* III-VIII (1878): 274, 336, 369; (1879): 150; (1880): 144, 175, 204, 235, 262, 299, 326; (1881): n.a.; (1882): 344; (1883): 46, 70.

59 Charles Nazzano, 'The Franciscan Mission of the Holy Land', *AOLA* IX, no. v (1884): 157. Fr Nazzano was Custos Provincial and Commissary of the Holy Land in New York at 135 West Thirty-First Street, a friary well known to Elizabeth Hayes.

60 The monthly index in 'Annals Index 1874–1902' recorded Elizabeth Hayes, 'Letters from the Holy Land', *AOLA* V, no. iii, iv, ix, x (1880): 73–7, 122–6, 272–6, 293–6.

61 'Letters from the Holy Land', *The Franciscan Annals and Monthly Bulletin of the Third Order of St. Francis* III-VI (1879): 3 parts; (1880): 6 parts; (1881): 6 parts; (1882): 2 parts.

62 Elizabeth took an article from the American *Catholic Visitor* by Bishop Keane, 'The Holy Land', *AOLA* IX, no. iii (1884): 87. 'Saint Anthony of Padua in the Holy Land' was taken from the *Little Bell of St Francis* (a periodical unable to be traced) yet received by its editor from a 'Father in Jerusalem'. Friar, 'Saint Anthony of Padua in the Holy Land', *AOLA* XIII, no. xi (1888): 346.

63 Elizabeth Hayes, 'Franciscan Devotions and Works', *AOLA* II, no. i (1875): 399–403. 'Franciscan Works and Devotions', *The Franciscan Annals and Monthly Bulletin of the Third Order of St. Francis* VI (1882): 312–16, 357–61; VII (1883): 81, 152.

64 Elizabeth's 1875 article 'Franciscan Devotions and Works', *AOLA* II, no. i (1875): 399–403 had the sub-heading, '1. Devotion to the Pope', as did the 1882 *Franciscan Annals* VI (1882): 312–16, so both began in the same way.

65 'St. Francis and Purgatory', *The Franciscan Annals and Monthly Bulletin of the Third Order of St. Francis* IV (1880): 281. Elizabeth Hayes, 'St. Francis and Purgatory', *AOLA* X, no. xi (1885): 327.

66 In 1892 Elizabeth, however, printed only part of it. Elizabeth Hayes, 'St. Francis and Purgatory' *AOLA* XVII, no. xi (1892): 346–8. It began at 'Thomas of Celano and Bernard of Besse, who were contemporaries with

S. Francis and S. Bonaventure, respectively, relate ...' etc.

67 The Capuchins slightly changed their index title to 'The Holy Souls in Purgatory' on the text page.

68 'Wadding, the Historian', *The Franciscan Annals and Monthly Bulletin of the Third Order of St. Francis* IX (1885): 264; Hayes, 'Wadding the Historian', 222–4. Irish-born Luke Wadding (1588–1657) was a famous historian and theologian, professor at Salamanca, representative in the Roman Curia and was guardian for many years of the Irish Franciscan College of St Isidore that he founded. His fame as writer and critic reached a pinnacle with his monumental edition of Scotus, on the 'Scriptores', and, especially, his 'Annales ord. minorum'. It was said that his piety equalled his great learning.

69 Elizabeth Hayes, 'Leo XIII and the Third Order', *AOLA* VIII, no. iv (1883): 97. 'The Sovereign Pontiff Leo XIII and the Third Order', *The Franciscan Annals and Monthly Bulletin of the Third Order of St. Francis* V (1881): 15–19. (Acknowledged as taken from *Annales Franciscaines*.) Also – 'Leo XIII and the Third Order of S. Francis', *The Franciscan Annals and Monthly Bulletin of the Third Order of St. Francis* VII (1883): 253, and 'Leo XIII and the Third Order', *The Franciscan Annals and Monthly Bulletin of the Third Order of St. Francis* IX (1885): 106.

70 Ibid., 28–9.

71 Capuchins, 'Peregrinus – Periodica', 1315–32. Titles and details are in the Alphabetical Directory of Franciscan Journals in Appendix 1.

72 *Annales des Franciscaines Missionnaires de Marie, Annales du Tiers-Ordre Séraphique, La Voix de Saint Antoine, Revue Franciscaine* and *Grusse aus Nazareth*. For details see Appendix 1.

73 Hayes, 'The Progress and Development of the Third Order in Europe', 28–9.

74 Goyau, *Valiant Women*, 192. Goyau says that de Chappotin ensured that part of young missionaries' training was to learn printing skills in order to take the benefits of the press to other countries and inculturate this skill for God's glory.

75 A number of bishops and priests received Elizabeth Hayes' *Annals* but the obituary lists confirm that a high proportion of the readers were seculars, often Third Order Secular Franciscans.

76 Friars Minor, 'Antonianum', no. 1162. Also in an 1899 Parisian copy; Michael Bihl, *Julian of Speyer*, New Advent – Catholic Encyclopedia, http://www.newadvent.org.cathen/08558a.htm; accessed 15 January 2002.

77 Friars Minor, 'Antonianum', no. 87. 'Literary Notices', *Irish Franciscan Tertiary* I (1891): 128; II (1892): 405.

78 Capuchins, 'Peregrinus – Periodica', 1320.

79 Ibid., 1322. Friars Minor, 'Antonianum', no. 418; 'Literary Notices', *Irish Franciscan Tertiary* I (1891): 128, 284; 'Literary Notices', *Irish Franciscan Tertiary* II (1892): 405; Friars Minor, 'Antonianum', no. 715. For details see Appendix 1.

80 The Villa Spada Convent, where Elizabeth lived in Rome, was identified

by the address – 'near Pietro in Montorio' where Spanish friars had a large monastery and old church.

81 Eliza Allen Starr, 'San Pietro in Montorio', *AOLA* XIV, no. i (1889): 1.

82 Chaffee, 'Memories', 42–5. Sr Chaffee wrote of Elizabeth's visit to Spanish holy places and of her wish to have a foundation in Rabida 'to honour Christopher Columbus' – a Tertiary.

83 Friars Minor, 'Antonianum', nos 1119–20; 'Literary Notices', *Irish Franciscan Tertiary* I (1891): 284; II (1892): 405; Louis Biersack, *The Saints and Blessed of the Third Order of Saint Francis*, 183. Other publications were *Sankt Franzisusblatt, Seraphischer Kinderfreund, Seraphischer Kinderfreund und Marienkind,* and Austria's *Die Posaune des hl. Kreuzes.* Details are given in Appendix 1.

84 Elizabeth's account is substantiated in Joseph Gerwing, *100 Jahre Franziskaner in Mönchengladbach 1889–1989.* Nearby Aachen had Franciscans living there in the 1850s with some going to USA in the 1860s.

85 P. Weiss, OP, 'The Religious Orders. Extracts from the Speech at the German Catholic Congress Recently Held at Coblentz', *AOLA* XV, no. xi (1890): 342–4. Elizabeth acknowledged that Revd P. Weiss was 'professor in the new Catholic University of Friburg'.

86 Pope Leo XIII, 'A New Step of the Sovereign Pontiff toward Alleviating the Social Miseries. Letter of His Holiness to the Archbishop of Cologne', *AOLA* XV, no. viii (1890): 246–50.

87 Hayes, 'Shrines of St. Anthony of Padua: The Miraculous Shrine at Kaltern in the Austrian Tyrol', 27–32, 90–6. 1892 letter in MFICAR, section A, box 3, folder 9.

88 Friars Minor, 'Antonianum', no. 689; 'Literary Notices', *Irish Franciscan Tertiary* I (1891): 284; II (1892): 405.

89 'Literary Notices', *Irish Franciscan Tertiary* I (1891): 160.

90 Doyle, *Canterbury and the Franciscans 1224–1974*, 79. Recollects, a renewal branch of the Friars Minor Observants, sought from the sixteenth century to live strictly in the spirit of St Francis and the early Franciscans.

91 Hayes, 'The Progress and Development of the Third Order in Europe', 58.

92 A complete set of year books from 1877 to 1894 was accessed at the Central Library of the Friars Minor Capuchins Historical Institute and International College, Rome; at the Capuchin's Curia Library, Erith (Kent) and at the Greyfriars Oxford University College Library. It was called *Franciscan Annals and Tertiary Record* in Capuchins, 'Peregrinus – Periodica', 1314; Also 'Literary Notices', *Irish Franciscan Tertiary* I (1891): 128, 284; II (1892): 405.

93 'The History of the Capuchin Order', *The Franciscan Annals and Monthly Bulletin of the Third Order of St. Francis* VI (1882): 8–11; 'A Model Professor', *The Franciscan Annals and Monthly Bulletin of the Third Order of St. Francis* VI (1882): 11>. (> means plus subsequent issues.)

94 'The Miraculous Tree of Sienna', *The Franciscan Annals and Monthly Bulletin of the Third Order of St. Francis* VI, (1882): 218>.

95 'A Sermon by S. Lawrence of Brindisi', *The Franciscan Annals and Monthly Bulletin of the Third Order of St. Francis* VI, no. 67 (1882): 169–73.

96 'Questions and Answers Appertaining to the Third Order', *The Franciscan Annals and Monthly Bulletin of the Third Order of St. Francis* VI, no. 71 (1882): 312.

97 'The Cathedral Chorister', *The Franciscan Annals and Monthly Bulletin of the Third Order of St. Francis* X (1886): 9 sections. 'Old Nurse Eleanor; or, Thirty Years Ago', *The Franciscan Annals and Monthly Bulletin of the Third Order of St. Francis* XI-XIV, many sections in 1887–90.

98 'Franciscan News', *The Franciscan Annals and Monthly Bulletin of the Third Order of St. Francis* XIV (1890): 342.

99 Friars Minor, 'Antonianum', no. 481. This is the only record found and it is not to be confused with *Franciscan Herald* of Chicago founded in 1921 which experienced a long life. Friars Minor, 'Antonianum', no. 480.

100 *Irish Franciscan Tertiary* I, Friars Minor ed. (Dublin: The Freeman's Journal Ltd Printers, 1891); reprint, 1890 (May) – 1891 (April). It is acknowledged, but its founding before 1890 is incorrectly indicated in Friars Minor, 'Antonianum', no. 565.

101 Provided in 1889 Prospectus. P. J. Cleary, 'Letter from Cleary to O'Reilly', *Irish Franciscan Tertiary* I, no. 1 (1891): 3.

102 'Correspondence', *Irish Franciscan Tertiary* I (1891): 32.

103 The journal carried news from the *Annales Franciscaines* of receptions of twelve, including four Irish-born, new Franciscan Missionaries of Mary at Chatelets. 'Franciscan Missionary Sisters', *Irish Franciscan Tertiary* I, no. 2 (1891): 64.

104 'The Seraphic Families in the United States', *Irish Franciscan Tertiary* III (1893): 242.

105 The Third Order of St Francis had been established by the Franciscan Recollects at Quebec in 1671 and some years later at Trois-Rivieres and Montreal. Confirmed by Danielle Julian mfic who accessed the French Canadian source, *The History of the Franciscans in Quebec*.

106 Reception as novices of five Canadian recruits took place on August 2, 1876. Chaffee, 'Memories', 30. (Sr Chaffee from Chicago made her novitiate with the Canadians in Belle Prairie). Ahles, *In the Shadow of His Wings*, 108–10; de Breffny, *Unless the Seed Die*, 134–6.

107 Friars Minor, 'Antonianum', no. 830. (Recorded as 1884–91 without acknowledging the change over to Tertiaries). 'The Third Order of St. Francis in Canada' in Cuthbert and al, *Third Orders: The Franciscans*, accessed. This publication became what the *Irish Franciscan Tertiary* acknowledged in 1892 as the *Revue du Tiers-Ordre, et de le Terre Sainte.* 'Literary Notices', *Irish Franciscan Tertiary* II (1892): 405. Confirmed by Danielle Julian mfic, personal communication, 12 February 2002.

108 Sr M. Edward Sherry, *Centennial Commemorative Volume: The Annals of Our Lady of the Angels 1874–1974*, 16.

109 'The Franciscan Capuchins in North America', *The Franciscan Annals and Monthly Bulletin of the Third Order of St. Francis* X (1886): 51.

110 Capuchins, 'Peregrinus – Periodica', 1330.
111 Dan Anderson, Franciscan archives, Cincinnati, Ohio, letter to Pauline J. Shaw, Brisbane, 22 May 2004. 'Literary Notices', *Irish Franciscan Tertiary* I (1891): 128; Biersack, *The Saints and Blessed of the Third Order of Saint Francis*, 183.
112 Anderson, letter, 22 May 2004.
113 Friars Minor, 'Antonianum', no. 1121. Biersack, *The Saints and Blessed of the Third Order of Saint Francis*, 183. Cincinnati Catholic Research, *Historical Research – Periodicals*, American Catholic Organization, http://www2.eos.net/dajend/biblio.html; accessed 26 April 2004. The first two Friars Minor who commenced the publication were Ambrose Sanning and John Forest McGee. Anderson, letter 22 May 2004.
114 Friars Minor, 'Antonianum', no. 1115; Biersack, *The Saints and Blessed of the Third Order of Saint Francis*, 183; Cincinnati Franciscans, *A Short Illustrated History of St. Anthony Messenger Press and Franciscan Communications*, American Catholic Organisation, http://www.americancatholic.org/About/History.asp; accessed 26 April 2004.
115 Dolores Liptak, 'Full of Grace: Another Look at the 19th-century Nun', *Review for Religious* 55, no. 6 (1996): 625–39.

Bell Prairie Log Cabin on church land, Minnesota. This replica stood on the original spot for many years and is now displayed nearby.

Front view of Elizabeth's first convent. This wooden building was destroyed by fire in 1889.

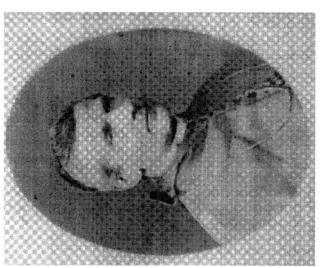

Elizabeth's personal photo of Fr Ludovico da Cassoria, a Franciscan described, according to Elizabeth, 'as the revived St. Francis of the nineteenth century'.

Frederica (Sr M. Benedicta) Law, an African-American from Georgia, was brought to Rome and received into the community by Elizabeth.

Elizabeth's writing desk in Rome at which she laboured at mission through journalism. LHS, her statue of St Anthony; RHS, samples of yearly *Annals*.

Carry bag which Elizabeth used when travelling.

Indian blanket which Elizabeth treasured, her diary, a copy of the *Annals* and her prayer book.

Villa Spada, Rome; the motherhouse where Elizabeth died in 1894.

F. De Federicis.   ROMA.

Elizabeth (Mother M. Ignatius) Hayes.

Chapter 5

Annals of Our Lady of the Angels:
an Analysis

The *Annals* encouraged readers to be more religious not only through inspirational or devotional content but also through interesting and educational articles. To illustrate how Elizabeth's Apostolate of the Press operated, we will consider samples of the major themes she chose for the general reader, followed by the dominant themes she presents to her Franciscan audience. As we do this, the story of how Elizabeth integrated her writing with the responsibilities of life in her community in Belle Prairie, Georgia and finally Rome, will be interspersed in the chapter.

Her Story 1878–79 and the *Annals*

Belle Prairie winters can be bitterly cold; they are such a contrast to its beautiful sunny days of mid-year. In early 1878 Elizabeth and her small yet growing community were surrounded with a great depth of snow and the only way they could move around outdoors was by sleigh. There seems to be truth in Sr Chaffee's memory of Mr Russell, their former printer in Brainerd, bringing a 'little Pearl printing press' to them by sleigh during the early months of 1878. The Sisters themselves printed monthly the 1878 issues and no doubt they welcomed the passing of the colder months when the extreme cold froze the ink, preventing it from flowing freely in the printing press. Today a large 'Belle Prairie Park' sign reminds a visitor of the extent of the former convent-school property. The exact position of the wooden convent in use in 1878, replaced later by a substantial convent, can be identified now by the renovated accommodation facility that reopened its doors in 2007.

Something of the 1870s fresh green environment was

acknowledged in Fanny Montgomery's description of the Franciscan Belle Prairie property. She wrote:

> Life lay in the far West, on the banks of the Mississippi, in a large quaint convent, built chiefly of wood, and with a church attached to it, a farm-yard close by, a well-stocked garden, many flowers for the altar, and some grand old trees spared by the recent settlers. Green meadows are all around ... where you hear the mighty river whispering along its banks amid the reeds and sedges.

This rare description from Fanny's first-hand account provides us with a pleasant picture of what Belle Prairie was like after the winter had passed. The description first appeared in an article Fanny wrote for the popular Catholic English periodical, *The Month*,[1] and later Elizabeth printed it in her *Annals*.

At Belle Prairie, five issues of Elizabeth's Volume III *Annals* had been printed and distributed, with the help of the Sisters, before Fr Daniel Hudson of Notre Dame, editor of the *Ave Maria*, indicated in his periodical of June 1878 that he was impressed by the publication. Prior to his June issue, Elizabeth and another Sister visited him in Notre Dame, Indiana, and the regular communications between these two 'distributors of good books' were soon to help her greatly as she considered transferring the printing of the *Annals* to a new location.[2] Sr Chaffee, at twenty-seven years, had come in 1876 from Chicago where she had learnt the printing skills that assisted Elizabeth to organize her own printing and binding office.

In her concern for practical missionary involvement Elizabeth wanted to establish a branch house in Augusta, Georgia, where assistance could be offered to children of emancipated slaves. Br Stan Clarke at Notre Dame University Press, often scribe for his editor, provided Elizabeth with detailed printing and purchasing advice which lessened the challenge of buying a new printing press and transferring the *Annals'* work to the South. The fact that Br Clarke was a friend of Bishop William Gross of Georgia was also an advantage.

The Augusta foundation that Elizabeth was negotiating included an industrial school for youth at which printing was going to be part of the syllabus. Besides time devoted to this and to her role as religious leader among her Sisters, Elizabeth kept herself abreast of the international periodical scene. She was aware that the 'New Journalism' connoted the shift toward a mass circulation commercial press to meet the needs of the increased numbers of literate citizens. So while Elizabeth still desired to journey to a foreign mission, in this period of her life she channelled much energy into helping others on their spiritual journey by using her literary talents. 1878 marked the death of Pope Pius IX, whom Elizabeth had known, followed by the election of Pope Leo XIII – the significance for her readers of these events was reflected in her *Annals'* articles.

Elizabeth, as editor and publisher of a successful Franciscan Catholic journal, not only selected enriching topics acceptable to her readers but in doing so she revealed dimensions of herself. Like many nineteenth-century editors, she did not sign her name to any articles, and was careful most times to acknowledge her sources. Authorship can be assigned only after careful reading of each *Annals* article, especially certain insightful lines. In the 1870s Elizabeth personally contributed a larger proportion of the *Annals* content than in later years when she took greater advantage of more readily available material for translating and editing. In these early days the Sisters printed yearbooks containing copies not only of the texts but also of the original monthly index by page order. While this meant that comparison of each separate year's index was possible, it proved unwieldy, particularly in regard to identifying the many serials that often were spread over two or more years. To overcome this challenge it was necessary for the present writer to build an alphabetical list of each year's content to supplement the original monthly index lists and so now a richer understanding of Elizabeth's editorial task and of her whole *Annals* enterprise is possible.

Present research shows that an oral myth about the content of the *Annals* circulating in the later twentieth century is inaccurate. A superficial glance at Elizabeth's overall *Annals'* content led some to say that her articles were composed merely of 'bits and pieces' of books, periodicals and news. Yet herein lay the partial secret of her success; a model also used by others. In 1881 George Newnes turned his hobby of collecting printed titbits into the publishing of a penny magazine, *Tit-Bits from all the Most interesting Books, Periodicals and Contributors in the World*. Its title was shortened later to just *Tit-Bits*, a sixteen-page weekly, while its successful founder was hailed as one of the British New Journalism's pioneers. *The Review of Reviews,* founded by Albert Shaw, sought similarly to condense material for the reader while the American *Readers Digest* also achieved its success by 1922 in addressing the need for concise reading matter. Just as *Tit-Bits* often contained short stories, snippets of information, pieces of advice and correspondence, so too did Elizabeth's *Annals*. However Elizabeth's criteria were fundamentally different from those of Newnes for she sought primarily the 'diffusion of good [God-centred] books'.

During 1878 Elizabeth travelled to Augusta in Georgia and, while biographical sources are not easy to synchronize, it is clear that in early 1879 Bishop William Gross had formally granted Elizabeth permission to work in his diocese of Georgia.[3] Children with differently coloured skin attracted Elizabeth, be they in her childhood dreams of China, or living in Jamaica, St Thomas Island or elsewhere. Gross wanted her to help in particular on the Isle of Hope so he offered her a former Benedictine house and land outside Savannah, the major 'Port City'.[4] The Sisters' initial ministry there commenced through giving coloured girls plain, simple English schooling and teaching domestic duties. Since Elizabeth considered any work inappropriate unless it also provided some personal assistance to the poor and sick, this was also undertaken by Elizabeth and the three Sisters with her. In this African-American community, the students numbered about one hundred and twenty and most of them were non-Catholic. During this period Elizabeth fostered a small noviciate for young women wanting to join the Sisters. However, gradually, due to several reasons, including the lack of a resident priest and the need for a more conveniently located administrative centre, she foresaw that it would be necessary to focus her personal attention again on Augusta. In September 1879, Bishop Gross gave his permission for purchase of a property at Harrisonville, a suburb of Augusta, and for the erection of a simple Franciscan Convent and industrial institute for coloured children. In the 1990s part of the original building, called Siloh, was still standing as a reminder that Elizabeth initiated an industrial school which included printing rooms for the youth.

At this point, it seems appropriate to look at the specific content of Elizabeth's *Annals*, for they need to be placed in their literary context and this includes other Franciscan journals discussed in the previous chapter. Her approach to content was different from the *Franciscan Annals* in Milan and the Franciscan publication in Naples because these two journals were specifically targeted at Franciscans, while the English *Franciscan Annals*, though also aimed at Franciscans, included some more general matter.[5] Elizabeth uniquely provided a balance of material for both the general reader and the Franciscans. In her *Annals*, she also showed a leaning toward the thematic approach of the Milan publication which expressed in its indexes the themes that were umbrella titles for the articles.[6] In Mario Finauro's analysis of Milan's publication, he describes the practice of relying on the Franciscans' rich literary heritage and of gathering together material from other magazines and publications;[7] Elizabeth's content matches his description yet, as will be seen, she did it uniquely her way.

Nineteenth-century periodical literature has enjoyed a revival of interest in the past forty years, and in general, scholars have concentrated either on the genre's formal properties or its subject matter. A thematic approach allows us to focus on the themes that Elizabeth selected yet it also provides a chance to note the *Annals'* formal properties. Elizabeth published not only for her Franciscan readers, but for those whom she called the 'general reader' as stated in her original 1874 aims:

> In the humble hope of making more widely known, and therefore more truly loved, the devotion to our Seraphic Patriarch, we have ventured on the publication of these ANNALS ... Besides affording matter of interest to the general reader, it will be our endeavour to make the ANNALS as much as possible a faithful medium of communicating to you the present progress and development of the Order, its Missions, new foundations, and good works, as well as its past history, legends, and traditions.[8]

Themes for the General Reader

Elizabeth set out to entertain and enlighten her general readers with a variety of themes including: original tales, historical and biographical sketches, poetry, lives of the saints and of contemporary holy people, pilgrimage accounts, stories of missionary enterprise and articles on devotions and Catholic life. Leaving poetry until we meet contributors to the *Annals* later, each of these six themes will be considered.

Original tales

At times Elizabeth chose popular authors who wrote on subjects that dealt with religious topics of interest to the general reader. From September 1880 to February 1883, she serialized 'Germaine', taken from one of Lady Georgiana Fullerton's lesser known works, *Germaine Cousin – A Dramatic Tale*. The writer's popularity since her first book *Ellen Middleton* (1844) obviously precluded the inclusion of her best sellers like *Grantley Manor* (1847), *Lady Bird* (1852) or

La Comtesse de Bonneval (Paris, 1857; London, 1858). For Elizabeth the serial 'Germaine' was considered an 'original tale' and there were others.

Five original stories by Revd Francis Drew were selected by Elizabeth for serials from 1883 to 1885 and all had a clear religious message.[9] Drew's style was typically nineteenth century with ample paragraphs devoted to descriptions of characters and natural settings. The commitment of a priest author is sensed throughout each tale and his conclusions were strongly religious while he also indicates his personal knowledge of Oxford University life. The author writes about conversion with the strength of personal conviction and refers to English works, including Carroll's *Through the Looking Glass* and Wiseman's *Fabiola*. One gripping serialized tale for the general reader was entitled 'Tristam's Friends' which began with a shipwreck and the story of the only survivor, a baby, who in the final episode was revealed to be Lord Catesby. The style is exciting and the threads of conversion and an English setting, characteristic of Drew's stories, are evident.

Like other contemporary Catholic journal editors, Elizabeth felt free, in 'the cause of diffusion of good books' as it was commonly described, to select original tales from Catholic journals and to edit and publish them. As mentioned earlier, in 1880 Elizabeth selected three different tales from an English *Messenger of the Sacred Heart* which she named, 'Scenes in a Soldier's Life', 'Story of a Recent Conversion' and 'The Holy Man of Tours'. Though the texts of Elizabeth's versions are unavailable, those of the *Messenger of the Sacred Heart* are, and for the first tale the editor adapted the title from 'Three Scenes from a French Soldier's Life', then she split the 'original' September 1879 article into two further parts for her April and May 1880 editions.[10] The delightful scenes, described in the first person and set around the 1830s to 1850s, involve in particular Cavalier Meyer, Sr Marthe (a French Sister of Charity) and the writer. The theme of Christian charity links the scenes together and the storyteller suggests that some highly educated people, even those who listened in Paris to the renowned eloquence of Fr Lacordaire, may understand less philosophy than an 'ex-soldier and peasant' who practised kind deeds that were 'clear and eloquent in the ear of God'.

Around the time that Elizabeth edited the story, she received news that all was not going well without her in Belle Prairie. She had left Sr M. Clare Peet in charge and while this talented Sister seemed to function well when Elizabeth was near, as she did in France, Germany, St Thomas and the early days in Belle Prairie, her leadership skills may have been over estimated. Now tension on the home front meant that Elizabeth had to travel north. Sadly, the outcome was that Sr Peet decided to distance herself totally from the Sisters and Elizabeth must have felt the pain of saying goodbye to the first woman who was professed in her Minnesota community. Sr Chaffee remembered that Elizabeth accompanied the departing ex-Sister for part of her journey and ensured that she was assisted in her transition back to secular life. Elizabeth decided on the temporary closure of Belle Prairie convent and the Sisters moved south. Returning to Georgia, Elizabeth was engaged in many tasks and ensured that the new noviciate provided the training necessary for young women to understand the Franciscan way of life and to be ready to serve others.

In her *Annals* work, Elizabeth acknowledged her indebtedness for educational material to 'A. T. Drane', a name familiar to educated nineteenth-century English Catholics. Like Elizabeth, Augusta Theodosia Drane read widely, was influenced by the Oxford Movement, consulted Dr Pusey, knew Revd Keble, converted and then, unlike Elizabeth, was attracted to the Dominicans whose community at Stone she joined.[11] Through the writings of Augusta (later Mother Frances Raphael) whose life spanned the same years as Elizabeth's, *Annals'* readers received the ideas of a respected convert educator. Newman, friend of the Stone Dominicans, remarked that there were two main reasons for Catholic writing: to edify Catholics, and to build up a moral and intellectual state of mind in converts.[12] These evangelical reasons were embraced by Mother Drane whose 1867 educational work, *Christian Schools and Scholars*, suited the aim of Elizabeth's publication, so she selected three topics from the text and presented them as a serial of five, four and six parts respectively.[13] As noted earlier, the *Irish Monthly* published works of 'Mother Raphael Drane' and Elizabeth's *Annals* also published two of her religious poems.[14]

Historical and biographical sketches

Catholic editors including Elizabeth predated and perhaps influenced the later recommendations of the Third Plenary Council of Baltimore of 1884, for they were already promoting 'good reading' that would lead the faithful 'to a love of history and biography'. This was exemplified in Elizabeth's three-part historical and biographical sketch, 'Edmund Gennings'.

In the sixteenth century Edmund Gennings converted to

Catholicism, received ordination at Rheims' English College and returned to England under the assumed name of Ironmonger when Queen Elizabeth's newly introduced statute 27 was being enforced.[15] At age twenty-four, the missionary career of Gennings was cut short for he was captured in London and executed in 1591. His death affected his brother John enormously.[16] The *Annals'* text indicates that Elizabeth had access to an unnamed old Franciscan source which relied on John Genning's biography of his younger brother and which provided her with numerous quotations. In this sketch which also illustrates a type of general catechizing, Elizabeth shows sensitivity to her general as well as to her Franciscan readers. Only in the story's final paragraph does she explain that Edmund's brother John 'entered the Franciscan Order, which by his instrumentality, was set up again in England, when ... he was appointed the first Provincial'.

Published between April 1886 and March 1887, 'The Royal Recluse', which was a biographical tale set in Spain for the general reader, was included as a serial of twelve parts. It gradually reveals the life and death of 'Charles V of Augsburg, King of Spain & Emperor of Germany'. Catholic Spain shines through the serial, the monastery of Yuste is an ever present theme and the descriptive flowing style of the unnamed author carries the reader to the final lines which recall the Battle of Lepanto where Europe, under the leadership of Don John of Austria, was saved from a second Muslim invasion. Another significant example of Elizabeth's selection of historical and biographical sketches is Vansittart's serial, 'Christianity under the Heptarchy: A Page from English history', which we will consider later.

Saints

Elizabeth emphasized the theme of Saints and explained the importance of saints' lives as follows:

> The glory of a Saint is always proportioned to the grandeur of his mission and the glory he has given to God; and as nothing glorifies Our Blessed Lord more than the redemption of souls, the more a Saint has co-operated in this work, the greater is his glory.[17]

'St Mary the Virgin' and 'St Mary of the Angels' are two Marian titles favoured by Elizabeth; in every volume she included particular Marian topics with the greatest number of Marian articles printed in the early 1890s when the *Annals* published a lengthy sequence focusing on 'Sanctuaries of Mary'. An 1890 article in the sequence, into which the editor drew three other writers, reminds the general reader why the periodical was called the *Annals of Our Lady of the Angels*.[18]

In 1891 four more Marian topics, spread over six articles, were 'translated from the Italian'; while in the next year their Italian source, Sanctuaries of Our Lady, was named for another six Marian headings featuring in ten articles. Included in 1892 was a two-part article, 'Our Lady 'Ad Rupes'', which Elizabeth ensured coincided with the Franciscan friars' return to the Ad Rupes ancient sanctuary at Castel Sant'Elia. She concluded the article's second part by updating her readers with the latest news on the sanctuary and assuring pilgrims that their spiritual needs would be accommodated. The *Annals'* article led to an immediate request from the friars' 'Father President' to prepare and print a separate booklet about the sanctuary. Letters acknowledged Elizabeth's commitment to a high degree of accuracy and truthfulness[19] and the friars satisfaction with her final work was expressed in Br Anthony's letter: 'Father President feels extremely grateful to Reverend Mother for all she has done for the 'Madonna ad Rupes'...'

The 1893 pattern was repeated the following year as Elizabeth presented nine different sanctuaries, mainly in Rome, where Mary was honoured under different titles. Finally in 1894 six Marian themes from Sanctuaries of Our Lady were spread over eleven numbers, amongst them one three-part serial, 'Our Lady of Galloro, in the Diocese of Albano, near Rome'. Mary's status as 'immaculate from conception' – long attributed to her by Franciscan theologians – was defined by the Vatican in 1854 and the title, 'of the Immaculate Conception', had been incorporated via the Glasgow Franciscan Sisters into the official name of Elizabeth's Institute. Hence it is not surprising that articles related to this title, and to the belief in Mary's apparitions to Bernadette Soubirous at Lourdes, appear in numerous volumes.[20] Elizabeth's desire to spread Marian devotion in volumes XI and XII is reflected in her selection from Revd T. E. Bridgett's work, *Our Lady's Dowry; or How England Gained and Lost That Title*. Bridgett's contribution will be discussed later as it provides an example of how Elizabeth edited another's text. She edified her early 1890s readers through two series, the saintly lives of Venerable Nunzio Sulprizio and Venerable Mary Christine of Savoy, translations from the *French Saints and Servants of God of the Nineteenth Century*.[21] Numerous other heroines and heroes were upheld by Elizabeth for imitation in most volumes through single articles, ranging from 'St. Frances of Rome' to 'Blessed Imelda', and from 'St. Benedict the Moor' to 'Edmund Campion'.

Her Story 1880–81 and the *Annals*

Elizabeth could identify readily with written pilgrimage accounts in her publication. Her biographers at times give the impression that her life was one personal pilgrimage after another, for example, in December in 1880, Elizabeth and Sr Chaffee set off for Rome with the intention of establishing a generalate, this initiating her third and final term of residence there. Elizabeth was now well into her fifty-eighth year, her health was not robust and she was concerned about the future welfare of her infant community. One biographer suggested that a house in Rome would seem to her to be a kind of insurance policy for the continuation of her Institute.[22] The Sisters in Augusta confidently continued to print the *Annals* while to the advantage of the publication, the travellers in Rome lived with a family whose relative was a Jesuit Brother, a printer, working on the influential Jesuit newspaper, *Civiltà Cattolica*. The tasks of Elizabeth and her companion involved a period of seven months yet the *Annals*' publication was uninterrupted, and they finally returned safely to Augusta. Elizabeth's trunk was hardly unpacked when within three months of returning she had to go back to Rome for it was time to take up permanent residence on the Via Alfieri. Even though she had signed a contract months earlier for a new villa there, it was not ready when she arrived. With two Sisters and a postulant as companions, Elizabeth was given the use of a villa on the Via Guilia while they waited. From her headhouse in Rome, Elizabeth hoped to send forth Sisters to distant dependent missions; finally the house was officially opened with papal permission in December 1881.

Pilgrimages

A good example of a pilgrimage account in Elizabeth's *Annals* was 'La Sainte Baume, St. Mary Magdalene's Retreat' which commenced with an explanation of the site's origin, then its destruction during the French Revolution and finally its partial restoration.[23] According to the article, by 1862 the celebrated Dominican writer-preacher, Père Lacordaire, had encouraged

Mademoiselle Lautard to build a hospice for pilgrims who wished to visit the retreat place where it was believed St Mary Magdalen lived as a solitary penitent after escaping persecution in Jerusalem. Elizabeth followed this article with 'Pilgrimage to la Sainte Baume',[24] in which Mrs Montgomery detailed her nine-day journey from England to Marseilles, the breakdown of her carriage and subsequent 'quick twenty minutes of hard walking in a pelting shower' and her overnight sleepless stay at the 'unfinished' hospice – 'roughing it in true pilgrim fashion'. While the author was pleased to visit St Mary Magdalen's grotto and to attend Masses and Benediction with her women's group, she concluded her article with a thankful prayer that 'pilgrimages were not the only road to Heaven'.

Elizabeth commenced 'Pilgrimage to Iona' with reference to Saints Cuthbert and Columba and painted a picture of pilgrims arriving in Oban 'from every quarter of Scotland, as well as from the north of England and some parts of Ireland'.[25] After a description of the journey and various religious events, Elizabeth concluded her account by quoting 'a correspondent who was present'. He explained the processions, told of sermons in English and Gaelic and provided the aristocratic names of pilgrimage participants. Another pilgrimage or travel theme is exemplified in 'A Peep into Spain' which was composed in letter-form under the pen name of 'Daisy': a series of ten articles spread over three volumes.[26] 'Daisy' wrote her supposed letters to 'Hattie', her younger sister back in England, telling of the family's journey to Spain and their religious adventures. This lengthy interesting story, Catholic in tone, had the potential to further readers' knowledge of European Catholic culture and to strengthen their relationship with God. Elizabeth acknowledged the author as 'A Tertiary', while the text provides hints that its author may have been Lady Herbert of Lea, a Franciscan Tertiary, who had published *Impressions of Spain* in 1866. Lady Herbert of Lea, a major contributor to Elizabeth's *Annals*, also published in 1867 another pilgrimage account, *Travels to the Holy Land*, sometimes called *Cradle Lands* (travels in Egypt and Palestine).

Missionary Activities

The comprehensive missionary involvement that marked the nineteenth century and Elizabeth's life and writings within this have been noted. The five-part serial, 'Echoes from Distant Lands', is

one example of how Elizabeth wove this mission theme into the
Annals,[27] and besides articles about foreign missions she also
created a special title, 'Missionary Notes'. It entered her *Annals* in
every issue of Volume V and flowed along, at times unevenly, until
the April issue of Volume X.[28] In Volume VIII alone through
'Missionary Notes' the editor provided the general reader with
news of missions in North Japan, Asia, Borneo, India and among
Southern Californian Indians, while three of nine missionary articles in 1884 recalled the story of the 'martyrdoms in Tonkin'. Since
journals were meant to contain up-to-date news, in 1886 Elizabeth
reintroduced news items on home and foreign missions under
'Miscellaneous'. The September issue of Volume XI published a
timely reminder of the value of diffusing news to home and foreign
missions, this time regarding the pope's jubilee celebrations; we
read that 'All Catholic journals of every country are invited to
republish' the article.

Devotions and Catholic Life

However, it was not just missionary endeavour that Elizabeth
sought to support and encourage as she also fostered particular
local devotions among the laity. Devotions, as part of American
Catholic life, had reached a more widespread community level
when Elizabeth commenced her journal. After the American Civil
War and a further immigration boom, the formation of devotional
confraternities and associations increased rapidly. Women parishioners joined the Sacred Heart Sodality, the men belonged to a
similar devotional group, later called the Holy Name Society, and
children were enrolled in the Holy Angels Confraternity. As each
local association recited appropriate prayers and received Holy
Communion together on a stipulated Sunday, a corporate sense of
belonging grew in the local parish community. Among the particular devotions that Elizabeth encouraged, through articles, were
devotion to the Sacred Heart of Jesus and to the Holy Angels. Like
the periodical, *Ave Maria*,[29] Elizabeth's *Annals* caught the contemporary devotional mood; in her first volume she included four
single articles on the Sacred Heart. The high point of Elizabeth's
writing on angels was her eighteen-part translation, 'The Holy
Angels', in Volumes XVI to XIX, based on an unnamed Italian
source. The articles provide evidence that Elizabeth felt at liberty
to edit the Italian original. Brownlow's *Angels Ever in our Midst* indicates the popularity of angels for numerous nineteenth-century

writers,[30] but Elizabeth waited until the 1890s to give the angel theme a high profile. In earlier issues she had certainly included stories of angels in her Christmas articles besides reference to the Queen of the Angels in her Marian ones. In Elizabeth's poetry selections she chose the work of Adelaide Anne Procter (1825–1864), popular English convert known for her writings in numerous magazines, who produced a narrative poem, 'The Angel's Story'. Elizabeth published Procter's 'The Angel of Prayers' in her Volume XVIII.

To further her Apostolate of the Press, Elizabeth selected material on two elements in particular of Catholic life, which she presented under the headings Christian Virtues and Spiritual Reading. For these topics Elizabeth turned to writings by high profile ecclesiastics, including Archbishop Ullathorne of Birmingham and Cardinal Manning. The *Annals* reproduced 'Cheerfulness' by Ullathorne in three instalments; then another original of his, 'Our Daily Duties', was presented in a four-part serial.[31] The two series could have been extracted from a major work since the topic of Christian Virtues had engaged Ullathorne's pen in publications during the 1880s.[32] Between 1888 and 1890 Elizabeth provided her readers with 'Confidence in God' by Manning in an eleven-part serial. Manning's style was straightforward and invited spiritual reflection:

> Remember God, forget yourselves, and forget yourselves in remembering God. The more you contemplate God the more you live with the eyes of your mind opened and illuminated, as the Apostle says, so as to gaze upon the length, and breadth, and depth, and height, and to know the love of Christ, which passes knowledge ... of His love, sanctity, tenderness, pity, compassion and Fatherly care.[33]

The *Annals*' articles, telling readers that the virtue of 'hope matures into confidence', were selected from Manning's major work, *Confidence in God*. While in general Manning's writings and ministry appealed to the editor, she printed only a few articles by him,[34] at a time when he was not always popular in certain English Catholic circles. Manning was known to be an ultramontane who challenged social pretensions and political conservatism.[35]

On the topic of Spiritual Reading, Elizabeth published articles by England's Archbishop of Westminster, Herbert Vaughn, to celebrate his reception of the cardinal's red hat from the hands of Leo XIII.[36] For such a major event, a description of proceedings, a biographical sketch, or an account of his former achievements as

Bishop of Salford could have been expected but Elizabeth chose
differently. Vaughn, after a United States visit in the early 1860s,
had developed a strong appreciation of the power of the press.[37]
Vaughn's words on Spiritual Reading sound like a justification of
Elizabeth's work and her inclusion of so many articles on saint's
lives:

> To see and understand, we must read and reflect. Doctrinal, moral,
> ascetical and mystical works teach us, either scientifically or popu-
> larly, to understand the service and the love of Christ. The lives of
> the Saints and servants of God present us with persuasive examples
> of the service and the love of Christ triumphing in frail human crea-
> tures like ourselves. The Saints are, therefore, our example and our
> encouragement in the midst of trials and difficulties.[38]

Her Story 1881–82

It was in the parish of St John Lateran, the mother church of
Rome, that Elizabeth had situated her generalate house. This was
the church to which St Francis and his early followers had come to
see the pope to have their Rule approved. It seemed certain that in
late 1881 permission would not be given for the Blessed Sacrament
to be reserved in the chapel because there was not the required
number of Sisters in the generalate. To overcome this, Elizabeth
decided to petition the Holy Father for a dispensation from the
Constitutions which required the Sisters to visit the Blessed
Sacrament. When the Holy Father heard of the request, he
exclaimed, 'What! Can it be that the Sisters can observe their
Constitution less exactly in Rome than in America!' Permission to
reserve the Blessed Sacrament was granted. During this same year,
Elizabeth also obtained an official 'Letter of Approbation for the
Zelatrices' (promoters) who worked on the distribution of the
periodical; gradually the approbation developed further and its
importance will be referred to later.

Elizabeth loved the town of Assisi with all its associations with St
Francis, so while in Rome she planned to build a house there. The
land she obtained was in front of and close to the basilica that shel-
ters the original chapel of Our Lady of the Angels on the plain
below Assisi. Evidence suggests that, while the plans were prepared
for her by an architect, the actual building did not eventuate and
another building in Assisi was rented for the Sisters. Young Italians
were asking to join the community so that in the following year
more women received the habit of St Francis. In 1882 Elizabeth was

delighted to publish the news that her periodical was acknowledged and 'honoured with the Blessing and Commendation of
Our Holy Father Leo XIII and encouraged by several Archbishops
and Bishops . . . and with the approbation of the Right Revd Bishop
of the Diocese'.[39]

Next there was the question of what the Sisters should do in
Rome. There were suggestions that they should help to care for the
poor and sick of the parish or open a school. To settle the question
Elizabeth had a private audience with the pope. His answer was,
according to Sr Chaffee's memory, 'You will bring to Rome young
women and train them for the missions'; another account also indicates that the pope expressed his desire for an international house
of formation for young women for the foreign missions. From this
time, Elizabeth's Franciscan Third Order Regular community was
officially known as a Papal Institute. Among the first postulants to
arrive in Rome was Frederica Law, an African-American from
Georgia. According to Sr Chaffee, Frederica previously worked
with the Sisters in the preparation of the *Annals* in Augusta, and in
October 1882 the postulants, Frederica Law and Julie Michaud,
received the Franciscan Habit in Assisi.

Themes for the Franciscan Reader

We have seen much evidence that Elizabeth was committed to the
Franciscan Third Order movement, especially to the many secular
Third Order members of whom the majority were women. As
Annals' editor, Elizabeth aimed to help her Franciscan readers find
God more deeply through original Franciscan stories, historical
and biographical Franciscan sketches – especially through the lives
of Franciscan saints – through accounts of pilgrimages to
Franciscan shrines, stories of Franciscan missionary activities and
through articles on Franciscan devotions. While each of these
themes can be identified in the content Elizabeth prepared for the
Franciscan reader, to single out each theme would fracture the
content which is often an interwoven combination of themes. So
while being aware that early Franciscan literature often amalga-
mated original stories, history, biography and other writings, we
will look at Elizabeth's work by commencing with her lives of major
Franciscan saints, followed by Franciscan literature, Franciscan
stories and then Franciscan devotions, ending with the special
focus on St Anthony of Padua in the *Annals*.

Franciscan saints' lives

A major feature in English culture for much of the nineteenth century was admiration of the hero or heroine. This was reflected in general English literature so religious writings took advantage of it by presenting saints as great heroes and heroines. Elizabeth ensured that one of the principal ways her *Annals* achieved its aims was through the promotion of biographies of Franciscan holy men and women. At times she highlighted Franciscan saints' feastdays and ensured that some of these particular saints' stories were included in the month containing their feastday according to the Franciscan Calendar.[40] The stories of major Franciscan saints' lives lent themselves to serials, a form popular in secular and religious journals of the period, and it proved successful for the *Annals* as readers looked forward to the next interesting instalment. Saints Francis and Clare of Assisi, Anthony of Padua, Elizabeth of Hungary, Collette, and John Vianney serve to illustrate her leading Franciscan saints.

Elizabeth's first *Annals'* serial on the life of St Francis appeared in 1884–5 in thirteen instalments, and while she had written much on the Franciscan Order in articles from 1874, the founder's biography waited a while. Elizabeth sprinkled 'sayings' and 'maxims' of St Francis in her later publications. An 1887 long single article, 'The Stigmata of St. Francis', reads like a traditional thirteenth-century chronicle and the unsigned text reveals no definite clue as to its origin. Another methodically laid out serial story, 'Legacies of the Seraphic Father St. Francis', appears also to have been edited by Elizabeth.

An analysis of Elizabeth's articles on St Francis' life raises questions about availability of sources. Celano in the thirteenth century was the first biographer of St Francis. Numerous lives of the saint were written later, including a popular late nineteenth-century translation from Chalippe's French life based on the labours of Irish Franciscan, Luke Wadding, and translated by Elizabeth's London Oratorian friends. The Allegany New York Franciscans, whom Elizabeth also knew, republished it in America.[41] The first American 1877 edition of Chalippe's work predated Elizabeth's 1884–5 articles while Moorman, Anglican Franciscan scholar, pointed out that the first *Life of St. Francis* to be written in English appeared in 1870, only four years before the commencement of Elizabeth's *Annals*. This *Life of St. Francis* by Mrs Margaret Oliphant (1828–1897) was credited as scholarly, based on medieval sources and written in a style that appealed to the mid-Victorian English reader.[42] Recognized as a fitting example of a professional woman journalist, Oliphant's name does not appear in Elizabeth's *Annals* and no explanation for this has been found. Of interest, Oliphant's words to Blackwood in 1870, 'Anonymity is a great institution', may offer a clue to Elizabeth's key to negotiating the masculine world of journalism as they did for Oliphant.[43] Elizabeth and her few assistants had the ability to translate French, Italian, German and Latin sources, yet in the reality of her mid-west and Georgian American mission convents, how far could she stretch her human resources? Even when working in Rome, one wonders how many translations she could include per month. Elizabeth Lockhart's death in 1870 ended her contributions to Franciscan translations but other Franciscans in England continued the work, at Baddesley and Taunton in particular, and Elizabeth availed herself of these.

The eight-part serial on the 'Life of St. Clare', the first woman to follow St Francis' way of life in Assisi, was organized by Elizabeth for November 1883 up to July the following year.[44] During its serialization it was accompanied, often in the same issue, with the 'Life of St. Anthony' but the sources of both remain a mystery amid the mountain of Franciscan Italian hagiography. Clare's writings provided by Elizabeth make up the basis of the Poor Clares' spirituality and charism, as well as being a primary source of historical information for the life of St Francis himself.

Elizabeth reserved for St Anthony of Padua (1195–1231) the greatest number of articles – above all other Franciscan saints – beginning an eleven-part serial on the 'Life of Saint Anthony' in her first issue.[45] Later 'The Life of St. Anthony of Padua' was presented again in the *Annals,* this time in sixteen sequential parts between April 1883 and September 1884. The author's anonymity and the lack of any particular named source strongly suggest that Elizabeth herself wrote the articles, using multiple and often foreign sources. The underlying mysteries of the Catholic faith that St Anthony strongly believed in, lived and preached, were what people of every age have sought to proclaim, remember and celebrate through commemoration of the saint's life. The editor foresaw the question as to why she gave so much attention to this saint and provided her answer in an article which commenced and concluded with:

> If then you ask why so much glory is paid to St. Anthony, I answer you in the words which the Church uses in the Office of the Apostle loved by Jesus. 'Children of men, listen and learn the glory of the Saint well-beloved of the Lord.'[46]

St Anthony's life which inspired devotion in Elizabeth and her readers will be further considered under Franciscan devotions because devotion to St Anthony created a unique inseparable association with the *Annals*.

Elizabeth's serial, 'Life of St. Elizabeth of Hungary', provides another example of how the *Annals'* editor read from sources and then composed her own articles on the subject.[47] A footnote in the first of her thirteen articles indicates that one resource at Elizabeth's elbow was written by the 'chivalrous biographer', the Comte de Montalembert. He married a descendant of the saint and had published his *Vie de Sainte Elizabeth de Hongrie* in 1836; this is claimed to have restored hagiography in France and restored a taste in Catholics for the supernatural as exemplified in saints' lives. The message to Franciscans in Elizabeth's introduction reveals her own attitude:

> There are few names in the calendar of the saints so full of tender and poetical associations as hers who has come down to us through six long centuries, as the 'dear Saint Elizabeth'. Her history has the brilliancy of a romance of chivalry with the deep pathos of a tale of human affection, added to the more sacred interest which belongs to the biography of a saint.[48]

Elizabeth's use of 'dear Saint Elizabeth' indicates her knowledge of the German people's favourite way of speaking of the saint who at her canonization was called 'the greatest woman of the German Middle Ages'. Elizabeth's other resources were 'chronicles' and historical accounts referred to and quoted in her articles. According to historians, Franciscans arrived in Germany in St Francis' lifetime and one of the first Germans who joined them was for a time the spiritual director of St Elizabeth at Wartburg. Along with her maids, St Elizabeth (1207–1231) later embraced the Franciscan ideals, wore the habit of St Francis, was among the first German Third Order members, built the Franciscan hospital at Marburg and devoted herself to the poor and sick. It is not possible to know which resource Elizabeth used as accounts are to be found as far back as the original letters sent by Conrad of Marburg to Pope Gregory IX in 1232. Around 1888 there began an upsurge in writings on St Elizabeth, especially in Germany and Austria, due to forthcoming celebrations in 1907 to honour the seven-hundredth anniversary of her birth. Elizabeth's articles of 1885–6 were forerunners in renewing the saint's popularity.

In 'St. Collette – Her Mission and Her Times', printed in the 1875 *Annals*, a few unique characteristics are evident. The four-part fifteenth-century based serial[49] began not with references or quotations from historians but with Elizabeth's consciousness of present papal difficulties in the seizure of the Papal States, comparable in some measure to those in St Collette's lifetime. We also have a rare glimpse into the writer's personal juggling of time commitments. Elizabeth, whose 'incessant labours' at this time included conducting both the Belle Prairie and Brainerd schools, wrote:

> I set myself to the work, but I must say, I required something more for the glory of St. Collette than the few shreds of time torn here and there from the requirements of the cloister, and the incessant labors of the apostolic life. I claim therefore the indulgence of the reader.[50]

Elizabeth stresses repeatedly how St Collette was a woman with a passion for unity in the Church, how she prayed and did penance and how she in practice brought about peace. This interesting serial tells of the problems related to anti-popes in the Church of St Collette's times, including the Great Schism (1378–1417). Elizabeth showed the strong character of St Collette, who in spite of being on good terms with the anti-pope Benedict XIII – who had approved her Poor Clare reform – joined with St Vincent Ferrer to oppose him when God directed her to do so. Numerous references are made to the General Council of Constance (1414–17) and the following interval of peace under Pope Martin V. Elizabeth called St Collette an 'oracle and pillar of the Church' because of her successful involvement in helping to bring about unity. The editor's serial informed readers that Collette founded seventeen Franciscan convents and was gifted with remarkable moral power over others, including the Cardinal Legate of the Holy See, bishops, King James of Aragon and the Duke of Savoy. Elizabeth concluded what she called her 'short study of the mission of our Saint', actually some twenty-three pages of small print, with the question:

> Does it not seem appropriate to propose St. Collette to the Christian people in the present afflictions as a help and model? In her life all the faithful may learn what is their duty during the sufferings of their common Father, and how efficacious prayers and intercessions are to obtain peace and blessing for the Church.[51]

As for the sources available to Elizabeth in frontier Belle Prairie, while she made no reference to French texts, research suggests that beside the possible availability of old Franciscan literature, a likely source would be a French life by Père Sellier or that of Abbé Douillé. In 1879 Mrs Parsons, at the request of the Poor Clare Colletines of Baddesley (England), published the first book on the saint in English.[52] Again Elizabeth outdated new publications.

The opening lines of 'The Cure of Ars', one of the *Annals'* longest serials,[53] leave the reader in no doubt as to why Elizabeth prepared and published this Franciscan life story:

> John Baptist Marie Vianney – universally known as the Cure of Ars, whose saintly life is still revered in living memories and whose Cause for Beatification we are told is rapidly advancing, was a Tertiary of the Third Order Secular of St. Francis of Assisi; whose simplicity of intention for God's glory, and the salvation of souls; whose charity, poverty, and marvellous self-abnegation would place him in the holy category of the first followers of his Seraphic Patron.[54]

Elizabeth's serial followed Vianney's life, 1786–1859, and included numerous references to Monseigneur Monnin who, as the articles explain, was friend and co-worker of John Vianney. Abbé Alfred Monnin on his bishop's request wrote *Le Curé d'Ars* which was published in Paris in 1861. The preface of the first English translation was completed by Dr Manning, Elizabeth's old friend, but the translator's name was omitted.[55] Evidence suggests that Elizabeth probably not only used this translation of Monnin's text as her basic source, with anonymity for herself again, and that it was the translation accomplished by her friend, Mother Elizabeth Lockhart.[56] Elizabeth's personal memorabilia contained John Vianney's photograph inscribed with the words, 'Four months before the death 2 April 1859' and a copy of this same photograph is in reprints of Monnin's popular translation. Analysis of this life story further clarifies how Elizabeth often read her sources and then wrote her own unsigned version. The lives of other significant Franciscan saints were also presented in *Annals* serials,[57] while at times Elizabeth published many single stories on lesser known Franciscan saints. A look at how Elizabeth used Fr Léon de Clary's *Lives of the Saints and Blessed of the Three Orders of St. Francis* to achieve her aims will be considered later.[58]

Franciscan literature

We have already mentioned Elizabeth's articles relating to the Order, so the Franciscan literature theme is limited to examples concerned with the Franciscan Order, Bonaventure's writings, the old classic – *Little Flowers of St. Francis* – and an account of the English Grey Friars. 'The Franciscan Order in England', Elizabeth's longest serial on the Order, was based on the 'Chronicle of the Franciscan Order in England' published between 1878 and 1883 in the English *Franciscan Annals*. In line with her aim to present the Franciscan Order's history, Elizabeth published a six-part serial, 'The Third Order of St. Francis', which she had translated in 1874 from the work of French expert on Franciscan literature, Monseigneur Louis Gaston de Ségur.

How Elizabeth used her application of St Bonaventure's writings to achieve her aims is intriguing. St Bonaventure (1217–1274) was described by Elizabeth as great in the science of God; a saint who 'passed successively from the lowest ranks of a simple religious to the honours of Doctor, General of the Order of Friars Minor, Bishop, and Cardinal'. While Elizabeth's inclusion of Bonaventure's works followed a strong Franciscan tradition,[59] she excluded, among his many famous writings, the important life of St Francis. Instead, her articles on Bonaventure drew attention to events that celebrated the sixth century after his death,[60] to news about Fr de Fanna's research and publications based on the *Echoes of the Vatican* – all of which indicate Elizabeth's enormous reading capacity.[61] She provided a succinct, well-resourced article on the saint's life,[62] while in later volumes moved into the practice of giving Bonaventure's words in snippets, for example:

> PERFECT Christians have always before their minds the shortness of life: they live as if they were to die each day, and prepare themselves with as much care for the future life as if they regarded the things of time with the light of eternity. *St. Bonaventure*

Elizabeth waited until 1893 to reproduce three of Bonaventure's more pastoral writings, followed the next year by three different selections from Conferences on the Gospel of St John and a serial on the Conferences on the Passion. About the unique source of these Conferences, Elizabeth wrote:

> The Latin text of this priceless treasure (Collationes in Evangelium S. Johannis) has been recently, *for the first time*, put into print, in the printing press of the Franciscan Order at Quaracchi near Florence, having previously lain hidden in the obscurity of ancient manuscripts.[63]

Elizabeth had not attempted to diffuse the deepest Bonaventurian

writings, particularly those described as using 'the language of
Pseudo-Dionysius the Areopagite', yet she did ensure that her
readers received something of Bonaventure's pastoral assistance,
particularly a taste of his scripturally-based sermons. A fuller appreciation of Elizabeth's broad and deep readings of St Bonaventure
which prefaced her selections of Bonaventure's work for the
Annals would be ideal; to present just one aspect of Bonaventure's
reflections, Elizabeth had to choose from seventy-nine conferences
on St John's Gospel.[64]

Sources suggest that Elizabeth was ahead of her time in introducing Bonaventurian literature to the English-speaking world
when availability of his works to English readers was extremely
rare.[65] The 1978 translation from the Latin by Ewert Cousins of
Bonaventure's trilogy, *Itinerarum mentis in Deum, Lignum Vitae* and
Legenda Maior, heightens awareness of Elizabeth's industry in
achieving her Apostolate of the Press.[66] Elizabeth's attitude
appears aligned with the comment of a later Franciscan author
who wrote of Bonaventure's work, 'presented are so many ways in
which he sought to understand and to nourish in himself and in
others, the love needed to heed that invitation of the Master'.[67]

Elizabeth evangelized not only through the Franciscan writings
in her *Annals'* content but also through her recommendations of
new Franciscan literary translations, as exemplified in two 1888
articles, different yet both entitled, 'The Little Flowers of St.
Francis', one by Elizabeth herself and the other by a 'P.F.'. The
Fioretti (Little Flowers of St Francis) is a Franciscan fourteenth-
century Italian literary masterpiece, a collection of charming and
instructive anecdotes about St Francis and his early friars.
Elizabeth wrote:

> We shall not attempt to quote any fragments for the benefit of those
> who may be unacquainted with the work, but prefer to recommend
> all such to lose no time in making it their own.[68]

Elizabeth rejoiced over the Bayswater Franciscans' second edition
of the *Fioretti,*[69] which she, among others, regarded not only as a
manual of devotional reading, but also of spiritual value and of
historical importance. She wrote:

> As a historical work the volume is a record of men whom many even
> of those who fail to appreciate the true soul animating their lives,
> have ranked among the chief benefactors of their kind, because of
> their genuine philanthropy, their recognition of the claims of the
> poor, their example and preaching of unselfishness, mutual help-

fulness and ceaseless beneficence. They were men whose lives ought to be known to all the world.[70]

The second article by 'P.F.' commenced with a tale of an unnamed convert, later priest, who became attracted to St Francis, then it moves on to resonate with Elizabeth's own article.[71] It praises 'the recent edition of a unique book' especially the quality of its translation despite being transplanted 'into our harsher tongue'.[72] Elizabeth's article concluded with a suggestion that study of the new publication would be fruitful:

> The real actual lives of the saints, when by rare fortune they find, as in the case of the early Franciscans, worthy chroniclers, present to those who study them with undarkened eyes, a combination of Truth and Poetry, of Beauty and Utility.[73]

A final example of Franciscan literature in the *Annals* is the historical article, 'The Grey Friars'. The editor's brief introductory words are, 'Dr. St. George Mivart contributes an interesting article to *The New Review,* in which he says:' – then the traditional, yet particularly Greenwich-orientated Franciscans' story of arrival and struggle in England commences.[74] The reader's attention is ensured because the famous contemporary name, Mivart, not normally associated with history but with scientific and philosophical works, explains the historical topic.[75] Once again Elizabeth shows her breadth of reading and her ability to pluck material from unexpected sources. The article concluded with a news update on the opening of Guilford's Observant Franciscan noviciate, an historical Franciscan event of 1887.

Franciscan stories

Among her Franciscan stories, Elizabeth created the 'Franciscan Record' as a regular feature in her *Annals* in 1878, as a means of reporting news and collecting stories about recent Franciscan events, and retained it until 1887.[76] The editor's method is exemplified in her 1879 'Franciscan Record' articles on the 'Archconfraternity of the Cord of St. Francis' which announced the two latest decrees promulgated that year on the Archconfraternity.[77] In Volume VII Elizabeth used her 'Franciscan Record' to provide her readers with news of the Capuchins' missions, stories from Europe and answers to correspondents. In 1884 the 'Franciscan Record' concluded with Roman news about 'another large Religious Congregation, all of whose members are Third Order Franciscans'.

The story of 'The Present State of the Franciscan Missions' throughout the world was reported by Elizabeth in three 1874 articles through her own explanatory introduction and notes, including a translated statistical type 'catalogue' as she called it.[78] The story covers Franciscan missions in Europe, the Holy Land, Asia, Africa, North and South America and, near the conclusion, missions in 'Oceanica' which includes:

> A Province with two hundred and seventy-eight religious, who direct sixteen missions amongst the Infidels, and supply the duty of one hundred and thirty-four Parishes, containing about 798,000 Catholics.[79]

Franciscan devotions

Nineteenth-century Franciscan devotions were numerous and many were woven into general Catholic practices,[80] yet traditionally Franciscan devotions to Christ's humanity revolved essentially around God's love expressed through the 'Crib', 'Cross' and 'Eucharist'. Elizabeth built many *Annals'* articles around these three topics and related ones, especially the love of the Sacred Heart. Illustrations of this are revealing as well as examples of articles that focus on Franciscan devotion to Mary, and, in particular, devotion to Saint Anthony.[81] Traditionally, Franciscans were also especially devoted to the Holy Father and so Elizabeth did not ignore this theme.

Devotion to the crib, according to the *Franciscan Annals*, was inaugurated by St Francis of Assisi.[82] Elizabeth, more restrained, reminded her readers:

> It was St. Francis who popularised, perhaps even inaugurated, in Italy the devotion of the crib. It was in 1223. Being at Rome he obtained the authorisation of the Soverign Pontiff to go and celebrate the birth of the Saviour at Greccio, to assemble his brethren and the neighbouring population, and give this feast unwonted honour.[83]

Alongside her use of poetry on Bethlehem, Elizabeth sometimes drew upon correspondence received from Franciscans in the Holy Land. The first occasion she did this was in the article entitled 'Christmas night at Bethlehem'. Late the same year, Elizabeth shared with readers her own Roman Christmas experience, entitled 'Christmas Day in Rome', and recalled:

Out again to wander among the countless churches of God's city, and visit some of the 'Bambinos', as the Italian name is, the images of the Divine Infant, which are placed in all the churches, to preach to the eye of the poor and the unlearned the gospel of God's birth, and to wake in the hearts of all thoughts of love for the Babe who stooped so low.[84]

Devotion to the Infant in the crib was encouraged through a number of general and specific articles. Franciscan devotion to the Cross was understood to focus on Christ's sufferings and death and traditionally Franciscans have been credited with spreading the devotion known as The Stations of the Cross. Under the heading, 'Stations of the Cross', Elizabeth republished for her Third Order Franciscan readers short questions to, and replies from, the Sacred Congregation of Indulgences in regard to this devotion.

The articles, 'Jerusalem and the Holy places', introduced with Pope Leo XIII's reminder that Christ became 'obedient unto death, even the death of the Cross' in Jerusalem, goes on to state that the Franciscans, the custodians of the Holy Places, in trying to restore the sacred sites were in need of the faithful's financial support and outlined a plan of action. Elizabeth then elaborated on the Pope's 'Brief' – calling the faithful's opportunity to assist, an 'act of devotion to the Gospel'.[85] Lady Herbert's 'Jerusalem and the Holy Sepulchre' contains similar references to the Franciscans' devotion to and care of Calvary, other holy places and the pilgrims whom, as a pilgrim herself, she describes at some length.[86] Other examples of articles intended by Elizabeth to produce increased devotion to the Cross are 'The Miraculous Cross', and the 'Legend of the Repentant Thief'.

First among Elizabeth's principal attractions in prayer was devotion 'towards our Blessed Lord in the Holy Eucharist',[87] so *Annals*' articles feature devotion to the Eucharist, with the most outstanding by Elizabeth's former mentor and friend, Cardinal Henry Manning.[88] This scripturally-based, theologically-rich devotional explanation is addressed in particular to English readers,[89] and its source, not indicated by the editor, is most likely Manning's book by the same title. Elizabeth encouraged Eucharistic devotion by publishing an article by her Franciscan friend, Fanny Montgomery, 'Corpus Christi, the Feast of the Most Blessed Sacrament' which highlights the experience of Fr Hermann Cohen, a converted Jew, to the Eucharistic Divine Presence and the establishment of his 'Association of Perpetual Adoration of the Holy Sacrament'.[90] The text indicates that Fanny Montgomery, when ministering with Elizabeth to wounded soldiers outside Berlin, was known to Fr

Cohen. Another *Annals* example is 'The Miracle of the Most Blessed Sacrament' which is a Franciscan story about the Blessed Sacrament, St Anthony of Padua, the people of Bourges including the unbeliever, Guillard, and a donkey – leading to Guillard's conversion.

Elizabeth's motivation in her selection of Franciscan devotions relating to the Crib, Cross and Eucharist could be considered encapsulated in Faber's 'God So Little Loved'.[91] Elizabeth made this selection in Belle Prairie when Faber's writings were very popular in the United States, especially his book *The Blessed Sacrament*, which Joseph Chinnici claims illustrates the connection between alienation, social identity, moralism and devotional feelings among migrant populations.[92]

The *Annals'* editor, wishing to evangelize through her selected themes, highlighted God's love in a special way through devotion to the Sacred Heart which she summarizes in one particular paragraph:

> The devotion to the Sacred Heart has for its object the adorable Heart of Jesus, and the immense love with which it was inflamed for us. It has for its end to render love for love, to thank Him for his benefits and to repair the outrages which He daily receives.[93]

Franciscans participated in the increased devotion to the Sacred Heart of Jesus developing through the nineteenth century, so Elizabeth provided her readers with news of a 'collective petition' to the pope. The petition was prepared by the three Franciscan Ministers General of the First Order, on behalf of Third Order members, regarding consecration to the Sacred Heart,[94] and included a summary of French Tertiaries' activities related to this same devotion.[95] Later Elizabeth read an old manuscript showing that Franciscans had a long tradition of this devotion while her own words best describe the source:

> In these few notes translated from a valuable work, entitled *Arbor Vitae*, written in 1305 by a holy son of Saint Francis, Friar Ubertino di Casale, we have a remarkable exposition of the devotion to the Sacred Heart of Jesus three centuries and a half before the revelation of the Blessed Margaret Mary; four centuries and more before the devotion to the Heart of Jesus was propagated in the Church.[96]

What Elizabeth called 'these few notes' actually consists of a three-part serial. This is not the place to discuss at length the significance of Friar Ubertino di Casale, author of *Arbor Vitae Crucifixae Jesu*

(The Tree of Life of Jesus Crucified) or his other fourteenth-century writings,[97] but this series included by Elizabeth using Ubertino's old manuscript, probably a Venetian copy of 1485, shows her again to be ahead of her times in reading, translating and presenting in English an old Franciscan writing. The whole text has been acknowledged as Ubertino's masterwork, an extended allegory. It contains stirring meditations on the inner life of Christ, his suffering prompted by love, and that love itself as the moving force of salvation.[98] It was the love in Christ's heart for herself and God's people that Elizabeth conveyed to her readers. An 1890s *Annals'* article on the devotion to the Sacred Heart in the Franciscan Order was also published.

Mary's place in Franciscan devotions is illustrated especially by Elizabeth's 1883 publication of a five-part serial, 'Our Lady of the Angels in Porziuncula'.[99] The initial article emphasizes that devotion to Mary on this site commenced some fifteen centuries earlier, before the property came into the possession of Benedictine monks and was later given to St Francis of Assisi. The latter's acceptance of the gift, also called 'the Church of St. Mary of the Porziuncula', is described as follows:

> Never any donation could have been more agreeable to him, and there was no difficulty in promising that his dear Porziuncula should always be the head and mother of his Order as by nature and origin it was already the mother and cradle of the Order of the Friars Minor.[100]

While Catholics have recited for centuries the Joyful, Sorrowful and Glorious Mysteries of the Rosary on beads with five decades, Franciscans have also prayed the traditional Franciscan Crown on beads with seven decades to recall the seven joys of Mary. On two occasions Elizabeth explained the origin and prayer method of 'The Franciscan Crown' to her readers and encouraged them to pray it.[101] She called on the Franciscan Doctor, St Bonaventure, to help promote devotion to Mary,[102] and she wrote of St Anthony of Padua's strong devotion to Mary, which also captures her own evangelizing missionary desire, as in the words:

> Would you have your life and your death sweetened by this devotion? then never forget that Mary ... must be obeyed with obsequious promptness; that she must be loved, and loved above all else, by observing the law given by her divine Son, which is Charity – love of God and neighbour.[103]

St Anthony of Padua and the Annals

In her many devotional stories of St Anthony,[104] Elizabeth encouraged Franciscans to believe that 'God only is glorious in His Saints'. Besides devotional stories, hymns and prayers to the saint,[105] in December 1884 she introduced the *Annals'* first article on the 'Association of the Clients of St. Anthony of Padua'. Significantly by then, under Elizabeth's leadership, the *Annals'* subscribers had formed an Association, known in brief as the Association of St Anthony. The Association's organization was composed of Clients (Associates), Zelatrices (Promoters) and Benefactors. From 1884 to 1893 Elizabeth edited a series of articles under the title of 'To the Clients of St. Anthony' in which she provided titbits of news about St Anthony's followers.[106] Pope Leo XIII, in a Brief dated 31 July 1886, declared that the work of the Association of St. Anthony of Padua was truly a spiritual work of mercy. Time would show how important this Brief was to Elizabeth's mission through the press, for it saved the work when it was later threatened. That same year Elizabeth published an article 'On Confraternities' in which she commenced, 'All the modern saints extol pious sodalities as the best means of enkindling and preserving the fervour of charity in the hearts of the faithful'.[107] Elizabeth also included a segment from Cardinal Raphael Monago La Valletta's 1884 instruction to all bishops regarding the desirability of associations and confraternities, concluding with the Franciscan Order's history of twenty-six confraternities since 1267.[108]

Elizabeth's Association of St Anthony of Padua was raised to the status of a Confraternity in May 1888 by the Cardinal Vicar of Rome, Cardinal Lucido M. Parocchi. It was canonically erected under that title in the Roman oratory of Elizabeth's Franciscan generalate, with the new Confraternity remaining under the protection of Mary. Statutes, containing the Confraternity's objectives, means of attaining these objectives, conditions for admission, the organization, spiritual advantages of the members and the Confraternity's principal feasts, were printed in the *Annals*. The first means of attaining objectives was stated clearly: 'to aid in the printing and propagation of good Books and pious Pictures'.

In 1891 in June, the month when the Church celebrates St Anthony's feast, Elizabeth devoted all the articles of the issue except one to topics around St Anthony. Of particular interest is the number of times reference was made to the *Annals'* 'Work of printing and propagating good books for the purpose of instruction in those things which lead to the acquisition of eternal life'.[109]

The Cardinal Vicar's 1888 Decree also reminded Associates of St Anthony of Padua how important it was 'to have good books spread among the people' when a 'multitude of bad books' existed and when a 'fierce war' was being 'waged both against religion and against the persons and things consecrated to religion'.[110]

Like other contemporary religious journal editors, Elizabeth aimed to foster a corporate feeling among her Associates, called 'Clients of St. Anthony'. She achieved this by uniting them through prayer in a number of ways. One means was the commencement of an *Annals*' 'Obituary' which appeared bimonthly from 1886 and always commenced with, 'The prayers of the Clients of St. Anthony of Padua are requested for the repose of the Souls of the following Associates deceased.' Such a list could only be composed after Associates' letters were received and this communication further fostered members' corporate feeling. The *Annals* often advised Associates of St Anthony to address their letters to 'The Secretary of the Confraternity of the Clients, Villa Spada, near San Pietro in Montorio, Rome. Italy'. Another means of bonding her associates was the printing during 1891–4 of twenty-one articles headed 'Intentions for St. Anthony's Association' which listed all the intentions the Associates had provided. These intentions could range from 'reconciliation and peace in seven families and between four friends living in discord' to 'the successful examination of six convent schools', or from the 'cure of mental malady of two afflicted patients' to protecting 'the voyages of two Associate Sea-Captains'. Elizabeth wrote:

> It is really wonderful when we consider amongst how many individuals, nations, kingdoms and empires has arisen so great a confidence in the powerful Thaumaturgus, St. Anthony of Padua, on account of the constant protection and innumerable benefits he continually lavishes upon all those who invoke him.[111]

Elizabeth concluded this two-part article by quoting St Bonaventure's advice: 'If you want miracles, go to St. Anthony of Padua; for whatsoever you ask, believing, you shall receive!' It was this kind of trust in God, in the saints and in the spiritual life that Elizabeth endeavoured to diffuse through her *Annals*' themes.

The different wide-ranging themes in the *Annals* provide a special insight into the mind and heart of Elizabeth Hayes. The editor delighted in history, revelled in biographical sketches, especially saints' lives, appreciated poetry and showed a sense of adventure through her travel and pilgrimage accounts. In particular, Elizabeth admired the courage, faith and endurance of missionaries in distant lands, and above all else, she held most precious her Catholic faith, her religious life and her Franciscan calling. Through the predominant themes in the *Annals*, it is evident that Elizabeth was a confident intelligent editor and a generous-hearted woman, who, besides leading her Franciscan Sisters, laboured tirelessly for the Apostolate of the Press. Elizabeth's strong commitment to journalism enabled her to share with her readers, the God she knew in the depth dimension of her experiences, and what she sincerely believed was most valuable, authentic and enduring.

Notes
1 *The Month* – a Catholic Magazine and Review, Vol. XLIX, no. 231, 1883: 109.
2 Fr Hudson's name is referred to in five of the seven extant letters that came from *Ave Maria's* Office to Elizabeth Hayes in 1878–9, MFICAR.
3 Ahles, 'The Southern Adventure', *In the Shadow of his Wings: A History of the Franciscan Sisters*, 140–5. The whole chapter provides a detailed background to this difficult mission in the South; Elizabeth and Bishop William are called 'kindred spirits' and it is worthy of note that the bishop's letters to Mother Ignatius (Hayes) were signed simply 'William'.
4 It appears to the writer that Sr Chaffee looked after the printery and binding in Augusta while Elizabeth took responsibility for the school on the Isle of Hope as requested by the bishop, and later also for the noviciate, for a period.
5 Lady Georgiana Chatterton's serial contributions, 'The Cathedral Chorister' and 'Old Nurse Eleanor', exemplify *Franciscan Annals'* general stories from 1885 to 1890 that were not specifically Franciscan.
6 Umbrella titles included: Spiritual Conferences, Franciscan History & Hagiography, Articles on the Third Order, Articles for Different Occasions, Franciscan History, News of the Franciscan Missions, Franciscan Thought – historical, literary and religious sketches – and Obituary.
7 Mario Finauro, 'Annali Francescani. Una Rivista Per Il Risveglio Spirituale Del Terzo Ordine Francescano in Italia (1870–1900)', Doctoral dissertation, Pontificium Athenaeum Antonianum, 1997, 304.
8 Elizabeth Hayes, 'To the Brothers and Sisters of the Third Order', *AOLA* I, no. i (1874): 1. The same aims were repeated in volume VII, December 1882.
9 Francis Drew, 'Justine's Martyrdom: (a Tale)', *AOLA* VIII, no. i-vi (1883); 'Two Good Fridays', *AOLA* VIII, no. vii-xi (1883); 'An Orphan Boy', *AOLA* IX, no. i-v (1884); 'Little Mildred', *AOLA* IX, no. ix-xii (1884), *AOLA* X, no. i-ii (1885); 'Veni Creator', *AOLA* X, no. iv-vii (1885).
10 'Three Scenes from a French Soldier's Life', *Messenger of the Sacred Heart*

VI, no. September (1879): 152–60.

11 These were Margaret Hallahan's Third Order Dominicans founded in 1844 and who sent a community to Adelaide, South Australia, in the 1880s. Mother Drane wrote a biography of Mother M. Hallahan.

12 Joyce Sugg, *Ever Yours Affly. John Henry Newman and His Female Circle*, 213–14.

13 Augusta T. Drane, 'Rise of the Christian Schools', *AOLA* XIV, no. vi, viii, ix, xii (1889), *AOLA* XV, no. i (1890); 'Schools of Britain and Ireland', *AOLA* XV, no. iii, v, vii, ix (1890); 'The Anglo-Saxon Schools' *AOLA* XV, no. xii (1890), *AOLA* XVI, no. ii, iii, v, ix, xi (1891).

14 Augusta T. Drane, 'O Mary, Help of Sorrowing Hearts', *AOLA* V, no. xi (1880): 331–2; 'Faith and Sense', *AOLA* XVII, no. viii (1892): 231–2.

15 Statute 27 gave all Jesuits, seminary priests and other priests in England, who had come from abroad, forty days to leave the country.

16 Hayes, 'Edmund Gennings', *AOLA* XIII, no. iv, vi, vii (1888): 109–16, 171–6, 211–18.

17 Hayes, 'Why Is So Much Glory Paid to St. Anthony?' *AOLA* XVIII, no. vi (1893): 162.

18 Hayes, 'Sanctuary of St. Mary of the Angels', *AOLA* XV, no. viii (1890): 221–32. The three other writers were 'F. B. Assisi', 'Hon. Mrs. Alfred Montgomery' and 'P. Barnabe'. The story of Our Lady of the Angels at the 'Porziuncula', or Mary's feast under this title, had previously appeared in volumes I, III, VIII, IX, and XV.

19 Seven letters between 12 September 1892 and 1 March 1893 were received by Elizabeth Hayes at Villa Spada from V. Revd Fr. President (Nicholas), from St Isidore's, Rome, and then from Castel Sant'Elia. MFIC archives, Rome, section A, box 3, folder 9.

20 Articles on 'The Immaculate Conception' appeared in volumes I, III, V, X, XI, XIV, XV and XVI. Besides single articles on Bernadette, two serials were printed; one entitled 'Bernadette' which ran through 1884. On its conclusion another commenced, 'Bernadette – a Translation', followed by an article in every 1885 issue, concluding the serial of twenty instalments with another seven 1886 articles.

21 The 1892 seven-part serial on Nunzio Sulprizio, a young artisan of Naples, was published unevenly from February to December in the Annals' volume XVII, while the life of Mary Christine of Savoy in twelve-part instalments was covered in volumes XVIII-XVIV, 1893–94, with six parts each year.

22 de Breffny, *Unless the Seed Die*, 151.

23 The introduction was written either by Elizabeth or by the Hon. Mrs F. Montgomery.

24 Hon. Mrs F. Montgomery, 'Pilgrimage to La Sainte Baume', *AOLA* XVII, no. i (1892): 6–10.

25 'Pilgrims to Iona' is part of a longer article by Hayes called 'Echoes from Distant Lands', *AOLA* XIII, no. viii (1888): 255.

26 Lady Elizabeth Herbert, 'A Peep into Spain', *AOLA* VIII, no. xii (1883): 381–4; *AOLA* IX, no. i-iii, viii, ix, xi, xii (1884): 7 segments and *AOLA* X,

no. ii, xii (1885): 2 segments.

27 Hayes, 'Echoes from Distant Land', *AOLA* XII, no. i, ii, iv, x (1887): 27–31, 54–61, 123–8, 304–14; *AOLA* XIII, no. viii (1888): 254–6.

28 'Missionary Notes' appears in every monthly issue in 1880, to be followed in succeeding issues. Borneo and 'Corea' (Korea) receive mention in December 1882, while there are articles in 1885 dealing with China.

29 *Ave Maria*, the American Catholic publication familiar to Elizabeth Hayes, was dedicated to popular piety and was reputed for its devotional tone. (Joseph P. Chinnici, 'The Immigrant Vision, 1830–1866', in *Living Stones: The History and Structure of Catholic Spiritual Life in the United States*, ed. Christopher J. Kauffman, 79.)

30 Brownlow included works on the theme of angels, e.g., ones by Thomas Carlyle, Elizabeth Barrett Browning, John Keble and John H. Newman. (*Angels Ever in Our Midst.*)

31 William B. Archbishop Ullathorne, 'Cheerfulness', *AOLA* XV, no. vii, x, xi (1890): 206–13, 297–303, 334–41; *AOLA* XVI, no. i (1891): 10–18. William B. Archbishop Ullathorne, 'Our Daily Duties', *AOLA* XVI, no. ii, iv, v, vii (1891).

32 William B. Archbishop Ullathorne, *The Groundwork of the Christian Virtues*; Ullathorne, *Christian Patience.*

33 Henry E. Cardinal Manning, 'Confidence in God', *AOLA* XV no. vi (1890): 183.

34 Henry E. Cardinal Manning, 'Selfishness', *AOLA* XI, no. ix (1886): 281–4; 'Pride', *AOLA* XI, no x (1886): 305–9; 'Love Not the World', *AOLA* XIV, no. vi (1889): 189–92.

35 Oliver Rafferty provides an insightful article on Manning and this point, taken from the London *Catholic Herald*, in Ian Boyd, ed., *The Chesterton Review: Cardinal Manning Special Issue*, vol. XVIII, no. 4, November (Saskatoon, Saskatchewan: Chesterton Society, 1992), 587–8.

36 Herbert Cardinal Vaughn, 'What Are Spiritual Reading Books', *AOLA* XIX, no. I (1894): 17–21. Herbert Cardinal Vaughn, 'The Advantages of Spiritual Reading', *AOLA* XIX, no. iii (1894): 88–9.

37 Vaughan's direct editorship of the *Tablet* was respected. 'Vaughan' is now more generally used, e.g., for his brother, Archbishop Roger Vaughan in Australia, as well as later spelling of the cardinal's name.

38 Vaughn, 'What Are Spiritual Reading Books', 17.

39 Hayes, 'The Annals of Our Lady of the Angels', *AOLA* VII, no. xii (1882): 366.

40 Apart from saints honoured in the Roman calendar, the Franciscan Order has its own calendar of saints.

41 Candide Chalippe, *The Life of S Francis of Assisi..*

42 John R. H. Moorman, *St. Francis of Assisi*, ix.

43 Joanne Shattock, 'Margaret Oliphant: Journalist', in *Victorian Journalism: Exotic and Domestic*, ed. Barbara Garlick and Margaret Harris, 100.

44 Elizabeth Hayes, 'Life of St. Clare', *AOLA* VIII, no. xi, xii (1883): 339–44, 365–72: *AOLA* IX, no. i-v, vii (1884): 9–12, 54–8, 76–80, 121–7, 139–43, 191–5.

45 Hayes, 'Life of Saint Anthony', *AOLA* I, no. i-v, vii-xi (1874); *AOLA* II, no. ii (1875). 1875s page numbering continued from 1874 but later each volume commenced with page one.
46 Hayes, 'Why Is So Much Glory Paid to St. Anthony?' *AOLA* XVIII, no. vi (1893): 164.
47 Hayes, 'Life of St. Elizabeth of Hungary', *AOLA* X, no. xi, xii (1885); *AOLA* XI, i-iv, vi-xii (1886).
48 Hayes, 'Life of St. Elizabeth of Hungary', *AOLA* X, no. xi (1885): 321.
49 Hayes, 'St. Collette – Her Mission and Her Times', *AOLA* II, no. i, iii, v, vi (1875): 383–7, 463–7, 532–8, 560–5.
50 Ibid., 384.
51 Ibid., 565.
52 Mrs Parsons, *The Life of Saint Collette: The Reformer of the Three Orders of St. Francis, Especially of the Poor Clares, among Whom She Revived the First Fervour of Their Illustrious Founder*. Parsons acknowledged that her two main sources, beside old documents, were the work of Père Sellier published at Ghent (1853) and another life by Abbé Douillé published in Paris (1869).
53 The seventeen parts were composed of four in 1887, seven in 1888, ending with six in 1889.
54 Hayes, 'The Cure of Ars', *AOLA* XII, no. viii (1887): 240.
55 Manning (later Cardinal) wrote numerous prefaces for texts and translations but he did not always name the translators. In the preface for the translation of *The Little Flowers of St. Francis* executed by 'three women', discussed earlier, at least he acknowledged the 'Rev. Mother Vicaress' who was Elizabeth Lockhart.
56 Sr M. Agatha McEvoy, *A Short Life of Mother Mary Elizabeth Lockhart and Brief History of Her Franciscan Sisters*, 20. Pauline J. Shaw, *London. Following Elizabeth Hayes – Pilgrim's Guide*, 28.
57 For example, a serial of seventeen articles on 'St. Angela Merici, Tertiary of St. Francis, Foundress of the Ursulines' was printed between August 1884 and June 1886.
58 Fr Léon de Clary's four French volumes, *L Auréole Séraphique*, were translated and printed by the Taunton Franciscans (1885–87). Elizabeth Hayes used these publications as direct and edited sources. De Clary's Italian edition, *L Auréola Sérafica* from Quaracchi (1898–1900) is not be confused with '*Saints of the Seraphic Order*' from which Elizabeth translated, e.g., five 1893 instalments of 'Venerable Bonaventure of Barcelona'.
59 In the fourteenth century the friars used a compendium of practical piety edited by Fra Giacomino of Milan who drew from Bonaventure's devotional writings. *Meditationes Vitae Christi and Stimulus Amoris* derived their inspiration from Bonaventure's mystical writings. Fr Cuthbert, *The Romanticism of St. Francis*, 187–8.
60 Hayes, 'The Sixth Century of the Seraphic Doctor of the Church', *AOLA* I, no. vi (1874): 180.
61 Hayes, 'New and Complete Edition of the Works of St. Bonaventure', *AOLA* I, no. vi (1874): 205.

62	Hayes, 'St. Bonaventure, the Seraphic Doctor of the Church', *AOLA* I, no. vii (1874): 220–1.

63	St Bonaventure, 'Omnipotence in Bonds', *AOLA* XIX, no. ii (1894): 43. Elizabeth Hayes' reference to the Quaracchi publications is timely. The *Conferences of the Gospel of St. John* were published, apparently more authentic this time, in 1893 by the 'Quaracchi editors' as part of volume six in their *Opera Omnia*, an Italian ten-volume print completed between 1882 and 1902. (J. Guy Bougerol, *Introduction to the Works of Bonaventure*, trans. Jose de Vink, *The Works of Bonaventure*, 97–8, 145, 185.)

64	Ibid., 145. Further appreciation may be gained in Peter Fehlmer, 'Foreword', in *Bonaventure: Rooted in Faith. Homilies to a Contemporary World*, x.

65	Ibid., x, xiii, xiv.

66	Only in the 1970s did the English-speaking world have easy access to three Franciscan literary masterpieces in one text; St Bonaventure, *Bonaventure: The Soul's Journey into God – the Tree of Life – the Life of St. Francis*.

67	Ignatius Brady in the preface of ibid., xviii.

68	Hayes, 'The Little Flowers of St. Francis', *AOLA* XIII, no. vi (1888): 183. Previously Elizabeth had in fact included a short quote. Hayes, 'Brother Juniper – from the Little Flowers of St. Francis', *AOLA* VIII, no. i (1883): 7.

69	The 2nd edition carried the Bayswater Franciscan's motto, 'Monast Immaculatae Conceptionis', representing the Sisters who led Elizabeth to be Franciscan. Elizabeth's own 2nd edition held in MFICAR is dated 1887.

70	Hayes, 'The Little Flowers of St. Francis', 182.

71	The initials may represent Paul Feval (1817–1887) whose work Elizabeth translated for another article. She recognized the translation's 'peculiar charm', how it retained 'the amiable simplicity of the original Italian style', yet admitted that, 'in spite of the translator's best efforts', the 'expressive diminutives cannot be translated into English'.

72	P. F., 'The Little Flowers of St. Francis', *AOLA* XIII, no. vii (1888): 223–4. Praise for the translation appears justified since by late the next year the *Franciscan Annals* were recommending its 3rd edition with a new preface by Manning. {Capuchins, 'Franciscan Publications', *The Franciscan Annals and Monthly Bulletin of the Third Order of St. Francis* XIII, no. 156 (1889): 378–9.}

73	Hayes, 'The Little Flowers of St. Francis', 184.

74	Dr St George J. Mivart, 'The Grey Friars', *AOLA* XIV, no. xi (1889): 342–6.

75	St George J. Mivart, Ph.D., MD, FRS, VPZS, FZS (1827–1900) was a London convert whom Darwin regarded as a 'distinguished biologist'. Mivart's article in Elizabeth's *Annals* provides a contemporary link to secular periodicals for he wrote for the *Quarterly Review, Popular Science Review*, the *Contemporary Review*, the *Fortnightly Review*, the *Nineteenth Century* and the *Dublin Review*, among others.

76 Per volume this topic ranged numerically from twelve insertions, one every issue as in 1880, to three as in 1884, 1885 and 1887. The contemporary *Franciscan Annals* called its own similar approach 'Franciscan Chronicles' initially and changed to 'Franciscan News' in 1886.

77 'Archconfraternity of the Cord of St. Francis' concluded in Elizabeth Hayes, 'Franciscan Record', *AOLA* IV, no. v (1879): 157. This Archconfraternity had been erected in 1585 by Pope Sixtus V in Assisi under the Conventual Franciscans' care. A contemporary Franciscan publication issued an associated item. Fra Bonaventura da Sorrento, 'Cordiglio Di S. Francesco' (Little Cord of St Francis) *L'Eco di S. Francesco D'Assisi* I, Anno I, no. November (1873): 314. Elizabeth in 1886, to link this old confraternity and her new one of St Anthony of Padua, continued this topic in an article by Fr Jarlath Prendergast whose Franciscan book, *The Cord of St. Francis*, was by 1885 into its 12th edition in Dublin. Jarlath Prendergast, 'On Confraternities', *AOLA* XI, no. iii (1886): 79.

78 Elizabeth Hayes and Bernardine of Portogruaro (OFM General), 'The Present State of the Franciscan Missions', *AOLA* I, no. vi, viii, ix (1874): 176–80, 238–41, 271–6. The story's facts, originally written by the Observant Franciscan General, were previously published, according to Elizabeth, in the September and December 1873 *Revue Franciscaine*.

79 Ibid., no. ix: 276.

80 In an article on Franciscan devotions, readers were reminded how much they owed to St Francis and the Franciscans. Constantina E. Brooks, *Ave Maria*, in 'Franciscan Notes', *The Franciscan Annals and Tertiary Record* XVIII, no. 214 (1894): 384.

81 Hayes, 'Franciscan Devotions and Works', *AOLA* II, no. i, iv, vi (1875): 399–404, 482–5, 565–71. No source was named but the contemporary English *Franciscan Annals* produced a similar article which suggests the same source was used. 'Franciscan Works and Devotions', *The Franciscan Annals and Monthly Bulletin of the Third Order of St. Francis* VI, no. 71 (1882): 312–16, 357–61; with more in 1883 and 1884.

82 The caption accompanying the detailed illustration of the Greccio crib indicates 'at midnight on 24th December, 1224'. {'Illustration', *The Franciscan Annals and Monthly Bulletin of the Third Order of St. Francis* V, no. 60 (1881): 334.} Other sources, including Hayes, indicate 1223.

83 Hayes, 'The Devotion of the Crib at Greccio', *AOLA* XVI, no. xii (1891): 367.

84 Hayes, 'Christmas Day in Rome', *AOLA* I, no. xi (1874): 329.

85 Leo XIII and Elizabeth Hayes, 'Jerusalem and the Holy Places', *AOLA* XIII, no. vi (1888): 161–5.

86 Lady Elizabeth Herbert, 'Jerusalem and the Holy Sepulchre', *AOLA* XI, no. ii (1886) 53–9.

87 Angelica Chaffee, 'A Brief Sketch of the Life of the Late Sister Mary Ignatius of Jesus, OSF, Foundress of the Association of St. Anthony of Padua for the Diffusion of Good Books', *AOLA* XIX, no. x (1894): 293.

88 Henry E. Cardinal Manning, 'The Blessed Sacrament the Centre of Immutable Truth', *AOLA* XII, no. vi, vii (1887): 178–86, 193–205.

89 With reference to the English preachers, Sts Augustine, Paulinus and Winifrid, Manning writes of the time 'when the truth and grace which went out from Canterbury and York spread throughout the whole of England … Jesus dwelt there in the Divine Mystery of the Holy Eucharist'. Ibid., 200–1. John Lingard's History of England is quoted to support the claim of 'the love of Jesus in the Holy Eucharist' by Catholics of Northern and Western England. Ibid., 204.

90 Hon. Mrs F. Montgomery, 'Corpus Christi, the Feast of the Most Blessed Sacrament', *AOLA* I, no. vi (1874): 187–92.

91 Frederick W. Faber, 'God So Little Loved', *AOLA* II, no. iii (1875): 471–2.

92 Joseph P. Chinnici, 'The Spirituality of Americanism, 1866–1900' in *Living Stones: The History and Structure of Catholic Spiritual Life in the United States*, 78.

93 Hayes, (Untitled), *AOLA* I, no. iv (1874): 116.

94 Hayes, 'Consecration to the Sacred Heart – Collective Petition', *AOLA* I, no. iii (1874): 77–8.

95 Hayes, 'St. Francis and the Sacred Heart', *AOLA* I, no. vii (1874): 222–3.

96 Hayes, 'The Sacred Heart of Jesus', *AOLA* VIII, no. vi (1883): 192.

97 Writings of Ubertino, a renowned spiritual leader, included *Sanctitas Vestra* (Your Holiness) and a famous exposition of the Rule of St Francis.

98 William J. Short, *Poverty and Joy, The Franciscan Tradition*, 71. Scholars today refer to the Venetian manuscript's reproduction, edited by C. T. Davis and published in Turin (1961).

99 F. B. (Assisi), 'Our Lady of the Angels in Porziuncula', *AOLA* VIII, no. v, vi, viii-x (1883): 129–31, 161–4, 225–9, 273–7, 308–12. F. B. of Assisi used numerous Franciscan sources to enrich the articles, including *Lumi Seraphiel*, St Bonaventure's writings, *the Legend of the Three Companions* (ch. v, ix) and Thomas of Celano's life of St Francis (chs xi, xii).

100 Ibid., 310.

101 Hayes, 'The Franciscan Crown', *AOLA* VIII, no. v (1883): 159–60; Elizabeth Hayes, 'The Franciscan Crown', *AOLA* XVII, no. xi (1892): 344–5. The articles are identical.

102 For example, St Bonaventure, 'The Most Holy Name of Mary', *AOLA* XVIII, no. v (1893): 136–49.

103 Hayes, 'Devotion of St. Anthony to Mary', *AOLA* XIX, no. vi (1894): 177.

104 Tales of St Anthony were sprinkled by Elizabeth in every volume from 1885 to 1893 then climaxed with eight articles in 1894. They range from the saint's wisdom to his humility, from his defence of Mary's Assumption to bread for the poor.

105 The famous hymn, *Si Quaeris Miracula*, words by St Bonaventure and music by Cavalier Antonio Quadrini (organist at Rome's St John Lateran Arch-Basilica), appeared in the June 1891 issue and is referred to in a number of other articles.

106 News included e.g., recent celebrations of St Anthony's feast in Rome and Padua or St Anthony's Brief, and a blessing which was a kind of talisman. Hayes, 'To the Clients of St. Anthony of Padua', *AOLA* XVII, no. ix (1892): 247–8.

107 Elizabeth Hayes' introduction to Jarlath Prendergast, 'On Confraternities', *AOLA* XI, 79.

108 Elizabeth credited Prendergast with the article which is prefaced with La Valletta's letter after her own introduction.

109 The *Annals* work was quoted in the 1891 volume XVI, no. vi, in 'The Apostolic Blessing of His Holiness Pope Leo XIII: 1866 Rescript', 183, also in the 'Confraternity of St. Anthony. Statutes', 180, and in 'Brief of His Holiness Pope Leo XIII. The Confraternity of St Anthony of Padua', 184.

110 Leo XIII, 'Confraternity and Work of Saint Anthony of Padua under the Protection of the Blessed and Immaculate Virgin Mary Queen of Angels. Directed by the Franciscans of the Immaculate Conception. Decree', AOLA XVI, no. vi (1891): 178.

111 Hayes, 'The Saint of the World', *AOLA* XVI, no. xi (1891): 344.

Chapter 6

The Editor and her Contributors

On examining Elizabeth's publication today, it becomes evident that in order to gain sufficient suitable prose and poetry for her Catholic journal, she relied on individual writers, women and men, whose lives and literary works exhibited deep religious commitment. Her contributors to the *Annals* are identifiable under four categories – Women Religious, Clergy, Third Order secular Franciscans and lay Catholic writers. While most writers contributed either prose or poetry, a few contributed both; our focus will be more on the contributor than on which genre provided the content. We will look at the <u>direct</u> contributors whose names are provided by the *Annals'* editor.[1] Acknowledgement of every named contributor and his/her work cannot be attempted here so major contributors in each category will be chiefly considered with a reference to minor contributors who were also high-profile contemporaries. Together with the inclusion of the four named categories, evolving events in Elizabeth's institute will be followed.

Women Religious as Contributors

Sr Brett

In her efforts to increase religious reading, Elizabeth published the poetry of an Irish religious, 'Sr. M. Josephine, Poor Clare, Dublin', when, according to Orby Shipley, other Catholic journals and hymn books were spreading the verses of Irish men like Aubrey de Vere, Dennis F. MacCarthy and Richard D. Williams.[2] In the *Annals* this nun's poetic contribution was numerically the greatest, some thirty-three identified titles, while the variety of genre within her devotional poetry is noteworthy. How Elizabeth found this Dublin contributor remains a mystery, even after a search in the Dublin archives and in the period's published Catholic verse. [3]

Sr M. Josephine Brett (1851–1906) belonged to a branch of the Second Order Franciscans known as the Poor Clares but who, with twentieth-century adaptations, are now known as the Sisters of Saint Clare.[4] Another writer, Margaret A. (Sr Francis Clare) Cusack, better known as the Dublin-born 'Nun of Kenmare' had made famous Sr Brett's convent at Harolds Cross.[5] Sr Brett contributed to the *Annals* from 1885 until after Elizabeth Hayes' death, with a pause in the years 1888–90; the variety of her work in the *Annals* includes verses, a sonnet, a sequence, translations and reflections.

In Sr Brett's devotional themes those surrounding Mary, the Mother of God, are conspicuous; one contribution includes a translation from the Latin of Pope Leo XIII's 'In Honour of the Blessed Virgin Mary' which lost its rhyme in the translation yet retained its spirit. This translation shows Sr Brett to be a well educated 'choir nun';[6] her versatility in Latin flows over into a few titles. Her Marian sonnet provides lovely imagery combined with religious beliefs. As a vowed Franciscan, she provided Elizabeth with verses about St Francis of Assisi appropriate for the Franciscan readers, with themes including St Francis receiving the stigmata on Mt Alvernia and the saint's death. One substantial poem on St Francis, Sr Brett entitled, 'The Saint of the Beatitudes', and for another, she presents a major event in the saint's life, 'St. Francis before the Crucifix in St. Damian's'. As editor, preparing the latter for publication, Elizabeth prefaced it with a lengthy explanation to help readers appreciate the full significance of Christ's call to Francis to 'repair God's house'. Verse twelve would have pleased Elizabeth especially because of her own love of and commitment to the Rule of St Francis:

> His Rule is like a living voice
> That tells us day by day:
> 'Be poor in spirit; your reward
> Shall never pass away'.[7]

Sr Brett's poetic contributions reveal that essentially her verses are God-centred, simple and reflect her Franciscan lifestyle. This is exhibited especially in 'To St. Clare', in which she neatly composed a play on the word 'light', the meaning of Clare's name both in both Italian and Latin. Traditionally, light is the Franciscan symbol for St Clare. Elizabeth's wide choice of Franciscan devotional themes was supplemented by Sr Brett's sequence on the Holy Name of Jesus. The poet sometimes chose to introduce her work with an inspirational quotation; in one instance it was Fr Faber's words, 'The years rob us as they pass'; in another it was, 'Pure lilies of eternal peace, whose odours haunt my dreams', Tennyson's line in 'Sir Galahad'.

Alert to Church celebrations, special events and feast-days, Elizabeth published poetry that was timely and appropriate in order to strengthen her reader's faith. The idea of death, which fascinated numerous nineteenth-century poets, found its way into sensitive poems whose content conveys the message of eternal life and hope. This was the case in Sr Brett's poem on the nineteen-year-old Nunzio Sulprizio, written after the pope's Decree of his Beatification and Canonization, and placed after Elizabeth's six instalments of her translation from the French story on him. A final instalment followed, and lastly, an account by Vincenzo Nussi of the 'Decree'.[8] The editor often highlighted Sr Brett's poetry by positioning it on the issue's first page.

When Elizabeth invited Sr Brett to commence contributing to the *Annals*, the poet was a hidden unknown female religious in her mid-thirties, yet Elizabeth appreciated her work and dared to publish her poetry among professional, highly respected names like Adelaide Procter, F. W. Faber, Lady Georgiana Fullerton, Augusta T. Drane, Matt Russell, Hon. Mrs Fanny Montgomery and Henry A. Rawes. Elizabeth recognized in Sr Brett a woman with a passion for her God and, through the inclusion of her many and varied contributions, was able to achieve better the goals of the *Annals*.[9]

Mother Drane

Another gifted woman religious whom Elizabeth selected as an *Annals*' contributor was Augusta T. Drane who, as noted earlier, entered a Third Order Dominican community in 1852 and was professed at Stone in Staffordshire. Sister, later Mother, Francis Raphael Drane's early life was somewhat like Elizabeth's for she had Anglican parents, was an avid reader from childhood and in her youth was influenced by the Oxford Movement. Mother Drane, as she was known, had published ten major works before Elizabeth commenced her *Annals* and was busy writing when Elizabeth was focused on foreign missionary work. However, when Elizabeth wanted a particular kind of poem she chose Mother Drane's 'O

Mary, Help of Sorrowing Hearts' and 'Faith and Sense'. Elizabeth had an abundance of Mother Drane's works to choose from and her choices contrasted with those of the editor of the *Irish Monthly* who in 1883 published three of Mother Drane's poems and credited them to 'the Author of Songs in the Night', her famous 1876 work.

With her special interest in music and hymns, Elizabeth must have been familiar with Mother Drane's verses on the Mother of God and St Dominic that were published as hymns, and which were credited to 'the author of *Lady Glastonbury's Boudoir*', another of her works. Elizabeth was aware of the public interest in Mother Drane's work and she took advantage of this. The editor read the author's *Christian Schools and Scholars,* described as 'one of the most able and learned works ever composed by a woman',[10] then in her *Annals* acknowledged her use of it when she wanted to spread its educational content.[11] Over two years in her monthly issues, Elizabeth cleverly intertwined this educational theme with another Mother Drane story entitled 'The Chapel of the Angels' which initially appears unrelated.[12] The story, a 'literary recreation', replete with chapter headings and concluding with 'Something about the Angels', had been selected from a longer tale to enhance Elizabeth's theme of angels. Comparison shows that this story consists of the first eight chapters of Mother Drane's work, 'Uriel; or The Chapel of the Holy Angels',[13] while the ninth section refers to Milton's knowledge of angels, to 'Uriel gliding through the even on a sunbeam', and to the 'Archangel Uriel, one of the seven' in God's presence.[14]

The confidence Elizabeth had in her own ability to write, translate or edit is obvious in that she knew Mother Drane had produced an article about a famous Franciscan, called 'A Page from the Life of Blessed Angela of Foligno',[15] but she did not include it in her *Annals.* Instead she chose other sources and edited a section from Brother Arnaldo's book on Blessed Angela of Foligno, as she wrote, 'for the edification of the children of St. Francis'. The editor probably used a French copy and supplemented it with the London 1871 translation of *The Book of the Visions and Instructions of Blessed Angela of Foligno* – 'as taken down from her own lips by Brother Arnold of the Friars Minor'.[16]

Clergymen as Contributors

Outstanding *Annals'* contributors from among over eighteen clergymen were the priests Léon de Clary, T. E. Bridgett, Louis G. de

Ségur and Francis Drew with poet priests, Henry A. Rawes and F. W. Faber. Elizabeth Hayes had the kind of personality, intelligence and character admired by male church leaders and the number of influential ecclesiastics who respected her is impressive.[17] Besides Elizabeth's dealings with two popes, she also knew to varying degrees numerous high-ranking church officials whose writings had added significance for her and her mission for the Church. These officials included Cardinal Parocchi – Vicar of Rome – Cardinals Barnabo, Ledochowski, Manning, Newman, Vaughn and Lavigerie; Bishops Murdoch, Smith, Dupanloup, Seidenbush, Grace, Ireland, Ullathorne, Gross, and other high profile clergy. On appropriate occasions Elizabeth included encyclicals, papal addresses and Briefs and letters of cardinals as contributions to her *Annals*.[18] Evidence confirms that the editor did things her own way and with a definite purpose; no stranger to the Vatican, Elizabeth printed papal communications very speedily after their official announcement and often waved aside part of a serial story to give preference to the 'voice of Rome'. This was the case with an 1886 papal encyclical, and with letters of the pope to Bishop Ireland and to the American Catholic Total Abstinence Union. Also, after printing 'The Apostolate of the Press' articles, Elizabeth next published an extract advocating the Catholic press taken from an encyclical of Leo XIII addressed to Italian archbishops and bishops.

Léon de Clary

Among those who heeded the pope's words and placed 'the salvation of souls and the integrity of the Cause' before their own peace and personal interests were two contemporary French Fathers called Léon.[19] In order to better carry out her mission, Elizabeth had turned to the Franciscan Léon de Clary's *Aureole Seraphique* (Paris, 1882) for stories of lesser-known Franciscan saints. The Taunton Franciscan Sisters translated de Clary's work, which Elizabeth simply called *Franciscan Saints*; she was quick to diffuse these lesser-known Franciscan saints' stories once she had de Clary's four volumes.[20] While Elizabeth was capable of translating the original source, her earlier contact with the Taunton Franciscans together with an examination of the text and dates of de Clary's editions, indicate that she used the Taunton translations.[21]

Identification of de Clary's contribution has been possible

mainly because of access to original volumes archived by Elizabeth. Comparison of thirty-two articles on nineteen saints shows that Elizabeth at times published from '*Franciscan Saints*' directly, although for many issues she edited de Clary's work in varying degrees. De Clary devoted seventeen pages to his life of St Jeanne of Valois so the editor, without changing one word, simply spread it over two instalments.[22] In the 'St. Margaret of Cortona' article, when de Clary's work was initially used, Elizabeth edited forty-one pages into ten for the *Annals*.[23] She felt free at times to omit scholarly footnotes if they did not serve her purpose, and at other times to include and even extend them in her article. It is clear that in editing de Clary's contribution, Elizabeth not only selected content carefully but was also very particular about grammatical correctness. Her former teaching skills as well as her command of language are revealed in her ability to reshape a story without disturbing the original flow. This is evident in the story of Blessed Jeanne Marie de Maille where Elizabeth basically presents de Clary's pages in four *Annals*' articles.[24] Whether she edited material or not, from the May 1890 article on 'Blessed Crispin of Viterbo' to 'Blessed Margaret Colonna, Virgin' in December 1891, the *Annals*' index acknowledges the *Franciscan Saints* as the source.

As a committed Franciscan, not seeking worldly fame or fortune, Léon de Clary would not have been concerned how Elizabeth revamped his work for, like her, his main concern was the 'diffusion of good books' for the extension of God's reign. Elizabeth, so

Elizabeth had her own way of selecting which lives of Franciscan saints were to be disseminated. It is certainly not a de Clary's volume by volume presentation, but a selection according to her distinct thematic needs. One of these was to provide a particular saint's story during the month in which the saint's feast-day was celebrated. When she prepared her November 1888 issue she knew that the feast of Blessed Helena Enselmini would fall on 6 November, so Elizabeth used de Clary's text as a resource. This author's stories were often sub-headed with facts about birth, death or celebratory events, data often converted by Elizabeth into a more interesting historical introduction. On one occasion, in order to help her reader better situate Jeanne Marie de Maille's story, she set the historical scene for the action between 1331–1414. In de Clary's fourth volume, he wrote 'Historical Sketch of the Order of Saint Francis' in which he explains the three Orders of St Francis with their numerous branches but Elizabeth decided not to use it and instead provided her readers with a similar history derived from other Franciscan literature.

As a committed Franciscan, not seeking worldly fame or fortune, Léon de Clary would not have been concerned how Elizabeth revamped his work for, like her, his main concern was the 'diffusion of good books' for the extension of God's reign. Elizabeth, so often ahead of her times, was diffusing de Clary's stories of Franciscan Saints to English readers well before the Quaracchi Franciscan press made them available in Italy.[25] Always sensitive to her general readers as well as the Franciscans, the editor planned that in each 1894 issue over consecutive months a saint's story was taken from a non-Franciscan source.

T. E. Bridgett

Redemptorist priest-contributor, Thomas E. Bridgett (1829–1899), was another English convert committed to the apostolate of the pen.[26] He successfully entered the arena of religious publishing with *In Spirit and in Truth* (1867) which became famous in later editions as *The Ritual of the New Testament: An essay on the principles and origin of Catholic ritual.*[27] In order to enrich her Marian devotion articles, Elizabeth turned to Bridgett's popular *Our Lady's Dowry: or How England gained and lost that Title* which illustrated from history and literature medieval England's devotion to Mary. Bridgett claimed 'that in the fourteenth century England was commonly called, throughout Europe, Our Lady's Dowry'.[28]

Elizabeth Hayes helped in the restoration of English Marian devotion, beginning with a serial, 'The Holy House of Loretto' which focused on Walsingham.[29] She was familiar with Our Lady's English shrines, the most famous being Walsingham; others included Aylesford and Buckfast Abbey, such shrines altogether being estimated to number thousands before the Reformation. In 1850, when Elizabeth joined the Wantage Community of Saint Mary the Virgin, only about 250 'Lady Chapels' were believed to exist in England and Wales. Initially Elizabeth did not indicate her serial's source and, without the text's availability, identification of this source and two others would have been impossible. The following year the source was revealed as Bridgett's work when Elizabeth edited two more Marian articles. How she edited these articles reveals much about the minds of editor and author. Elizabeth's selections from Bridgett's text show her to be painstaking in her choices and indicate that she copied or edited only passages with which she fully agreed and genuinely wanted for her readers. Bridgett divided his book into three parts, one containing doctrine, written by 'native writers', current in earlier centuries, and the second containing illustrations of the various methods by which English forefathers showed their love and veneration for God's Mother. Thirdly, he asked, 'How did their Lady lose her

English Dowry?' then answered it by tracing a phase in Reformation history.[30] Elizabeth accentuated Bridgett's work on English and Irish Franciscan writers who defended Mary's Immaculate Conception and included Alexander of Hales and others mentioned in the *Collectanea Anglo-Minoritica* and in Wadding's famous *Annales Minorum.*

In the search to discover what further guided Elizabeth's selections, three modes of her use of selection and adaptation emerged. In the article, 'Our Lady Invoked at Death', which was based on Bridgett's chapter thirteen by the same title, Elizabeth selected only the first four of his twenty-two pages and deleted his footnotes. In the same year, her *Annals* had a four-page article called 'Our Immaculate Mother's Joys'. The sixteen pages of Bridgett's third chapter were entitled 'Our Lady's Joys' but only the content of the first two and last two pages of the original chapter were included. Elizabeth changed the original heading to another encapsulating two traditional Franciscan devotions, namely the Immaculate Conception and the Joys of Mary. Scholarly references were omitted yet key names, like St Peter of Blois and St Anselm, were retained in her article. In keeping with the *Annals'* Franciscan emphasis, Bridgett's illustration of humility was included through reference to 'the first celebration of the Christmas crib by Saint Francis in Greccio'. In the 1887 issue, the title of Bridgett's chapter six appears, 'Our Lady's Glory';[31] the editor skipped over the first eight pages of the original, then used four pages which she rearranged, omitted a few Latin words, then rounded it off herself with the omission of Bridgett's next two pages. The three patterns indicate that the editor accomplished her task with a clear sense of purpose and confidence in her own ability.

Bridgett's praise of Miss Adelaide Procter's 'purified imagination' confirmed Elizabeth's inclusion of this poet's verse in her *Annals.* In *Our Lady's Dowry* this apostle of the pen also opposed the anti-Catholic writer, Hallam, and proffered a contradiction to Mrs Anna B. M. Jameson.[32] The *Franciscan Annals'* editor, like Elizabeth but later, appreciated Bridgett's work and published his 'Merit of Martyrdom'. Burns and Oates, at the conclusion of *Our Lady's Dowry,* advertised Bridgett's *Infamous Publications: An Answer to Mr. Lecky and Mr. Fitzgibbon,* which further serves to show that Bridgett's works were intended for the Apostolate of the Press and the 'diffusion of good books', to which Elizabeth also was so committed.[33]

Louis G. de Ségur

Another clerical contributor was Mgr Louis Gaston de Ségur
(1820–1881), French apologist and Franciscan Tertiary. Elizabeth
recognized Mgr de Ségur's Franciscan and other literary works at
the beginning of her editorial career while in subsequent years the
Italian *Franciscan Annals* regarded him as one of their four most
important contributors.[34] Much was written about Mgr de Ségur
because of his recognized standing, and he was constantly quoted
in the Italian *Franciscan Annals* as an undisputed authority on
Third Order Franciscan spirituality.[35]

Before Elizabeth commenced a translation on Gaston de Ségur's
life, she wrote an article explaining the importance of the young
de Ségur's priestly work. She explained that he was a leader in the
'Christianising of the teeming world of the young artizan life of
Paris', and in the rescuing of youth and workers from evil and 'the
socialists of the day'.[36] The translation is 'From the French', *Mgr.
de Ségur – Souvenirs et récits d'un frère*, written by Gaston de Ségur's
brother, the Marquis de Ségur, and was presented by Elizabeth in
a fourteen-part serial. This translation, with little editorial
comments by Elizabeth, began:

> Few names in our time have been more honoured among Catholics
> than that of Mgr. de Segur, the 'blind saint'; and his brother, the
> Marquis de Segur, has earned the gratitude of all those who have
> penetrated more deeply into the sanctuary of that holy life than
> would have been possible except by the guidance of the loving and
> skilful hand which has penned the deeply interesting *Souvenirs d'un
> frère*.[37]

Mgr de Ségur wrote for the people, rather than for learned scholars and his spirited ascetical works had a popular style that aimed
above all to spread the tested insights of Catholic spirituality.[38] Mgr
de Ségur's literary ability, his contribution (through Elizabeth's
translation) of the six-part *Annals'* serial on 'The Third Order of
St. Francis' and Elizabeth's further 1883 editing of this translation
have already been mentioned. The *Annals'* editor in her first
volume also included a translation of Mgr de Ségur's interpretation of indulgences. Regarding Fr Francis Drew, attention was paid
to him and his work in our earlier discussion under contributions
of original tales.

Frs Rawes and Faber

Analysis of the religious poetry in Elizabeth's *Annals* shows that, from among six contemporary priests who feature,[39] Henry A. Rawes and F. W. Faber made the highest contribution. There were a number of personal and professional reasons related to Elizabeth's choice. Elizabeth knew Fr Rawes, an original member of Manning's Oblates of St Charles at Bayswater.[40] Qualified with an MA and DD, Rawes produced numerous poems and hymns, religious books and translations, with his best work preserved in *Foregleams of the Desired: Sacred Verses, Hymns, and Translations.*[41] Elizabeth published at least eleven of Rawes' poems from 1883 to 1893. Characteristic strains of Rawes' rapt devotion and Elizabeth's are heard in this reflection on Isaiah 9:3:

> Thought of man can never fathom,
> Tongue of man can never tell,
> But thine Angels and Thy Ransomed,
> Rapt, adoring, know it well.[42]

This same poem was selected for publication a year later by Orby Shipley in his *Annus Sanctus.*[43] Shipley acknowledged his gratitude to editors of Catholic journals for numerous contributions included in his book, and it is likely that Elizabeth borrowed some poetry from the same sources. When the editor needed a poem for a May number, May being traditionally Mary's month, she chose Rawes' work on 'The Month of Mary' with its homely simplicity of language and awareness of nature's beauty. Elizabeth selected Rawes' poetic hymns – often marked with a strain of mysticism – and appears to have been in agreement with Manning who believed that the use of English hymns was one of the most effectual means of spreading and keeping alive the devotion of the faithful.[44] In Rawes, Elizabeth had chosen a contributor whose devotionalism resonated with hers:

> May all who read these lines stand one day, glorified in the Beloved, before the Throne of God, where there is the beauty of peace, and see Jesus, 'the DESIRED,' in the house of the glory of the Lord.[45]

F. W. Faber (1814–1863), renowned preacher and spiritual author, was also an outstanding hymn writer and, in selecting his verses for the *Annals,* Elizabeth evidenced both wisdom and foresight as his verses attained leading success in shaping the spirituality of countless Catholics for a century.[46] However, Faber's verses in the *Annals* were lengthy, so while it is possible to find the same Faber poem shortened in hymnology, the latter was not the source of Elizabeth's selection. She probably took Faber's verses from his own volume of poems, or from Catholic period-icals.[47]

In her own desire to reach out spiritually to others through the *Annals*, Elizabeth selected a Faber poem that in part expressed this desire in 'The Infant Jesus'.[48] A further poem, 'Desire for God' provides an example of Faber's personal approach to a personal loving God, as in the lines:

> For the heart only dwells, truly dwells with its treasure,
> And the languor of love captive hearts can unfetter;
> And they who love God cannot love Him by measure,
> For their love is but hunger to love Him still better.[49]

Faber had a special devotion to the 'Precious Blood of Christ', reflected not only in his establishment of a Confraternity by this title, and in his work of spiritual reflection, *The Precious Blood* (1860), but also in his poem chosen by Elizabeth for the *Annals,* 'Hail Precious Blood', a translation from Italian. Elizabeth opted for Faber's doctrinally sound, subjective and personal verses in preference to a wide choice of vigorous dogmatic verses, many in Latin, by another Oratorian, Edward Caswall.[50] Caswell's verse became known through his hymns, with Elizabeth selecting his 'Hymn for the Ascension'. She opted not to include Caswell's translation of the famous 'Stabat Mater Speciosa', attributed to the Franciscan poet, Jacopone da Todi, published in the contemporary *Franciscan Annals.*

Just as Rawes, Faber and Caswall did not exhaust the impressive list of well-known nineteenth-century clerical poets, neither did they in the *Annals*, for Elizabeth also included the verses of Matt Russell, Francis Stanfield and Henry Oxenham, yet omitted those of John H. Newman and Henry Ryder.[51] Matt Russell's lines were frequently full of thanks to God for life's simple things and reminded the reader that 'In each moment my heart can discover a Fatherly Hand on my head.' The editor selected these poets' verses mainly to highlight a Church feast – Christmas, Easter or New Year – and to promote a special devotion to the Sacred Heart of Jesus, the Crib or the Precious Blood.

Third Order Secular Franciscans as Contributors

In her *Annals of Our Lady of the Angels*, Elizabeth's inclusion of contemporary women's prose and poetry was contrary to the general pattern in Victorian journals where, though a significant number of women were journalists and writers, their contributions were far outweighed by male contributors.[52] The editor valued women's contributions and the names of three Tertiaries: Hon. Mrs Fanny Montgomery, Lady Georgiana Fullerton and Lady Herbert of Lea, grace its pages.[53]

Hon Mrs Fanny Montgomery

Fanny Montgomery's major prose contributions spread from volume one to seventeen, the year before her death. Her *Annals'* obituary contains the following:

> The general reader is doubtless acquainted with one or more of her interesting works of fiction *My own Familiar Friend, The Bucklyn Shaig,* etc. It seems hardly credible that the same hand should have also given us such proof of deep study in dogmatic theology as is afforded by her really valuable works *The Divine Sequence, The Eternal Years* and *The Divine Ideal* of which the late Archbishop Porter said 'that they would survive the bulk of the literature of the century.' Perhaps no other woman has more ably mastered subjects with which few men, even, outside the priesthood, have attempted to grapple.[54]

In the *Annals'* volume one, Elizabeth acknowledges three selections from Fanny Montgomery's *The Divine Sequence,* publishing them to encourage readers to recognize God as revealed through Mary and the Church. In the same volume, on Saints and Church infallibility, Elizabeth simply introduced another three articles 'By author of *The Divine Sequence'*, suggesting she knew just how well Fanny Montgomery's book was known and respected in Catholic circles.[55] Fanny's study of theology is evident in a serial of three instalments published by Elizabeth under the Marian title so much associated with her journal, 'Mary Immaculate, Queen of the Angels'. Both editor and author's wish to spread devotion to Mary, the Mother of God, was evidenced also in a prose rendering of 'The Magnificat'. In her desire to further the knowledge of God's love and to draw a response in love, Elizabeth published articles from Fanny reflecting Franciscan devotionalism, including themes on God's love, love of the Sacred Heart of Jesus, the Eucharistic presence of love, and love's proof in the Stations of the Cross.

Faber, a favourite of Elizabeth as we have seen, provided the words of inspiration for one of Fanny Montgomery's articles which began:

> I would fain persuade some one – one would be good enough – to love God a little more for His own dear sake. Faber's *All for Jesus*

> Would to God, my dear reader, that one might be *you!* ... Just look into your own heart, and see if you cannot make room somewhere, for a little more love of God. ... And, oh! how can you *help* loving God? Why, He is always loving *you!* And all He has ever done in this great wide universe of His Creation, He has done to show you His love. The earth is full of God's love ...[56]

Elizabeth and Fanny were very familiar with Faber's writings and, like him, they wanted to share their spirituality, optimism and devotion with ordinary Christians.[57] Fanny displays this unison in spirituality – friendship with God and with each other – in her article on the Eucharist. The author observes Fr Hermann Cohen's fervour in distributing the Eucharist to French soldiers during the Franco-Prussian war, and then requests the *Annals'* readers to allow her to share a personal experience. She provides a unique insight into her ministry with Elizabeth and this well-known convert priest at Spandau, near Berlin, when they nursed sick and dying French prisoners of war. Fr Cohen planned to write music for Fanny's concluding Eucharistic poem but died while ministering in Spandau.[58] All past biographers, as noted in an earlier chapter, were unaware of Elizabeth's presence in Spandau; outside Berlin yes, but not Spandau – another example of how the *Annals* reveal both new insights and factual details about Elizabeth.

The *Annals'* editor did not fail to appreciate Fanny's ability to weave some of her life experiences into her writings and this is evident in another contribution. Fanny Montgomery's 'My Aunt's Journal' is an amazing article constructed around a character named Emm, Aunt Catherine's desire to assist him, and her waiting for letters from him.[59] It is a beautiful piece of literature containing poetic descriptions of the Italian countryside, striking imagery, deep philosophical insights, and revelations of the author's 'three lives' which are attributed in the story to Aunt Catherine.[60] In reality, Fanny saw one of her three lives situated in Belle Prairie 'with the children of St Francis' and the 'large-hearted Mother Superior, the person in the world who best knows me, the person in the world I best love'.[61]

The story was supposedly written by Aunt Catherine's nephew who travelled to her Naples home after her death and through the reading of a diary-type manuscript learnt of his aunt's long concern for Emm – the other beneficiary of her will.[62] This story, as published by Elizabeth, reveals over three months the riches of Fanny Montgomery's mind and heart.[63] If one can judge a person by their friends, then Elizabeth is to be admired for her choice of Fanny's friendship. The story indicates Fanny's philosophy of life, her understanding of people and especially her faith in a loving God who answered Aunt Catherine and others' prayers.

'My Aunt's Journal' also has a line, 'What we have once touched sticks to us', expanded by Fanny in other contributions that exhibit a psycho-religious approach in dealing with children – 'Early Influences', 'Improvement of Character' and 'Good Impulses and Moral Influence'. There is no reference in Elizabeth's *Annals* to Fanny's book, *Misunderstood,* yet it, like these contributions, shows the author's deep understanding of, and love for, children. Fanny's articles helped to raise awareness of parental influence on young children; 'lessons which linger in the heart of a full-grown man long after the lips that pronounced them are silenced for ever'.[64] Elizabeth's teaching background and Catholic belief that 'grace builds on nature' found her including Fanny's articles on early education, reminding adults of children's need for moral and religious training. These articles, forerunners of today's theories on child psychology and adult religious education, contribute in no small measure to the religious and educative nature of Elizabeth's *Annals*.

Elizabeth also appreciated Fanny's ability to write on a broad range of religious topics as evidenced in her historically based contribution, 'Letter of Saint Hilary to his Daughter', which introduces the reader to 'A Bourbon Princess in Hindustan'. Religious fervour and Franciscanism are poured out in Fanny's seven-part story of Blessed Angelina Marsciano, foundress of the first community of Third Order Regulars of St Francis, with whom she cherished association.[65] Of Fanny's single longest running contribution published in the *Annals*, 'Clare; or, The Child of Our Lady of the Angels', twenty-four instalments have survived, while others are no longer extant. Appearing in volumes one to four, the tale represents a children's reading genre which the author presents in small segments. The tale's main character, Clare, not St Clare, was a seventeen-year-old girl living with her family in a plantation mansion on a tropical island in the West Indies. The story resonates with the vibrancy of youth while Christian virtues and values are presented – 'there is a gleam of light behind every cross, and strength proportioned to its weight'. No doubt Elizabeth's missionary heart approved of her friend's ability to write a lively narrative demonstrating a teenagers' excitement over the arrival of a priest-relative who would share mission stories and Eucharist with them:

> In one instant the joyful cry arose from each one of the little party, 'Father Bernard! dear Father Bernard is come to see us!' 'How glad Aunt Gertrude will be!' exclaimed Clare. 'And what fun we shall have!' cried Charlie: 'no more dull time! We will make him talk and tell stories all day long.'[66]

The evidence is compelling: Elizabeth's evangelizing mission through journalism was strengthened and made more fruitful because of Fanny's constant contributions. When Elizabeth wanted to enrich her *Annals* with devotional poetry she again turned to her friend Fanny, a 'singularly gifted' writer. A contemporary view of Fanny's important contribution, related in her obituary, was written by Mrs R. Vansittart and published by the editor:

> Mrs. Montgomery was a fervent Tertiary of S. Francis, a most devoted Benefactress of the Association of S. Anthony, and for 16 years a constant contributor both in prose and poetry to the ANNALS OF OUR LADY OF THE ANGELS.[67]

Franciscan devotions, associated with Fanny's Franciscan Tertiary membership, are often evident in her verse, as found in her five 1874 poems, these appearing in the first year of publication of the *Annals*; in December and January issues, Elizabeth needed Christmas themes so Fanny provided, 'A Christmas card and the reply' and 'The Nativity'. Devotion to the Holy Name of Jesus was propagated greatly in the fifteenth century by the Franciscans, St Bernardine of Siena and St John Capistran, and Fanny's poem, 'The Holy Name', encourages the reader in this devotion; it shows sensitivity to nature and serves as a reflection.

The editor chose Fanny's poems to strengthen traditional Marian devotion expressed in English poetry for many centuries.[68] This is evidenced in her writing of 'The Statue of Our Lady and the Divine Infant' and 'The Two Journeys'. While Sr Brett's poetic contributions outnumber Fanny's, there is compelling evidence that both these women wrote original poems for the *Annals*. Some *Annals'* poetry is identical to that in Catholic hymn books, not so Fanny's; the richness of her contribution suggests that just as

Wordsworth influenced the devotional poetry of John Keble, she was in turn influenced in her youth by Keble, as were many other converts.[69] Every Christian story should end with a Resurrection so Elizabeth did not overlook Fanny's Resurrection poem, the title of which reflects Abraham's words, 'Give me a burying place that I may bury my dead out of sight'.[70]

While Fanny Montgomery stood out as the 'constant contributor', other Tertiaries including Lady Georgiana Fullerton and J. A. Jackman, each contributed only a few extant poems, but they may have written more as some Tertiaries simply signed their work 'A Tertiary' or used only their initials. This abbreviated style of Tertiary authorship was common in other Franciscan journals and it did not detract from the spiritual insights they brought to Elizabeth's *Annals*.

Lady G. Fullerton

Elizabeth and Fanny's high-profile contemporary, Lady Georgiana Fullerton, a Franciscan Tertiary since 1856 and distinguished for her prose, contributed only a few poems according to extant records. In her compassion for the poor, Elizabeth chose to include the lovely poem 'Sister Clare', a long and touching incident of the Irish famine reflecting the people's religious faith and the kindness of a Sr Clare who, guided by a child, delivered food to her starving family. The response to the child's plight reads:

> 'Enough, my child; come, wipe your eyes!
>   They will not die to-day,
> Nor yet to-morrow. God Forbid!
>   He hears us when we pray.'
> The Nun has ta'en her basket up,
>   Cathleen has led the way,
> To where the fisher's cottage stands,
>   Within the lonely bay.[71]

Lady M. E. Herbert

Also outstanding among Tertiary contributors was Lady Mary Elizabeth Herbert of Lea who also signed herself M. E. H.; it was under these initials that she entered volume one of Elizabeth

Hayes' publication.[72] The Christian life of Lady Herbert of Lea is reflected in the kind of religious and secular literature she produced – books, articles and translations including numerous biographies and autobiography; all were intended to spread her convert faith and to inspire others. Elizabeth depended on this woman's significant contribution for twelve years; 'The Marshall: or, a good Confession' and 'The Brigand Chief: or, the Penitent Son' were both presented in the same month of 1875.[73]

From May 1878 to March 1880, Elizabeth chose to serialize a very significant contribution, 'Life of Mary Cherubini Clare of St. Francis'. The book, *Life of Mary Cherubini Clare of St. Francis,* had been written by the Assisi Superior of St Clare's Convent, then prefaced and translated by Lady Herbert.[74] Elizabeth, with her special love for Assisi and the Poor Clares there, was particularly sensitive to this story and knew that the proceeds from the book's sale assisted the Italian nuns suffering from government persecution. Evidence suggests that Elizabeth probably knew Sr Mary Cherubini Clare and the Italian writer for she stayed in Assisi on a number of occasions in the 1860s and 1870s. Before this lengthy serial concluded, in her first 1880 issue Elizabeth commenced another serial by Lady Herbert entitled 'A Saint in Algeria'.[75] Again in 1882 and 1883 Elizabeth acknowledged Lady Herbert's religious contribution of 'The Priest of the Eucharist' while the writer's single articles describe the author's pilgrimage visits to Jerusalem and Bethlehem. A modern writer lists Lady Herbert among nineteenth-century 'Nunnish Ladies', a term created by Newman, and claims that Fr Herbert Vaughn, later Cardinal, not only critiqued some of her work but that they both spiritually guided and helped each other.[76] As a Franciscan and an authoress of many years, well-known in Catholic circles in Rome as well as London, Lady Herbert practised the Christian life style she preached through her pen; she was known as a great promoter of many charities and worthy causes.

Other Lay Contributors to the *Annals*

Members of the Vansittart family

The contributions of E. C. Vansittart and Mrs C. Vansittart, two lay women of strong Christian faith, assisted Elizabeth to carry out her goals.[77] They accomplished this not so much through devotional or theological articles but through interesting, informative and historical stories. For the general reader, E. C. Vansittart contributed a compassionately written account of her visit to 'The Refuge of Anglet';[78] after quoting Elizabeth Browning's appropriate words – 'Guide the poor bird of the snows through the snow-winds above loss' – this writer introduces the reader to the stark realities of a French Bernardine convent, orphanage and women's refuge. The editor welcomed its clear message on the values of prayer and compassion as the author shared her empathy with the hitherto abused women in the refuge. Quite different and set in Germany, Elizabeth published a shorter tale by E. C. Vansittart, a sensitive account of a poor child and her death at Christmas.[79]

Another contemporary Catholic life story is set in Rome where E. C. Vansittart had been 'a regular visitor at this Hospital [children's Hospital of the Infant Jesus] for several years'. Besides providing descriptive passages on Rome's beauty and attractions, the writer grapples with the mystery of suffering, especially the pain of disabled children in the care of St Vincent de Paul's Charity Sisters. The patience of the little sufferers is tenderly described and the reader's sensitivity heightened by the story of a blind, deaf and dumb child's response to the loving touch of the author. While encouraging and suggesting the type of donations that would bring joy to the children, the writer attempts to cope with the mystery of children's pain in her reflection:

> We may well look with awe and reverence on what the world calls 'victims', for 'their Angels do always behold the face' of our Father in Heaven, and He Who is Love, He Who said: 'Suffer the little children to come unto Me, and forbid them not,' must have some good reason in allowing them to suffer thus on earth. There is no bond like the bond of common and mutual suffering, nothing else brings us so near other souls, nothing else breaks down every barrier, and unites in the true sense of the word.[80]

In the month of September 1892 when the feast of the Stigmata of St Francis occurs, Elizabeth introduces another Vansittart woman, Mrs C. Vansittart. She does it through a translation of a 'Popular Hymn to the Seraphic Father St. Francis' for which the editor also published Galli's accompanying music. Mrs C. Vansittart provided much entertainment in her major contributions and focused mainly on pilgrimages and English history. As she herself explained, she contributed three original tales about personal pilgrimages to 'the three Great Sanctuaries of Tuscany', to Mount Alvernia, Camaldoli and Vallombrosa; each one shows the author's historical insights and reveals something of the flourishing life of religious Orders at the time, a topic close to Elizabeth's heart. For Franciscan and general readers, Mrs C. Vansittart's two-part story on the 'Sanctuary of the Stigmata of St. Francis' is attractively introduced with an illustration of the event, Dante's words on the stigmata and a short reflection on God's mercy and love for St Francis.[81] It not only describes the landscape, weather conditions and accommodation but also covers centuries of religious and artistic history. Besides dwelling on Franciscan saints associated with Mt Alvernia, the writer devotes space to explaining the hours of prayer and devotions she experienced, and includes even the antiphons of the Latin hymns.

Vansittart's second pilgrimage account which the editor chose to publish describes a journey in a horse-drawn carriage to the ancient Cistercian Monastery at Camaldoli whose tenth-century original founder was 'Romuald, a scion of the family of the Onesti – dukes of Ravenna, mentioned by Boccaccio as one of the noblest families in Italy'. While recounting Romuald's story, of conversion from a life of luxury and recklessness to one of religious commitment, Mrs C. Vansittart's style captures the reader's imagination through lively historical events and reminiscences of the monks' skill in carving, illuminating, embroidering and goldsmith's work.[82] Railway problems, something that Elizabeth experienced often in her many travels, introduced the third pilgrimage but finally the pilgrims reach the refreshing atmosphere and towering walls of the Vallombrosa monastery. The history of the old Benedictine church and the monks is unfolded, including the story of one of their distinguished lay-students, Galileo, while a portion of the story depicts the country people and their contemporary activities.[83]

Elizabeth's publication of Mrs C. Vansittart's 'Christianity under the Heptarchy: A Page from English History',[84] can be enjoyed still by the reader who appreciates Bede's *Historia Ecclesiastica* or who delights in Canterbury's old religious stories – especially those of St Augustine, Queen Bertha and other interesting figures of Saxon England. This major contribution is lengthy; the editor considered the total contribution worthy of fifty-six pages spread over seven non-consecutive issues in 1893–94. In brief, Mrs C. Vansittart set out to discredit a 'dictum' that had been initiated by a High-Church party, that 'All that S. Augustine did was to revive the Faith in England a little'. This dictum had become an issue because it had been repeated by 'one of the most advanced Ritualists in a church in S. Devon'.[85] Mrs C. Vansittart, with a wealth of resources by her side,[86] told her readers that she intended 'to consider the state of things at the time of S. Augustine's arrival and what <u>he</u> did for the nation amongst whom he found himself'. However, the author was not content to examine just the period around St Augustine of Canterbury;[87] her argument went back to 'Apostolic times' and the second century in order to show the richness of Catholic history in England, well before the coming of St Augustine and his monks from Rome. The well-read editor delighted in this exploration of English church history.

The phrase 'journeyed to Rome' was repeated regularly not merely to emphasize the physical journey of 'British saints' to Rome but also to acknowledge conversions to Catholicity. The reader is whisked through centuries up to the year '586, ie. quite nine years before S. Augustine's advent'. The scene is set for the arrival of the mission of St Augustine to reconvert England to Christianity, following the Anglo-Saxon invasions that had caused reversion to paganism. The story includes famous people and places,[88] still fascinating modern tourists and historians.[89] Mrs C. Vansittart relied partially on John Lingard's *History of England,* a Catholic ecclesiastical history of England in ten volumes, published when Elizabeth was around London in 1849. The author considered him a 'very exact Catholic historian' and supported her argument with numerous quotations from Canon Routledge to Dr O'Connor, from Gotcelinus' *History Magazine* to the '*Dublin Review* of January 1890'.

The author, sustaining her argument for the important link between the Roman Catholic Church and the English Catholic Church – strengthened as she illustrates by St Augustine in earlier times – wrote:

> St. Aidan was succeeded by Bishop Finan who built there [in York] a church of oak, covered with reeds, which was consecrated by Theodore Archbishop of Canterbury – another proof of the perfect solidarity of faith and communion between Rome, England and Scotland at the time.[90]

As in so many *Annals* issues, saints' names proliferate in the article because Mrs C. Vansittart, like Elizabeth Hayes, recognized the influence of old stained-glass windows of Catholic saints in cathedrals and churches that were later places of Anglican worship. Vansittart's conclusion is bolstered with facts about the 'British Church' that built and dedicated so many churches to St Peter, Rome's first pope.

The author's final reference is to the contemporary writer, Count de Montalembert, who said of the English Catholic Church that 'No people on earth have received the Christian faith more directly from the Roman Church and more exclusively from the monks and their agency, than the English.' Elizabeth's successor published Mrs C. Vansittart's final allegorical contribution, thus ending the Mrs C. Vansittarts' ministry of assisting Elizabeth's journal in its 'dissemination of good books'.

A third member of the Vansittart family, Mrs R. V. Vansittart, remembered for her 'In Memoriam' on the Hon. Mrs F. Montgomery, was invited by Elizabeth to contribute at least seven religious poems to three *Annals*' volumes.[91] R. V. Vansittart's first contribution was 'The Meaning of Life' followed the next year by three poems of substantially equal length and depth, with 'The Church of the Martyrs' neatly reverencing past generations of martyrs while encouraging contemporary saints-in-the-making.

Lay women of deep Christian spirituality, Mrs R. Vansittart, Adelaide Procter, Mary Howitt, Emily Bowles, Lady C. Petre and Rosa Mulholland, contributed to the *Annals*' poetry far more than the lay men, Aubrey de Vere, Denis MacCarthy, Richard Williams, Dr Reeves and John Earle. While Elizabeth employed the term 'women' in only two *Annals*' titles, and did not comment on contemporary Irish women's rights advocate, Margaret A. Cusack,[92] she certainly included women's contributions generously and especially through poetry.

A. A. Procter

The name of Adelaide A. Procter, popular English writer of verse, ranks second after Sr Brett in a tally list of the highest number of contributions by women poets in Elizabeth's *Annals*.[93] Adelaide Procter, well known for contributions to periodicals,[94] was a regular contributor to women's publications.[95] With regard to the query as to where Elizabeth obtained Adelaide Procter's and other verses, a partial answer is found in Orby Shipley's edited *Annus Sanctus*. His book was in Elizabeth's possession after 1884 and acceptable to Elizabeth were Shipley's 'Two main objects, one being devotional and one literary'. Shipley reminded readers that he was greatly indebted 'to editors of periodicals, especially of the *Month*, the *Messenger* and the *Irish Monthly*' and since Elizabeth acknowledged reading the first two, they may have been her source also.

Supported with a delicate Alexander Deberny nativity illustration, Elizabeth included Adelaide's seven verses of the 'The Christmas Moon' in her December 1890 issue. She selected this poem from Procter's 1862 publication of *Chaplet of Verses,* mostly of a religious nature, which raised finance to support a refuge for homeless women and children under the care of Catherine McAuley's Sisters of Mercy. In publishing Adelaide Procter's poetry Elizabeth was not only furthering her aim to spread the Christian message, which Adelaide embodied by her practical support of charities as well as her poetry, but was in tune with the general reader's approval of the poet.[96] Besides the dozen single Procter poetry contributions selected by Elizabeth over a number of years, she chose a series of her poems, 'The Shrines of Mary' for her 1893 *Annals.* The editor used this series of poems to preface an Italian serialized translation of a Marian theme, positioning one poem at the beginning of each issue after a delicate illustration of Mary. For the 'Young Associates of Our Lady of the Angels' Elizabeth chose Adelaide's long poem, 'Offerings to Mary, for the Month of May' which concluded:

> Give her now – to-day – forever,
> One great gift – the first, the best;
> Give your heart to her, and ask her
> How to give her all the rest?[97]

M. B. Howitt

The sensitive religious poem, 'A Child's Prayer', was a translation by Mary Botham Howitt (1799–1888), another 'lost' English Victorian author and poetess. The poem appears to have been Elizabeth's tribute to this highly respected woman who translated the Swedish novels of Frederica Bremer and Hans Christian Anderson's fairy tales, for she published it in the April volume shortly after Mary's death. The sentiment in the poem was in tune with the translator's life for Mary had watched most of her children die young. In the poem a mother dreams of the Christ child playing with her own child and the dream becomes a reality.[98]

Elizabeth's large-heartedness and convert experience made for inclusiveness as Mary Howitt and her author husband, William, followed Quakerism and spiritualism; they were known for a range of publications and produced journals including Spiritualist magazines.[99] Like Adelaide Procter whom Mary Howitt knew, she contributed at Dickens' request to his *Household Words*. Other members of the Howitts' social circle included Mrs Gaskell, Tennyson, Wordsworth, Elizabeth Barrett Browning and John Keats. Elizabeth Hayes may have personally known Mary Howitt who lived with her family for many years in Rome where Mary converted to Catholicism in old age, six years before her death. No record of Elizabeth's meeting Mary exists but English-speaking Catholics living in Rome had regular gatherings. Mary Howitt is best remembered for the well-known verse, 'Will you walk into my parlour said the Spider to the Fly?'

E. Bowles and Lady C. Petre

While Elizabeth overlooked Cardinal Newman's poetry, she included 'The Epiphany' by Emily Bowles, a convert and gifted writer (1818–1904) who looked upon Newman as mentor and friend.[100] Among her impressive literary output, Emily Bowles wrote a life of St Jane Frances de Chantal which Newman appreciated as did Elizabeth's Franciscan friends in Bayswater; she translated Mrs Augustus Craven's long, French work, *The Story of a Soul,* produced a history textbook for Irish children, contributed articles to various journals including *The Lamp* and *The Month* and published a volume of poetry.[101] The obvious reason for Elizabeth's choice to include Emily Bowles' poem in the January issue was that it met with the criterion of association with the Church's feast of the Epiphany.[102]

Three extant *Annals'* poems indicate that Elizabeth accepted contributions by Lady Catherine Petre, who had published 'for the cause of God and of truth' a collection of short poems, *Hymns and Verses.* This two-part volume contained first those verses which the author wrote before her 'conversion', with the second part produced after that event. Lady Petre's verse was known for a particular tenderness with the rhythm always correct and its metre regular. Her volume was considered suited to families and religious communities so it attracted Elizabeth who was publishing for the religious development and entertainment of both Catholic families and Franciscans. Lady Petre's life had involved much sorrow and her verses offered support for those carrying a cross.[103]

A. de Vere

Aubrey de Vere (1814–1902), critic and essayist who published in London, was prominent as a poet among his nineteenth-century Irish contemporaries. Elizabeth installed de Vere as one of her major poetry contributors from 1883 to 1891 in order to enrich her publication's religious tone. Shipley, in his well-known 1884 publication, included some of de Vere's work but none of these were chosen by Elizabeth whose selection process was based mainly on the requirement to highlight a particular church feast or a saint's feast-day. De Vere's background prepared him well to contribute to numerous religious periodicals including the monthly *Irish Ecclesiastical Review*, the *Irish Monthly* and the *Tablet* – as noted earlier.[104]

The editor of the *Irish Ecclesiastical Record* had published de Vere's 'Sonnet on St. Peter' while later Elizabeth's choice was 'The Feast of St. Peter's Chains'.[105] This poem, as with a number of de Vere's poems, was honoured by the editor with placement on a cover page. Aubrey de Vere's literary aim was to illustrate the supernatural and the quality of his verse was not only strong and vigorous but also musical and imbued with spirituality. In Elizabeth's selection of de Vere's poems an example of his vigorous style appears in the lines:

> He willed to lack; He willed to bear;
> He willed by suffering to be schooled;
> He willed the chains of flesh to wear;
> Yet from her arms the worlds He ruled.[106]

The quality of de Vere's musical and spiritual verse is exemplified in Elizabeth's reprint of the lengthy 'Hymn for the Feast of the Annunciation', chosen by her to celebrate the feast of Mary's Annunciation, 25 March.

R. Mulholland

Another contributor of special interest was the contemporary Irish writer/poet, Rosa Mulholland (Lady Gilbert), whose works became famous in secular and Catholic journals and through numerous other publications.[107] Rosa Mulholland (1841–1921), under the pseudonym 'Ruth Murray', had her long poem 'Irene' accepted by *Cornhill*, wrote the serial, *Hester's History*, for Dickens' *All Year*

Round and saw *The Wild Birds of Killeevy* first published in 1883 in the *Irish Monthly*. The *Academy*, the *Spectator* and other London critics praised it warmly. *The Wild Birds of Killeevy*, with its scenes of brutal evictions, was quoted in the *Freeman's Journal* and cited by J. H. Murphy in *Catholic Fiction and Social Reality in Ireland, 1873–1922*. Elizabeth had a sixth sense for selecting material of high quality.

Rosa Mulholland was related to an *Annals* contributor, already noted in this chapter: Matt Russell, Irish Jesuit priest and long-term editor of the *Irish Monthly*.[108] Russell regarded Mulholland's life-work of writing, her apostleship of the pen, as 'a holy and sublime vocation'. She was referred to as 'the eminent Irish *litteratrice* whose works are so generally read and appreciated';[109] Elizabeth included Rosa's 'Angels Everywhere' when she needed a poem that suited her prose theme on angels. This bright poem includes:

> They sing to us in music, they smile on us in dreams -
> They talk to us in echoes the worldly spirit deems
> But chirruping of wood-birds and chattering of streams.[110]

Other lay contributors

Katharine Tynan was a regular contributor to the contemporary *Irish Franciscan Teritary*, and though her love for all things Franciscan was evident her name did not appear in Elizabeth's *Annals*.[111] While William B. Yeats considered two of Katherine Tynan's poems on St Francis among his favourites, Elizabeth looked elsewhere. No explanation has been found as to why Elizabeth omitted the notable contemporary Irish poet, Denis F. MacCarthy,[112] while his fellow countryman Richard D. Williams, pseudonym 'Shamrock', made only one known appearance but inclusion was merited by its quality and length.[113] Irish antiquarian, Dr Reeves, whose views earned much respect, made a single but significant contribution, 'Rebuke to rebel Reason'. This 'high authority on all matters of antiquarian investigation' wrote:

> Why this zeal to deny,
>   Honouring doubt as a faith?
> Surely such scrutiny
>   Ferrets out nothing but death![114]

A December *Annals* choice of John C. Earle's poem, 'Adeste Fideles', suited the feast of Christmas.[115] Elizabeth's appreciation of the work of Earle, BA Oxon, echoed that of the *Irish Ecclesiastical Record's* editor who praised the author's article, 'English Men of Letters', published in the *Dublin Review*.[116] Earle's verses were printed in Shipley's *Annus Sanctus* while five of his poems were published in *The Oxford Book of English Mystical Verse*. In the Lenten season Elizabeth printed Earle's reflective 'Agony of Jesus in the Garden'.[117]

Aware that the majority of *Annals'* readers were American, we note that Elizabeth showed a clear bias towards English and Irish contributors. She did not select American Christian poets who were contributing to the 'golden age of the American magazine'. American poet, Emily Dickinson (1830–1886), for example, was just as reflective in her seclusion,[118] as Sr Brett or Mother Drane, while Whitcomb Riley wrote poetry featuring the Midwest region with which Elizabeth was familiar. A prose exception to these omissions was Eliza A. Starr's contributions.[119] The Franciscan editor would have known that Eliza Starr befriended the Chicago Poor Clare nuns and, by her publication on their cloistered life, made these foreign Second Order Franciscans better understood and socially acceptable in the general milieu of the United States. Starr's contribution on St Agnes suited the editor's need, according to her pattern and aims, for a story in January when the saint's feast was celebrated. The accusation put forward by the American 'Knownothing' Movement that non-American born religious leaders were strongly European in their thinking was accurate in regard to Elizabeth's choice of poetry and prose. Whatever the reason for the omission of American writers in the *Annals*, it did not weaken the religious content that Elizabeth included in her journal nor prevent its successful propagation. Elizabeth's whole literary climate was more European than American; considering her life and literary background this is not surprising.

Regarding contributors to Elizabeth's *Annals*, what is finally noteworthy is their non-competitive style for, as in many other religious journals, contributors were inspirational and in keeping with their Christian apostolate. Co-operation among the Apostles of the Press showed itself in exchanges and especially in their expressions of praise of one another's articles and literature, together with encouragement to their readers to make purchases of others' publications. To disseminate good reading among Catholics was the cherished desire of Elizabeth and her contributors; together they opposed 'writing to writing', as Pope Leo XIII had hoped for, and they helped to make her Franciscan journal a 'powerful instrument for salvation'.

Further Evolving of her Institute (1883–88)

It is easy to imagine that in Rome as Elizabeth edited material for the Sisters to print back in Augusta, she desired to have her co-workers closer; hence 1883 witnessed the transfer of the printing of the *Annals* to Rome. Sr Chaffee recalled many years later that when Elizabeth was on the other side of the Atlantic and she was in charge in Augusta, she felt that the *Annals* work struggled 'without the presence and influence' of their leader. It was a happy event when Elizabeth called the helpers to join her for they were delighted to work beside her again on the *Annals*.

Elizabeth, still brimming over with mental energy and enthusiasm at the age of sixty, clearly understood the importance of the Sisters' apostolate of the press as they shared in the war being waged against what Christians believed to be a deluge of irreligious books, newspapers and other organs promoting disorder and violence. Seven years later, Leo XIII's words, would be shouted from hilltops and printed in many Catholic journals, including the *Annals*, but in 1883 Elizabeth already was actioning her commitment to his words promoting the dissemination of 'good writing'. She determined, in his words, to 'oppose writing with writing' and, of the 'powerful engine for ruin', to make an equally 'powerful instrument for salvation'.[120]

The *Annals* editor published in the midst of enormous journalistic outpourings in which the Catholic output comprised only a fraction of the current periodical press. Even then, from a wide range of contributors to Catholic literature, Elizabeth needed to select those who would provide the type of content that matched her particular advertised aims.[121] Elizabeth, whose breadth and depth of personal reading were paramount for the success of her *Annals*, was poised in an advantageous position. Yet, besides the better-known writers and poets, she also introduced some new contributors whose work was unique to her publication. There is also a bulk of unsigned poetry that enriched the *Annals* and, while it seems likely that Elizabeth herself wrote some of these poems to suit thematic topics, proof is lacking.

With the settling in of the Sister-printers and the *Annals* work now running well in Via Alfieri, Elizabeth and Sr Chaffee set off to visit Spain. This Spanish adventure is reflected in an *Annals* article beginning in 1883 and continuing into 1885. The editor published 'A Peep into Spain', a series of ten articles written by an unidentified 'Tertiary', probably Lady Elizabeth Herbert, yet complete proof is lacking. Places named by Sr Chaffee in her memories match places described in the articles. Sr Chaffee recalled Elizabeth's visit to Spanish holy places and of her wish to have a foundation in Rabida 'to honour Christopher Columbus' – a Tertiary;[122] however, the Spanish foundation never eventuated. While they were away, the novice Frederica (Sr Benedicta) Law, the first African-American to join the Sisters, became gravely ill and Elizabeth could not have anticipated how their lives were about to be filled with great concern and then sadness. Her institute consisted only of her Roman motherhouse, an establishment in Assisi, and the Belle Prairie and Augusta convents/schools in North America.[123] On the 30 December that year, the Sisters in Rome witnessed the first death in the institute; the novice Frederica, who had come from Georgia and had inspired others by her gentle and recollected manner, died to the grief and sudden sense of loss of her companions.

'Freddie', as she was fondly called, made her profession of vows on her deathbed in the presence of the Franciscan Fr Lauer and witnesses, Elizabeth (Mother M. Ignatius) and Sr M. Agnes Riley. Mention was made earlier of Fr Lauer in relation to Germany and we will meet him again. Frederica had known much suffering because she chose a vowed Franciscan life instead of following her family's wishes to marry the man of their choice. On the morning after her death, the Franciscan Capuchin Confraternity carried her body to the baptistery of St John Lateran Basilica for burial. We can only imagine the Sisters' sorrow as on the first day of January 1884 Requiem Mass was chanted for her and her body was laid to rest. This event inclines one to reflect on the action of Elizabeth, a white European foundress who, despite social protocol, accepted a coloured woman into community in the 1880s. Before she joined the noviciate in Rome, Freddie was an early lay associate with the Sisters as was Fanny Montgomery.[124]

Around this time there was concern over financial responsibility for the two establishments in Italy, the needs of the growing institute and care of the postulants who continued to arrive. Understandably in 1884, the foundress did not attempt to visit her American convents but focused her energy on the building up of the community around her, especially in assisting the young women in formation, and of course editing and supervizing the *Annals*. In the 1880s it was difficult to attract priests to serve in the

northern part of Minnesota and just how unfortunate the consequences of accepting unsuitable and unstable clergy, vagrants from
other dioceses, was borne out in the experiences of the Franciscan
Belle Prairie Sisters. Sadly, one such a priest, Adelard Lemay was
accepted into the Vicariate; Bishops John Ireland and Rupert
Siedenbush were prepared to give him a trial and initially
supported him. The 'import' had to be moved, or he requested to
be moved a number of times between 1881 and March 1885, at
which time he was placed again for a trial at Belle Prairie. This
happened just a few months before Elizabeth's visit when the
Sisters were looking forward to having their Mother Foundress
with them again.

In the northern hemisphere's summer of 1885, Elizabeth arrived
in New York, went to Montreal to gain candidates and then travelled to Belle Prairie. Earlier in Rome she had officially accepted
two young local women into the Belle Prairie community, Adzire
Doucette (later she formally changed her name to Doucet) and
Mary Blaise. Adzire had been a boarder at the Belle Prairie convent
school and with Mary she looked forward to receiving the
Franciscan habit from Elizabeth during her visit. All was in readiness for the ceremony when a violent storm struck down the priest
from Brainerd causing him such serious harm that the intended
celebrant for the reception ceremony, Fr Buh, was urgently called
to help. As a result of the cancellation and maybe because some
Sisters expressed continued opposition to the Generalate being in
Rome, Elizabeth decided that Adzire and Mary should accompany
her to Rome, along with the Canadian women she recruited, to
receive the habit there. It was the practice of Fr Buh, well known
since 1872 to Elizabeth and to Sr Chaffee, to visit and spiritually
support the Belle Prairie Sisters, as well as to keep in mail contact
with those in Rome. As weeks passed and Fr Lemay began to show
his true colours, Fr Buh was to become a significant intermediary
as problems in Belle Prairie increased.

Lemay showed that he had no regard for the Belle Prairie
Sisters' Constitutions in regard to the practice of receiving daily
Holy Communion in their chapel rather than in a public church
and in various ways he caused them much suffering. In the twenty-
first century this may not appear a big issue but in 1885, when the
privilege of receiving the Eucharist daily was viewed differently,
this was a serious problem. By his action he showed much arro-
gance,[125] so unlike Bishop Gross in Savanna, in disregarding the
Sisters' obligation to follow their Rule and Constitutions as
approved by the Sacred Congregation of the Propagation of the

Faith. During her visit, Elizabeth discerned the growing tensions and, being a sensible woman, had instructed the Sisters to attend Mass in the parish church when it was not possible to celebrate in the chapel. Elizabeth saw only the tip of a problematic iceberg that would later emerge for the local leader, Sr M. Francis Beauchamp, her Sisters and some parishioners.

Elizabeth really cared for the Zelatrices, the Sisters who personally undertook the promotion and distribution of the *Annals*, and while she was in New York she asked the Sisters working on the *Annals* there to attend to the needs of those canvassing for their sale in Philadelphia, namely Srs M Anthony Lyons and Rose Ethier. Accompanied by her ten postulants, Elizabeth left New York at the beginning of November, but not before the two Belle Prairie postulants had a little taste of sharing in the *Annals* work with the New York Zelatrices, Sr M Leonard Kennedy and Sr M Hyacinth Leydon.[126] At sixty-three years of age, Elizabeth felt the strain of her six months' travel and visitation, yet more excitement awaited her as the Atlantic crossing was very rough and their steamer, *Scotia* of the Fabre Line, was nearly wrecked in a fog off the coast of Spain. According to Sr Doucet's detailed account, they hit a sand bank, lifeboats were lowered, local fisherman were of little help and only through the captain's commands and the 'manoeuvres' of the 'ship's men' was mobility finally gained. The group did eventually arrive in Rome in time to celebrate Elizabeth's favourite feast, Mary's Immaculate Conception, on 8 December. Meanwhile, back in Belle Prairie, Lemay became more headstrong and, as one historian described it, he initiated a 'poisonous ferment' that began affecting the school, convent, church and the surrounding countryside and it devolved on the local people to try to deal with it.[127]

What was evolving for Elizabeth in 1886? The Rome printing operation was thus described by Adzire Doucet (soon to receive the name of Sr M. Columba):

> Mary Blais and I were employed at the composition and printing of the *Annals* while most of the other postulants were occupied at the binding, printing of addresses, etc. We were very happy together and our dear Mother Foundress did all she could to look after our comfort.[128]

One of Elizabeth's happiest days must have been 18 February 1886 for this was the day when the ten women she had brought across the Atlantic were due to receive the habit of St Francis. A day traditionally known in religious institutes as Reception Day, this marked the occasion when women who desired to begin a new life with the Franciscan Sisters would, in a rich and meaningful ceremony, receive not just the habit but also a new name in order to show family, friends and the world that their new life would be 'in Christ', a life as the 'spouse of Christ'. These young women had already bravely said goodbye to their loved ones at home, now Elizabeth and the other Sisters determined to ensure that they would be made very welcome in the Franciscan family and that their life's journey would be enriched by all that Franciscan spirituality could offer.

Back in Belle Prairie the Sisters were blamed for the bishop's discovering that Fr Lemay had organized a three-day bazaar in the church building, an event to raise finance for which Lemay was obliged to have the bishop's permission but had not asked it. One incident led to another, progressively threatening the peace of the whole community. Factions began to form, replicating the experience of St Paul, when it was echoed, 'I'm for Appollo' or 'I'm for Paul' – but in Belle Prairie, it was 'I'm for the Sisters' or 'I'm for Lemay'. It is not hard to guess on whose side were the parents of Adzire Douchette and others who regularly visited the Sisters. For the Belle Prairie Sisters the real problem was their pastor versus the Rules and Constitutions of Elizabeth's Institute but what could the local people do in a situation where the clergyman was a man determined to dominate and control unreasonably? No one could have foreseen how in time the situation would escalate into irrational animosity and violence.

During 1886 the Belle Prairie situation worried Elizabeth greatly, for amid her many other responsibilities, reports reached her that Lemay had accused the Belle Prairie Sisters of being inferior teachers. He himself was a French Canadian yet he showed no compassion for the French Canadian Sisters who worked hard to do their best in the school; he distorted facts and caused trouble yet was able to enlist followers to his cause. On one hand he reported the Sisters to church authorities yet on the other he complained that they would not take on more teaching in the public school. In August Bishop Seidenbush had tried to calm the storm but by October he took the step of suspending Lemay who then defied this direction. Further official letters followed. Lemay did not leave before causing further trouble, actually using the pulpit to abuse the local Sisters and to label them bad women. In fact serious allegations regarding his own behaviour grew and the whole distasteful business became a total scandal; however, a defender of Lemay took his case to Rome for the Sacred Congregation to examine.

In the same city, Elizabeth and her Sisters had gained the approval and attention of church authorities, including that of the vicar of Rome, Cardinal Parocchi. He was knowledgeable about publishing matters; in 1878 he had founded the Italian Catholic journal, *Scuola Cattolica,* embracing all branches of theology and discipline, and he asked Elizabeth to publish a very large work in Latin that would be used in his administration and in other dioceses. Besides this and at the same time, he asked for a book, *Against Heresy,* to be translated from Italian into English and then to be printed. In the *Annals* of July of the same year, Elizabeth published a striking article by Cardinal Parocchi, 'Against Heresy in Catholic Garb', subtitled with 'Notification of the Most Eminent Lord Cardinal Parocchi, Vicar General of His Holiness the Pope' and followed by 'Translated and published by order of His Eminence'. The seven-page article targeted 'these heretical teachers desiring to destroy the Catholic education of our people' and who 'raise the standard of discord'. This article which speaks of the Church's desire for 'justice, love and clemency', together with the translation and printing of the book, provides an insight into the confidence which Parocchi and church authorities placed in Elizabeth.

Cardinal Parocchi and the Prefect of Propaganda Fide, Cardinal Simeoni, visited Elizabeth at the Sisters' convent in Via Alfieri this same year and inspected all the departments of the printing work, including the press and the bindery. Later, when Elizabeth petitioned Leo XIII for a Rescript that would classify the printing and sale of the *Annals* as a 'Work of Spiritual Mercy' for the 'propagation of good books', rather than an industry or a commercial venture, her request was granted. Her lengthy letter of petition acknowledged the encouragement she had received from the pope and Cardinal Parocchi. However, it seems that in 1886 Elizabeth may have overcommitted herself and, as she worried more deeply about news from the American houses, she became quite ill during the summer. News reached the Sisters that Lemay finally left Belle Prairie at the beginning of November but this was not to be the end of the Belle Prairie struggles.[129]

On 12 January 1887, Elizabeth Hayes grieved on hearing of the death of her own dear sister, Frances (Fanny) Sophia Hayes in England. In contrast, it was at a time when the general English populace began celebrating the jubilee of Queen Victoria. The death of one of the pioneer workers for the distribution of the

Annals occurred in Assisi on 4 October. Although Elizabeth had brought Sr M. Leonard Kennedy back from New York earlier and given her needed rest, bouts of sickness interrupted her work and finally death claimed this selfless woman at only thirty years of age. On a happier note, 13 May marked a day of great rejoicing in Rome when the ten novices made their first profession of vows. Records suggest that Elizabeth and her assistants had prepared and inspired these women so well that they persevered for the rest of their lives in their chosen vocation.

Among the difficulties and joys of that year, in June Elizabeth opened a convent known as Villa Pavoncelli in Naples for sick Sisters. She guided the training of fourteen young members in Rome – some of whom were due to return to North America to help distribute the *Annals* – and she worried over the continuing unrest among her Sisters in Belle Prairie. Elizabeth wanted to visit America again but was prevented because of ecclesiastical pressure on her to open another Roman establishment. For Elizabeth, as a Franciscan journalist, it must have been both a joy and a penance to apply herself continuously to the editorial work required as well as being a foundress handling her role of leadership. She received news from Minnesota that Lemay had been ordered out of Belle Prairie but that the parish community was divided and shattered.

In February 1888, Elizabeth opened a convent in the Testaccio area beside the River Tiber; working class people were moving into this area, an unhealthy, low-lying mosquito-infested riverside zone. The Sisters were not well received by the boisterous people among whom an anti-clerical tone was evident. This mission caused Elizabeth great anxiety as, against her better judgement and that of the Fathers at the Franciscan Curia, the convent site was located in a rough area, beset with constant fighting and even homicides. Eventually Elizabeth had to withdraw the Sisters because their health degenerated. In the following May, the new province of St Paul was erected in Minnesota and Elizabeth received news that her regular correspondent, Bishop Ireland, was appointed first Archbishop of St Paul; as noted earlier, he became a particularly powerful figure in the US hierarchy. Disturbing communications continued to reach Elizabeth and the deep involvement of the Belle Prairie Sisters in the Lemay affair threatened to bring about further problems.

This same year under Elizabeth's guidance, the Association of St Anthony was established as a Confraternity on 30 May and this further strengthened its association with the *Annals*. The significance of the Confraternity of St Anthony will be further explored later. Moving house is never an easy task and it was another challenge for Elizabeth and her Sisters in 1888 as they organized the transfer of the motherhouse from Via Alfieri to 'Villa Spada', an impressive building on Rome's Janiculum Hill. It was to become a source of great anxiety because of legal problems, orchestrated by corrupt contractors, but the assistance of a Don F. Martino would be an answer to Elizabeth's prayers.

Notes

1 Contributions to the *Annals* may be described as direct and indirect. The present writer has interpreted indirect contributors as those whose work Elizabeth Hayes used as a resource for her edited articles. Some overlap is unavoidable.

2 Orby Shipley, ed., *Annus Sanctus: Hymns of the Church for the Ecclesiastical Year*, 17.

3 Elizabeth had connections with Continental Poor Clares; she had brought the Bentivoglio Poor Clares from Via Panisperna to New York, but no links with Dublin's Poor Clares have been discovered. Sr M. Josephine Brett lived at Harolds Cross. Poor Clare archivist, Sr Marie Feely, claims that neither their archives nor oral history reveal any knowledge of Sr Brett's poetic gift. The poet's name does not appear in contemporary journals named earlier.

4 These Sisters are often called the active or teaching Poor Clares. Poor Clare nuns have been associated with Dublin since 1629.

5 Margaret A. Cusack (1832–1899), from an Irish aristocratic family, was once a member of Lydia Sellon's Puseyite Sisters, converted to Catholicism, joined the Poor Clares, became a prolific religious writer and was outspoken on befalf of Irish women and the poor; this gained attention and caused her much suffering. In the early 1880s, Margaret came to seek shelter at Harolds Cross Convent – much to the nuns' anxiety. Sr Brett was probably one of the anxious nuns; if not, she lived among those acquainted with the event.

6 'Choir nuns' recited the Office in Latin; a 'lay sister' did not. A choir nun was essentially a solemn-vow religious as recognized in canon law. Lay Sisters, who were not canonically nuns, had simple vows. It was only in 1900 that those with simple vows were canonically recognized as religious.

7 Sr Brett, 'St. Francis before the Crucifix in St. Damian's', *AOLA* XVIII, no. x (1893): 280.

8 Elizabeth Hayes, trans., 'Saints and Servants of God of the Nineteenth Century: Venerable Nunzio Sulprizio, A Young Artisan of Naples', *AOLA* XVII, no. ii, iv, vi-vii, x-xi (1892): 38–44, 118–26, 176–80, 211–20, 300–2, 329–36, 357–61; Sr Brett, 'To Venerable Nunzio Sulprizio', *AOLA* XVII, no. xi (1892); 337; Vincenzo Nussi, 'Decree of the Beatification and

Canonization of the Venerable Servant of God Nunzio Sulprizio', *AOLA* XVII, no. xii (1892): 361–4.

9 A few months after Elizabeth Hayes' death, the *Annals* recorded the death of 'Mrs. Mary Brett, the beloved mother of Sr. M. Josephine, Poor Clare ... late of Ireland'.

10 Matt Russell, 'Preface', *Irish Monthly: A Magazine of General Literature*, eleventh (1883): iv.

11 The *Annals'* fifteen articles were examined previously under educational themes.

12 Augusta T. Drane, 'The Chapel of the Angels', *AOLA* XIV, no. i, iii, iv, v, vii, x, xi (1889): 10–15, 73–9, 121–6, 143–9, 195–206, 312–18, 325–32; *AOLA* XV, no. ii, iv (1890): 44–7, 123–8.

13 Elizabeth had 'selected' eight from twenty-four chapters, published initially in another Catholic Journal. Augusta T. Drane, 'Uriel; the Chapel of the Holy Angels', *Irish Monthly: A Magazine of General Literature*, eleventh (1883): 175, 178, 183, 233, 238, 242, 291, 296. Published as a book at Christmas 1883.

14 Drane, 'The Chapel of the Angels', *AOLA* XV, no. iv (1890): 124–5.

15 Augusta T. Drane, 'A Page from the Life of Blessed Angela of Foligno', Irish Monthly: A Magazine of General Literature, eleventh (1883): 189–90.

16 Hayes, 'Counsels of Perfection by Blessed Angela of Foligno', *AOLA* XVII, no. v (1892): 154–8. Br Arnold's book in MFICAR.

17 This kind of male helpfulness and appreciation from church authorities toward religious foundresses was not common. The history of many women's congregations involved power struggles for clerical dominance over women religious, incidents often exacerbated by an unclear canonical situation.

18 Elizabeth's use differed from the way some Catholic journals handled like material, e.g., the contemporary *Irish Ecclesiastial Record* included such church items in an appendix.

19 The surname de Clary was rarely used for Fr Léon who was for a time provincial leader of the French Observant Friars Minor. The second well-known writer was Abbe Léon Monnier.

20 Léon de Clary, *Lives of the Saints and Blessed of the Three Orders of Saint Francis*, trans. Taunton Franciscan Sisters, 4 vols, vol. 1. It was followed in 1886 by volume 2 and 3; in 1887 volume 4. The 1894 issues with de Clary's contributions were headed slightly differently, 'Saints of the Seraphic Order'. The major Franciscan saints' lives had already been printed in the *Annals* before 1888.

21 After a short time in Exeter Sr M. Annunciata Roberts, who was professed in Glasgow with Elizabeth, spent the rest of her life with the Taunton Franciscans. de Breffny, *Unless the Seed Die*, 79.

22 de Clary, *Franciscan Saints*, 140–56. (The title, *Franciscan Saints*, is Elizabeth's invention for de Clary's lengthy book title.) Léon de Clary, 'St. Jeanne of Valois', *AOLA* XVI, no. ii, iii (1891): 47–56, 70–2.

23 Hayes, 'St. Margaret of Cortona', *AOLA* XIII, no. ii (1888): 55–64; de

Clary, *Franciscan Saints*, 272–312.

24 Léon de Clary, *Lives of the Saints and Blessed of the Three Orders of Saint Francis*, trans. Tauton Franciscan Sisters, 4 vols, vol. 2, 106–30; Hayes, 'Blessed Jeanne Marie de Maille', *AOLA* XVI, no. iv, v, vii, ix (1891): 108–15, 148–54, 203–7, 255–62.

25 The Italian translations of *Aureola Serafica* were not published until 1898 and 1900. The *Irish Ecclesiastical Record* praised volume one, printed a segment of Manning's introduction in it and claimed it was 'the best panegyric of the Third Order, the lives of its Saints.' A. Murphy, 'Notice of Books: *Lives of the Saints and Blessed of the Three Orders of Saint Francis*', *The Irish Ecclesiastical Record* VII (1886): 382–3.

26 Bridgett's books include *Our Lady's Dowry* (1875), *Life of Blessed John Fisher* (1888) and *Life of Blessed Thomas More* (1891). These and more are in Braintree's MFICAE.

27 High praise came from the *Tablet, English Churchman, Freeman's Journal, Month, Watchman and Wesleyan Advertiser, Literary World, Brownson's Quarterly Review, Christian Observer* and *Church Times*. T. E. Bridgett, ed., *Our Lady's Dowry; or How England Gained and Lost That Title*, 487.

28 Bridgett, ed., *Our Lady's Dowry*, 1. 'The origin of this title of honour, conferred by popular assent as much as by royal command had been lost over the centuries, yet in the Middle Ages official documents frequently referred to England as 'Our Lady's Dowry''. *The Story of Catholic England*, 47.

29 Hayes, 'The Holy House of Loretto', *AOLA* X, no. iii, v, vi (1885): 89–95, 155–9, 169–70.

30 The *Franciscan Annals* praised this work of Bridgett, which Hayes had recognized years earlier, when he preached at the 1893 re-dedication of England to the Mother of God at London's Oratory. 'The Dowry of Mary', *The Franciscan Annals and Tertiary Record* XVII, no. 199 (1893): 221.

31 Hayes, 'Our Lady's Glory', *AOLA* XII, no. v (1887): 129–32.

32 Bridgett, ed., *Our Lady's Dowry*, 102. The author refers to Mrs Anna B. M. Jameson's claim that the title, Our Lady's Dowry, first became appropriated to Mary in medieval times.

33 William E. H. Lecky (1838–1903) was an Irish historian, atheist and freethinker, who published among other anti-Christian works, *History of the Rise and Influence of the Spirit of Rationalism in Europe* (1866).

34 Besides the French Mgr de Ségur the other three major contributors were Italians, Timothy of Brescia, Venanzio of Lagosanto and Rocco Zagari.

35 Mario Finauro, 'Annali Francescani', 64–5.

36 Hayes, 'A Leaf from an Apostolic Life', *AOLA* IX, no. i (1884): 25–9.

37 Marquis de Ségur, 'Souvenirs of Mgr. de Ségur', *AOLA* IX, no. ii (1884): 33.

38 Bayswater Franciscans with whom Elizabeth had lived read two of Gaston de Ségur's books in French and his versions on St Francis and St Clare in English. MFICAE.

39 The six were Henry A. Rawes, Frederick W. Faber, Edward Caswall, Francis Stanfield, Matt Russell and Henry N. Oxenham. A notable absence among these contemporary clerical poets' names is that of Cardinal Newman, yet from his circle of poet friends the editor included Fr Faber, Emily Bowles, Aubrey de Vere and Lady Georgiana Fullerton.

40 It was common knowledge that Rawes had been an Anglican minister, converted in 1856, and was ordained the next year. Directed by Manning, he became pastoral leader in the poor district of Notting Hill. Ward, *The Life & Times of Cardinal Wiseman*, 354.

41 *Foregleams of the Desired*, published in London by Burns and Oates, was by 1881 into its 3rd edition; this edition was in Elizabeth Hayes' possession. MFICAR.

42 Henry A. Rawes, 'The Epiphany of Jesus', *AOLA* VIII, no. i (1883): 6. Also in Henry A. Rawes, *Foregleams of the Desired: Sacred Verses, Hymns, and Translations*, 98–9. Other hymns in this text republished in the *Annals* are (1892) 'Our Blessed Lady's Glory', 'St. Joseph', 'The Graces of Mary', 'To My Guardian Angel' and (1893) 'The Assumption of Our Lady'.

43 Shipley, ed., *Annus Sanctus*, 35. Shipley's work includes the names of forty contributors, sixteen of whom feature in Elizabeth Hayes' *Annals*; he used a symbol or initials for seven contributors, two of which Elizabeth also used.

44 Manning's Letter of Introduction, Rawes, *Foregleams of the Desired*, 11.

45 Ibid., 24. Elizabeth Hayes' own final words in life were, 'I desire my God'. Chaffee, 'Memories', 59.

46 Today English-speaking Catholics over fifty years of age can recall Faber's well known hymns: 'Jesus My Lord, My God, My All', 'Faith of Our Fathers', 'Mother of Mercy, Day by Day' or 'Hail, Glorious Saint Patrick'. The highly popular St Basil's Hymnal contains thirty-five of Faber's verses accompanied by tunes ranging from Hadyn to traditional melodies. Willan, ed., *St. Basil's Hymnal.*

47 Shipley acknowledged taking verses from *The Month*, the *Messenger* and the *Irish Monthly*. Shipley, ed., *Annus Sanctus*, 20.

48 Frederick W. Faber, 'The Infant Jesus', *AOLA* IX, no. xii (1884): 351. Shipley published a few verses of 'The Infant Jesus' for his hymnal while Elizabeth Hayes printed seven. Shipley, ed., *Annus Sanctus*, 23.

49 Faber, 'Desire for God', *AOLA* IX, no. xi (1884): 343.

50 Among Caswall's principal works was his *Lyra Catholica*, a translation of all of the Breviary and Missal hymns with some others; it was reprinted in 1884 but Elizabeth made no selection for the *Annals*.

51 Matt Russell, brother of Lord Russell, was Jesuit longstanding editor of the *Irish Monthly*; during this time he accepted, like Elizabeth, contributions from de Vere, Bridgett, Drane, Fullerton and Mulholland. Francis Stanfield (1835–1914) is best remembered for his hymns, in particular 'Sweet Sacrament Devine'. Henry N. Oxenham (1829–1899) educated at Harrow and Oxford, was an English controversialist, writer and poet who moved in the Manning, Lockhart, Pusey and Dollinger circle. Many of J. H. Newman's verses became Latin hymns and not suitable for the

Annals' purpose. Henry Ryder was a Birmingham Oratorian.

52 Lloyd Davis, 'Journalism and Victorian Fiction', in *Victorian Journalism: Exotic and Domestic,* ed. Barbara Garlick and Margaret Harris, 201.

53 Hon. Mrs Fanny Charlotte (née Wyndham) Montgomery (1820–1893), with an impressive genealogy, married Alfred Montgomery in 1842 and had two daughters, Mrs Finch of Burley-on-the-Hill and the Marchioness of Queensberry, Mrs Douglas. The parents separated, wealthy Fanny embraced Catholicism, was free to travel, write and assist church/charitable groups. One of her homes was in Rue St Honore close to the Louvre, and she was Elizabeth Hayes' friend and benefactor from the 1860s. Lady Georgiana Fullerton (1812–1885) was a distinguished English novelist, a verse and religious writer, who converted to Catholicism in 1846. Her contribution to the Apostolate of the Press has been acknowledged in a number of biographies while Yonge paid her credit among *Women Novelists of Queen Victoria's Reign.* Lady Herbert of Lea (1822–1911) assisted Miss Stanley, Florence Nightingale and others during the Crimean Campaign. A philanthropist, author and translator, she wrote to support the cause of religion and to better finance her seven children after her husband's death.

54 Mrs R. Vansittart, 'In Memoriam', *AOLA* XVIII, no. iv (1893): 122. English-born George Porter (1825–1889) was Archbishop of Bombay; as a Jesuit he had formerly lived and ministered among the literary men of Farm Street, Mayfair, and the many converts known to Elizabeth Hayes and Fanny Montgomery.

55 Fanny Montgomery, 'Why Do We Invoke the Saints?' *AOLA* I, no, iii (1874): 65–70. Fanny Montgomery, 'The Infallibility of the Church', *AOLA* I, no. iv, v (1874): 97–101, 133–6.

56 Fanny Montgomery, 'The Love of God', *AOLA* I, no. v (1874): 152.

57 Pauline J. Shaw, *Companion to the Diary,* 69–70.

58 Montgomery, 'Corpus Christi, the Feast of the Most Blessed Sacrament', *AOLA* I, no. vi (1874): 191. Fr Hermann Cohen (1821–1871) was a famous German Carmelite convert from Judaism. Taken to Paris by his mother, he became a pupil of Franz List, enjoyed the highest social circles of Europe, and had a hectic career as an internationally acclaimed concert pianist. In 1847 through a religious experience when conducting a Parisian church choir, he converted to the Catholic faith and led many others in the same path. He received the Carmelite habit in 1849, was ordained priest (1851) and commenced a lifelong preaching ministry in all the capitals of Europe. With the blessing of Pius IX, Cardinal Wiseman invited him to England where he was appreciated by London Catholics, including Elizabeth Hayes and Fanny Montgomery, and by 1867 he was in the French Alps. Amongst his numerous works is *Thabor* (1870), five collections of sacred songs with accompaniment. As chaplain to some 5,300 French prisoners in terrible conditions at Spandau, he contracted smallpox and died there.

59 Montgomery, 'My Aunt's Journal', *AOLA* VIII, no. x – xii (1883): 302–7, 334–8, 373–80.

60 Fanny Montgomery, alias Aunt Catherine, with all her wealth did not locate her 'three lives' in the places where she owned houses – Paris, London, Naples and probably Rome also – for, as noted earlier, she described the Belle Prairie convent beside the Mississippi and called her associations her 'second life'. As a mother with two married daughters, surely her family was her first life and possibly her writing her third.

61 Montgomery, 'My Aunt's Journal', *AOLA* VIII, no. xii (1883): 373–4.

62 Emm, so the reader learns in the final paragraph, was also known as Captain C. and later Fr Ambrose of the Franciscan Order.

63 Also published by Montgomery in *The Month*, vol. XLIX, no. 231, 1883:107–28. The story is so convincing that the present writer at first believed that Fanny Montgomery's 'mysterious' nephew wrote it about her. Signing it A. Montgomery, Alfred being her former husband's name, assisted the initial confusion.

64 Montgomery, *Misunderstood*, 49. MFICAE.

65 Montgomery, 'Blessed Angelina Marsciano: Foundress of the Third Order Regular of St. Francis of Assisi', *AOLA* VIII, no. i-vii (1883): 1–5, 13–39, 65–9, 98–104, 132–6, 183–9, 211–14. The contribution's concluding article was dated, 'Rome. May 6, 1882', evidence that Fanny Montgomery at times wrote specifically for the *Annals*.

66 Montgomery, 'Clare – a Tale', AOLA I, no. i(1874): 32.

67 Mrs R. Vansittart, 'In Memoriam', *AOLA* XVIII, no. iv (1893): 122.

68 The earliest vernacular poetry to celebrate Mary is credited to Cynewulf, before the time of Alcuin and Charlemagne.

69 Keble was professor of poetry at Oxford from 1831 to 1841; *The Christian year* (1827), his volume of poems for Sundays and feast days, was a major influence during the Oxford Movement and familiar to converts from Anglicanism.

70 Montgomery, 'Bury the Dead', *AOLA* II, no. iv (1875): 486–7. It was signed simply, 'F.M., Member of the Third Order of St. Francis'.

71 Georgiana Fullerton, 'Sister Clare', *AOLA* I, no. xi (1874): 333.

72 Lady (Mary) Elizabeth Herbert, 'Human Respect or What will People Say?' *AOLA* I, no. ix (1874): 255–63. She may have contributed some articles signed, 'A Tertiary'. Mary Elizabeth Ashe A'Court moved in the highest early Victorian social circles and married Sidney Herbert, a politician who became Secretary of War.

73 Herbert, 'The Marshall: Or, a Good Confession', *AOLA* II, no. v (1875): 511–19. It reappeared in December, 1882. Herbert, 'The Brigand Chief: Or, the Penitent Son', *AOLA* II, no. v (1875): 522–31. The latter was unsigned but bears the hallmarks of Lady Herbert, including her experience of Palermo.

74 'Life of Mary Cherubini Clare of St. Francis', *The Month and Catholic Review* III (XXII), no. xi (cxxv) (1874): 363–4. This book was acknowledged also in the *Dublin Review* and recorded in Bishop Ireland's scrapbook. *John Ireland Papers – Index Book (of Five Reviews) 1863–93*.

75 *A Saint in Algeria* was published (1883) in book form which suggests Elizabeth Hayes may have had early access to the script or part of it.

76 Joyce Sugg, *Ever Yours Affly*, 225, 228, 230. Lady Herbert remained on friendly terms with Newman and Lady Fullerton and like the latter reflected in her writing a great admiration for the French Sisters of Charity.

77 Based on limited personal evidence in their work combined with the story of the Vansittart family, who once owned the former Bisham Abbey in Berkshire, these Vansittart women appear to be sisters-in-law. Their names have not been found in contemporary journals.

78 E. C. Vansittart, 'The Refuge of Anglet', *AOLA* XIV, no. iii (1889): 68–72.

79 E. C. Vansittart, 'Lina's Christmas', *AOLA* XV, no. ii (1890): 61–3.

80 E. C. Vansittart, 'Hospital of the Infant Jesus at Rome', *AOLA* XIV, no. v (1889): 140.

81 Mrs C. Vansittart, 'A Pilgrimage to 'La Vernia' or Mt. Alvernia' *AOLA* XVII, no. ix, x (1892): 267. (Sanctuary of the Stigmata of St Francis). Dante was a Franciscan Tertiary.

82 Mrs C. Vansittart, 'A Pilgrimage to Camaldoli', *AOLA* XVII, no. xi, xii (1892): 338–43, 67–72.

83 Mrs C. Vansittart, 'A Pilgrimage to Vallombrosa' *AOLA* XVIII, no. ii (1893): 45–54.

84 'Heptarchy' means government by seven rulers, a reference to the early Anglo-Saxon kingdoms in England.

85 This was Bishop Phillpotts of Exeter, a Camdenian or member of a movement much concerned with ritual solemnities, church structure and decoration. This movement contrasted with the Oxford Tractarians whose emphasis was doctrinal. Owen Chadwick, *The Victorian Church, Part One, 1829–1859*, 213.

86 Resources named by the author: Bede's fundamental *Historia Ecclesiastica* (History of the English People), books written by Protestant and Catholic writers, journals and pamphlets, including the work of Protestants Rees, Sharon Turner and Archbishop Parker; writings of Hume, Gildras, Dr Trench, Revd A. D. Crake and Green; Smith's *Ancient Geography* and his *History of England Literature* and a Romily Allen pamphlet.

87 Augustine arrived in 595; the Heptarchy's period was seventh and eighth centuries.

88 King Ethelbert and Queen Bertha, Edwin, Lindisfarne, Columba, Queen Ethelburga, Cuthbert, Wilfrid, Hilda, Canterbury, Jarrow and Whitby.

89 A Kent historian claims that Queen Bertha's father had controlled Tours, her mother had been a friend of Tours' bishop and that her sister in Tours was a nun; this further confirms Queen Bertha's connections with the St Martin of Tours church in Canterbury, the oldest extant Christian place of worship in England. Richard Gameson, *Saint Augustine of Canterbury*, 12.

90 Mrs C. Vansittart, 'Christianity under the Heptarchy: A Page from English History', *AOLA* XVIII, no. xi (1893): 325–6.

91 Mrs R. Vansittart basically wrote poetry while the two other Vansittart women contributed prose; she remains something of a mystery.

92 *The Month* reviewed Margaret A. Cusack's, *Woman's Work in Modern Society* (1874) and *Donahoe's Monthly Magazine* printed 'The Ex-Nun and Her 'Libels''. 'Catholic Review: 5. Woman's Work in Modern Society', *The Month* III (XXII), no. IX (CXXIII) (1874): 118–23. Peter McCorry, 'The Ex-Nun and Her 'Libels'', *Donahoe's Monthly Magazine* 21, no. 6 (1889): 541–8.

93 Often only the *Annals'* index, not the text, carried the poet's name and in some years or months even this was absent. Calculations are based on evidence available.

94 Dickens' *Household Words; All the Year Round; Merry and Wise;* and *Reformatory and Refuge Journal.*

95 Emily Faithfull's *Victoria Magazine, Home and Work* and the *English Woman's Journal.*

96 Adelaide Procter's 1858–60 poems collected under Legends and Lyrics reached a tenth edition by 1866 and her works were published in America and translated into German. By 1877 this sympathetic woman's poetry, praised by Dickens, was in greater demand in England than those of any living writer except Tennyson.

97 Adelaide A. Procter, 'Offerings to Mary, for the Month of May', AOLA I, no. v (1874): 162.

98 Mary Botham Howitt, 'A Child's Prayer', *AOLA* XIII, no. iv (1888): 108.

99 The Howitts are credited with writing 180 books between them. One of the Howitts' major works is *The Literature and Romance of Northern Europe* (London: Colburn and Co., 1852).

100 Emily Bowles, 'The Epiphany', *AOLA* XVI, no. i (1891): 1–3. Felicity O'Brien, *Not Peace but a Sword: John Henry Newman*, 154.

101 Sugg, *Ever Yours Affly*, 157, 243.

102 Bowles, 'The Epiphany', 2–3. Also published, as *Three Kings*, by the *Dublin Review* in Jan. 1874.

103 Catherine Petre, 'Road to Calvary', *AOLA* XII, no. vii (1887): 206.

104 Aubrey de Vere, an admirer of Wordsworth and Coleridge and a convert influenced by Manning and Newman, had published many works including ones with strongly religious themes.

105 Aubrey de Vere, 'Sonnet on St. Peter', *Irish Ecclesiastical Record* (1867): 601, in Revd P. J. Canon Hamel, *Indexes to the Irish Ecclesiastical Record from 1864–1963* (Dublin: Browne & Nolan Ltd., 1963), n.p. Aubrey de Vere, 'The Feast of St. Peter's Chains', *AOLA* XIV, no. vii (1889):193–4.

106 de Vere, 'Mater Christi', *AOLA* IX, no. ii (1884): 59.

107 Rosa Mulholland's work was commented upon in the *Irish Monthly, The Month, Donoghue's Monthly Magazine* and in Shiply's *Annus Sanctus;* the *Irish Ecclesiastical Record* praised her editing for children of Defoe's *Robinson Crusoe*. Glasgow: James McLehose and Sons (Publishers to the University), 1911. 'Notice of Books: Robinson Crusoe. Edited by Rosa Mulholland', *Irish Ecclesiastical Record* VII (1886): 671–2.

108 Matt Russell, a Jesuit, was youngest of a large upper middle-class family. His famous brother, Sir Charles Russell, QC, MP, married Ellen Mulholland, the sister of Rosa Mulholland. Matt's sister, Katherine (Sr

M. Baptist Russell), was California's first Sister of Mercy. C. W. Russell, an uncle, was contributor to various papers and journals, including Matt's, for thirty years.

109 Description of Mulholland in an article on Sir Charles Russell. ATS, 'Memoir of Charles Russell, Q.C., M.P.', *Donahoe's Magazine*, June 1889, 598–601.

110 Rosa Mulholland, 'Angels Everywhere', *AOLA* XV, no. i (1890): 30.

111 Katharine Tynan (1859–1931, Mrs Hinkson) published collections of poems, over one hundred novels and five volumes of autobiography. She contributed to the *Irish Franciscan Tertiary* which in 1890 alone printed her poems 'St. Francis and the Ass', 'St. Francis and the Birds', the serialized tale 'A Lost Bairn' and 'Maurice and Eugenie Guerin'.

112 His poem, 'For the Epiphany', is in Shipley's book and was chosen in 1895 by the next *Annals*' editor, a fact that suggests Elizabeth used this book.

113 R. D. Williams, 'Imitation of 'Dies Irae'', *AOLA* XIX, no. xi (1894): 303–5. R. D. Williams, known for his promotion of Irish periodical literature, wrote devotional poetry for the Sisters of Charity as well as famous patriotic songs for his countrymen. (Shipley, ed., *Annus Sanctus*, 17.)

114 B. Reeves, 'Rebuke to Rebel Reason', *AOLA* XIX, no. vi (1894): 184. Irish Catholic journals acknowledged his work as in 'Notice of Books – the Culdees of the British Isles by Dr Reeves', *Irish Ecclesiastical Record* I, no. October 1864 – September 1865: 444–9.

115 John C. Earle, 'Adeste Fideles', *AOLA* XIX, no. xii (1894): 351–2.

116 'Notice of Books – the *Dublin Review*. January 1882', *Irish Ecclesiastical Record* III, 3rd series (1882): 125–6.

117 John C. Earle, 'Agony of Jesus in the Garden', *AOLA* XV, no. ii (1890): 33–4.

118 Mabel L. Todd & T. W. Higginson, eds, *Favourite Poems of Emily Dickenson*, 15.

119 Elisa Allen Starr, 'San Pietro in Montorio', *AOLA* XIV, no. i (1889): 1–7. Starr, 'St. Agnes, Virgin and Martyr', *AOLA* XV, no. i (1890): 22–9. Elizabeth Hayes' source – Eliza Allen Starr, *Pilgrims and Shrines*. MFICAR.

120 Pope Leo XIII, 'The Catholic Press: Extract from an Encyclical Address by His Holiness Pope Leo XIII to the Archbishops and Bishops of Italy', *AOLA* XV, no. vii (1890): 189.

121 Her aims, named earlier, were to provide 'matter of interest to the general reader' and to present 'the progress and development of the Franciscan Order – its missions, new foundations and good works, as well as the past history, legends and traditions of the Franciscan Movement'.

122 Chaffee, 'Memories', 42–5.

123 The term 'institute' is used to mean the whole religious community or congregation.

124 The term 'lay associate' is used with today's meaning in mind not the description provided by Elizabeth in relation to the Association of St Anthony for the *Annals* yet both women were *Annals*' helpers.

125 'Hitlerish determination' according to one biographer, Ahles.

126 Adzire Doucet, 'Memoirs of Mother M. Columba Doucet', written 1950, typescript privately circulated by MFIC Generalate, Rome, May 1982, 3.
127 Ahles, *In the Shadow of His Wings*, 184.
128 Doucet, 'Memoirs', 4.
129 Further details of 1886 in Ahles, *In the Shadow of the His Wings*, 192–212.

Chapter 7

Her Strategies in Production and Distribution

In order to do battle with her pen through 'the propagation of good books'; Elizabeth weighed up the factors critical to her journal's success. These essential factors, basically production strategies, involved reading widely, the skill of editing, availability of printing facilities, publication capacity with substantial financial backing, all-weather distribution plans and a targeted audience. Through consideration of these factors her successful methods of production and distribution demonstrate that she was a significant contributor to Catholic journalism.

Elizabeth knew the importance of reading as preparation for the genre of journal she published, and reading had been her delight since childhood. As we have seen, one of the texts Elizabeth chose to edit for her first volume was the 'Life of St. Anthony' which is indicative not only of her admiration for this illustrious Franciscan saint but also of her desire to imitate Anthony's opposition to the heresies of the times. From the outset Elizabeth's monthly publication was to be a means of spreading good reading and of combating what she understood to be the heresies of her day being propagated at the time through a deluge of anti-Christian and anti-Catholic newspapers, journals and books. She responded with originality to a challenge later issued by Pope Leo XIII – 'of this powerful engine for ruin make an equally powerful instrument for salvation'[1] – but it had to be preceded by continuous reading. Living in pioneer Minnesota and later in Georgia, Elizabeth collected an impressive range of international material from which to select, according to her chosen criteria,[2] the various books, manuscripts and articles she wished to edit and publish.

Editing Skills

During her twenty-one years of editing material for her journal, Elizabeth established her main editorial offices at Belle Prairie (Minnesota), Augusta (Georgia) and in Rome's Trastevere.[3] The most successful editors often modelled their publication on other journals that met a particular demand or had attracted large readership due to superior quality. There is no reason to suspect that Elizabeth did otherwise. She once had access to London's successful models which, though not necessarily favouring Catholicism, included well-known secular journals. Often the place of publication was considered significant for nineteenth-century journals, but for Elizabeth, who was more focused on achieving her stated aims than on providing local stories, her place of editing and publishing was of small consequence to topics except in a few instances. However, access to Vatican and Italian materials did increase the number of articles and illustrations about Rome when she published there, especially in the early 1890s.

Around the mid-1850s, when Elizabeth was surrounded by English journals, John Henry Newman observed that journalists 'wrote so much and so well', and in terms of style, he considered '*The Times* writers surpassed even Dryden and Swift'.[4] According to Newman, if the interests of religion were to be promoted and edification was to result, then Catholic journalists needed to look first to their prose.[5] Elizabeth appreciated the importance of quality prose, which included maintaining a good style and a high tone in a journal. It was her 'high toned and interesting' prose, even before the first print rolled off the press, that attracted praise in *The Brainerd Tribune*,[6] and again after the first volume was published, when the printer 'determined to bring it, typographically, up to the standard of its merit and high tone'.[7]

At the beginning of her publishing career Elizabeth wrote many of the articles and expressed herself with depth, flair and clarity. In addition, she edited many original articles. Her editorial approach is revealed in an article, originally by Léon de Clary, called 'Jane of Signa',[8] where Elizabeth disapproved of the original's long paragraphs so she broke them into shorter ones; she considered some of de Clary's footnotes significant enough for the text and rewrote them. Elizabeth's actions in this and numerous other articles indicate her confidence in editorial work. In general, she showed herself to be a rigorous editor and was not prepared merely to reprint a chapter of a book or another's journal article but fashioned content in a style that met her exacting standards.

At times Elizabeth applied or selected the narrative style for which her friends, Fathers Hecker and Lockhart, were famous. This was to put Catholic teachings into conversational form and link them together with a narrative thread in order to produce a story. This style is similar to that adopted by the *Annals* contributor Mrs C. Vansittart and not unlike that used by Newman and other successful Catholic journalists, who applied the method of conversationally discussing a Protestant's statement or criticism clearly used to introduce the script.[9] A contemporary and regular reader of the *Annals*, Bishop John Ireland, considered Elizabeth's literary skills a 'talent' and he expressed himself as delighted that her 'talent' was used in his diocese of Minnesota.[10]

As editor, Elizabeth was aware that all Catholic journals treating of religious or theological matters must be submitted for censorship. The official Church believed that not only was 'bad press' a danger to faith and morals but that it had the responsibility to ensure that all Catholic publications adhered to sound teaching, as expressed in Catholic doctrines and dogmas; hence bishops were authorized to appoint qualified and impartial censors. Elizabeth (Sr M. Ignatius) Hayes' name did not appear on the *Annals*; instead each number concluded with the church approval, 'Cum Approbatione Auctoritatis Ecclesiasticae'.[11] This censorship was required even though Elizabeth held an ecclesiastical Rescript, Brief and Decree approving of the *Annals*' work as a 'Spiritual work of Mercy' and granting the *Annals*' Confraternity of St Anthony canonical status. Over the years the censors' names changed but one of special note is that of Joseph Doebbing, a highly qualified Franciscan censor, because it further underlines Elizabeth's journalistic capability.

Munster-born Joseph (Bernard) Doebbing (1855–1916) migrated to America from Germany during the *Kulturkampf*, was ordained and became a professor.[12] He was director of the Irish College of St Isidore in Rome when he censored Elizabeth's *Annals*. The fact that Doebbing in this role was delegate general, whose jurisdiction at a period extended over Capranica and St Elia, throws light on Elizabeth's letters to and from Castel St Elia regarding her research; this culminated in a pamphlet for the Friars and in material for *Annals*' articles.[13] These letters provide the best insight into the enormous amount of work, correspondence and translations required of Elizabeth to achieve accurate results when editing old manuscripts.[14] Her difficulties are acknowledged in a part of Doebbing's letter regarding proofs she submitted which read:

You must understand from the corrections which you may see it is deemed necessary to make, that the approval of translations from this book is a matter of no small delicacy and difficulty, because the book though containing much that is interesting and useful, is certainly a very strange book.[15]

Another letter from Doebbing acknowledges Elizabeth's zeal and hard work:

I know that changes are troublesome when the work has reached a certain stage, but it has not been easy to get at the truth in regard to some matters mentioned in the first part of the little sketch, and I feel sure that your zeal will lead you to admit that this work of yours is worth doing well.[16]

Time and again Elizabeth applied to the Vatican for its approval of new censors and papal authorities would reply saying that the undersigned authorized the named priests 'to re-read and sanction for publication the periodical entitled the Annals of Our Lady of the Angels'.

Printing of Words and Illustrations

In the fifteenth century printing was called the 'divine art'; in the next century Franciscans as far away as Mexico were committed to printing, but it was through the nineteenth century's improvements in printing and illustration techniques that the 'divine art' became big business. This resulted in reduced production costs and mass circulation, especially in the United States. St Paul, the main city in Minnesota Territory, boasted of Goodhue's Press which produced its first newspaper, the *Minnesota Pioneer* in 1849. In the 1850s Goodhue's printers were composing lead type in a gallery while Goodhue dedicated himself to promoting Minnesota's image, with his issues reaching major Eastern newspapers, which ensured even further circulation.[17] By coming to Minnesota Territory, Elizabeth was not beginning her *Annals'* venture in a printing backwater; as already mentioned, besides St Paul, there was St Cloud, close to where Elizabeth launched her 1874 journalistic mission, which had a number of printing houses.

For Elizabeth to have her first issue printed in January 1874, and for Mr Russell, her printer, to have promoted her forthcoming publication in his Brainerd newspaper the previous December,[18] many decisions had to be completed well ahead. These decisions included layout, costs and printing matters including diversity of typefaces, quality of paper, cover style, number of pages, deadlines and more. While women compositors, though few in number by comparison with men, had succeeded in some printing offices,[19] Elizabeth had to wait until her community expanded enough to employ young Sisters as typesetters. Meanwhile, Russell's Brainerd establishment accomplished the printing. In the 1870s type foundries published illustrated specimen books, with related costs, showing the range of typefaces from simple to ornamental and a variety of borders, corners and other stock for lead and wooden presses.[20] We noted earlier that it was in Chicago that Angelica (Sr M. of the Angels) Chaffee learnt the printing skills that assisted Elizabeth to gradually organize her own printing office. Sr Chaffee's memories indicate that for a period a 'little Pearl print-ing press' was used in Belle Prairie, with Mr Russell, their former printer in Brainerd, bringing the press monthly even in winter across the snow,[21] but for the Augusta printing office better equip-ment was purchased in late 1878.[22] However, this still meant the typesetting Sisters experienced the fatigue of standing at the case for long hours as they prepared each line of words and justified it by hand ready for the printer.[23] Elizabeth understood the spirit of commitment needed for the Apostolate of the Press and its associ-ated hard work of typography. In an article she published her admiration for the young women, such as those of the newly founded Society of St Paul, who dedicated their lives to this mission.[24] Extant *Annals* printed in Augusta show that Sr Chaffee also acted as *Annals'* secretary and that her work, and that of the other Sisters, was vital to the *Annals*. Sr Chaffee recalled that when Elizabeth was away in Rome, she was left in charge of the *Annals'* work which involved:

> ... the arranging of the articles, proof-reading, the mailing etc. Sr. M. Agnes had charge of the composition and the binding, and Rosaline aided Frederica on the printing, also aided now and then in every department of the work ... we were all called to Rome together... the *Annals* work went on lamely ... following the counsel of the Cardinal Vicar and the Secretary of Propaganda, she [Elizabeth] had it transferred to Rome.[25]

Mother M. Columba Doucet recalled her involvement in 1887:

> As soon as I was professed (13 May 1887) I was left in charge of the printing and composition of the *Annals*. Except for a couple of months spent in Assisi and about three or four months in Posillippo,

Naples, I remained in Rome busy with the *Annals.* I remember going
one day to Mother Foundress' room with a proof sheet of an
article...[26]

Illustrations and general presentation were important elements in
the success of Elizabeth's periodical. She witnessed not only the
increasing nineteenth-century use of illustrations in books and
journals, but also the great appeal that illustrated articles had for
readers, so she ensured that illustrations were an aesthetical
component of the *Annals. Punch* had firmly established comic illustrations in the Victorian periodical field but, as to be expected in a
religious journal, Elizabeth's *Annals* were dominated by religious,
often Franciscan, illustrations. The illustration had the capacity to
bring an image close to the Victorian reader and, while images
could be improved through the technique of lithography, wood
engraving continued to dominate journal illustrations. Wood
engraving contained finer detail than wood cut and had become
popular for reproducing illustrations from the end of the eighteenth century.

Elizabeth selected, in particular, images of Christ, Mary, saints
and angels. The frontispiece of the 1887 January issue was unusual
with the Christ Child framed with intricate delicate figures; at the
top was Christ surrounded by children, while on both sides
hovered an angel and each corner was filled with a bunch of grapes
(appendix 6.1, fig. i).[27] One Marian illustration (appendix 6.1, fig.
ii) focused readers' attention on 'The Patronage and Cultus of the
Most Blessed and Immaculate Virgin Mary'.[28] The *Annals* oldest
extant frontispiece is a half-page illustration of 'Saint Veronica
Galiani' and this particular mode of presentation was repeated.[29]
The editor made 1886 a benchmark for illustrations by increasing
the number and variety. An innovative example is a portrayal of St
Francis on Mt Alvernia, incorporating the saint's love of creation
by setting the crucifix in a leaf background (appendix 6.2, fig. i).[30]
A lace-like border around a picture of St Joseph reproduced the
delicate frame formerly used for 'St. Elizabeth of Hungary' (appendix 6.2, fig. ii).[31]

Among the various illustrations of St Anthony of Padua, three in
particular are worth a comment. Positioned in the article, 'St.
Anthony's Tuesday', was 'Vera Effigie di St Antonio di Padova', a
full-length illustration of St Anthony reclining. Under it was
printed in Italian and in English, 'True likeness of St. Anthony
which is venerated in Arcella under the Altar where the Saint
expired in the year 1231',[32] (appendix 6.3, fig. i). Another picture

(appendix 6.3, fig. ii) also entitled 'True Likeness of St. Anthony of Padua', is explained by Elizabeth's caption:

> A copy of the true likeness of St. Anthony of Padua, which through the kindness of His Grace the Archbishop of Spoleto has been taken for the Association of St. Anthony, from the original fresco, preserved in the Palace della Genga in Spoleto. This fresco was brought from Padua to Spoleto in the year 1232, on the occasion of the Saint's Canonization, and presented by the Delegates of the citizens of Padua, to the then reigning Pontiff Pope Gregory IX residing at that time in Spoleto, and who with the solemn ceremonies of the Church, inscribed the Blessed Anthony in the Catalogue of the Saints.[33]

Elizabeth's admiration for this painting, copied for the Association of St Anthony, is significant for it is recorded in the Association's Statutes that she valued the importance of religious illustrations. Under 'Means' for Statute 2, Elizabeth wrote, 'To print and publish good books, and pious pictures: to propagate Catholic literature ...'[34] The Statutes of the Association, later Confraternity, became slightly changed but the 'propagation of pious pictures' was retained.[35] When Elizabeth directed a separate printing of the Statutes, the picture of St Anthony was prominent.[36] The picture of St Anthony with the Mother and Child encircled with the words 'Societas S. Antonii de Padua' (appendix 6.3, fig. iii) appeared regularly because it introduced the 'Intentions for St. Anthony's Association', followed by the 'Obituary'. The 'Obituary', often introduced by the picture of a decorated cross, commenced with: 'The prayers of the Clients of St. Anthony of Padua are requested for the repose of the Souls of the following Associates deceased.'[37]

As well as the images printed in many nineteenth-century illustrated magazines, landscapes were also popular. Elizabeth chose vistas of churches, chapels, and places of retreat or of religious significance. Frontispiece full-page vistas appeared from the 1886 October issue introducing a delicate series on Roman buildings and churches beginning with 'The Basilica of S. Peter and the Castle of S. Angelo, in Rome, as taken from a distance', to be followed by others.[38] The 1890 issues strongly favoured landscapes of Rome with seven different scenes framed in identical artistic style frontispieces.[39] This impressive style is illustrated by 'Piazza Navona and the Church of St. Agnes, Virgin and Martyr, Rome' (appendix 6.4).[40] Elizabeth's original aim, to entertain the Franciscan reader as well as the general public, was reflected in this selection of 1890s frontispieces, for, besides the scenic public

places, she included four Franciscan frontispieces.[41] 'The
Sanctuary of the Portiuncula, in the Basilica of St. Mary of Angels,
Assisi', is shown in appendix 6.5. These Franciscan illustrations
were chosen to match the month in which the saints' feasts were
celebrated. 'La Sainte Baume, St. Mary Magdalene's Retreat' was a
full-page image that illustrated Fanny Montgomery's French
pilgrimage article of the same title.[42]

A selection of smaller religious illustrations,[43] like most others
carrying no signature, were used creatively by Elizabeth, such as on
an issue's title page, for an appropriate theme or to fill a spare
space on a page so that a major article could begin on the following new page. A set with various Marian images was used regularly
for title pages. The *Annals* also regularly used attractive ornamental initials for the first letter of the word at the commencement of
poems or special articles. Elizabeth's favourite one encased the
delicate form of an angel within the ornate letter. Another method
used to make the journal pleasing to the reader's eye was the
regular use of dainty borders and frames. The Sister-printer's skill
in linking fancy corners to one another by differently shaped line-
work to form a frame became more and more evident over the
years. Elizabeth's *Annals* always adopted an undivided page layout
and never, like some journals, presented its contents in columns.[44]

Elizabeth's use of illustrations grew as the years passed so that
gradually a variety of religious and other suitable subjects were
depicted through line drawings and halftones of different shapes
and sizes in each month's issue. This growth reflected the particular woodblock and type-foundry business with which Elizabeth and
Sr Chaffee dealt. It was a business that possessed picture and type
libraries from which buyers could select, and so they had increasing access to the kind of illustrations required to match Elizabeth's
text. Growth in the number and quality of the illustrations also
reflects Elizabeth's growing ability to defray the purchasing costs of
wood blocks and fonts. The *Annals'* cover, like most other contemporary Franciscan journals, featured a printed illustration of the
Franciscan coat of arms, yet Elizabeth chose her own distinctive
style (appendix 6.6).[45] The *Annals'* cover remained much the same
in the years up to 1884 but by then illustrations needed to improve
to keep abreast of other Franciscan journal covers, for example,
the *Irish Franciscan Tertiary.*[46]

For the signed illustrations, Elizabeth ignored line drawings and
half tones of famous English artists and chose repeatedly the work
of French-born Alexander Deberny (1809–1881) of Paris. While
artists had depicted saints' lives for centuries, it was Deberny's St

Francis, St Clare and St Anthony that adorned the *Annals*. Deberny's work, 'St. Francis of Assisi', showing the traditional Franciscan habit and cord, stigmata and halo of sainthood, appears in a number of issues. The illustration of St Clare is a rare one in Franciscan literature while Deberny's St Anthony had to compete with numerous other more popular images (appendix 6.7). Deberny's symbolic illustrations for Mary, the Eucharist and the papacy were finely detailed and appealing while his delicate floral settings graced many pages. The artist's daintily etched nativity scene with its reverent angels (appendix 6.8, fig. i) was applied by Elizabeth to illustrate two poems, 'The Christmas Moon', and later 'The Nativity'. By comparison, the contemporary English *Franciscan Annals* contain far fewer illustrations yet they produced a larger remarkable nativity scene by the artist, W. T. Beane Piux.[47] Adelaide Procter's poem, 'The Angel of Prayers', was illustrated by Deberny's image of an agile angel carrying a large fish (appendix 6.8, fig. ii).[48]

Two contrasting Assumption illustrations, in the same 1894 *Annals* issue, are Spagna's illustration of Mary's Assumption that introduces the article 'St. Anthony Defender of the Assumption of Our Lady' and a line-drawing frontispiece, 'The Glorious Assumption of Our Blessed Lady' (appendix 6.9).[49] Other extant *Annals*' illustrations that bear signatures include three religious pictures – a monstrance surrounded by angels and signed F. Simon S., an angel in knight's armour watching at a bedside by L.B., and a Papal Coat of Arms signed B.L.[50] Elizabeth's commitment to religious illustrations in her journal with their related costs and work contrasts with the boast of the *Franciscan Annals'* editor who wrote in 1893 that the friars aimed to make their publication 'the cheapest of magazines'.[51] The meaningful illustrations in Elizabeth's *Annals* set the publication apart, provided added pleasure to the reader and dignity to the religious content. Through her arduous search for appealing illustrations, she lived out the words of another pioneer who said, 'I am ready to ... wear out my head for the Apostolate of the Press'.[52] The successful publishing of the *Annals* by Elizabeth and her 'Members of the Third Order Regular of Saint Francis of Assisi', as the covers acknowledged, was a source of admiration to others. St Paul's Bishop Grace believed the *Annals'* work would be repaid with fruitful results,[53] while Savannah's Bishop Gross recommended the *Annals* to all in his diocese, describing them as interesting, well written and 'replete with useful and edifying information'.[54]

Publishing – including finance

Elizabeth had a recipe for success when so many other secular and religious journals failed. Besides her ability as a talented prose writer and the commitment of the members of her institute to this apostolate, careful examination suggests that the combination of three key elements – financial stability, dependable regularity and communication skills – contributed especially to her successful publishing. Many Victorian periodicals that failed did so because of financial difficulties; it was vital to have financial stability. From the beginning of her enterprise, Elizabeth had the support of her very wealthy friend, the Hon. Mrs Fanny Montgomery, who continued to aid Elizabeth financially from their early days together in France. In Fanny's obituary she is described as 'a most devoted Benefactress of the Association of S. Anthony' which implied 'pecuniary aid'.[55] A printing enterprise also needed to exhibit prudence in its expenditures, to gain regular income, and to ensure profit, and the *Annals'* publishers achieved this.

The survival of Elizabeth's institute, which depended so much on the *Annals'* income, was proof of this financial success. Many contemporary journals contained advertisements in order to gain income that would supplement subscriptions and balance the expenses but the only advertisement ever printed in the *Annals* was one for itself which, with slightly varied format, appeared seldom. As *Annals'* secretary for much of the period discussed, Sr Chaffee's involvement was a key factor in financial matters.[56] Earlier we mentioned that Sr Chaffee praised her editor's dependable regularity; she was always on time and this is a key element in successful publishing. Another aspect of regularity meant delivering to readers what they had learned to expect in a publication. Elizabeth, by her faithfulness to her aims, determined a level of expectation to which she measured up continually.

Archival materials in particular are proof of Elizabeth's communication skills in regard to her publication. In her memories Sr Chaffee highlights the earliest letters about the *Annals* from Bishop Thomas Grace.[57] In replying to Mother M. Ignatius (Elizabeth Hayes), Bishop Rupert Seidenbush communicated his approval and recommendations through numerous letters and not only for publishing the *Annals* in English but also in French and German.[58] There is no other existing reference to this, nor any proof, that French and German companion issues existed. Franciscans from Teutopolis in Illinois to Calvary in Wisconsin, together with correspondents from Washington and New York, rejoiced over the *Annals* in their communications with the editor.[59] Archival packets of letters, cards and permissions provide some indication of the communication that was expected of Elizabeth in regard to every aspect of publishing. One wonders if she ever slept. A series of incoming letters from the *Ave Maria* printing office at Notre Dame, Indiana, provide an insight into the bulk of information requested by Elizabeth when she planned purchasing a new press for Augusta, along with details about paper, ink and other printing necessities to be purchased from southern companies.[60] Over the years, Elizabeth had a reputation for communicating face to face about her *Annals* and took advantage of railroad travel to visit and converse, for instance, going to the Santa Barbara Mission in 1873, Notre Dame (Indiana) in 1878 and when passing through New York on a number of occasions.

Other important communications successfully engaged in by this pioneer Franciscan journalist were petitions to the pope for approval of *Annals*' censors,[61] while intimately associated with the *Annals* work were the communications related to the Association (Confraternity) of St Anthony of Padua. Elizabeth made the final decision about the amount of associates' correspondence to be included in the regular articles, 'Intentions for St. Anthony's Association' and the 'Obituary'.[62]

Distribution

The *Annals*' distribution with its emphasis on personal delivery by Zelatrices, supported by rail and sea transport, contributed highly to its success and fruitfulness. Such a service was not trouble-free as Mother Doucet recalled about New York in 1884:

> We had some sort of an office there for the *Annals* which were sent from Rome in large sacks. The Zelatrices (as the Sisters on the *Annals* apostolate were called) often had one kind of difficulty or another with the post office officials so their presence was needed to settle these problems.[63]

From the outset, Elizabeth knew that her method of distribution would depend significantly on railroads and so 'Brainerd on the Northern Pacific Railroad' was her first choice as the town from which circulation would commence.[64] Around this time, laws were passed providing inexpensive mailing rates for periodical literature, so she took advantage of this and mail orders were encouraged through her Brainerd post office box number.[65] Not only was the journal destined for distribution in the USA but requests from overseas were welcome.[66] According to Sr Chaffee, who was one of the first Zelatrices chosen in 1878, the *Annals* was first propagated through 'a lady' who travelled for subscriptions and gained the first sixty.[67] Gradually circulation became largest in North American cities, New York and Philadelphia, then Boston and later Chicago. These were the cities in particular where the Zelatrices walked from home to home to gain subscriptions and then returned with the *Annals*.[68] Later we will see that nine of these ten Zelatrices were lost from the *Annals* work when they separated to join the Little Falls diocesan foundation. One Zelatrice from Philadelphia, Sr M. Gabriel Keenan, wrote to Elizabeth, 'I must say that I love the Annals very much ...'[69] However, eight fresh, full-time Zelatrices were working in the USA in 1890, led by the experienced Sr M Anna Flannery, and this number alone indicates how the Franciscan Sisters' Apostolate of the Press could soon regain lost ground and continue to flourish.[70]

The distribution of the *Annals*, the collection of the *Annals* subscription, and the general work of the Zelatrices were inter-woven.[71] Elizabeth described her organisation of the Zelatrices' work:

> Zelatrices are those who, being so authorized by the head of the Direction, co-operate in the propagation of good books, labour to increase the number of new Associates, and collect and send into the office of the Association the subscriptions and offerings of the Associates.[72]

The words, 'being so authorized by the head of the Direction', were vital since begging was prohibited,[73] and so Elizabeth had to ensure that her Sister Zelatrices had her authorization to distribute and personally collect money for the *Annals*. Besides the 1881 Letter of Approbation for the Zelatrices, in 1886 Sr Chaffee explained that Elizabeth:

> Obtained a special rescript of the Sovereign Pontiff, acknowledging the work of the Association as a SPIRITUAL WORK OF MERCY, and afterwards an Apostolic Brief, raising it to the rank of a Confraternity.[74]

A copy of the Rescript was published in the editor's fuller article on the Association, sub-headed, 'Rescript from the Holy Audience of July 31st 1886', and should have been understood by all bishops. It stated:

Our Most Holy Lord Pope Leo XIII having listened to the relation of the undersigned Cardinal Vicar, graciously acceded to the prayer of the petitioner, that the Work of printing and propagating good books for the purpose of instruction in those things which lead to the acquisition of eternal life, shall be regarded as a true Work of Mercy, which, the other conditions not wanting, will be followed by the promise of Eternal Beatitude. (Signed) L. M. Card. Vicar.[75]

The Sister Zelatrices knew that they, as well as editor, compositors, printers and other workers, co-operated as Franciscans in a ministry that reached out to people through the journal and in this fulfilled a Christian work. By propagating the *Annals*, which meant tramping the streets in all kinds of weather and lodging with people away from their community, Zelatrices were Apostles of the Press. A 2001 interview with a retired Zelatrice, Sr Katherine Collins of Newton, Boston, revealed that those who visited homes of *Annals*' recipients extended care and compassion to those they met besides delivering the journal. Zelatrices, also called 'Advocates', 'Sister Promoters' or 'Sisters on the *Annals*', knew that their unique role in the organizational structure was different from that of the Associates and the Benefactors. 'Associates are those who have their names and surnames inscribed upon the Register of the Association and contribute towards its object', while 'Benefactors are those who in a more special manner give their protection and personal influence to this holy work and who also strengthen it with pecuniary aid.'[76]

The Zelatrices' method of collection included recording in their accounts the amount of money received, then showing the deduction of their small weekly living expenses and finally sending the remaining amount to Elizabeth's office. This collection system, with Sisters working in pairs, differed from that of other contemporary organizations; for example, Pauline Jaricot for the Propagation of the Faith introduced a pyramid collection system with a widely branched well-organized network.[77] When the first journals were sold the subscription price was $2.00 annually for the twelve monthly issues per year, $5.00 for three annual subscriptions to one address, $10.00 for six such subscriptions, while single numbers cost 20 cents each.[78] At the time of issue of the third volume, when the publishing in Belle Prairie became 'exclusively the work of the Sisters themselves', the subscription price was announced as $1.25.[79] During the years when the printing office was in Harrisonville (Augusta), Sr Chaffee recalled that, 'Our Annals subscriptions increased to upwards of 10,000'.[80] The terms of subscription were then described as:

Post-free; $1.25 a year, in advance. Clubs of five to one address, $5.25; Clubs of ten ditto, $10.00. All who desire to subscribe are requested to forward their names and addresses with the amount of subscription, to the Secretary. Money may be sent either in Registered Letter or by Post-Office Order.[81]

In 1881, the income from the *Annals* subscriptions more than doubled from the previous year, from $4087 to $9047.[82] Growth in the numbers of young women joining Elizabeth's Franciscans meant a significant increase in the number of helpers for the Apostolate of the Press. Regarding 1887, Doucet wrote:

We were sixteen for Profession which number included the six novices who were clothed in April 1885. The older of the newly professed sisters were sent out as Zelatrices for the Annals, the subscriptions for which were rapidly increasing.[83]

Sr Ahles examined some extant and incomplete archival account sheets and concluded that the *Annals*' income was significant, presumably including profit, and for 1887 she calculated an income of around $10,135.[84] In 1888 and again in 1893, the Rome printing office published the yearly subscription, including postage, for the United States, as $1.25 in advance, with European subscriptions set at five shillings.[85]

Even though Elizabeth obtained her Letter of Approbation for the Zelatrices in 1881, her fears over misunderstandings about distribution and collection were justified, for it became a controversial issue in the United States. Later, some Zelatrices were disturbed when they encountered bishops who either misinterpreted or were unaware of the Letter of Approbation. Sr Chaffee recorded that at this time, another motivation was unsettling the Minnesota group, namely a desire by some for 'the separation of the American houses from the Roman'.[86] (The session of the Little Falls group will be recalled later in this chapter.) In spite of the Letter of Approbation, confusion increased when some Sisters from the Little Falls diocesan group shared a concern that Zelatrices did not have the necessary church approval for their *Annals* work. Perceptions and motivations were complex for those involved, resulting in most Zelatrices joining the Little Falls group and thus lost from the *Annals* ministry in 1890. This created serious repercussions, including the dramatic drop in the 1891 *Annals* income, when receipts fell from $15,000 to $4,000.[87] However, through Elizabeth's tireless leadership, Sr M. Anna Flannery returned to the USA in January 1891 with a new group of

Zelatrices; they overcame many and varied obstacles, resulting in the recovery of the *Annals* circulation. Somewhat reminiscent of Elizabeth's distribution of Oxford Movement Tracts with Puseyite women, her method of *Annals*' distribution by women was successful. Through the subscriptions collected by the Sister Zelatrices, Elizabeth's Franciscan institute was able to support itself, but more importantly, Elizabeth and her Sisters continued to contribute to the mission of the Catholic Press.

Readers

Readers associated with Elizabeth's *Annals* were called subscribers, associates, clients and members, and they appear to reflect the nineteen-century readers who preferred to read periodicals to books in the ratio of ten to one.[88] Elizabeth often used the term, 'dear reader', thus giving the subscriber the feeling of being personally addressed with a message from the editor. When the editor commenced her journal she stated clearly that she was writing for the 'general reader' and for Franciscan readers. Along with contemporary editors of Franciscan journals, Elizabeth believed that the Franciscans should provide quality journalism for the Third Order readers but she ventured a step further by also publishing for a wider audience. This approach meant that the *Annals* readers came from a larger clientele and it guaranteed greater potential for success among readers with an appetite for Catholic journalism. As time went by and the association/confraternity for the 'propagation of good books' was formalized through papal approval, her twin aims remained the same, namely that everyone who became a subscriber became an associate as well.

While nineteenth-century journal analysts write of 'targeted' or 'common' readers, I believe that Elizabeth had a somewhat different approach. She wanted everyone to find God, 'to be a saint' as one early companion said, so she wrote for inquiring readers who desired material that would enrich their spiritual life, strengthen their Catholic faith and bring them closer to God. More than this, because every Catholic journal claimed to address this search, the number of *Annals*' readers was directly related to the subscribers' desire to share in the spiritual life of Elizabeth's Franciscan Sisters and other Franciscan communities. As she explained:

> The Subscribers to the Annals, share in the spiritual advantages accorded to the Association of St. Anthony of Padua, under the

> Protection of the Immaculate Conception, Queen of the Angels, for
> the Publication and Propagation of Good Books, to which our Holy
> Father Pope Leo XIII, has granted His special Approbation. The
> Holy Sacrifice of the Mass is celebrated daily for the Associates, and
> on Saturday during the Adoration of the Most Blessed Sacrament in
> honour of the Immaculate Conception, prayers are offered for the
> same intention. They also participate in the Masses, Prayers and
> good works of numerous Communities of the Franciscan Order in
> Europe and America.[89]

Elizabeth related to her individual readers, as part titles and
contents of articles and readers' correspondence indicate. This is
instanced by, 'To the Clients of St. Anthony' and 'Thanksgiving
and Obituary'; also the *Annals* created space for readers to feel
personally involved through correspondence. Readers, and at
times contributors, felt integrally related to and associated with the
Franciscan Sisters and their ministry. While some subscribers were
religious or clerics, most were in secular employment or caring for
families at home. The laity apparently valued their association with
the Franciscans. How Fanny Montgomery felt involved and part of
the Sisters' life and ministry is recorded:

> Three young girls, full of ardour, full of the talents required
> specially for missionary work in a new country, ingenuous, active,
> brightly pious, as the children of St. Francis always must be, were
> professed on the first of this month of May. And there lay before me
> the letter assuring me beforehand how much I, and those I love,
> would be in their thoughts and prayers on that happy occasion.[90]

Elizabeth related to her readers also through her hard-working
Sister Zelatrices, who knew her personally, had been attracted by
her and looked on her as a mother.[91] Besides the assurance of
prayers through Zelatrices, one advertisement informed readers
that their intentions would be remembered in the sacred places of
Assisi, Padua and Rome:

> The subscribers to the Annals, in addition to pleasant and profitable
> reading, share in the spiritual advantages ... The Holy Sacrifice of
> the Mass is celebrated for their intention every week within the
> Sacred Chapel of the Porziuncula in St. Mary of the Angels, Assisi;
> at the Shrine of St. Anthony in Padua; and in the Franciscan Chapel
> of the Immaculate Conception in Rome.[92]

Elizabeth promoted her *Annals* by providing content that suited
the readers' spiritual needs. Franciscan Catholic readers desired to

be prayed for, to join others in prayer and to hear God's voice through spiritual reading. Vaughn's article confirmed for readers that spiritual reading was equivalent to listening to God and that reading, combined with talking to God, was essentially prayer. The editor ensured that Vaughn's article concluded with her own journalistic aspirations:

> We ought frequently to read good books, such as the Holy Gospel, the lives of the Saints, and other spiritual works, which nourish our faith and piety, and arm us against the false maxims of the world.[93]

Many nineteenth-century readers, surrounded by a sea of journals, newspapers and books, experienced the need for concise, good reading matter and lower-waged readers could stretch their budget only so far. Elizabeth's publication met these criteria and also provided readers with a record of current Catholic thought as well as Catholic views for non-Catholic inquirers.

The *Annals* also measured up to another desire of the Victorian reader, to access material of a topical nature. One way Elizabeth achieved this was in her many articles on the progress of new missions, particularly Franciscan ones, in America, in the United Kingdom and foreign lands. Finally and most significantly, *Annals'* subscribers were more than readers with needs and interests; they collaborated in a seven-hundred-year-old Franciscan way of life with its rich history, traditions, missions and Franciscan spirituality. This was the cornerstone of the ultimate success of Elizabeth Hayes' mission through journalism and why, after over a hundred years, it is opportune to acknowledge her as a pioneer Franciscan journalist.

The Institute's Story Continued (1889–90)

While happenings of 1889 and 1890 (in the institute's American and Roman houses) are not indicated in Elizabeth's *Annals*, these events had major repercussions for a few years on the publication's distribution and finances. To retell even the outline of this story today is fraught with difficulty for in trying to write the perceived truth with sensitivity, one is aware of other perspectives. Valued relationships exist among Franciscan Sisters of various branches of the Order and some of the early members of Elizabeth's institute struggled with trials beyond our imagination, with localized constraints, movements and 'isms', yet all acted in 'good faith'.

Elizabeth sometimes asked her readers to be patient; the same is asked again now as an attempt is made to be impartial in an abbreviated telling of the complex struggles of Elizabeth and her early Sisters.

On 25 April 1889 adversaries of the Belle Prairie Sisters set fire to and completely burnt down the Franciscan convent-school buildings. While the troublesome Fr Lemay had been expelled and Fr Payette installed, resentment among Lemay supporters still percolated until it boiled over into this act of violence, a not uncommon reaction of outraged communities on the American frontiers. The four Sisters, then known as Francis Beauchamp, Angela Michaud, Magdalene Michaud and Elizabeth Ethier, and their twenty-four boarder-pupils escaped, but with stunned shock to all involved. Immediate shelter was provided for the Sisters and children by the parents of Sr M. Columba Doucet, Elzear and Lucile, who lived close by. On the next day, after a seven-mile walk to Little Falls, the Sisters gained help and returned to Belle Prairie with short-term necessities such as food, clothing, bedding and financial assistance. Fr Payette moved to a room in Doucette's house and the presbytery became home and school for the Sisters and also for some boarders, unable to return home as they were orphans and time was needed to contact their guardians.

News about the fire spread quickly to Fr Buh and to Archbishop Ireland who was, at this time, administrator of the Vicariate of Northern Minnesota in place of Bishop Seidenbush. Through these two, the main details about the fire gradually reached Elizabeth and the Sisters in Rome. Over the years, numerous interpretations of events have evolved as to what actually happened as the months passed. The 'Memoirs' of Sr M. Angela Michaud are critical to the story.[94] Archbishop Ireland suggested to Elizabeth that it would be unwise to rebuild in Belle Prairie at once for he feared that a new building 'would share the fate of the other'.[95] He also advised her as leader of the institute to give the Sisters living in North America 'certain Provincial autonomy'.[96] The archbishop encouraged Sisters belonging to various religious groups in his archdiocese to seek more local autonomy; he advised the Josephite Sisters of Carondelet against central government.[97] While the Franciscan Sisters in Minnesota were encouraged by Ireland to 'have another government', which meant he did not have 'to deal with a superior residing in Rome',[98] it seems that Elizabeth was possibly unsure of exactly what he had communicated to the Sisters in Minnesota. With her wide experience and sound knowledge of women's religious traditions and developments, she remained committed to centralized government, while membership of her institute was still too small for the formation of provinces. Not to follow the advice of a powerful archbishop must have taken much courage and personal conviction. Elizabeth knew that papal approbation made it possible for geographically separated communities to remain connected to a motherhouse, through a provincial structure, yet it appears that either through illness, lack of receiving her letters or the influence of negative advice in Rome, she became immobilized while her Sisters in America faced a desperate situation.[99] What kind of mental pressure was Elizabeth under in Rome while her naturally empathetic heart was with her Sisters? The Belle Prairie fire served as the activator of a new situation which had serious implications for her *Annals*, as well as Elizabeth's entire institute.

It seems that after the fire the four Belle Prairie Sisters indicated to supporters and locals that they intended to restart in Little Falls, or maybe the Little Falls newspaper reported the matter incorrectly. After some delay the Sisters received directions from Elizabeth to join their three Franciscan Sisters in Augusta via Sr Chaffee, Elizabeth's secretary, who was in New York at the time. During this year of 1889 she was promoting subscriptions for the *Annals* and in general seeking finance to help the institute and so Elizabeth asked her to be the intermediary.[100] The Belle Prairie Sisters proceeded to Augusta only to discover that Bishop Becker – successor to Bishop Gross who had invited and welcomed Elizabeth and her Sisters to his diocese – preferring women religious directly under diocesan control, refused to allow the Belle Prairie Sisters to remain in his diocese. At this time there was a movement among bishops to want to retain the religious congregations directly under their control while secular organizations were also strengthening their attempts at greater American independence in the wider milieu.[101]

As anxiety and unrest among the now united seven Franciscan Sisters increased, and believing that they had support from Archbishop Ireland, they wrote in August asking Elizabeth for a diocesan structure; the letter also included a suggestion of going to higher authority, *Propaganda Fide* (as their prelates had advised), if need be.[102] No one will ever fully know what Elizabeth, unwell at the time, understood and concluded from this letter but she did not answer it; later however she revealed to the Cardinal Prefect of Propaganda that she did not reply because she did not want to be the cause of action against her Sisters.[103] When the seven Sisters in a now impossible situation did not receive a reply in due time, they

decided, without Elizabeth's blessing, that a few should go immediately to Minnesota with the others to follow later.[104]

With the return of these Sisters to Minnesota, with only a barn to
live in, Fr Payette became involved again and put the matter before
Bishop Otto Zardetti, bishop of the newly erected diocese of St
Cloud in which Belle Prairie was now situated. The new bishop was
intelligent, highly educated and a very able speaker and writer.[105]
At first Zardetti was reluctant to become entangled and suggested
that the Sisters should join other existing religious communities.
One thing led to another and before long a kind of desperation
drove the Minnesota Sisters to write again to Elizabeth; still no
answer. Payette had interceded again and Zardetti relented.
Similar situations were replicated in England, Ireland and
Australia – they stemmed from the historical and canonical context
and the very real differences between the demands of a new environment and an overseas centre of administration. He now
decisively recommended that the Minnesota Sisters remove themselves from Elizabeth's authority as Mother General in Rome, that
the Sisters separate, yet remain Franciscan under certain conditions and establish their own diocesan autonomy. This meant the
involvement of German Fr Ferdinand Bergmeyer, provincial of the
Franciscan friars in St Louis, to ensure the continued Franciscan
identity of the group, who now became established at Little Falls in
the St Cloud diocese, where they were to take root and expand in
later years.

It is worthy of note that other bishops also encouraged the idea
of creating an independent American identity in their local sisterhoods. So while this situation was so difficult for Elizabeth and all
the Sisters involved, it was not unique; the Josephite Sisters of
Carondelet had similar experiences in North America, and the
history of women religious reveals that these struggles were
repeated in many branch houses of religious communities when a
motherhouse was situated in Europe.[106] A Vatican II shared deci-
sion-making model for local levels was still a long way off. It is
significant that today we see the struggle of the past in the context
of those times. How can we, 120 years later, hope to really grasp or
even partially understand the experience of Elizabeth and the
Sisters in 1889, whether we look at it from the Mother Superior's
perspective in Rome, through the eyes of the Belle Prairie and
Augusta Sisters who pondered together in Augusta, through
understandings and insights of the clergy and bishops involved or
through documentation? What must have been their feelings, their
anxiety, unanswered questions, sense of loss, abandonment, isola-

tion and confusion? Yet Elizabeth and all involved struggled to somehow see the hand of God in their experience and to make the decisions that they thought were appropriate at the time. Today the extant letters written at this time of struggle still cry out to be heard; some express sincere love and gratitude to Elizabeth for her 'bounty', while others accuse her of lack of guidance and rapid definite action in time of crisis. One letter from the French-Canadian Sr M. Bernardine Bergin appears to contain an astute observation, she wrote:

> What I desired Sr. M. Magdalen and Sr. M. Francis to do instead of going from priest to priest and Bishop to Bishop, was to go quietly to Rome to Reverend Mother and explain all to her, by letter it is impossible and to continue as we are is impossible...[107]

Had this happened the outcome may have been different; perhaps Elizabeth could have reconsidered the possibility of increased local autonomy for Minnesota, and on the other hand, this may not have been enough freedom and independence to allow the pioneer Sisters to achieve their potential for fruitfulness, as was to be recorded later in their history.[108] Suffering was endured by the original seven Sisters, the four from Belle Prairie and three from Augusta,[109] leading their anxiety and desire for autonomy to spread to the ten Zelatrices living and working on the *Annals* ministry in Chicago, Boston, New York and Philadelphia.[110] Before long these Sisters joined the Minnesota group, except for the one Irish woman, Sr M. Anna Flannery, who stood resolute in her personal convictions and, on Christmas Eve 1890, returned to Rome as Elizabeth directed in her cable that came too late for most of the Zelatrices. Meanwhile, the Sisters remaining in the US lived in the Little Falls Community.

Elizabeth found it very difficult to accept the bitter disappointment of losing her much loved daughters due to this separation. One wonders, in the light of Sr Chaffee's comments about Elizabeth being 'stunned' when two Sisters from the American group were sent to her by the Cardinal Prefect;[111] perhaps she felt crushed because she had failed to 'read the signs'. Sr Chaffee wrote, 'She [Elizabeth] received them, and told them kindly that she would not oppose them, nor quarrel with them. Thus they obtained their autonomy.' Elizabeth had to cope with learning that, along with giving autonomy, there followed the loss of nine Zelatrices for promoting and delivery of the *Annals* and the associated new financial losses resulting from declining *Annals* subscriptions. Sr Chaffee wrote that it meant for a time 'total cessation of all remittances, upon which we were dependant for our daily bread, not to speak of the expenses of this affair of Villa Spada'.[112]

1890 had also brought a lawsuit over Villa Spada due to the deception of Prince Sciarra regarding the terms of payment; this was accompanied by further financial troubles, and so this year became for Elizabeth what could be described as a kind of *annus horribilis*, when her state of inner exhaustion led to near prostration. In September of this year she went to Naples to assist at the deathbed of Sr M. Lucy, a further cause of grief for her. As a woman of prayer, 'zeal and labour', Elizabeth was not alone in her trials for she never lost confidence that God's grace was with her. She much appreciated the human support and encouragement of those around her, among whom was Cardinal Vicar Parocchi, her longstanding friend for whom she had done so much work in earlier years on translations and printing.

Notes

1 Leo XIII, 'The Catholic Press', *AOLA* XV, no. vii (1890): 189.

2 As noted earlier, provision of educational and religious articles of interest to the general reader and stories about Franciscan life and developments

3 Sketch of the *Annals'* office in the Belle Prairie Convent, MFICAR, section A, folder 11, item 13, no. 7. The Augusta office was in the Barrat property, Harrisonville, Augusta. Trastevere's printing address was 40 Via Garibaldi; the building still stands but as far as can be ascertained Elizabeth also worked at her desk in the convent nearby.

4 John H. Newman was aware of the costly failures of some sixty-seven Catholic newspapers, journals and periodicals that had been launched in Britain during the first half of the nineteenth century. Neil Byrne, 'Dunne's Vision: Catholic Press Teacher of Humanity', The Catholic Leader (Brisbane), 28 October 1992, 15.

5 Newman in Ibid.

6 Morris C. Russell, 'News Item', *The Brainerd Tribune*, 27 December 1873.

7 Ibid.

8 Leon de Clary, *Lives of the Saints and Blessed of the Three Orders of Saint Francis*, vol. IV, 160–64. Elizabeth here shortened de Clary's title to *Franciscan Saints*. Hayes, 'Jane of Signa', *AOLA* XV, no. xii (1890): 349–52.

9 Owen Chadwick, *Newman* (Oxford: Oxford University Press, 1983), 59. Newman's outstanding example of this approach was his *Apologia Pro Vita Sua*.

10 Revd John Ireland, St Paul, MN, letter to Mother M. Ignatius Hayes, 23 September 1874, MFICAR.

11 Archival evidence shows that censors always also wrote 'Nihil Obstat' followed by their signature on a copy sent to them of each monthly *Annals* that was then returned to the editor.

12 P. Friedhelm Scheiwe, *Our Lady of the Cliffs: A Papal Shrine. Castel S. Elia*, 29.

13 Hayes, 'Miraculous Picture and Sanctuary of Our Lady of 'Ad Rupes', Castel Saint Elia, near Rome', *AOLA* XVII, no. viii, ix (1892). 'Near Rome' meant thirty miles north of Rome.

14 Letters via secretaries from Franciscan 'Convento di San Guiseppe, Castel Saint Elia' and St Isidore's College to 'Rev. Mother', MFICAR, section A, box 3, folder 9, no. 17.

15 Letter from St Isidore's College, 26 October 1892, signed on behalf of the 'President', Doebbing, by 'Br. Nicholas OSF'. MFICAR, section A, box 3, folder 9, no. 17.

16 Letter from 'Convento di San Guiseppe, Castel Saint Elia', 15 November 1892, signed on behalf of 'President', Doebbing, by 'Fr. Nicholaus OSF'. MFICAR, section A, box 3, folder 9, no. 17.

17 William E. Lass, *Minnesota – a history*, 141.

18 Morris C. Russell, 'News Item', *The Brainerd Tribune*, 27 December 1873, p. 1, col. 5.

19 Women compositors had set in type *Victoria Regis*, edited by A. A. Procter (1825–64) and worked at Emily Faithfull's Victoria Press. Faithfull (1835–1895) initiated *Victoria Magazine* – printed by women until 1881. (Lennox, *Adelaide Anne Procter*, accessed. R. W. Davidson, *Emily Faithful*, Princeton University, http://libweb2.princeton.edu/rbsc2/ga/unseenhands/printers/Faithful.html; accessed 9 August 2004. Mademoiselle M. Durantet and other women (1870s), originally in Roanne then in Fribourg, Paris and Bar-le-Duc, printed and published 'several important Catholic Journals'. (Hayes, 'The Apostolate of the Press', 39.)

20 Two such Chicago foundries were Great Western Type Foundry and Marder, Luse & Company. Books used by the Sisters were *Chicago's Great Western Type Foundry Specimen and Price List* and *Specimens of Printing Type and Printers' Purchasing Guide*. MFICAR.

21 Angelica Chaffee, 'Memories', 26, 32.

22 Confirmed in the letters that passed between Mother Hayes and the *Ave Maria* Printing Office, MFICAR, section A, folder 9, no. 16, a-g. Some Belle Prairie printing materials were transported to Augusta also. Adzire Doucet, 'Memoirs of Mother M. Columba Doucet', (Privately circulated by MFIC Gencralate, Rome, May 1982: written in 1950), 1.

23 This method is known as monotype. The first linotype machines were introduced in New York in 1886 but only at the century's end was Ottmar Mergenthaler's linotype machine invented with its automatic device. Retired Brisbane printer, R. A. Shaw, recalls learning monotype in the 1950s before proceeding to linotype; between invention and purchase for general use, much time could elapse.

24 The three women of the Society of St Paul mentioned were Sisters

Marguerite Marie Durantet, d. 1879; Marie Praxede Weber, d.1884 and Catherine Pauline Sturney, d.1884. (Hayes, 'The Apostolate of the Press', 164–9.)

25 Chaffee, 'Memories', 41–2.

26 Ibid., 5. The article referred to was republished in the month Elizabeth Hayes died. (Hayes, 'Devotion to the Blessed Tongue of Saint Anthony of Padua', *AOLA* XIX, no. v (1894): 150.)

27 'Jesus advanced in wisdom and age, and grace before God and men', *AOLA* XII, no. i (1887).

28 'The Patronage and Cultus of the Most Blessed and Immaculate Virgin Mary', *AOLA* XV, no. xii (1890): 361. The tiny signature on the inner image is 'Deberny', an artist whose work appears often in the *Annals*.

29 'St. Veronica Galiani', *AOLA* IX, no. i (1884). Similar illustrations are 'St. Philip Neri', *AOLA* X, no. v (1885); 'St. Anthony of Padua: The Miracle of the Blessed Sacrament', *AOLA* X, no. xi (1885); 'St. Francis Preaching by the Wayside', *AOLA* XI, no. iv (1886).

30 'The Stigmata of St. Francis', *AOLA* XI, no. ix (1886): 256. The editor repeated this illustration in September 1892, in the appropriate month for the feast of St Francis' Stigmata.

31 Frontispieces: 'St. Joseph', *AOLA* XV, no. iii, (1890). 'St. Elizabeth of Hungary', AOLA XI, no. i (1886). Repeated use of blocks indicates they were stored at Elizabeth Hayes' Roman printing office and re-used years later.

32 'Vera Effigie di St Antonio di Padova', *AOLA* XV, no. xi (1890): 321.

33 'True Likeness of St. Anthony of Padua', *AOLA* XVIII, no. vi (1893): 156; frontispiece for June during which the Saint's feast is celebrated. After Elizabeth Hayes' death this oil painting was given a place of honour, along with a Reliquary, 'in the oratory where formerly she [Elizabeth] suffered, laboured and prayed'. (Chaffee, 'Two Signal Graces', *AOLA* XIX, no. vii (1894): 208–9.)

34 Hayes, 'Association of St. Anthony of Padua', *AOLA* XI, no. xi (1886): 350.

35 'The object of this publication [*Annals*] is threefold: (a) to aid in the printing and propagation of good books and pious pictures ...' in a five-page article on 'Confraternity of St. Anthony of Padua', n.d., MFICAR, section A, folder 14.

36 Besides a reprint in the 1893 and 1894 *Annals*, the Statutes in a twelve-page pamphlet included the *Annals*' print of the 'True Likeness of St. Anthony of Padua'. 'St. Anthony's Press near San Pietro in Montorio Rome' published the pamphlet, containing the Rescript, Decree and Brief originally printed in the *Annals*. 'Near San Pietro in Montorio' served as address for Hayes' two establishments, printing office and convent.

37 Next were printed names, age, date and place of death with many North American towns and cities figuring prominently. The 'Obituary' was printed bimonthly – appearing six times a year.

38 'The Basilica of S. Peter and the Castle of S. Angelo, in Rome, as taken from a distance', *AOLA* XI, no. x (1886). Others include e.g.: 'Exterior

View of the Coliseum in Rome', *AOLA*, XI, no. xi (1886); 'Interior view of the Coliseum in Rome', *AOLA* XII, no. ii (1887).

39 While all 1890 issues and most of 1891 commenced with a full-page frontispiece illustration, it was not until 1892 that the word, 'Illustration' with its title, appeared in the 'Contents' list.

40 The 1890s Roman series in volume XV consisted of 'Piazza Navona and the Church of St. Agnes, Virgin and Martyr, Rome' (Jan.); 'The Fountain of Trevi, Rome' (Feb.); 'Fontana Paolina, Rome' (April); 'The Capitol with a distant view of Church of St. Maria in Aracoeli, Rome' (May); 'Arch of Titus, Rome' (July); 'Piazza di Spagna and Church of the Trinita de Monti, Rome' (Sept.); 'One of the Fountains before St. Peter's Basilica, Rome' (Dec.).

41 The Franciscan illustrations: 'St. Anthony of Padua: The Miracle of the Most Blessed Sacrament' (June); 'The Sanctuary of the Portiuncula, in Basilica of St Mary of Angels, Assisi' (Aug.); 'St. Francis of Assisi giving the Holy Habit to St. Clare' (Oct.); 'St. Elizabeth of Hungary' (Nov.). Another full-page Franciscan illustration is included in the middle of 'St. Anthony's Tuesday', *AOLA* XV, no. xi (1890): 321.

42 'La Sainte Baume, St. Mary Magdalene's Retreat', *AOLA* XVII, no. i (1892): 2.

43 Illustrations include: a trumpeting angel in an intricate decorative pattern (one of a series), the combination of Passion symbols (crown, cross and lance; inter-woven also into the 1884 cover), two angels worshipping the Eucharist, Mary framed in a decorative gateway and children with a guardian angel.

44 Among other contemporary examples, *The Builder* favoured three columns while the *Ave Maria* two. Julian Tenison Woods' religious journals of 1867–72 published in Adelaide always had two columns.

45 *Annales Franciscaines* (appendix 2.10, fig.i), *Annali Francescani* and *L'eco di S. Francesco D'Assisi* displayed the Franciscan coat of arms in slightly different illustrative styles. This simple cover style, minus the Franciscan coat of arms, had been popularised by many contemporary secular journals, e.g., *The Builder, Strand Magazine* and the *Gentleman's Magazine and Historical Review*. North (ed.), *The Waterloo Directory of English Newspapers and Periodicals 1800–1900*, accessed 16 August 2004.

46 *Irish Franciscan Tertiary*: A monthly journal for the Third Order of St. Francis (Dublin: The Freeman's Journal Ltd Printers, 1891, vol. 2, no. 13, June. Coverpage).

47 'The Inauguration of the Devotion to the Crib by St. Francis of Assisi, at Midnight, December, 24, 1224'. *Franciscan Annals* V, no. 60 (1881): 334. The woodcutter provided only his initials, F.B.

48 Adelaide Procter, 'The Angel of Prayers', *AOLA* XVIII, no. iv (1893): 95–6.

49 'Assumption of Our Lady', *AOLA* XIX, no. viii (1894): 212 & 215. Additional to Spagna's name on the illustration is that of Halleiz, responsible for the printing woodblock. Elizabeth had selected this particular Spagna illustration for two previous Marian articles. {Hayes, 'What We

Owe to Mary', *AOLA* XI, no. v (1886): 129–33. Hayes, 'The Patronage and Cultus of the Most Blessed and Immaculate Virgin Mary', *AOLA* XV, no. ix, xii (1890): 259–67, 361–5.}

50 The monstrance illustrates St Bonaventure's words regarding St Francis' affection for the Blessed Sacrament. *AOLA* XIX, no. vii (1894): 194. The bedside angel illustrates 'The Holy Angels: Our Defenders at the Judgment of God', which Elizabeth translated from the Italian. *AOLA* XIX, no. ix (1894): 255–62. The papal coat of arms accompanied 'The Catholic Press', *AOLA* XIV, no. vii (1890): 190. The signatures retain their anonymity.

51 'To Our Readers', *Franciscan Annals and Tertiary Record* XVII, no. 193 (1893): 1.

52 Marguerite Durantet's words quoted by Elizabeth in 'The Apostolate of the Press', *AOLA* XIV, no. vii (1890): 164.

53 Bishop Thomas L. Grace, St Paul, letter to Mother M. Ignatius Hayes, 29 August 1879, MFICAR.

54 Bishop William Gross, Savannah, Georgia, letters to Mother M. Ignatius Hayes, 16 September and 10 December 1879, MFICAR.

55 Mrs R.Vansittart, 'In Memoriam', *AOLA* XVIII, no. iv (1893): 122.

56 Chaffee's support of Hayes was especially evident when Elizabeth's health was frail during three periods, in 1886, in 1889 and just before her death; Chaffee carried on and the *Annals* in no way suffered. Another Sister filled the breach when Chaffee was absent visiting the USA in late 1889. (de Breffny, *Unless the Seed Die*, 179, 204–5.)

57 Chaffee, 'Memories', 25.

58 MFICAR, section A, Folder 9, nos 4, 5, 9, 10 and 11.

59 MFICAR, section A, folder 9, nos 8, 15, 12, and 14.

60 MFICAR, section A, folder 9, no. 16, series a-g of Clarke's letters.

61 For example, a request for Franciscans – Fr Bernard the lector of sacred theology at St Isidore College and Fr Pietro Battista at San Pietro in Montorio – to be censors of the English *Annals* and of other Italian publications respectively. MFICAR, section A, folder 9, no 17.

62 The inclusion of associates' requests for prayers, for particular intentions or the deceased, was not unique to Elizabeth Hayes' *Annals,* e.g., the contemporary *Ave Maria* did much the same through their 'Association of Our Lady of the Sacred Heart'. A. Granger, 'The Annals of Our Lady of the Angels', *Ave Maria* XIV, no. 23 (1878): 370.

63 Doucet, 'Memoirs', 3.

64 The *Saint Paul Northwestern Chronicle* on August 1, 1874, p. 5. col. 1.

65 Elizabeth Hayes' post office address was provided initially in *The Brainerd Tribune* of 27 December 1873.

66 Sr M. Edward Sherry, *Centenial Commemorative Volume: The Annals of Our Lady of the Angels 1874–1974*, 14, 16.

67 Chaffee, 'Memories', 26.

68 The name of New York City was repeated countless times in the *Annals'* obituaries over the years.

69 de Breffny, *Unless the Seed Die*, 221.

70 The number of eight Zelatrices was stated in a letter from the Little Falls Sisters to Cardinal Simeoni. Ahles, *In the Shadow of His Wings*, 159.

71 More on the work of the Zelatrices is found in ch. 9 of de Breffny, *Unless the Seed Die*, 171–233.

72 Hayes, 'Association of St. Anthony of Padua', 349–52.

73 The Third Plenary Council at Baltimore in 1884 prohibited begging in any diocese without express authority of the bishop. For some clergy, Sisters and potential customers the distinction between collecting money as payment for the *Annals* and collecting money for charities (begging) was blurred at times.

74 Chaffee, 'In Memoriam', 146–7. As early as 1882 Hayes was at pains to have her journal seen as one that was 'honoured with the Blessing and Commendation of Our Holy Father Leo XIII and encouraged by several Archbishops and Bishops ... and with the approbation of the Right Rev. Bishop of the Diocese'. {Hayes, 'The Annals of Our Lady of the Angels', *AOLA* VII, no. xii (1882): 366.}

75 Hayes, 'Association of St. Anthony of Padua', 352.

76 Ibid: 350.

77 Peter Gates, 'Women in Mission', *Mission Today* 7, no. 2 (1997): 10. MacGinley, *A Dynamic of Hope*, 93.

78 Morris C. Russell, 'News Item', *The Brainerd Tribune*, 27 December 1873, p. 1, col. 5.

79 Daniel E. Hudson, 'The Annals of Our Lady of the Angels', *Ave Maria* XIV, no 23 (1878): 370.

80 Chaffee, 'Memories', 35. In her analysis Ahles found it difficult to acknowledge the 10,000 figure because she thought that it was not until the transfer of the printing office to Rome that numbers reached this height and higher. However, she admitted archival evidence was lacking to refute Chaffee's claims. (Ahles, *In the Shadow of His Wings*, 156.)

81 Hayes, 'The Annals of Our Lady of the Angels', 366.

82 de Breffny, *Unless the Seed Die*, 169.

83 Doucet, 'Memoirs', 5.

84 Ahles, *In the Shadow of His Wings*, 157.

85 Hayes, 'The Annals of Our Lady of the Angels', *AOLA* XIII, no. xii (1888): 386. It cannot be fully substantiated, but some time after 1888 at the Via Nicola Fabrizi office, it seems that a member's subscription was $2.00 annually.

86 Chaffee, 'Memories', 57.

87 de Breffny, *Unless the Seed Die*, 224–5.

88 North (ed.) *The Waterloo Directory of English Newspapers and Periodicals 1800–1900*, accessed.

89 Hayes, 'The Annals of Our Lady of the Angels', 386.

90 Fanny Montgomery, 'My Aunt's Journal', *AOLA*, 374.

91 Letters of farewell from Zelatrices who joined the Minnesota diocesan community, including the seven previously mentioned, attest to this genuine love for Elizabeth Hayes, as in, 'Never, never could I forget you very Revd. Mother because I have received too many graces through your

favour and I thank you for all the bounty you have had for me ...' (de Breffny, *Unless the Seed Die*, 220).

92 Hayes, 'The Annals of Our Lady of the Angels', 366. From 8 December 1888 subscribers knew that in Rome their Confraternity was 'seated' in the 'Church of the Blessed and Immaculate Virgin Mary Queen of the Angels', in the Franciscan Sisters' Convent of 'Villa Spada' on the Janiculum Hill.

93 Herbert Cardinal Vaughn, 'What Are Spiritual Reading Books', *AOLA* XIX, no. i (1894): 21.

94 Marie Emilie (Sr M. Angela) Michaud (1845–1925), one of the Belle Prairie Sisters, experienced the events of 1889–90 at first-hand and became a Little Falls Franciscan in 1890. Sr Ahles used Sr M Angela Michaud's 'Memoirs' in her publication.

95 Archbishop Ireland, St Paul, Mn., letter to Mother Mary Ignatius, 9 May 1889. FSALF. Chaffee, 'Memories,' 55.

96 John Ireland, St Paul, Mn., letter to Mother M. Ignatius, 19 June 1889, MFICAR.

97 The Josephite Sisters of Carondelet are a large congregation who opened a school in St Paul, MN, in 1851; among the Josephites were three close relatives of the archbishop. For bishops encouraging an independent American identity see Carol K. Coburn and Martha Smith, *Spirited Lives: How Nuns Shaped Catholic Culture and American Life, 1836–1920*, 57–61. Photo of Ireland's relatives, ibid., 69.

98 The seven Franciscan Sisters (of the Belle Prairie and Augusta group), letter to Mother Mary Ignatius, 19 August 1889. FSALF, a similar copy MFICAR. Ahles, *In The Shadow of His Wings*, 225.

99 Roman officials would have strongly supported centralisation; this influence is seen in Chaffee's account recording that on a particular day Cardinal Vicar Parocchi paced the Roman convent parlour floor and repeated in Italian words that showed his disapproval of Franciscan happenings in Minnesota. (Chaffee, 'Memories', 57.)

100 Chaffee provides an account of the fire and her understanding of events but not regarding her part in it while in New York. She was much distressed after her return to Rome because she saw Elizabeth suffering so much over 'the separation of the American houses from the Roman'. (Chaffee, 'Memories', 55–7.)

101 Canonically, until the emergence of new legislation developed over the course of the nineteenth century, women's religious institutes were under the authority of the bishop in whose diocese they were located or, if they were affiliated to a male religious order, as were Elizabeth's Franciscan Sisters, they were under the jurisdiction of the relevant Provincial or Minister General. In the nineteenth century, Rome began to approve women's congregations with centralized government and this caused problems when they began to expand beyond their diocese of origin. The first expedient was that they remained subject to the bishop in whose diocese the motherhouse was situated. Much conflict ensued, with many cases referred to Rome for settlement. By about 1850 Rome

vested more authority in the female Superiors General of the new centralized institutes and they were given a Cardinal Protector in Rome, whose authority superseded that of a bishop and who could thus be appealed to in the case of disputes. Rome encouraged first, and then required, all new institutes to be completely centralized. Archbishop Ireland was aware of the strongly centralizing movement in Roman policy; he suggested a provincial arrangement to Elizabeth. Then soon Bishop Zardetti was appointed, so Ireland left the concerns of Elizabeth's Sisters to the new bishop who decided on complete separation. Elizabeth's community, like most modern women's congregations operated originally on the authorization of a local bishop; she ensured that her institute had an approved Franciscan Rule and Constitutions and she later gained Roman or papal approbation. However foundations with an overseas female central motherhouse, without self-directing provinces, have regularly experienced dissatisfactions and Elizabeth's institute was no exception. Many examples of historical and canonical developments, conflicts and resolutions are provided by Rosa MacGinley in *A Dynamic of Hope.*

102 The seven Franciscan Sisters to Mother Mary Ignatius, letter, 19 August 1889. FSALF, MFICAR.

103 Mother M. Ignatius Hayes to Cardinal Prefect of Propaganda, letter of 1891 in de Breffny, *Unless the Seed Die*, 222–3.

104 One account claims that five Sisters went first and two others followed. (Ahles, *In the Shadow of His Wings*, 228.) Another account says that Srs M. Francis (local superior in Augusta), Angela and Magdalene set out first and four other Sisters followed later. (de Breffny, *Unless the Seed Die*, 207.) Two biographers vary, indicative of the different interpretations of the same events in this whole episode.

105 In 1891, Bishop Zardetti initiated his own diocesan publication, *The Diocese of St Cloud: Official Record and Messenger.* Accessed St Cloud Diocesan Chancery Archives.

106 The Sisters of St Joseph of Carondelet had formed their generalate in St Louis, approved by the Holy See, but at the request of the local bishop, the group at Philadelphia retained its autonomy. Not long before, Philadelphia on the broader scene had witnessed riots and numerous acts of violence spurred on by the Knownothing spirit, so belief in the benefit of independence was so to speak 'in the air'. In 1819, the Lyons' motherhouse of the Sisters of St Joseph of Bourg made a foundation at Belley and four years later at the bishop's request these Sisters were constituted an independent diocesan congregation.

107 de Breffny, *Unless the Seed Die*, 211.

108 Ahles, *In the Shadow of His Wings*, 251–467.

109 Srs M. Bernardine Bergin, Bonaventure Harrison and Joseph White.

110 Srs M. Rose Ethier, Anthony Lyons, Baptista Blaise, Anna Flannery, Hyacinth Leydon, Pacifica Marion, Ferdinand Boyer, Michael McClarney, Gabriel Keenan and Cherubina Vincent.

111 The two Sisters were Magdalene and Joseph; they had been sent to Rome

by Bishop Zardetti to present their appeal for a canonical separation to the Sacred Congregation of Propaganda and they carried official letters addressed to Cardinal Simeoni. They left Little Falls in March 1890, were staying with another community in Rome during May and arrived back home in mid June. (Ahles, *In the Shadow of His Wings*, 238–9.)

112 Chaffee, 'Memories', 57.

Chapter 8

Final Challenge and Legacy

Elizabeth was well grounded for the literary challenge she set herself, for love of reading accompanied her through life and, with the assistance of different circles of friends, she was usually surrounded by good literature. Having internalized what she read, Elizabeth spread the essence of her reading through her periodical, motivated by her desire for the 'propagation of good books'. While the best documented life of a person can still be enveloped in much obscurity, perhaps this story of Elizabeth as pioneer Franciscan journalist has decreased the shadows and allowed her to be appreciated in a fuller and more accurate light. Elizabeth acted in a different way from the majority of nineteenth-century women religious by embarking on an editing-publishing career in an ambiguous cultural context for women writers, demonstrating that she was strongly and absolutely committed to the Apostolate of the Press as it became a central strategy of the Church's evangelizing mission.

Feminist historians who are writing women back into history like to discover women like Elizabeth Hayes who held their own in a man's world. She had enough confidence in herself to assume confidence as an equal when dealing with leading male figures of her time, with the exception of her last few years when support from Cardinal Parocchi was relied upon and appreciated. Many great women lived in the aura of a particular eminent man but Elizabeth did not. She responded to external factors that were active in her society and made a significant literary contribution because of this, knowing that she had the literary talents and aptitude for bringing to birth the world's first Franciscan journal in English. She set out bravely to achieve her goals and was successful and fruitful in attaining them, yet now, the early 1890s, instead of earned rest, she was to face the final challenge.

Events of 1891–94

Eager young women continued to join Elizabeth's Franciscans; however, in 1891 her numbers in Italy counted only twenty-five professed Sisters and four novices. In Rome, with Elizabeth still as editor, the Sisters continued the printing, stitching, binding and dispatching of the *Annals* and a committed fresh group of Zelatrices, with the experienced Sr M. Anna Flannery at the helm, were back in North America busy promoting and distributing the Franciscan publication. In March that year a formal decree was issued by Bishop Zardetti approving the diocesan congregation, composed of her former Sisters at Little Falls, Minnesota. During this period, because of the changed situation in the institute, Elizabeth was required to produce much official documentation for the Vatican; it indicates not only her integrity but also her special gift for writing with clarity and conciseness. She was an intelligent, informed and confident woman who negotiated a difficult path; in journalism she swayed neither toward over-conservatism nor liberalism, she knew the purpose of her mission in life and to her *Annals* publication she remained steadfast. Passionate, talented, self-contained and focused on her objectives in the midst of trials, she balanced her approach to those around her with consideration and spiritual insight.

It was noted earlier that Elizabeth hoped to restore the failing health of some Sisters by directing them to the Naples' convent, 'Villa Pavoncelli'. Three years later, Elizabeth travelled there to be present at the bedside of the dying Sr M. Lucy Ryan, a native of Tipperary. While in Naples she realized that the Roman Curia was asking for something new. Elizabeth was disturbed at being told that her Sisters were living for themselves, concerned for their internal affairs and not working for their neighbours as expected of missionary Sisters, an accusation which constituted another trial for her.[1] She was a woman of great faith and prayed fervently to know the will of God. One request was that the Sisters should open and maintain a public chapel in a new quarter of the city, a challenge which proved difficult to implement. The Sisters in Naples made an effort to comply but rents in the city were extremely high and it was impossible to find a house that could be used as a public chapel. Elizabeth keenly felt the inability to meet this need of the Church.

At this time, Cardinal Sanfelice D'Acquavilla, Archbishop of Naples and former Benedictine Abbot of La Cava, showed a pastoral interest in the little community at Villa Pavoncelli and visited often. During one of his visits he suggested that some type of apostolic work be undertaken – printing, for example, and the free distribution of good reading material among his people. Around this same time in 1892 Elizabeth was involved in a lawsuit in connection with Villa Spada. As a security measure and to ensure that the work and printing of the *Annals* would not be interrupted, she had all the printing equipment transferred to Naples. In that way, the Sisters did some printing in Italian to the satisfaction of the cardinal, who appointed a theological adviser for the work, a practice noted earlier in connection with publishing in Rome. He had the Sisters' Office registered with the municipality.[2]

Elizabeth always had a great love for Assisi and visited it many times before and after she established a community of Sisters there. She purchased land outside the old walls, in front of the basilica of Our Lady of the Angels, in order to build a convent but financial barriers proved too much and the Sisters continued to live in a rented house. Even though finance was a struggle, Elizabeth's generosity is shown in a letter to her around this time. Fr Francesco M. Galli ofm, Guardian of St Mary of the Angels, Assisi, writes on 16 July 1892:

> Being placed here by obedience as Guardian of this Sanctuary, looking over what has been done, I find myself reading your precious name among other benefactors of this poor parish ... I take the liberty to ask for charity for the poor families who come for bread which I have not and where can I get it?[3]

In September 1892 Elizabeth rejoiced over the growth in the institute's numbers when she professed, in Villa Spada's chapel, Sisters M. Annunziata, Purification, Antonia and Visitation; they would be the last group to be professed by the foundress.[4] When Sr Chaffee later reflected on the next period in Elizabeth's life she wrote:

> While the spirit was not wanting, her poor body could no longer hasten to its promptings. And now it was God's time to refine her in the crucible of pain, of which the last four or five years were full to overflowing; ... Yet in all these sufferings she was upheld by her superiors, and in a most particularly by His Eminence Cardinal Parocchi, Vicar to His Holiness, who throughout her trials, even to the breathing out of her soul to God, was never wanting in paternal sympathy and aid.[5]

Attempting to ignore the infirmities of her body, Elizabeth decided to make another transatlantic journey to the United States in June 1893; however the journey was cut short, as she had travelled only as far as Naples when she was stricken with a severe internal inflammation, an illness that would develop into dropsy.[6] After months of acute suffering, during which time she was unable to lie down but needed to sit in a chair at night as well as day, she returned to Rome, arriving just before her favourite Marian feast of the Immaculate Conception. Sr Chaffee recalls that everything that was medically possible was done and the Sisters did their best to ward off the calamity of the loss that now seemed to be inevitable.[7] Elizabeth knew that the days of her missionary and literary endeavours were drawing to a close.

However, all mortals must finally face death; 'Sister Death', as Franciscans say, approached Elizabeth in early May 1894. Preparing to return to her God, Elizabeth's editorship of the *Annals* was assumed by her faithful companion and secretary, Sr Chaffee; without this woman's recorded memories, much of Elizabeth's extraordinary life would be unknown. Sr Chaffee, with Elizabeth in her last days, published her contemporary account of May events in the following October 1894 *Annals;* later she edited it slightly and wrote it in a more personal way in her 'Memories'. This account reads:

> On Tuesday the 1st of May 1894 our dear Mother received the last Sacraments at the hands of her Confessor, Rev. Father Luigi Da Rocca Priora O.S.F., guardian of the venerable monastery of St. Peter in Montorio. 'I feel this to be the happiest day of my life,' she whispered to me, being no longer able to speak audibly, 'Oh, the happiness of dying a child of Holy Church. I would like to let everyone know of my happiness.' She had already received the Blessing (in articulo mortis) from our Holy Father Pope Leo XIII; also the Seraphic Blessing was administered to her in the name of St. Francis from the Minister General of the whole Order at the hands of the Very Rev'nd P. Aloysius Lauer, O.S.F. ... She entered the 'midst of the shadow of death,' fearing no evil, for her Divine spouse was with her, his rod and his staff comforted her.
>
> On the afternoon preceding her death, she asked that a candle should be lighted, as she thought it was growing dark. One was immediately lit. Shortly afterwards, perhaps fifteen minutes, she repeated the request, and at once a lamp was brought near, and placed so as to shine upon her eyes. Another while passed, and a third time she plaintively asked for a light, I replied, 'Dear Rev. Mother, a lamp is on the table near you, and shining at its fullest in your eyes.' She made no allusion to it afterwards for she knew that she had lost her sight.
>
> ... Once she appeared to want something, her hand reached out.

She searched for her crucifix, again she whispered. 'What is it dear Rev. Mother that you desire,' I asked. 'I desire my God' was the reply. It was towards evening that she began to grow cold. She allowed some of the stronger young Sisters to come and rub her feet and limbs. (Our present Mother General Sr. M. Columba [Doucet] was one of them ... when she saw it was the hand of Death that was chilling her, she told them to cease. The agony of our beloved Mother continued till five o-clock Sunday morning, and as the bells of the Eternal City were ringing the Angelus, then without token or sign of pain, but like one who falls into a gentle sleep, her holy soul took silent flight to its Creator...

Her solemn obsequies took place on the morning of the 7th of May in our chapel at Villa Spada, at which the Very Rev. Franciscan Father of St. Peter in Montorio officiated, and her remains were placed in a temporary deposit in the cemetery of San Lorenzo in Campo Verano, from whence they were born in solemn procession on the feast of St. Ignatius of Loyola, to the chapel of the Arch-confraternity of the Most Precious Blood; and after a Mass of Requiem and the Absolution, at which Rev. Father Benedict de Milia, and several other Capuchin friars, she was placed within a vault of the same chapel.[8]

Sr Chaffee also recalled a particular 'coincidence'; after Elizabeth left the Wantage Anglican Sisterhood and became a Catholic in the 1850s, she joined Mother Lockhart and her Greenwich community composed of converts, both Sisters and secular women. Mother Lockhart's Sisters at the time were known as the Rosminian Sisters of the Most Precious Blood. After Elizabeth's death 'the resting place of her body' was in a chapel dedicated to the Most Precious Blood.[9]

Continuity yet Changes

Thanks to Elizabeth, her institute enjoys a rich heritage and a long spiritual tradition. It is part of the large Franciscan family and, in the her spirit, follows the Rule of the Third Order Regular of St Francis of Assisi accompanied by modern Constitutions that have been renewed over the years. Following the example of Elizabeth, the institute honours as its special patrons Saints Francis and Clare of Assisi, Saints Anthony, Bonaventure, Elizabeth of Hungary and many other holy women and men, about whom Elizabeth wrote at length in her *Annals*. The term Franciscan is synonymous with mission and all missionaries need a spirit of contemplation if they are to be fruitful; the example of contemplation combined with action is found in the lives of these patron saints.

On taking over her role as editor of the *Annals*, Sr Chaffee was quick to remind readers that all Associates of St Anthony were called on 'to labour for the honour of Our Patrons with new fervour.' She wrote:

> Whilst closing our records of 1894 with its many pain-tinted and grief-bordered pages noting the loss of the beloved Foundress of the Association, our Mother of holy and ever cherished memory ... let us offer an act of heartfelt thanksgiving to God for the glory He has received through both grief and joy, and for the honour which has redounded through all to our Heavenly Patrons, Our Lady of the Angels, St. Francis of Assisi and St. Anthony of Padua; and let us prepare to serve His glory with still greater zeal, in the new year.[10]

Sr Chaffee was more aware than anyone that Elizabeth's project had been enormous for it embraced not just reading widely, extensive correspondence and editing but also the responsibility for overseeing production and distribution. She was prepared to carry it on and to retain Elizabeth's twin aims of providing literature of interest to the general reader and of presenting the Franciscan Order's progress and development. Sr Chaffee admired Elizabeth as an insightful and intelligent woman who clung to her belief in the *Annals* power for good, despite the painstaking work it demanded. She embraced Elizabeth's conviction that journalism could facilitate God's reign only when accompanied by the spirit of love, prayer and service.[11]

It was to be almost another seventy years before the preliminary process for the beatification of Elizabeth (Mother M. Ignatius) Hayes was introduced in Rome in February 1962. The first vice-postulator of the Cause for Beatification was Fr Canice Mooney, OFM, former research-professor at the Dublin Institute for Advanced Studies, but he died suddenly in late 1963. Early the following year, Fr Benigus Millett, OFM was appointed to succeed him. As a pledge of the support of the then Superior General, Mother M. Helena Flynn, she assigned her assistant and secretary, Sr M. Redempta Power, to help him in the motherhouse archives. This Sister had previously searched, with Sr M. Assumpta Ahles of the Little Falls Franciscan Sisterhood, the archives of the Sacred Congregation of *Propaganda Fide* where much relevant documentation was available. Millet worked on until March 1976 when other official duties and pressure of academic work obliged him to sever his official connection with the Cause for Beautification.[12] The research accomplished for the Cause was not lost,[13] but it was allowed to lapse, while another project replaced it. This was Brian de Breffny's impartial biographical text, *Unless the Seed Die*, printed in 1980 with a foreword by Fr Benignus Millet. The Roman generalate decided that, due to high costs related to beatifications, difficulties in finding another vice-postulator, and with the likelihood of groups of foundresses being beatified together, further investigations be placed on hold.

As the story of Elizabeth and her pioneering enterprise in Franciscan journalism has unfolded, there were two names in particular, Angela (Sr Mary of the Angels) Chaffee and Adzire (Sr Mary Columba) Doucet, that intertwined with hers right from the early years in Belle Prairie. Among other valued contributions, these two Sisters were outstanding workers for and promoters of the *Annals*. After Elizabeth's death, at which they were both present, they became in turn, the second and fourth 'Mothers General', leaders of the institute. So as we draw the threads of the institute's story to a published 'conclusion', it seems appropriate to look briefly at how these two women ventured on and reached outward in the charismatic spirit of Elizabeth over the next nineteen years. Since both of them recorded their memories, it is possible to gain personal insights.

Angela (Sr Mary of the Angels) Chaffee (May 1894 to 1900)

Elizabeth lived and died in the Roman motherhouse, Villa Spada, from 1888 to 1894.[14] There had been legal complications attached to the property of which she was totally ignorant at the time of signing the contract and by 1892, as mentioned earlier, she had been involved in a stressful lawsuit. The expenses connected with Villa Spada were alarming and far beyond her means. However, despite intrigues and exorbitant rents, Elizabeth's community, now under the guidance of Mother Chaffee, managed to remain there until 1895. By this time, the latter was forced by necessity to transfer the motherhouse to a building with a more reasonable rent; the place chosen was at 21 Via Goffredo Mameli, Trastevere. The Franciscan community remained here until a permanent motherhouse could be built in later years.[15] The community in Assisi continued to receive its support from the motherhouse while the Sisters were engaged in weaving cloth from which the Franciscan habits were made and in making sandals for community wear. Though poor in the goods of this world, they shared their spiritual treasures with their neighbours and, in a limited way, the

Sisters' charity also extended to the temporal needs of the poorer local people.[16] Mother Chaffee was responsible in 1896 for overseeing the construction of St Michael's Mortuary Chapel in the St Lawrence Cemetery, Rome, for deceased members of the Institute.[17]

In 1897 Mother Chaffee sent Mother M. Antonia Thomas (later 3rd Superior General) to visit the Savannah mission in Georgia in the hope of rekindling Elizabeth's early missionary vision. St Benedict Orphanage for African-American girls had been, since 1886, under the supervision of Mother Beasley, the first African-American Sister in Savannah,[18] but lack of personnel and finance threatened closure so an invitation was extended to Elizabeth's Franciscan Sisters. This time the Sisters were welcome again at the request of Bishop Becker of Savannah and the following year Sr M. Columba Doucet was sent as the superior of the new community while Mother Beasley and two of her local Sisters stayed on, according to Mother Doucet, for an interim period.[19] The locality, which was basically white and Protestant, provided many challenges including difficulty in obtaining monetary support even for the basics of life, but the Sisters continued their mission there.[20]

Some months prior to Elizabeth's death, when she was confined to her sick bed in Naples, she considered again the African mission fields and spoke especially of Egypt as a future field of activity for her Sisters. Franciscans have laboured throughout Egypt since the thirteenth century and their mission for hundreds of years was under the jurisdiction of that in the Holy Land. Elizabeth edited a number of articles and reprinted others in the *Annals* that dealt with the missionary work of the Franciscan friars.[21] In 1686 the mission in Upper Egypt was separated and later became an independent Prefecture Apostolic, while Lower Egypt continued its connection with the Holy Land until 1839, when both were formed into a Vicariate Apostolic. In Upper Egypt a mission was established among the Copts in 1892 and new developments were taking place in parishes and schools under the Franciscan friars. Hence when Fr Giulio Gianola, OFM, a missionary from Fayoum, Upper Egypt, asked Mother Chaffee in March 1898 to send Sisters to Upper Egypt to open an orphanage, he met with a generous response.

For Mother Chaffee, events all seemed to fit into the plan of God when Fr Gianola was forced by ill health to return to his native land. He arrived at Naples and met Mother Chaffee while there. She not only agreed to undertake work in Upper Egypt but she and a companion set out in May 1898 from Naples to visit the mission of the Franciscan Fathers in Fayoum, southwest of Cairo. They spent two months there assessing the situation and researching the possibilities of a future apostolate there. Mother Chaffee and her companion were touched on seeing the primitive conditions, health hazards and absolute poverty, along with mothers, young girls and children in extreme need. What would St Francis or Elizabeth Hayes wish to do for the *fellaheen* (soil-cutters), the poor inhabitants who worked for the wealthy landowners? It carried overtones of Elizabeth's days in Kingston, Jamaica. Trusting in God and her patrons, Mother Chaffee returned to Rome, obtained permission from the Sacred Congregation of *Propaganda Fide* to open a mission in Fayoum, and in October 1898 sent a community of five Sisters.[22] While Elizabeth yearned to see this foreign mission become a reality, it was her successor who actioned the dream. In the following month, the Sisters rented a house for an orphanage and a small dispensary for medical supplies. 'The orphans and the poor knocked continuously for assistance' and so began the simple work which was to continue through many trials and hard times, later extending into other parts of Egypt.[23]

While the mission in Jersey City, New Jersey, did not open until 1899, five years after Elizabeth's death, this place had been part of her vision. With Sr Chaffee present, she discussed it with Fr Isaac Hecker who recommended that she consult the dependable Bishop Wigger of Newark, New Jersey. Faithful to Elizabeth's practice of honouring St Anthony of Padua, a house on Sixth Street for the Sisters was opened on the patron's feast, 13 June. Beginning with Sisters Margaret Michaud and Coletta Menconeri, followed later by three more, they understood that the promotion of the *Annals* was part of the community's responsibility. Two Sisters were assigned as Zelatrices in New York City while the others moved into visitation in the parish.[24] After recognizing local needs, it was decided that the opening of a day care centre was a priority. The next year, even though much hard work and zeal, like that shown by Elizabeth, was needed, St Francis Orphan Home was established. After six years in office, regular elections were held and Mother Chaffee was free of the role of 'Mother General'.

Interval – 1900–01

Between the leadership periods of Mothers Chaffee and Doucet, part of 1900 and the next year, Mother Antonia Thomas should be noted as she was also part of the early story. Back in 1870, Elizabeth

looked after Annie Rosalie S. Thomas, an English orphan who was
born in London in 1862 and lived with her as a student-boarder in
Sèvres. Abandoned by her guardian, she became Elizabeth's ward.
Known as Rosalie, she seems to have attended another boarding
school while Elizabeth, Sr Clare Peet and Mrs Fanny Montgomery
moved around Germany and France after the Franco-Prussian
War. Rosalie made her first Holy Communion in Belle Prairie in
1873, went with Elizabeth to Canada in 1876, met Angela (later
Mother) Chaffee in Chicago and then, aged twenty, went to Rome.
In 1883 she joined the Sisters as a novice, along with four young
Italian women, and became Sr M. Antonia.[25] In 1900 when Mother
Chaffee's term of office concluded, she was elected as 'Mother
General', but she died in August 1901.

Adzire (Sr M. Columba) Doucet (1901–13)

In her memories of late August this same year, Mother Doucet told
of her Atlantic journey from New York to Naples and thence on to
Rome. Having no idea of what the outcome of the Chapter elections would be, she participated along with 'fifteen to eighteen'
other Sisters and appreciated the presence of the Vicar of Rome as
the Presider at the Chapter, who was none other than Elizabeth's
old friend and supporter, Cardinal Parocchi. Mother Doucet
wrote:

> When the elections were over, I spoke to his Eminence about the
> black Sisters we had in Savannah and said I thought that in the
> future all black candidates should make their novitiate in the States
> and not be brought to Rome for that purpose. The Cardinal Vicar
> readily agreed to this. He then suggested that we help the Copts in
> Egypt print their missal as they were very poor and could ill afford
> such a big expense. Since we had a printing office he, no doubt,
> thought we were organized enough for that purpose. We made no
> promises and time counselled us otherwise as neither our printing
> equipment nor our purse allowed us to undertake such a work.[26]

The work and printing of the *Annals* had been returned to Rome
and as a result fewer Sisters formed the community in Naples.
Requests from bishops and pastors asking for Sisters to work in
their respective dioceses and parishes were pouring into Mother
Doucet in the motherhouse and this was especially true regarding
the United States. Mother Doucet was an energetic and broad-
minded woman who looked at the overall needs of the Church and

the pressing needs of the institute, wishing to send her Sisters where the need was greatest. She was aware that Elizabeth's institute now had convents and ministries in Assisi, Naples, Fayoum, Jersey City and Savannah. She longed to see the earlier work in Augusta, Georgia, reinvigorated, and decided on booking a passage to New York, following in Elizabeth's footsteps.[27] This would be just one of the many transatlantic journeys she would make as Mother Superior of the institute; no doubt the events of the early 1890s in Elizabeth's lifetime had taught her the importance of her regular presence in the North American convents.

1901–2 was to witness the reopening and construction of a new orphanage for coloured girls in Augusta. It had been founded by Elizabeth in 1878 and abandoned when Sisters returned to Minnesota in 1890 before the separation from the motherhouse in Rome. Mother Doucet had received formal requests to resume an apostolate in Augusta and on arrival rented a house on Broad Street in Sacred Heart Parish. With a Sister companion, she investigated the possibility of gaining a property in a healthier area than that occupied before, thus setting the wheels in motion for the establishment of a new beginning.[28] Back in 1885, Mother Doucet who had entered in Belle Prairie had left there to accompany Elizabeth to Rome. Since that time she had not seen her now aged parents, who were still living in Belle Prairie, so she travelled to visit them and to investigate the situation regarding the original site where the convent had been burnt down. She had difficulty in uncovering the legal dimensions of the whole business but did learn that the original property was entangled in a law suit, so she let the matter rest while trusting in God for the best outcome. Mother Doucet, in later years, remembered returning again the same year to Augusta, purchasing property, directing plans for a convent and orphanage for African-American children and, once satisfied construction was underway, returned 'to Rome in April via New York and Naples on the S.S. Città di Milano of the Dominican Line'.[29] She returned to Rome in high spirits for she had in her company eight young women who were eager to pursue a Franciscan vocation in the spirit of Elizabeth Hayes.

This same year (1902) with the authorization of Archbishop Williams of Boston, St Anthony's School for the Italian Children of St Leonard's Parish in North End opened with the Sisters living at 9 Snowhill Street. By August the community purchased a house on Sheafe Street in the North End and so the Boston convent in Massachusetts was opened. Later in the year, after Mother Doucet had visited the Augusta mission again, she spent time with the

Sisters, saw their work and so it was not surprising that in the next year, she initiated the opening of a novitiate in this convent. Another development this year in the United States saw an orphanage annexed to the convent in Jersey City. News of a fire in the Jersey City orphanage reached Mother Doucet in 1903 and it must have revived memories of the fire at Belle Prairie, though accidental this time. She was relieved to hear that, once again, no harm had come to the children due to the bravery this time of Mother M. Michael Gaffney with assistance from the other Sisters. Changing circumstances required the transfer of St Francis Orphanage to the West Hoboken estate of Sarah Kerrigan in 1904; this was followed by the purchase of the Kerrigan Homestead and Brazeau Estate and later the orphanage building was converted to Holy Rosary School. Unfortunately, Mother Doucet had to withdraw the community in 1910.[30]

In February 1903 Mother Doucet was accompanied by Sisters M. Patrick Moriarty and Pancrazia Batarse as she set out for Fayoum, sailing first from Naples to Alexandria. Great was their delight on their arrival to be welcomed by Mother Chaffee, now local superior, and what stories were exchanged among the Sisters.[31] However, the expenses of this mission were many; locally there was no income and she was forced to ponder just how effective were the community's efforts in this place. At least on the return journey to Rome, the visitors were able to be spiritually uplifted through a visit to the Holy Land whence they travelled through Jaffa, to Alexandria and on to Naples. Later the same year, Mother Doucet was back in the United States visiting and trying to assist the Sisters in Jersey City. More accommodation was necessary, finance was inadequate as usual and the Sisters started to take in orphans. This house in Jersey City also proved to be a very useful stopping place for the Sisters who promoted the *Annals* work for it provided interim accommodation when travelling to and from Rome.[32] Mother Chaffee, worried about the health of her novices in Rome, had gained permission from the Sacred Congregation of *Propaganda Fide* for young women to complete their novitiate in Boston.

A gift that Mother Doucet had developed over the years through her involvement with the *Annals* was the ability to write, edit, and compile different documents and books for printing by her Sisters. In 1903, when the Sisters continued to recite the Office of the Blessed Virgin Mary in Latin accompanied by the traditional rubrics, she was able to move toward producing, with formal approval the next year, a much improved institute Office Book which was certainly appreciated by the Sisters, especially since the rubrics were printed in English and Italian. She also produced a Prayer Book for Sisters throughout the institute and this she believed 'created greater regularity and unity in prayer and in the community spiritual exercises'.[33] A few years later these same skills of Mother Doucet proved invaluable when, after presenting much documentation to the Sacred Congregation in Rome, she updated the institute's Constitutions and ensured that copies by the *Annals* press were spread to each community.[34] Through her efforts the *Decretum Laudis,* or Decree of Praise, from the Sacred Congregation of *Propaganda Fide* was given in 1906, formally establishing the institute's canonical status as a congregation of pontifical right.

During Mother Doucet's term of office, St Michael's Mortuary Chapel in Rome was dedicated, and the mortal remains of Elizabeth (Mother M. Ignatius) Hayes were transferred to it. Mother Chaffee recounted the story:

> On the eve of the feast of the Sacred Heart (1904) the body of our venerable Foundress Mother Mary Ignatius of Jesus, was translated from the Mortuary chapel of the Confraternity of the Precious Blood, and deposited in that of St. Michael. The Very Rev Father Provincial was assisted by several of his fathers. The tomb being opened and the dear remains of our Mother was lifted by the pall bearers and borne thither, accompanied by a long procession, headed by the Cross, and composed of Franciscan Fathers, Acolytes, Sisters of our Institute, little girls dressed in white carrying lilies, and a considerable number of friends, all carrying lighted tapers. It was truly an impressive sight; and the solemn chanting of the Psalms and prayers made it all the more awe-inspiring. Taken from the *Annals of Our Lady of the Angels,* September, 1904.[35]

October 1904 brought with it an adventure for Mother Doucet and Sr M. Margaret Michaud who travelled to Canada, following in the footsteps of Elizabeth and for the same reason, to gain young women for the Lord's work in the mission areas. In Montreal, where Franciscan secular tertiaries were printing their own periodical back in 1869 and where Elizabeth found valiant women prepared to accompany her to Belle Prairie, the Franciscan Guardian, Fr M. Raymond, made them welcome. In no time the recruiting was successful and the 'first postulant in this renewed effort of getting candidates from Canada' was packing her luggage.[36]

Early in 1905 Mother Doucet was back in Egypt visiting, assisting the Sisters, ensuring that Eucharistic devotion was central in the convents, and doing practical things for the mission, like searching for a suitable plot of land upon which to build a bigger school and convent to match growing needs. Back in Rome she continued her search for another plot of land; this time it was for a new mother-house. She successfully purchased land on the corner of Viale Glorioso and Via Nicola Fabrizi on the Janiculum; the foundation stone was laid that year on the feast of St Anthony. With untiring commitment Mother Doucet was soon back in Augusta again, this time with the intention of adding a chapel to the Sisters' building which could serve as a meeting place for the African-American Catholics in the parish. The home dedicated to St Benedict the Moor continued to expand so she helped with building plans in order that more accommodation for the increased number of orphans and for more Sisters would become available.

The pace of life appears not to have slowed down for Mother Doucet; next she ensured that novices in Rome should receive better training so that they would have the necessary skills for teaching in the schools for this, she believed, was 'imperative for the development of the institute'. Time and again Mother Doucet reflected the attitude and understanding of Elizabeth who was progressive in her endeavours in the schools of her day. Travel consumed more of her time and a modern observer, ignorant of her lack of funds, would be inclined to wonder why she did not buy shares in one of the shipping companies that she so regularly used. In any case, a gift of finance given from one source, when she was drawing up plans for a new convent in Savannah, was never forgotten by Mother Doucet. The amount donated in 1906 was $5000 and was given through the generosity of the now famous Katherine Drexel, later the foundress of the Sisters of the Blessed Sacrament for Indians and Coloured People.[37] The financial gift carried only one condition, that the money must be used for ministry to the African-American people of the city of Savannah.[38]

In the motherhouse, Mother Doucet continued to receive requests from bishops and pastors who were looking to the Franciscan Sisters for assistance in the work of spreading God's reign. She knew that expansion was well underway in the United States so she turned her attention to Egypt where the Sisters were establishing themselves in Fayoum. They looked to her for direction, especially when they received a telegram from Monsignor Aurelio Briante, OFM, telling them to take over a school in Boulac, a section of Cairo well known for excessive poverty. Sisters from another religious community had to withdraw from the school and

he wanted Franciscans to assume the responsibility of this apostolate among European Catholics.[39] Could a second mission in Egypt
be part of God's plan?

Mother Doucet, having heard of this demand, sent two Sisters
from Fayoum to resume the work impossible for others. The
poverty of the mission in Fayoum was so great that Sisters were
even obliged to borrow enough money just to take them to Boulac-
Saptieh. The Franciscan pastor, Fr Andrea Azzopardi, received the
news of their coming with joy and, after difficulty, succeeded in
obtaining two rooms for accommodation near the church. He
begged for some basic furniture and Monsignor Briante offered to
pay the rent for the first scholastic year which commenced in
September 1907. On the feast of St Francis, 4 October, the Sisters
reopened the school with an enrolment of forty pupils.[40] The dire
poverty and privations of all kinds were no less trying than those of
the early days in Fayoum; they were forced to move house a
number of times yet the Sisters, in the spirit of their foundress,
demonstrated the same zeal and commitment.

Back again in the USA in 1908 and passing through New York,
Mother Doucet delighted in knowing that authorization was
underway for another convent and school for Italian migrant children and this time in Newcastle, Pennsylvania. This year also she
encouraged the opening of a mission in New York City, namely
Our Lady of Pity School in the Bronx. She travelled again to Belle
Prairie to inquire into the legal state of Elizabeth's former property. Six years had passed since her earlier visit; this time the parish
priest learnt of her family connections to many parishioners and of
her leadership of Elizabeth's missionary institute. An invitation was
extended to build a new school. Mother Doucet set her heart on
regaining the original property and providence favoured her
dream. After certain legal procedures were overcome, Mrs
VanBeck of Hastings, Minnesota, niece and benefactor of Fr
Koering who once held a mortgage on the property and who
retained possession until his death, was visited by Mother Doucet.
She offered to buy the property, whereupon the owner promised
her first option, then later instead of stating a reasonable sale
price, she offered it to the Franciscans for the sum of $700, 'the
identical price paid for it by Elizabeth Hayes'.[41] Unfortunately,
Mother Doucet did not have a wealthy friend with a 'purse' the size
of Fanny Montgomery's, so construction of the building on this
land had to wait until 1911.

The continued story of this Belle Prairie property is too long to
relate here; however, to round off Elizabeth's association with it,

readers may appreciate a final tale of events. At the gathering, 'Celebrating Family History and Community History' held at Belle Prairie on 16 September 2007, Franciscan Sisters from Little Falls sat beside Missionary Franciscan Sisters and many locals. Photographs of events were downloaded to power points and shared among the Franciscans to record not just the special outdoor liturgy but the memorabilia on display. These included a large stone plaque honouring the names of the early Franciscan Belle Prairie Sisters. Elizabeth had purchased the property next to the parish church, so today Mary's statue from the former chapel and a statue of St Francis stand outside the church to welcome visitors. A replica of Elizabeth's log cabin has been given a sacred space in the new 'Peace Garden' nearby. Another plaque records the dedication of the Sisters' chapel of Our Lady of the Angels by Bishop Trobec, who assisted Mother Doucet's project of 1911, and honours the fact that this place is respected as the 'Cradle of the Franciscan Order' in Belle Prairie. On the original property a four-storey building that was once a convent still stands, the middle section of which was built by Mother Doucet in 1911. Later the former convent became church property; now the building has been restored and provides low-cost accommodation. Last but not least, the large old Franciscan convent bell, appropriately positioned near the church, rings again in Belle Prairie.

While 1909 saw the mission reactivated on the original property at Belle Prairie, Mother Chaffee also rejoiced that 20 Manet Road, Chestnut Hill, Massachusetts, was purchased for a noviciate. The year also marked the construction of a new chapel in connection with the Augusta mission and the opening of a day school there for African-American children. In November 1910, Mother Doucet decided to withdraw the Sisters from Naples and send them forth to bring the gospel message elsewhere. Thus ended the mission in Naples, which had been instrumental in opening up to the Missionary Franciscan Sisters the mission field of Egypt.[42]

In Fayoum, Monsignor Gaudenzio Bonfigli, OFM, Vicar Apostolic of Egypt and Apostolic Delegate to Egypt and Arabia, mediated for the Sisters so that their small orphanage developed into an elementary school for the education of Coptic Catholics. The Sisters, dedicated to this particular apostolate with the poor, were imbued with the spirit of the foundress who wrote in her diary, 'A mission without work for the poor and sick, doing little or nothing for the place in which we live, has not a very enticing aspect.'[43] In true simplicity, they worked and prayed with the conviction that God had chosen them as his instruments of peace and love and that their needs would receive Divine intervention. Heroic sacrifices and steadfast faith received the reward of a hard-won triumph when the new school opened in December 1910. Monsignor Aurelio Briante, OFM, successor to Monsignor Bonfigli, officiated at the solemn blessing of the convent and school dedicated to St Michael. The number of pupils enrolled exceeded the capacity of the school; as well as the basic elementary school subjects taught through the medium of Arabic and French, art, embroidery, sewing and also the English language were included in the programme. The Sisters also engaged in teaching religion, visiting the sick and attending to those who came to the dispensary.'[44]

In Rome, having completed more work on the revised Constitutions in 1911, Mother Doucet returned to Belle Prairie with two other Sisters, and the school was opened for boarders in November. School ministry continued to expand in general as new teachers were sent by Mother Doucet to work in Our Lady of Peace School, Brooklyn, and in Our Lady of Pompeii School, South Side, Chicago. Fr Joseph Vella, OFM, advised Mother Doucet to purchase land and to build in Boulac-Saptieh in Egypt. For progress in the mission work, both the pastor and the Sisters real-ized that a school and a convent should be provided in proximity to the Catholic population. After having secured enough money, the institute purchased an appropriate site for a school and a convent. However, the Sacred Congregation of Propaganda Fide would not allow the added incurring of a building debt and then the First World War deferred construction for another interval.[45]

Finally, amid great rejoicing, in 1912 Mother Doucet and her community moved into the new Roman motherhouse which was to be, with justifiable pride, an international centre of Franciscan life, prayer, training and hospitality for many years.[46] In the same year in Canada, the Sisters celebrated the opening of a mission in Montreal called Our Lady of Defence. In the USA there was not only the opening of Mount Alvernia convent and a canonically established noviciate, in Newton, Massachusetts, but also the opening of a mission in Pittsburgh with St Peter's School, the dedi-cation of the convent at Manet Road, Chestnut Hill, and significant developments at St Mary's School, Savannah, Georgia. The next year (1913) saw a foundation in Damanhour, Egypt, where the school opened with ninety-nine pupils.

Conclusion

This book ends in 1913 when Mother Doucet completed her second term of office but since we have followed, from its birth, the life of Elizabeth's *Annals of Our Lady of the Angels*, it seems right to bring its story to a conclusion. With the events of the First World War that brought changes in censorship of the press and postal restrictions in Italy, the printing and processing of the *Annals* was transferred to Union City, New Jersey, in 1914.[47] The Sisters' hard work and zeal ensured the continuation of this Franciscan journal until it was decided, after 100 years, that its mission – seen by Elizabeth as 'an instrument of salvation' – was accomplished. There were now more widespread avenues of media communication to be utilized. Sr M. Edward Sherry, the last editor, ensured that the *Annals* would be remembered as a milestone in the Apostolate of the Catholic Press through a final Centennial Commemorative Volume in 1974.

Today, when modern researchers ask how the spirituality of women religious was expressed in written and visual sources, Elizabeth Hayes as *Annals* pioneer editor, would want to be remembered more as a Franciscan than be highly regarded as an outstanding educator, missionary, foundress and journalist. She was all of these and certainly a most extraordinary woman yet it was her life as a Franciscan that was most precious to her; she even dared in her diary to call this gift a 'miracle'. Down the years, Sisters have attributed to Elizabeth the virtues exemplified in St Francis, the spirit of poverty, humility, simplicity, joy, and love of God overflowing into love for all,[48] yet just what kind of spiritual heritage does she offer to the twenty-first century? It is not easy to define her spirituality; one is delving into mystery and the ground one walks on is holy.

Like every other religious foundress, Elizabeth developed a unique spiritual culture within the broad Christian tradition and she certainly exemplifies a particular Franciscan one. She had a profound respect for the Franciscan Rule, believing that the Gospel of Christ was essentially expressed in the Rule; she was convinced that the Constitutions she attached to it were vital for the spiritual life and outreach of her own Third Order congregation. Her understanding of and commitment to sharing the history of the Franciscan Order, news of its missions, traditional devotions and the stories of Franciscan holy women and men, diffused through her *Annals*, enabled her to make a significant contribution to the growth in numbers of lay people who were becoming

Franciscan tertiaries or strengthening their life as Franciscans.

This woman understood that writing, editing and publishing the *Annals* was a 'heavy vocation' yet for her it was an expression of carrying the Cross and following in the footsteps of Christ, essential for a Franciscan. It was significant that Elizabeth chose for the title of her journal, Our Lady of the Angels, a name synonymous with the little chapel, just outside the town of Assisi, which St Francis restored, where he founded the Order and where St Clare received the Franciscan habit. At the core of Franciscan Spirituality is the value of conversion and this chapel, like Elizabeth's journal, called herself and others to conversion, a 'turning again' to Christ and his Gospel way of life. Sr Chaffee was convinced that Elizabeth's ongoing inner conversion and prayerfulness focused on the silent Christ in the Eucharist, invoking the Holy Spirit to discern the will of God and celebrating Mary's Immaculate Conception, followed by 'devotion to the Seraphic Love and Poverty of St. Francis, and the Universal Charity and Apostolic Zeal of St. Anthony'.[49]

Key emphases in Elizabeth's developing institute were strongly influenced after her death by her breadth of spiritual awareness and resulting convictions; the institute spread in the missionary activity she had always envisioned. Recurring central motifs can be identified, in her life and writings, as facilitating the reign of God, evangelization, service to the poor and outreach to those beyond the salvific Christian message. While individual members can and do exhibit a range of personal motivations for undertaking their religious life, Elizabeth's Sisterhood, in its ready commitment to mission fields and risk taking, exhibits a communal sense of being strongly drawn to missionary outreach. Women desire to follow in the footsteps of Elizabeth Hayes in order to be Franciscans and especially because they desire to be missionaries.

Notes

1 Sr M. Redempta Power, 'Italy' in *Missionary Franciscan Sisters of the Immaculate Conception 1873–1973. Italy, Egypt, England, Ireland*, 15.

2 Ibid.

3 'Correspondence relative to the Progress of the Institute' in Power, 'Italy', 14.

4 Angelica Chaffee, 'Memories', 59.

5 Chaffee, 'A Brief Sketch of the Life of the late Sister Mary Ignatius of Jesus, OSF, Foundress of the Association of St. Anthony of Padua for the Diffusion of Good Books', *AOLA* XIX, no. x (1894), 290.

6 This was the same illness that caused the death of St Anthony of Padua. Elizabeth was singularly devoted to St Anthony and chose him as Patron of the Association founded by her.

7 Chaffee, 'Memories', 58.

8 Ibid., 58–9 (b). Edited and based on her October article, 'A Brief Sketch of the Life of the late Sister Mary Ignatius of Jesus, OSF, Foundress of the Association of St. Anthony of Padua for the Diffusion of Good Books' *AOLA* XIX, no. x (1894), 291–3. Fr Aloysius Lauer mentioned in the account is the same German friar known to Elizabeth as far back as her first visit to Fulda.

9 Chaffee, 'Memories' 59 (b).

10 Chaffee, 'To the Clients of St. Anthony' *AOLA* XIX, no. x (1894), 301.

11 Elizabeth Hayes, 'The Apostolate of the Press', 76.

12 His interest in Elizabeth lived on and in 2001 in an interview with the present writer at the Franciscan friary in Killiney, a coastal town south of Dublin, he praised Elizabeth and asked, 'From where did Mother M. Ignatius get all her material for the *Annals of Our Lady of the Angels?*' This key question stimulated research.

13 Canice Mooney, OFM, Benignus Millett, OFM, and Redempta Power, MFIC, 'First Installment of Facts about the Life of Mother Mary Ignatius Hayes, Foundress', typescript privately circulated, Rome: MFICAR, 1976.

14 Villa Spada is today owned by Ireland's Embassy to the Holy See. The history of the building and surrounds date back hundreds of years, see Gearoid Ó Brión, 'Villa Spada – A Historical Note' in *Passageways*, ed. Helene Byrne. There is a plaque commemorating Elizabeth (Mother M. Ignatius) Hayes in the chapel; Ambassadors over the years have welcomed visits by her Missionary Franciscan Sisters.

15 Power, 'Italy', 12.

16 Ibid., 14.

17 It was designed by the young Italian engineer, Federico Martino, good friend and adviser to Elizabeth in a few projects, e.g., legal matters re Villa Spada, designing a convent for Assisi (not built).

18 Maltilda (née Taylor) Beasley (1834–1903), born in New Orleans, said to have been of mixed Creole, African-American and Indian ancestry, taught African-American children before the Civil War, married, and after her husband's death in 1877, made a novitiate with the Poor Clares in York, England. She founded a Third Order Franciscan community and, when it finally dissolved, she lived in a cottage adjoining the Sacred Heart Church, Augusta, and continued to help others.

19 Doucet, 'Memoirs of Mother M. Columba Doucet' *c.*1950, typescript privately circulated by MFIC Generalate, Rome, 1982, 6.

20 Further information is given in Sr Eileen Cahalane, *History of the Immaculate Conception Province*, 87–8.

21 In chapter 4, references are made to these articles and a quotation given from Elizabeth's account of Fr Nazzano's article on 'The Franciscan Mission of the Holy Land'. At the friar's house in New York, Elizabeth probably met Fr Nazzano, Custos Provincial and Commissary of the Holy

Land. Both St Francis and St Anthony visited the Holy Land.

22 Power, 'Italy', 15.
23 Sr M. Antoinette Sheridan, 'Egypt' in *Missionary Franciscan Sisters of the Immaculate Conception 1873–1973. Italy, Egypt, England, Ireland*, 22.
24 Cahalane, *History of the Immaculate Conception Province*, 22–3.
25 de Breffny, *Unless the Seed Die*, 109, 116, 134, 162, 164.
26 Doucet, 'Memoirs', 8.
27 Ibid.
28 Ibid.
29 Ibid. Mother Doucet when recalling her many transatlantic crossings was always able to provide the exact name of the ship and its line. To follow this interesting story through would provide a project in itself.
30 Cahalane, *History of the Immaculate Conception Province*, 23–4.
31 Doucet, 'Memoirs', 9.
32 Ibid., 10.
33 Ibid.
34 Ibid., 13.
35 Chaffee, 'Memories', 59 (b). Mother Chaffee wrote the reference in *AOLA* (1904) and while by that time she was no longer Superior General, it seems she was still writing for the *Annals* and quoted her own previously published article.
36 Doucet, 'Memoirs', 11. In her written memories, Mother Doucet reminded readers that the postulant took the religious name of Sr M. Raymond and that she continued in the institute.
37 Katherine (1858–1955) was the daughter of extremely wealthy railroad entrepreneurs and philanthropists; her parents taught their children to use wealth for the benefit of others and Katherine eventually gave away millions of the family fortune. Known also to Mother Frances Cabrini, she is now St Katherine Drexel and her institute's mother house is in Pennsylvania.
38 Doucet, 'Memoirs', 13.
39 Sheridan, 'Egypt', 16.
40 Ibid.
41 Doucet, 'Memoirs', 16. Records vary as to the acreage of the property; it appears to have been either seventy-two or ninety acres.
42 Power, 'Italy', 15. It is estimated that, at one point, some 100 Sisters were serving in Egypt, with many of them Italians.
43 Shaw, ed., *Diary*, 41.
44 Sheridan, 'Egypt', 23.
45 Ibid., 24.
46 Via Nicola Fabrizi was the location of the motherhouse from 1912 to 1969. Faced with the need for major renovations, it was sold and a new convent built at Via Lorenzo Rocci, 64. The present motherhouse is in Via Raffaello Sardiello, 20.
47 This also meant that the printing of pamphlets and periodicals in Italian had come to an end and so the Sisters in the Assisi community, who not only contributed material to the *Annals* work but also circulated the

printed matter, were withdrawn in 1915.

48 *Missionary Franciscan Sisters of the Immaculate Conception 1873–1973.* (Illustrated generalate edition), 5.

49 Chaffee, 'A Brief Sketch of the Life of the Late Sister Mary Ignatius of Jesus, O.S.F., Foundress of the Association of St Anthony of Padua for the Diffusion of Good Books', *AOLA* XIX, no. x (1894), 293.

Former Chicago printing worker, Angela (Mother M. of the Angels) Chaffee, second Mother General (1894–1900).

From Belle Prairie, Minnesota, came Adzire (Mother M. Columba)
Doucet. Fourth Mother General (1901–1913).

MFIC symbol in the Centennial Commemorative Volume (1874–1974), the final publication of the *Annals.*

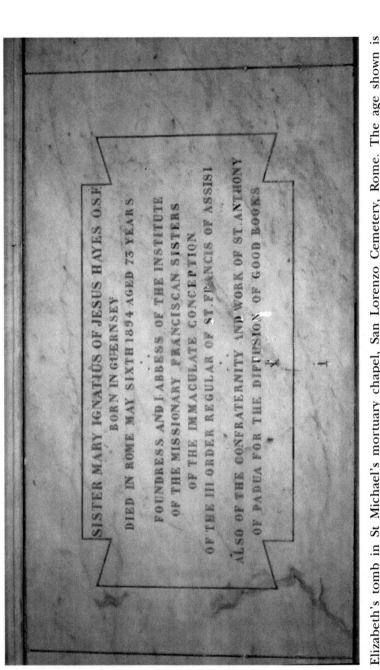

SISTER MARY IGNATIUS OF JESUS HAYES O.S.F.
BORN IN GUERNSEY
DIED IN ROME MAY SIXTH 1894 AGED 73 YEARS

FOUNDRESS AND I.ABBESS OF THE INSTITUTE
OF THE MISSIONARY FRANCISCAN SISTERS
OF THE IMMACULATE CONCEPTION
OF THE III ORDER REGULAR OF ST. FRANCIS OF ASSISI

ALSO OF THE CONFRATERNITY AND WORK OF ST. ANTHONY
OF PADUA FOR THE DIFFUSION OF GOOD BOOKS

Elizabeth's tomb in St Michael's mortuary chapel, San Lorenzo Cemetery, Rome. The age shown is inaccurate; Elizabeth died aged seventy-one.

Appendix 1

New Directory of Franciscan Journals To 1894[1]

Acta Ordinis Minorum. Grottaferrata (Rome), Friars Minor, 1882–97; 1897 to present.

Analecta Ordinis Minorum Capuccinorum. Rome, 1884–1888>

Annales des Franciscaines Missionaires de Marie. Paris, Franciscaines Missionaires de Marie, 1886–1963.

Annales du Tiers-Orde Seraphique. Caen, 1890–93>

Annales du Tiers-Ordre de Saint Francois d'Assise. Avignon, Aubanel Freres, 1865>

Annales Franciscaines: revue menssuelle du Tiers-Ordre de S. Francois. Paris, Capuchins, Librairie de Mme Poussielgue – Rusand, 1861–91>

Annali Francescani. Milano, Capuchins, 1870–91.

Annals of Our Lady of the Angels. Elizabeth (Mother M. Ignatius) Hayes. Belle Prairie (MN), Augusta (GA), Rome, Union City & Tenafly (NJ), TOR, 1874–1974.

Annuario Sacro Francescano Sorrentino. Sorrento, S. Agnello da Sorrento, 1876>

De Bode. Antwerp, 1890–91>

Der Sendbote des Gottlichen Herzens Jesu. Cincinnati (Ohio), Friars Minor, 1875–1946.

Die Posaune des hl. Kreuzes. Vienna, 1890–91>

El Eco Franciscano. Santiago de Compostela, Osservanti (Friars Minor), 1884–92>

El Mensajero Serafico. Madrid, Capuchins, 1883>

El Misionero Franciscano: revista religiosa. Angol, Brossura, <1892>

Franciscan Annals and Monthly bulletin of the Third Order of St. Francis. Crawley (Sussex), Pantasaph (Holywell, North Wales), Peckham (London), Capuchins, 1877–95 >

Franciscan Herald: Monthly Remembrance for English Speaking Tertiaries. Somerset, 'Mercury' Office – Clevedon, <1887>

Gazette des Familles. Montreal, TOSF, 1869–77.

Grusse aus Nazareth. Strasbourg, Capuchins, 1893–96.
Guida al terziario francescano nel secolo. Novara, Riformati, 1887–89.
Il Cittadino Cattolico. Rome, 1884–
Irish Franciscan Teritary: A Monthly Journal for the Third Order of St. Francis. Dublin, Friars Minor, Freeman's Journal Ltd. (Printers), (May) 1890 – (May) 1899.
L'eco del Vaticano. Sorrento, 1875–79.
L'eco di S. Francesco: periodico mensile sacro-francescano. Naples. Capuchins. 1873–1904.
L'Oriente serafice. Assisi, Friars Minor of S. Mary of the Angels, 1889–
La Crociata. Torino, 1884–90.
La Palestina. Roma, 1890–92>
La Revista Franciscana. Barcelona, Osservanti (Friars Minor), 1873–92>
La riforma sociale: Periodico per la propaganda de Terz'Ordine Francescano. Bologna. 1882–83.
La Strenna del Terz'Ordine Francescano. Sorrento, 1882–1904.
La Vergine di Loreto. Loreto, Capuchins, 1893–97.
La Voix de Saint Antoine. Brive-la-Gaillarde, Les Franciscains, <1890–97> Paris, 1899.
Le Messager de Saint Francois d'Assise: Revue mensuelle du Tieis. Brussels, Friars Minor, Mathieu Closson et C., <1875–1931> [Antwerp, 1890–92>].
Le Saint aux Miracles. Padua, 1891–92>
Letture Francescane: peridico mensile religiso dedicato ai figli Ferziarii di San Francesco d'Assisi. Cuneo, 1871–1904.
Lo Svegliarino Francescano. Caltanissetta (Sicily), 1883.
Miscellanea francescana. Pulignani, Foligna. 1887–
Miscellanea francescana: revista trimestrale di scienze teologiche e di studi francescani. Rome, Conventuals. 1886–
Petite Revue du Tiers Ordre et des interets du Coeur de Jesus. Montreal, Jesuits, Chapleau J. & Fils, 1884–91.
Revue du Tiers-Ordre. Montreal, TOSF, 1892–1915. [It became *Revue du Tiers-Ordre, et de Terre Sainte.*]
Revue Franciscaine. Bordeaux, 1890–99>
Revue Franciscaine. Montreal, Friars Minor, 1871–1886>
Revue Franciscaine: bulletin mensuel du Tiers-Ordre de Saint Francois. Paris, Tolra et Haton (Editeurs), 1870–1910.
Sanct' Francisci Glocklein. Innsbruck, 1877–78. 1890–92>
Sankt Franzisusblatt. Limburg, 1879–1934>
Seraphischer Kinderfreund und Marienkind. Ehrenbreitstein, 1890>
Seraphischer Kinderfreund. Altotting, Capuchins, (pub. Verlag des 'Seraphischen Liebeswerkes'), 1890–1902>

St. Anthony Messenger. Cincinnati (OH), Friars Minor, 1893–2009 (Online).
St. Franziskus Bote. Cincinnati (OH), Friars Minor, 1892–1917.
Stelle e Fiori. Sorrento, S. Agnello da Sorrento, 1876–95.
The Echo. Herman (PA), Capuchins, 1891>
The Sodalist. Cincinnati (OH), Friars Minor of St. Francis Seraph Parish, 1884–1938.

Note
1   The symbol > as used here indicates further publications but research on these dates is not possible within the present writer's time constraints.

Major Sources for Directory

Capuchins, 'Peregrinus – Periodica', In *Lexicon Capuccinorum. Promptuarium Historicum – Bibliographicum Ordinis Fratrum Minorum Capuccinorum (1525–1950)*, 1315–32 (Rome, 1951).
Capuchins, *Annales Franciscaines*, vol. Tome Premier. September 1861 to August 1863 (Paris, Library of Mme Ve Poussielgue-Rusand, 1863). *Annali Francescani. Periodico Religioso Dedicato Agli Ascritti Del Terz'ordine Di S. Francesco D'assisi*, 31> vols, vol. Anno I. Volume I (Milan, Libreria Religiosa di Serafino Majocchi, 1870). *The Franciscan Annals and Monthly Bulletin of the Third Order of St. Francis*, vol. I (London: Capuchins, Crawley & R. Washbourne, 1877).
Fra Bonaventura, OFMCap., ed., *L'eco Di S. Francesco D'assisi*, 32 vols, vol. Anno I, Volume I (Naples, Libreria Festa, 1873).
Finauro, OFMCap., Mario, 'Annali Francescani. Una Rivista Per Il Risveglio Spirituale Del Terzo Ordine Francescano in Italia (1870–1900)' (Doctoral dissertation, Pontificium Atnenaeum Antonianum, 1997).
Friars Minor, 'Elenco Alfabetico Delle Riviste Presenti Nel Catalogo Elettronico Della Biblioteca Dell'antonianum' (Rome, Franciscan Library, Pontificium Atnenaeum Antonianum, 1950).
Friars Minor, 'Franciscanae Ephemerides' in *Acta Ordinis Minorum* (1883–84), Archive Library, College San Bonaventura, Grottaferrata, Rome.
Friars Minor, *Irish Franciscan Tertiary: A Monthly Journal for the Third*

Order of St. Francis (Dublin, The Freeman's Journal Ltd Printers, (May) 1890 – (May) 1899).

Hayes, Elizabeth (Mother M. Ignatius), ed., *Annals of Our Lady of the Angels* (Belle Prairie (MN), Augusta (GA), Rome, Union City & Tenafly (NJ), Franciscan Sisters of the Third Order, 1874–94).

Steck, OFM, Francesco B, *Glorie Dell 'Ordine Francescano* (Verona, Italy, L'araldo, 1921).

Biersack, OFMCap., Louis, *The Saints and Blessed of the Third Order of Saint Francis* (Paterson, NJ, Saint Anthony Guild Press, 1943).

Appendix 2

Pre-1874 European Franciscan Journals – Commentary and Resources

The first nineteenth-century Franciscan journal, *Annales Franciscaines,* was founded in 1861 by the Capuchins of Paris,[1] and its significance has been recognized by numerous authorities.[2] Another French Franciscan publication, *Annales du Tiers-Ordre de Saint Francois d'Assise,* was produced by the Aubanel friars of Avignon in 1865 but information on it is scarce.[3] 1870 marked the beginning of *Annali Francescani,* published by the Capuchins of Milan. In its first number the editor, Fr Egidio, stated that its goal was 'to revive the spirit of the Seraphic S. Francis' so that there would be a return to Christian practices, to virtue, and 'to faith in Christ for our troubled humanity'.[4] *Annali Francescani* intended to 'attract spirits and minds and above all hearts to the imitation of the exemplary life and works of Saint Francis of Assisi'.[5] Tertiaries especially were encouraged, as well as friar preachers and directors, to diffuse the periodical's message and through it to be united in the spirit of the Seraph of Assisi.[6] (By 1890, Fr Cyprian of Dugnano, another editor, wrote of the periodical's main purpose and described it as 'the growth, and better still, the organisation of the Holy Third Order of Penance'.[7])

1870 also gave birth in Paris to the French journal, *Revue Franciscaine.*[8] The next year the Cuneo Friars Minor published *Letture Francescane,* a periodical that continued until 1904.[9] In 1873 the Capuchins at Naples launched their monthly periodical, *L'eco di S. Francesco D'Assisi,* which continued for thirty-one years although it had 'a laboured existence', with a five-year suspension at one period.[10] Friar Bonaventure, the editor of the monthly periodical, *L'eco di S. Francesco D'Assisi,* introduced the friars first volume with a greeting to Franciscans and Catholics everywhere, followed by a strongly worded claim that the journal would counteract the evils of the day. Friar Bonaventure compared 'evil doers', who write and work against the Church, with wolves and wild beasts.[11] References to *L'eco di S. Francesco D'Assisi* appeared in numerous sources[12] and it was different from most other journals in that it was not a periodical for the secular Third Order Franciscans but rather for First Order friars and intellectuals, as shown by its sub-title, *periodico mensile sacro-francescano.*[13] For the Tertiaries, Bonaventure (of Sorrento) edited another publication, *La strenna del Terz'Ordine Francescano* (The Gift of the Third Order of St Francis) which was an illustrated monthly supplement provided, free of charge, to receivers of his publications, *L'eco di S. Francesco D'Assisi* and *Stelle e fiori.*[14] Early in 1873 in Spain the Franciscan Fathers commenced their *La Revista Franciscana*, a monthly publication.[15]

Notes

1 *Annales Franciscaines*, Capuchin ed. Tone Premier. September 1861 to August 1863 (Paris, Librairie de Mme Ve Poussielgue-Rusand, 1863).
2 Friars Minor, 'Antonianum', no. 89. Capuchins, 'Peregrinus – Periodica', in *Lexicon Capuccinorum. Promptuarium Historicum – Bibliographicum Ordinis Fratrum Minorum Capuccinorum (1525–1950)* (Rome, 1951), 1320. Friars Minor, 'Literary Notices', *Irish Franciscan Tertiary: A Monthly Journal for the Third Order of St. Francis* 1 (1891), 128, 160, 284. Francesco B. Steck, *Glorie Dell 'Ordine Francescano* (Verona, Italy, L'araldo, 1921), 128.
3 Friars Minor, 'Antonianum', no. 88.
4 Fr Egidio, 'Program', *Annali Francescani* I (1870), 1.
5 Ibid., 2.
6 Mario Finauro, 'Annali Francescani: Una Rivista Per Il Risveglio Spirituale Del Terzo Ordine Francescano in Italia (1870–1900)' (Doctoral dissertation, Pontificium Athenaeum Antonianum, 1997), 81.
7 Third Orders for lay people were generally known in the Middle Ages as Orders of Penance.
8 *Revue Franciscaine.* Bulletin mensuel du Tiers – Ordre de Saint François – Paris: Tolra et Haton, Editeurs, 1870 in Friars Minor, 'Antonianum', no. 968.
9 *Letture Francescane.* Periodico mensile religioso dedicato ai Figli di San Francesco d'Assisi, a cura di sacerdoti della citta di Cuneo (Cuneo, 1871–1904) noted in Finauro, 'Annali Francescani', xi. Also an 1871 copy is recorded in Friars Minor, 'Antonianum', 641.
10 Capuchins, 'Peregrinus – Periodica', 1326, Finauro, 'Annali Francescani', 323, f'n 13.
11 Fra Bonaventura da Sorrento, 'Program', *L'eco di S. Francesco D'Assisi* I (1873), 1.
12 For Example, *Irish Franciscan Tertiary* I (1891), 284.
13 Finauro, 'Annali Francescani', 82.
14 Ibid., xi.
15 Elizabeth Hayes, 'The Progress and Development of the Third Order in Europe', *AOLA* I, no. i (1874), 29.

Appendix 3

Rome

April 21st 1875. Elizabeth's Day of Anguish

Characters involved:-

'Pope' – Pius IX

'Cardinal Vicar' – Cardinal Patrizi

'*Propaganda*' - Cardinal Alexander Franchi

'Nuns' - Poor Clares who volunteered to go with Elizabeth

'Confessor' and 'Fr General' – Minister General, Fr Bernardine of Portogruaro

'Fr Ludovico' – Saintly Franciscan and friend of Elizabeth.

AS WRITTEN BY ELIZABETH HAYES

April 21st. A day of anguish! I went to the Cardinal Vicar (Eminence Patrizi) but he would have nothing to say about the (Poor Clare) Nuns. He said it was their Confessor's and Propaganda's responsibility, and was very angry that they (ecclesiastics) had thrown it on him. I am quite upset. Will no one take responsibility? So little faith! Did Saint Francis and Saint Clare act so? In my anguish at all this uncertainty, I prayed for a solution.

In came Father Ludovico (of Casoria) like an angel from heaven. I told him all. At first he opposed the idea on the same grounds as all the others (ecclesiastics). 'If they were sick, how were they to return? How would the Convents do without them and so forth?'
I said, 'All this is human questioning. God would reward them. Could they

(those in authority) not give Him (God) two out of thirty? Saint Francis, when he sent his children to Morocco, didn't fret about where he should get more! Saint Clare gave Saint Agnes.'

'Times have changed,' he (Cardinal Patrizi) said.

'No, no.' I cried, 'faith never changes. Confidence in God never changes.'

Then reverting to the responsibility, he (Cardinal Patrizi) said, 'It belongs with the Father General (Fr Bernardine); he is the Poor Clares' confessor; he knows the vocations. He judges the spirit in which it is done and would not advise it if he had not seen the Nuns were capable. The Pope and Propaganda Fide (Cardinal Franchi) should say they give consent if the General (Fr Bernardine), as Confessor and Superior, is favourable and believes the vocations to be of God.' At this point we agreed perfectly.

What a picture! Elizabeth Hayes lecturing the Cardinal Vicar of Rome. It is priceless. This is an exceptional scene in which a nineteenth-century woman is standing up for what she believes. Still the Cardinal Vicar vacillated so Elizabeth had more to say:

I said, 'Had there been no vocations, none formed, then I could understand; but to have encouraged all these women up to this point, and then leave them because <u>they</u> (ecclesiastics) won't take responsibility I cannot understand. They (Poor Clares) have committed themselves before their Superior and Sisters and now to forsake them half-way?' He (Cardinal Patrizi) agreed perfectly.

'What right have any of us to claim authority and not take responsibility?' I continued, 'If we poor women can take responsibility, why not a General of a great Order like ours?'

'I am flesh and blood,' he (Cardinal Patrizi) said, pinching his hand.

'Nonsense,' I cried, 'so are we.'

'What a life these nuns will have. *Un inferno* (Hell),' he (Cardinal Patrizi) replied.

I said, 'It all hangs on this. Are they (2 nuns) moved by the Spirit of God? That is the question. Have they true vocations?'

He (Cardinal Patrizi) went away to seek the General (Fr Bernardine). He (Cardinal Patrizi) returned, not finding him. He (Cardinal Patrizi) said, 'There are only two ways, the ordinary way of human prudence and the extraordinary way of faith and confidence in God. If you walk in the way of human prudence, this is all contrary to it, you will suffer an inferno (hell), a torture of responsibility. If you will embrace it in faith and say 'Come evil, come good, it's all the same. I do it for God and then go on. Andare, avante

(Go ahead).' The natural and the supernatural.

This was an inexpressible comfort and light to me. I felt we had all begun in faith, and they (ecclesiastics) were now trying to choke us with human prudence. I said, 'If you consider your responsibility and the General his, it is impossible on human grounds.'

He (Cardinal Patrizi) said, 'You have spoken to the Pope, the Cardinal (Cardinal Franchi), etc. If you fail, your reputation is gone with them.' I assented. We concluded that it could only be done for God and in God.[1]

Note
1 Elizabeth Hayes, 'Diary of Sister Mary Ignatius Hayes', n.d., manuscript, MFICAR, 70-4. Pauline J. Shaw, ed., *Diary: Sister Mary Ignatius of Jesus (Elizabeth Hayes)* (Brisbane, Qld, Rapid Offset Pty Ltd & MFIC, 1995), 65–7.

Appendix 4

Elizabeth Hayes' *Annals of Our Lady of the Angels*

Summary of Availability

Year	Vol.	All	(12 issues)	Part	Text	Index
1874	I	1	Yes	-	Yes	Yes
1875	II	2	–	6 Issues	Jan-June	Yes
1876	–	–	–	–	–	–
1877	–	–	–	–	–	–
1878	III	3	–	No	No	Yes
1879	IV	4	–	1 Issue	May	Only May
1880	V	5	–	No	No	Yes
1881	VI	6	–	No	No	No
1882	VII	7	–	1 Issue	Dec.	Only Dec.

1883–94: III–XIX (vols 8-19) **All 12 issues – all Texts and all Indices**

Summary re Texts

From 1874 to 1894 inclusive (i.e. twenty-one years) nineteen volumes (eighteen volumes with monthly issues and one volume with only six issues) were published. There was a pause in publishing in the second half of 1875, all of 1876 and 1877.

Of the nineteen volumes, MFICAR and CDs hold texts of:
– the year book/twelve issues bound for thirteen years (1874, 1883–94)
– six issues for one year (1875)
– one issue for two years (1879 and 1882)
– no printed issues/texts at all on hand for three years. (1878, 1880, 1881)

(i.e. 13+1+2+3=19)

Of the nineteen years of publication, MFICAR and CDs have Index records:
– the whole year's index of the twelve issues for fifteen years
– index of the six issues of one year
– index of one issue for two years
– no index for one year

(i.e. 15+1+2+1= 19)

Appendix 5

Franciscan Terms and Insights

It was important for Elizabeth Hayes that her readers understood the origin and structure of the Catholic Franciscan family that is composed of three Orders. The First Order for male religious, the Second Order for solemn-vowed nuns and the Third Order for lay men and women. The Third Order led to two categories, the Third Order Regular (religious communities like Elizabeth's with simple vows) and the Third Order Secular (Tertiaries living in their own homes).[1] Elizabeth edited and published in a seven-part serial the traditional story of the foundation of the three Orders and their evolution.[2]

A desire for renewal within the three Orders led to the development of numerous branches of the one Franciscan family tree. Elizabeth's group is an example of a Third Order Regular branch. Elizabeth initially belonged to a Third Order Franciscan community called the Bayswater Franciscan Sisters, then she transferred to the Glasgow Franciscans because they had a mission in Jamaica; next she founded the short-lived Sèvres Franciscan community and finally she founded her enduring Franciscan institute at Belle Prairie, Minnesota. Later, from this foundation other independent groups were also formed and all belong as branches of the Third Order Regular. Elizabeth had an excellent understanding of the Third Order Sisters of her time and provided an overview in 'The Order of Penance'.[3]

St Francis is of course the first person alleged to have received the stigmata – the crucifixion wounds of Christ. According to tradition, Francis received the stigmata directly from the crucified Christ who appeared in the form a six-winged seraph. So over the centuries St Francis has been called the Seraph of Assisi, with the term 'Seraphic Order' regularly substituted for the whole Franciscan Order.[4]

In 1888 Elizabeth published an article on the First Order, that of the Friars Minor, to explain to her readers how the Discalced,

Recollects and Reformed (from the Observants) evolved. It concluded with, 'The Friars Minor of the Observance are still the most numerous and important family in the Seraphic Order and that which has produced the greatest number of Saints.'[5] In the article Elizabeth reveals her knowledge of all the localities in Europe, Asia, Africa, North and South America and Oceania (including Sydney) where the Friars Minor served. She also lists the old Franciscan sanctuaries that the friars cared for, beginning with 'St. Mary of the Angels', the chapel which had inspired the choice of her *Annals'* title. The friars were known by numerous names at different times and in different places. From 1897 just three First Order groups have existed, the Friars Minor (Observants), the Capuchins and the Conventuals. The multiple names will be simplified here, even though periodicals before 1897 are being examined. Popular nicknames like 'Greyfriars', 'Barefeet' or 'Cordeliers' were interchangeable in the First Order and were used in some nineteenth-century Franciscan journals. Within the First Order the Capuchins were quicker than the Observants to develop their own periodical press with its Franciscan tradition and they also published a greater number of journals that became better known and continued longer.

No nineteenth-century periodicals produced by the Second Order groups have been found. Franciscan and Catholic Church periodicals at times conveyed the Second Order history and stories, for example, a paper written on the occasion of the septi-centennial commemoration of Saint Clare's 'conversion' which appeared in 1912 in *The Catholic World* of New York.[6] Although the Third Order Regular Franciscans were numerous in the late nineteenth century,[7] the only two recorded communities that contributed to the growth of Franciscan periodicals were Elizabeth's Franciscan Sisters and, later, Helen de Chappotin's Franciscan Missionaries of Mary. De Chappotin, like Elizabeth, believed in the printing press's value for the rapid diffusion of Christian teaching.[8] Numerous Tertiaries were involved in the Apostolate of the Press; among the most famous were Cardinal Manning, Lady Georgiana Fullerton, Canon Oakley[9] and Lady Herbert of Lea who, besides their major writings, contributed generously to Franciscan journals, including Elizabeth's *Annals*.

Notes

1 Further explanations are available e.g., Introduction to Leopold de Cherance, *Saint Francis of Assisi*, trans. R. F. O'Connor, 3rd edn (London, Burns & Oates, 1900); Patrick Conlan, *Franciscan Ireland* (Mullingar, Co. Westmeath: Lilliput Press, 1988), 89; 'Who are the Franciscans?' in William J. Short, *Poverty and Joy: The Franciscan Tradition* (Maryknoll, New York, Orbis, 1999), 18-19; 'All in the Family: A Quick Guide to the Franciscans', *Franciscan News*, Friars Minor Provincial Office, Waverley, NSW, Australia, 4 October 2005. Websites on all things Franciscan are countless.

2 Elizabeth Hayes, 'The Seraphic Order', *AOLA* xiii–xiv, no. iii, v, viii, x, xi (1888): 87–93, 143–51, 225–30, 289–99, 330–8; no. iii, v; (1889), 90–6, 130–5.

3 Elizabeth Hayes, 'The Seraphic Order - the Order of Penance', *AOLA* xiv, no. v (1889): 130–5. The term, 'Order of Penance' was the original thirteenth-century label for tertiary movements.

4 Elizabeth Hayes, 'The Sacred Stigmata of St. Francis', *AOLA* xii, no. ix (1887), 260–70. The following year Hayes provided 'The Sacred Stigmata'.

5 Hayes, 'The Seraphic Order', 330–8.

6 Fr Cuthbert, *The Romanticism of St Francis* (London, Longmans, Green & Co, 1924), vii.

7 Literally hundreds of women's congregations were founded in the nineteenth century and the re-emergence of Third Order Regulars seems part of the nineteenth-century 'neo-monastic movement' which gained impetus from the 1850s. Among the many Third Order Regular Franciscans, communities followed the rule and constitutions to different degrees, and sometimes, by necessity or local clerical influences, they diverted from the original Franciscan charism. Elizabeth Hayes was thoroughly Franciscan-minded in leadership, ideals and missionary aspirations.

8 Georges Goyau, *Valiant Women: Mother Mary of the Passion and the Franciscan Missionaries of Mary*, trans. Mgr George Telford (Sydney, NSW, O'Loughlin Bros, 1953), 191.

9 Oakley was a friend and mentor of Fr Julian Tenison Woods who became a press apostle and significant religious founder in Australia. As a youth, Julian joined a lay Franciscan group in London.

Appendix 6

Illustrations

From the *Annals of Our Lady of the Angels*

1. i Jesus advanced in wisdom and age … 1887, vol. XII, no. i.
   ii The Patronage and Cultus of the Most Blessed … 1890, vol. XV, no. xii.

2. i A Pilgrimage … Sanctuary of the Stigmata of St Francis, 1886, vol. XI, no. ix.
   ii St Elizabeth of Hungary, 1886, vol. XI, no. i.

3. i Vera Effigie di St Antonio di Padova, 1890, vol. XV, no. xi.
   ii True Likeness of St Anthony of Padua, 1893, vol. XVIII, no. vi.
   iii Societas S. Antonii de Padua.

4.   Piazza Navona & the Church of St Agnes, V. & M., Rome, 1890, vol. XV, no. i.

5.   The Sanctuary of the Portiuncula, in Basilica of St Mary of Angels, Assisi, 1890, vol. XV, no. viii.

6.   *Annals* cover with Franciscan coat of arms, 1882, vol. VII, no. xii.

7.   Deberny's St Francis, St Clare and St Anthony.

8. i Deberny – The Nativity, 1890, vol. XV, no. xii; 1892, vol. XVII, no. iii.
   ii Deberny – The Angel of Prayers, 1893, vol. XVIII, no. iv.

9. i The Glorious Assumption of Our Blessed Lady, 1894, vol. XIX, no. viii.
   ii Spagna's Assumption illustration, 1886, vol. XI, no. v 1890, vol. XV, no. ix.

The Patronage and Cultus
of the
Most Blessed and Immaculate Virgin Mary.

Figure ii.

Figure i.

Figure ii.

Figure i.

VIDEO DOMINVM MEVM

VERA EFFICIE DI S.ᵗᵒ ANTONIO DI PADOVA
che si venera nell'Arcella, sotto l'Altare, dove il Santo spirò un 1231

TRUE LIKENESS OF ST. ANTHONY
which is venerated in Arcella under the Altar where the Saint expired in the year 1231.

Figure i.

Vera ritratto di S. Antonio da Padova.

TRUE LIKENESS OF ST. ANTHONY OF PADUA.

Figure iii.

Piazza Navona and the Church of St. Agnes, Virgin and Martyr, Rome.

THE SANCTUARY OF THE PORTIUNCULA,
IN THE BASILICA OF SAINT MARY OF THE ANGELS, ASSISI.

Vol. cii.   December.   1882

Annals

of our

LADY OF THE ANGELS.

Published by

Members of the Third Order Regular

— of —

SAINT FRANCIS OF ASSISI.

Augusta.   Georgia.

St. Francis of Assisi.

To St. Clare.

St. Anthony of Padua.

The Nativity.

Fig i

Vol. xviii.   April, 1895.   No. iv.

The Angel of Prayers.

Fig ii

Figure ii.

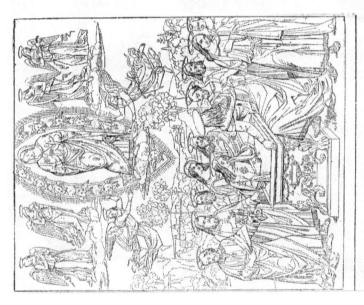

THE GLORIOUS ASSUMPTION OF OUR BLESSED LADY.

Feast, August 15.

Figure i.

Bibliography

Ahles, Veronica (Sr M. Assumpta), *In the Shadow of His Wings: A History of the Franciscan Sisters,* St Paul, MN, The North Central Publishing Company, 1977.

Altholz, Josef L., *The Religious Press in Britain, 1760–1900,* Westport, CT, Greenwood Press, 1989.

Beck, George Andrew, ed., *The English Catholics, 1850–1950: Essays to Commemorate the Centenary of the Restoration of the Hierarchy of England and Wales,* London, Burns & Oates, 1950.

Biersack, Louis, *The Saints and Blessed of the Third Order of Saint Francis.* Paterson, NJ, St Anthony Guild Press, 1943.

Bonaventure, Saint, *Bonaventure: The Soul's Journey into God – the Tree of Life – the Life of St. Francis,* translated by Ewert Cousins, New York, Paulist Press, 1978.

Bougerol, J. Guy, *Introduction to the Works of Bonaventure,* translated by Jose de Vink, *The Works of Bonaventure,* Paterson, NJ, St Anthony Guild Press, 1963.

Bridgett, T. E., ed., *Our Lady's Dowry; or How England Gained and Lost That Title,* London, Burns and Oates, 1875.

Brownlow, ed., *Angels Ever in Our Midst,* Fort Worth, TX, Brownlow, 1995.

Burnquist, Joseph A. A., ed., *Minnesota and Its People,* Vol. 2, Chicago, The S. J. Clark Publishing Company, 1924.

Butler, Arthur J., ed., *Life and Letters of William John Butler. Late Dean of Lincoln and Sometime Vicar of Wantage,* London, MacMillan and Co, 1897.

Cahalane, Eileen, *History of the Immaculate Conception Province,* Boston, MA, MFIC, 1994.

Cameron, Jennifer, *A Dangerous Innovator: Wary Ward (1585–1645),* Sydney, NSW, St Pauls Publications, 2000.

Carey, Patrick W., *Orestes A. Brownson: American Religious Weathervane,* Grand Rapids, MI, Eerdmans, 2004.

Chadwick, Owen, *Newman,* Oxford, Oxford University Press, 1983.

Chadwick, Owen, *The Victorian Church, Part One, 1829–1859.* 2nd edn, London, SCM Press Ltd, 1972. Reprint, paperback, Trowbridge, Wilts., Redwood Burn Ltd, 1980.

Chadwick, Owen, *The Victorian Church, Part Two, 1860–1901,* 2nd edn, London, SCM Press Ltd, 1972. Reprint, paperback, Trowbridge, Wilts., Redwood Burn Ltd, 1980.

Chalippe, Candide, *The Life of St. Francis of Assisi,* translated by Congregation of the Oratory of St Philip Neri, American edn, New York, D. & J. Sadlier, 1889.

Chinnici, Joseph P., 'The Immigrant Vision, 1830–1866', in *Living Stones: The History and Structure of Catholic Spiritual Life in the United States,* edited by Christopher J. Kauffman, New York, Macmillan, 1989.

Chinnici, Joseph P., 'The Spirituality of Americanism, 1866–1900', in *Living Stones: The History and Structure of Catholic Spiritual Life in the United States,* edited by Christopher J. Kauffman, New York, Macmillan, 1989.

Coburn, Carol K., and Martha Smith, *Spirited Lives: How Nuns Shaped Catholic Culture and American Life, 1836–1920,* Chapel Hill and London, The University of North Carolina Press, 1999.

Concannon, Mrs Thomas, *At the Court of the Eucharistic King,* Dublin, M. H. Gill and Son Ltd, 1929.

Cuthbert, Fr, *The Romanticism of St Francis,* London, Longmans, Green & Co., 1924.

Davis, Lloyd, 'Journalism and Victorian Fiction', in *Victorian Journalism: Exotic and Domestic,* edited by Barbara Garlick and Margaret Harris, St Lucia, Brisbane, Queensland University Press, 1998.

de Breffny, Brian, *Unless the Seed Die: The Life of Elizabeth Hayes (Mother M. Ignatius O.S.F.). Foundress of the Missionary Franciscan Sisters of the Immaculate Conception,* Rome, Don Bosco Press, 1980.

de Clary, Léon Fr, *Lives of the Saints and Blessed of the Three Orders of Saint Francis,* translated by Taunton Franciscan Sisters, 4 vols, Taunton, Somerset, Taunton Franciscan Convent, 1885–7.

Delaney, Francis X., *A History of the Catholic Church in Jamaica B. W. I. 1494 to 1929,* New York, Jesuit Mission Press, 1930.

Devas, Francis Charles, *Mother Mary Magdalen of the Sacred Heart: Fanny Margaret Taylor: Foundress of the Poor Servants of the Mother of God (1832–1900),* New York, Cincinnati, Chicago, Benziger Brothers, 1927.

Dickenson, Donna, ed., *Margaret Fuller: Woman in the Nineteenth Century and Other Writings, The World's Classics Series,* Oxford, Oxford University Press, 1994.

Dillan, Ingolf, *Brainerd's Half Century,* Brainerd, MN, press not indicated, 1923.

Doyle, Eric, *Canterbury and the Franciscans 1224–1974,* Canterbury, Kent, Friars Minor & Guildford Offset Service, 1974.

Engelhardt, Zephyrin, *Santa Barbara Mission: The Missions and Missionaries of California,* San Francisco, CA, The James H. Barry Company, 1923.

Fehlmer, Peter, 'Foreword' in *Bonaventure: Rooted in Faith. Homilies to a Contemporary World,* translated and introduced by Marigwen Schumacher, Chicago, Franciscan Herald Press, 1973.

Fiege, Marianus, *Princess of Poverty: St Clare of Assisi and the Order of Poor Ladies,* 2nd edn, Evansville, IN, Monastery of St Clare, 1909.

Franciscan Sisters of the Immaculate Conception: Celebrating 150 Years in Glasgow 1847–1997, Glasgow, Franciscan Sisters & Milton Press, 1997.

Franklin, R. William, 'The Impact of Germany on the Anglican Catholic Revival in Nineteenth-Century Britain', *Anglican and Episcopal History,* Volume LXII, no. 3 (1993), in E. G. W. Bill, *University Reform in Nineteenth Century Oxford 1811–1885,* Oxford, 1973.

Freunden, Unseren, und Wohltatern Gewidmet, *200 Jahre Kirche und Kloster: Frauenberg/Fulda 1763–1963,* Fulda, Ludwig Fleischmann, 1963.

Fullerton, Lady Georgiana, *Mrs. Gerald's Niece,* 3 vols, vol. 2, London, Richard Bentley, 1869.

Gameson, Richard, *Saint Augustine of Canterbury,* Canterbury, Kent, The Dean and Chapter of Canterbury, 1997.

Gerwing, Joseph, *100 Jahre Franziskaner in Mönchengladbach 1889–1989,* Gladbach, Rhenania Franciscana, Dietrich-Coelde-Verlag, Weri, 1989.

Goyau, Georges, *Valiant Women: Mother Mary of the Passion and the Franciscan Missionaries of Mary,* translated by Mgr George Telford, Sydney, NSW, O'Loughlin Bros, 1953.

Hales, E. E. Y., *The Catholic Church in the Modern World: A Survey from the French Revolution to the Present,* 2nd reprint, New York, Image, 1961.

Hamel, P. J. Canon, *Indexes to the Irish Ecclesiastical Record from 1864–1963,* Dublin, Browne & Nolan Ltd, 1963.

Holmes, J. Derek, and Bernard W. Bickers, 'The Church, Revolution and Reaction, 1789–1914' in *A Short History of the Catholic Church,* Tunbridge Wells, Kent, Burns & Oates, 1984.

Houghton, Walter E., *The Victorian Frame of Mind: 1830–1870,* New Haven and London, Yale University Press, 1957. Reprint,

Clinton, MA, Colonial Press Inc., 1973.

Koester, Sr M. Camilla, *Into This Land: A Centennial History of the Cleveland Poor Clare Monastery of the Blessed Sacrament,* Cleveland, OH, Robert J. Leiderbach Co., 1980.

Lass, William E. *Minnesota – A History,* 2nd edn, New York, W. W. Norton & Company, 1998.

Liptak, Dolores, 'Full of Grace: Another Look at the 19th-century Nun', *Review for Religious* 55, no. 6 (1996), 625-39.

Lockhart, William, ed., *Life of Antonio Rosmini Serbati: Founder of the Institute of Charity,* 2nd edn, 2 vols, vol. 2, London, Kegan Paul, Trench & Co, 1886.

Lockhart, William, ed., *The Old Religion; or How Shall We Find Primitive Christianity?* London, Burns, Oates & Washbourne Ltd, 1914.

Lumley, Sarah, 'A Tale of Bad Times; or, Ecological, Sustainable Development and Harriet Martineau', *Australasian Victorian Studies Journal* 6 (2000), 60–7.

Macfarlane, Leslie J. and Revd J. McIntryre, eds, 'Emancipation and Catholic Revival 1793–1878' in *Scotland and the Holy See: The Story of Scotland's links with the Papacy Down the Centuries,* Edinburgh, Heritage Commission of the Scottish Catholic Hierarchy, 1982.

MacGinley, M. R., *A Dynamic of Hope: Institutes of Women Religious in Australia.* 2nd edn, Sydney, NSW, Crossing Press for Australian Catholic University National, Research Centre for the Study of Women's History, Theology and Spirituality, 2002.

MacGinley, M. R., *A Lamp Lit: History of the Poor Clares Waverley Australia 1883–2004,* Sydney, NSW, St Pauls Publications, 2005.

McCarthy, Sr M. Cuthbert, 'Elizabeth Hayes – a Woman of Her Time: An Examination of the History of Victorian England and an Attempt by an Englishwoman to Trace Its Influence on Mother Mary Ignatius Hayes, 1823–1894', in *Passageways,* edited by Helene Byrne, Rome, MFIC, 1995.

McClelland, V. A., 'Manning's Work for Social Justice', *The Chesterton Review* XVIII, no. 4 (1992), 525–38.

McEvoy, Sr M. Agatha, *A Short Life of Mother Mary Elizabeth Lockhart and Brief History of Her Franciscan Sisters,* London, Quick & Co, 1959.

McKenzie, Judy, 'Review of *Periodicals of Queen Victoria's Empire: An Exploration*', edited by J. Don Vann and Rosemary T. VanArsdel, *Disreputable Profession: Journalists and Journalism in Colonial Australia,* by Denis Cryle, *Australasian Victorian Studies Journal* 3, no. 2 (1998), 136–8.

Meadows, Denis, 'Loss and Gain in the 19th Century', in *A Short History of the Catholic Church*, New York, All Saints Press, 1959.

Missionary Franciscan Sisters of the Immaculate Conception 1873–1973, illustrated generalate edn, Rome, MFIC, 1973.

Montgomery, Hon. Mrs Fanny, *Misunderstood*, Leipzig, Bernard Tauchnitz, 1872.

Moorman, John R. H., *St Francis of Assisi*, 2nd edn, London, SPCK, 1982.

Mother Mary Ignatius – Foundress of the Missionary Franciscan Sisters of the Immaculate Conception, 1823–1894, Rome, Tipografia Poliglotta Vaticana, 1954.

Moynihan, James H., *The Life of Archbishop John Ireland*, New York, Harper & Brothers, 1953.

Newman, John Henry Cardinal, *Apologia Pro Vita Sua*, reprint, 2nd edn, London, Sheed & Ward, 1946.

O'Brien, Felicity, *Not Peace but a Sword: John Henry Newman*, Australian edn, Sydney, NSW, St Pauls Publications, 1991.

O'Connell, Revd Marvin, 'James J. Hill and John Ireland', in *'You Shall Be my People': A History of the Archdiocese of Saint Paul and Minneapolis 150th Anniversary*, edited by John Christine Wolkerstorfer, St Paul, MN, Catholic Archdiocese of Saint Paul and Minneapolis, 2000.

Osborne, Francis J., 'J. Sidney Woollett, S.J., and His Times' in *History of the Catholic Church in Jamaica*, Chicago, Loyola University Press, 1964.

Parsons, Mrs, *The Life of Saint Collette: The Reformer of the Three Orders of St. Francis, Especially of the Poor Clares, among Whom She Revived the First Fervour of Their Illustrious Founder*, London, Burns and Oates, 1879.

Philip, Kathleen, *Victorian Wantage*, Witney, Oxon, The Witney Press, 1968.

Power, Sr M. Redempta, 'Italy', in *Missionary Franciscan Sisters of the Immaculate Conception 1873–1973: Italy, Egypt, England, Ireland*, Rome, MFIC, 1973.

Rawes, Henry A., *Foregleams of the Desired: Sacred Verses, Hymns, and Translations*, 3rd edn, London, Burns and Oates, 1881.

Scheiwe, P. Friedhelm, *Our Lady of the Cliffs: A Papal Shrine. Castel S. Elia*, Rome, Franciscan Friars, 1971.

Shattock, Joanne, 'Margaret Oliphant: Journalist' in *Victorian Journalism: Exotic and Domestic*, edited by Barbara Garlick and Margaret Harris, Brisbane, Qld, University of Queensland, 1998.

Shaw, Pauline J., ed., *Diary: Sister Mary Ignatius of Jesus (Elizabeth Hayes)*, Brisbane, Qld, Rapid Offset Pty Ltd & MFIC, 1995.

Shaw, Pauline J., ed., *London: Following Elizabeth Hayes – Pilgrim's Guide*, 2nd edn, 3 vols, vol. 2, International Charism Renewal Programme, Brisbane, Qld, MFIC, 1994.

Shaw, Pauline J., *Companion to the Diary: Sister Mary Ignatius of Jesus (Elizabeth Hayes)*, Brisbane, Qld, MFIC & Parish Youth Ministry Services, 1996.

Sheridan, Sr M. Antoinette, 'Egypt', in *Missionary Franciscan Sisters of the Immaculate Conception 1873–1973: Italy, Egypt, England, Ireland,* Rome, MFIC, 1973.

Sherry, Sr M. Edward, ed., *Centenial Commemorative Volume: The Annals of Our Lady of the Angels 1874–1974,* Tenafly, NJ, MFIC with Freeman & De Troy Corporation, 1974.

Shipley, Orby, ed., *Annus Sanctus: Hymns of the Church for the Ecclesiastical Year,* vol. 1, London and New York, Burns and Oates, 1884.

Short, William J., *Poverty and Joy: The Franciscan Tradition,* Maryknoll, NY, Orbis, 1999.

Starr, Eliza Allen, *Pilgrims and Shrines,* 2 vols, vol. 1, Chicago, Union Catholic Publishing Company, 1883.

Stead, W. T., 'To the English-Speaking Folk under the Southern Cross: Why the *Review of Reviews* Takes Root in Australia', *Review of Reviews,* Australian edn 1, no. 1 (1892), 10–13.

Sticker, Anna, *Florence Nightingale Curriculum Vitae,* 3rd edn, Dusseldorf, Daikoniewerk Kaiserswerth, 1987.

Stuart, Lurline, *Nineteenth Century Australian Periodicals: An Annotated Bibliography,* Sydney, NSW, Hale & Iremonger, 1979.

Sugg, Joyce, *Ever Yours Affly: John Henry Newman and His Female Circle,* Leominster, Herefordshire, Gracewing, 1996.

The Story of Catholic England: Commemorative Publication – a Hundred Years after the Restoration of the English Hierarchy, London, Catholic Truth Society, 1950.

Todd, Mabel L. and T. W. Higginson, eds, *Favourite Poems of Emily Dickenson,* New York, Avenel, 1978.

Ullathorne, William Archbishop, *Christian Patience,* London, Burns & Oates, 1886.

Ullathorne, William Archbishop, *The Groundwork of the Christian Virtues,* London, Burns & Oates, 1882.

Vann, J. Don, and Rosemary T. VanArsdel, eds, *Victorian Periodicals and Victorian Society,* Aldershot, Hants, Scolar Press, 1994.

Ward, Wilfred, *The Life & Times of Cardinal Wiseman,* 2 vols, vol. 2, London, New York & Bombay, Longmans, Green & Co, 1897.

Watts, John, *A Canticle of Love: The Story of the Franciscan Sisters of the Immaculate Conception,* Edinburgh, John Donald, 2006.

Willan, Healey, ed., *St. Basil's Hymnal: An Extensive Collection of English and Latin Hymns for Church, School and Home,* 36th edn, New York, J. Fisher & Brothers, 1935.

Yonge, Charlotte M., 'Miss Yonge's Recollections', in *Life and Letters of William John Butler: Late Dean of Lincoln and Sometime Vicar of Wantage,* edited by Arthur J. Butler, London, MacMillan and Co., 1897.

Index

Note: Page references in *italics* indicate illustrations. The abbreviation EH is used for Elizabeth Hayes.

LaVergne, TN USA
13 November 2009
164007LV00001B/39/P

9 780852 442098